HACKING EXPOSED™
COMPUTER FORENSICS
SECRETS & SOLUTIONS

"*Hacking Exposed Computer Forensics* gives the reader, whether they are experienced or just starting out, a good solid guideline for designing, building, and operating their forensic lab."

—Curtis Tomlinson
CPP, Manager of Investigations, Advanced Micro Devices, Inc.

"Not just theory. Solid information a business can use in the security investigation trenches."

—Christopher Joerg
CISSP, CISM, Lead Security Manager, Harrah's Entertainment, Inc.

"*Hacking Exposed Computer Forensics* provides in-depth, real-world information presented by proven industry experts and illustrates the practical use of industry standard tools and practices, not just the theory of forensic examinations."

—Travis Good
*CISSP, IAM, Associate Director of Professional Services at the
Center for Infrastructure Assurance and Security*

"*Hacking Exposed Computer Forensics* is an excellent book to balance formal issues related with procedures in computer forensics and a practical way to understand technical strategies to face technological challenges in digital forensics. This book is a solid reference advance in IT forensic topics."

—Jeimy J. Cano, Ph.D
Forensics Researcher, Universidad de los Andes, Columbia

HACKING EXPOSED™
COMPUTER FORENSICS
SECRETS & SOLUTIONS

CHRIS **DAVIS**
DAVID **COWEN**
AARON **PHILIPP**

McGraw-Hill/Osborne

New York Chicago San Francisco
Lisbon London Madrid Mexico City Milan
New Delhi San Juan Seoul Singapore Sydney Toronto

McGraw-Hill/Osborne
2100 Powell Street, 10th Floor
Emeryville, California 94608
U.S.A.

To arrange bulk purchase discounts for sales promotions, premiums, or fund-raisers, please contact **McGraw-Hill/**Osborne at the above address. For information on translations or book distributors outside the U.S.A., please see the International Contact Information page immediately following the index of this book.

Hacking Exposed™ Computer Forensics

1234567890 CUS CUS 01987654

ISBN 0-07-225675-3

Executive Editor	**Indexer**
Jane K. Brownlow	Valerie Perry
Project Editor	**Composition**
LeeAnn Pickrell	Apollo Publishing Services
Acquisitions Coordinator	**Illustrator**
Jessica Wilson	Apollo Publishing Services
Technical Editors	**Series Design**
Tanya Baccam, Erik Harssema	Dick Schwartz
Copy Editor	Peter F. Hancik
Lisa Theobald	**Cover Series Design**
Proofreader	Dodie Shoemaker
Susie Elkind	

This book was composed with Corel VENTURA™ Publisher.

To my beautiful and patient wife Sarah,
my grandfather LaVaughn who is the greatest man I know,
my loving mother,
and God, whose providence brought me here.

—*Chris*

To my soul mate and wife Mireya
who sacrificed much to let this book come to be.
To my mother for teaching me how to write
and my father for giving me the motivation to do so.

—*Dave*

To my mom and dad, thanks for teaching me to follow my dreams.
To my sister, Renee, for always being there for me.
To all of my friends and teachers at The University of Texas at Austin,
for making me what I am and showing me what I can be.
Hook'em Horns.

—*Aaron*

About the Authors

Chris Davis

Chris Davis, CISSP, of Texas Instruments, leverages practical experience from a global corporate environment. Mr. Davis has managed worldwide teams in security architecture, design, and product management. Mr. Davis has trained and presented at Blazck Hat, ISSA, CISA, ConSecWest, McCombs School of Business, 3GSM World Congress, and others in areas including advanced computer forensic analysis of various platforms and devices, information security, and hardware security design. His contributions include projects for Gartner, Harvard, SANS, CIS, and the McCombs School of Business. He has enjoyed positions at eForensics, Cisco Systems, Austin Microsoft Technology Center, and currently Texas Instruments. Mr. Davis was a US Navy Submariner on the USS Nebraska and Submarine NR-1. He holds a bachelor's degree in Nuclear Engineering from Thomas Edison, and a master's in Business from the University of Texas at Austin.

David Cowen

David Cowen, CISSP, is a sr. consultant at Fios, Inc. Mr. Cowen has extensive experience and training in security research, application security testing, penetration testing, and computer forensic analysis in both computer and telecommunications systems and software. He has conducted forensic investigations, developed methodologies for use by incident response teams, and managed teams of forensic consultants. As a sr. consultant for Fios, he has served as an expert witness and consultant in a large variety of legal matters, ranging from internal investigations to anti-trust lawsuits.

Aaron Philipp

Aaron Philipp, CISSP, has extensive experience in the field of forensics. He was the team lead in the Forensics and Survivability Research group at the McCombs School of Business, University of Texas at Austin. He holds a patent in the field of web server survivability. He has consulting experience with U.S.- and foreign-based companies, and in performing network architecture design, cryptographic consultation, penetration testing, and incident response. He also has performed litigation support and contributed expert witness knowledge in multiple court cases, on levels ranging from civil to federal criminal. In addition, he has spoken at several conferences (Black Hat 2002, FBI Infraguard, and more) on the topics of forensic investigation and toolkits, intrusion detection, and hacker methodologies. He holds a BS in Computing Science from the University of Texas at Austin.

About the Contributing Authors

Rafael Gorgal is the manager of evidence collection services at Fios, Inc. He has consulted extensively in the area of information systems security, as well as computer forensics over the past nine years. Mr. Gorgal has also taught information security at Southern Methodist University and at the University of California at Los Angeles. His professional affiliations include President, Southwest Chapter, High Technology Crime Investigations Association; the North Texas Crime Prevention Association; and the American Society for Industrial Security.

Brian H. Karney, CISSP, is director of product management at Guidance Software, where he is responsible for the direction and vision of incident response and computer forensic solutions. Brian brings deep technical expertise and a broad-based business knowledge with experience in forensics, incident response, enterprise security management, system architecture, infrastructure analysis, and directory services. Prior to joining Guidance Software, Mr. Karney worked for CenterBeam, a Silicon Valley–based services company focusing on directory services, IT operations, security architecture, and securing Microsoft environments. Past experience includes expertise as a virus security consultant at Network Associates and infrastructure management consultant at PricewaterhouseCoopers.

Andrew Rosen, a forensic computer scientist, offers unique litigation support services to the legal, law enforcement, and investigative communities. With over a decade of experience in the recovery of computer data and forensic examination (computer forensics), Rosen regularly provides expert testimony in federal and state courts. Along with training attorneys and law enforcement officials in computer investigation techniques, Rosen frequently speaks and writes on emerging matters in the field. Rosen has a worldwide reputation for developing cutting-edge computer crime investigative tools and is frequently consulted by other professionals in the industry.

David Weber practiced law with a boutique complex civil litigation/white collar criminal defense law firm for seven years. During that time, he appeared before both state and federal courts. Mr. Weber's portfolio includes valuable experience in healthcare fraud, misappropriation of trade secrets, environmental law, and cyber intelligence. Following his tenure as an attorney, Mr. Weber directed a regional office of a national consulting firm specializing in investigative and intelligence work for publicly and privately held corporations and their counsel in the United States and abroad. Mr. Weber is now a client executive for Fios, Inc. As a member of the American Bar Association and the State Bar of Texas, he has written numerous articles and presented several seminars on issues ranging from the need for a cohesive cyber security plan in corporate America, to sanctions for discovery abuse. Mr. Weber is honored as a Fellow in the Texas Bar Foundation.

Tomas M. Castrejon's background includes 10 years of computer forensics experience. Prior to founding Digital Disclosure, Inc., Mr. Castrejon managed all computer forensic lab operations and staff for Deloitte & Touche in Northern California and Hawaii for two years. In addition, Mr. Castrejon conducted and supervised litigation support projects and computer-related investigations, including the theft of intellectual property, procurement fraud, and revenue recognition issues. Prior to entering the private sector,

Mr. Castrejon served as a law enforcement officer in California for more than eight years. During that time, he developed a solid grounding in investigative techniques, chain of custody, authentication, and other evidentiary matters. Mr. Castrejon is an active member of the High Technology Crime Investigation association (HTCIA), InfraGard, the Information Systems Security Association (ISSA), and the International Association of Computer Investigative Specialists (IACIS), where he also serves as a coach for students during the rigorous certification process.

About the Technical Reviewers

Erik C. Harssema, CISSP, is a security engineer with Southwest Airlines, responsible for the development and management of the intrusion detection systems, computer incident response program, and computer forensics program. Throughout his eight years of experience in the professional IT security field, he has worked with Ernst and Young LLP, Deloitte and Touche LLP, and AMR Corporation. He has spoken at select security conferences, public and private. He holds a BBA in International Marketing from Texas Christian University and is pursuing a master's in International Business.

Tanya Baccam is an instructor and courseware author for the SANS institute. She provides training on a wide variety of security topics such as system auditing, consulting services, and perimeter protection. She also functions as the director of assurance services for Vigilar, where she is responsible for providing system auditing, penetration testing, vulnerability and risk assessments, computer forensic services, incident response, and training for clients. Prior to joining Vigilar, she served as the manager of infrastructure security for a healthcare organization, as well as being a manager at Deloitte & Touche in the security services practice. Throughout her career, she has consulted with many clients regarding their security architecture, including topics such as perimeter security, network infrastructure design, web application security, and database security. She played an integral role in developing and programming multiple business applications. Currently she holds multiple certifications including CPA, GCFW, GCIH, CISSP, CISM, CISA, and Oracle DBA, as well as being a SANS-certified instructor.

AT A GLANCE

IV   **Presenting Your Findings**

V   **Appendixes**

CONTENTS

Part II

Collecting the Evidence

Part III

Forensic Investigation Techniques

Part IV

Presenting Your Findings

Part V

Appendixes

FOREWORD

Trust me when I tell you that six months from now this industry will have gone through more changes than my peers and I could have imagined. That is the very reason why many of us find computer forensics to be the most fascinating industry of our time.

By the end of the 1980s, personal computers made the workplace more efficient, and slowly but surely they found their way into the home. Color graphics cards and monitors, along with the modem and communication software, gave the home-computer user access to new avenues of exploration, including both legal and illegal activities. The growing computer market introduced new types of storage media every six months and the amount of available storage grew exponentially. Users could now go to shows and buy parts to build and upgrade their computers.

Despite the growing amount of data on the personal computer, it was common for law enforcement personnel to overlook the computer during an investigation. Even with the very small sizes of the early media and the then-advanced DOS-based tools, computer forensic investigations were tedious and time-consuming.

In those days, there was neither formal training on this new science, nor books on the subject. The first recognized book on computer forensics, per se, was Que's *Guide to Data Recovery*, which was copyrighted in 1991. It's no longer in print but is still treasured by early computer forensic examiners, like myself.

In the spring of 1998, I participated in the Treasury Department's four-week Seized Computer Evidence Recovery training at the Federal Law Enforcement Training Center. Five years after my IACIS training in Portland, and just a few months prior to the release of Windows 98, we were still being trained on the exact same DOS-based tools. The problem now was that investigations involved a lot more media, with a lot more storage.

One of the other special agents in the class was talking about the Open Source operating system, Linux, which most of us felt we did not need; it was an entirely new file system, with completely new and different evidentiary artifacts. My peers and I were soon to learn of the forensic possibilities from Linux-based computer tools.

During the summer of 1998, I conducted a computer forensic exam on two hard drives for the Riverside County Sheriff's Office. The case started out as a simple child-pornography possession investigation, but it soon revealed journals chronicling 30 years of child molestation with photographs of almost every victim. The examination was time-consuming and in the end produced 25 six-inch binders of evidence. That was the last major investigation that I conducted with DOS tools. The corporate environment requires efficiency. Using today's computer forensic tools, this same investigation would have only taken far less time and could have been far more thorough.

In December of 1998, I received formal training on the commercial Windows-based computer forensic program, EnCase version 1, and spent the Christmas holidays reviewing old cases with this new tool. That prior investigation that had consumed my summer could have been accomplished in less than half the time.

The introduction of Linux and EnCase caused an industrial revolution in computer forensics. Many of my "DOS Dinosaur" computer forensic peers looked down their nose at the new Windows program because it made computer forensic examinations easier and less of a "black art." Worse than that, you had to buy it and most law enforcement agencies were not properly funding the computer forensic efforts.

Very quietly, the Open Source community expanded through the end of the 90s. Many of the DOS Dinosaurs jumped on the Open Source train to avoid being associated with the unwashed masses jumping on the Windows one and conducting "point-and-click" computer forensics.

As time rolled into the first decade of the 21st century, we saw the birth of physical write-blocking hardware devices, making Windows acquisitions possible, as well as computer hardware manufacturers, who specialized in computer workstations designed for computer forensics. Of course, the Penguin-loving Linux enthusiasts poo-pooed the write-blocking device progress, as Linux could already mount media read-only.

After the tragic events of 9/11/2001, special agents with the Federal Bureau of Investigation seized thousands of personal computers, requiring very fast computer forensic examinations. That event made the public aware of the term *steganography*: the art and science of hiding information by embedding messages within other, seemingly harmless messages.

Computer forensic examinations now support investigations involving narcotics transactions, money laundering, identity theft, false identification, counterfeiting, child sexual exploitation, murder, suicide, financial fraud, sexual harassment, and stalking to just name a few. People now use not only personal computers but also PDAs and cell phones, which can also hold potential evidence.

Computer professionals and data recovery specialists have now joined the onetime law enforcement–exclusive computer forensic community. There are now at least a half a dozen write-blocker manufacturers and at least that many commercial computer forensic software tool companies based on Windows, Linux, and Macintosh. College campuses have added computer forensic classes to their curriculum. The federal budget for 2005 includes millions of dollars to fund the expansion of computer forensics training and cyber investigations. There are now at least a dozen books, and a number in second editions, on the computer forensic practice.

The hardware, software, and training revenues from this industry easily exceed $150,000,000. I can't even fathom the hundreds of millions of dollars billed for computer forensic and electronic discovery consultation work. Large-scale computer investigations now involve terabytes of data, which didn't seem possible 20 years ago. There will be new issues with new files systems, large network data sets, seamless encryption, and data destruction/privacy protection tools in our future.

As the computer industry has changed, so have the investigative tools and techniques, but one thing has remained constant: that is the power of knowledge and the requirement for training. If you are not learning something new or being reminded of something you forgot in this industry, then you are not paying attention. It is my hope that this book will both shed light on something fresh and help you remember those things you previously knew.

For anyone who is tasked with performing a computer forensics investigation, *Hacking Exposed Computer Forensics* is a must-have reference in your arsenal of tools. Complete with information that has yet to be adequately covered in the market, such as the sections on remote investigations, Macintosh forensics, enterprise storage, and PDA/cell phone forensics, *Hacking Exposed Computer Forensics* provides you the necessary tools for completing investigations in a thorough and forensically sound manner, and will challenge your thinking so you will become more effective in your investigations.

Bill Siebert
Guidance Software
October 16, 2004

Bill Siebert has successfully recovered critical digital evidence pursuant to computer forensic examinations, in support of federal, state and local law enforcement criminal investigations involving the sexual exploitation of children, drug trafficking, money laundering, financial fraud, commercial fraud, and the illegal exportation of munitions list items.

During his law enforcement career with the United States Customs Service, Office of Investigations, he conducted over one thousand computer forensic examinations. He has testified in state and federal courts on computer evidence issues as they relate to the distribution of child pornography and the proper means of processing computer evidence, and he has been accepted by the courts as a qualified expert witness on these subjects.

For two years, Mr. Siebert worked off-duty as a member of Guidance Software Incorporated (GSI) training staff. This elite group of law enforcement computer forensic examiners provides instruction on the EnCase software and digital evidence artifacts, as well as on the proper computer-evidence handling and examination procedures. He has also provided training to other federal agents and to state and local law enforcement personnel on the *U.S. Attorneys' Guidelines for Searching and Seizing Computers* and the best ways of presenting computer evidence.

In December 2000, Senior Special Agent Bill Siebert received an award from the United States Attorneys Office for his contributions in digital evidence recovery in support of critical criminal investigations and prosecutions in the Central District of California.

In January 2001, Mr. Siebert joined the management team at Guidance Software and has held a number of positions in the company.

ACKNOWLEDGMENTS

We simply could not have done this without the help of many, many people. It was an amazing challenge coordinating the necessary depth of corporate, legal, criminal, and technical expertise across so many subjects. Many old and new friends donated knowledge, time, techniques, tools, and much more to make this project a success. We are truly grateful to each of you.

The wonderful and overworked team at McGraw-Hill/Osborne is outstanding. We sincerely appreciate your dedication, coaching, and long hours during the course of this project. Jane Brownlow, this book is a result of your tireless dedication to the completion of this project. We congratulate you on your marriage and wish you the best. We look forward to working with you again in the future. We would also like to extend a big round of thanks to LeeAnn Pickrell, our senior project editor, for her coordination and work with Lisa Theobald on the copy edits. Jane and LeeAnn, you are truly amazing. Thank you so much for being a part of this. We also would like to thank the wonderful efforts of Athena Honore, Agatha Kim, Jessica Wilson, Lisa Theobald, Valerie Perry, and Susie Elkind.

A special thank you goes to Brian Karney, Rafael Gorgal, Bill Siebert, George Hinkle, Andrew Rosen, David Weber, Tanya Baccam, Tomas Castrejon, and Erik Harssema for their contributing works and deep reviews.

Your involvement truly made the difference. Thank you also to the several reviewers, including Curtis Tomlinson, Jeimy José Cano Martínez, and Darren Windham. Your reviews were wonderful, detailed, and significant in providing a useful product for the readers.

In particular, Brian Karney—you went way above and beyond, and came to the table with excellent contributions and reviews. Rafael Gorgal, with all that you have going on, thank you for taking the time on this project. We know the readers will appreciate your expertise. Bill Siebert, you did an outstanding job outlining the history of computer forensics, helping people remember the origins of this field. Thank you for writing the foreword. George, you're going to go far, and we sincerely appreciate your help and expertise! Andrew, David, Tanya, Tomas, and Erik, you each juggled multiple responsibilities including your home lives and extensive work responsibilities to work on this book. We thank you for that time and know the readers will appreciate the effort you put into this project.

Vendors were gracious in donating tools and technical expertise. We want to thank Jennifer Dedrick, Brian Karney, and Bill Siebert at Guidance Software; Amber Schroader and her wonderful group (Rob, Will, and many others) at Paraben Forensics; Nii Larnyoh at OutIndex; Shawn M. Strickler at eMag Solutions; and Paul Sanderson at Sanderson Forensics. Additionally, we would like to thank Ken Lucke at www.stopspam.org and Elizabeth at dtSearch.

—*The Authors*

To my wonderful wife Sarah, I love you so much. Thank you for the many long nights you sat by me and loved and supported me. This book would not exist without you. I'm thankful to have you as my wife and look forward to the many wonderful years we have left. I love you!

Aaron and Dave, thank you for sharing the load and investing your time into this work. You are good friends, and I appreciate the opportunity to learn from you. Through all of this project's challenges, among the three of us, we pulled it off. Brian Karney, Rafael Gorgal, Bill Siebert, George Hinkle, Andrew Rosen, David Weber, Tanya Baccam, Tomas Castrejon, Erik Harssema, Curtis Tomlinson, Jeimy José Cano Martínez, David Weber, and Darren Windham—thank you for your generous time and reviews. Many of you balanced active work and home lives to fit this into your schedule. Thank you for your tremendous help.

To the crew at McGraw-Hill/Osborne, especially Jane Brownlow, LeeAnn Pickrell, and Lisa Theobald, you're a wonderful group to work with. I am grateful for the outstanding guidance and continual support. You're an amazing team, and I'm blessed for having worked with you.

A special thank you goes to my family for their love and support. I'm grateful to Rob for his wisdom and for introducing me to Larry and IT security. Jon, thank you for the best demonstration of work ethic I have ever seen. David, good luck as you rise in the ranks at GE; I'm proud to have you as a brother and mentor. Thank each of you for your wisdom, love, support, and guidance.

Finally, a special thank you goes to Jennifer Dedrick and Amber Schroeder, who convinced me to move forward with the project in the beginning stages. Thank you to all the friends and influences along the way, including Dr. Larry Leibrock for the opportunities to learn, Brian Kearney for your ideas, Chris McAbee of Dallas, Texas, for always being there for a game of hoops, and many, many others. I sincerely appreciate you all.

—*Chris*

It is hard to put into words that anyone can read the thanks and praise you have for another. First and foremost this book would not exist if it where not for my wife Mireya, who gave up countless hours of our first year of marriage to allow me to write this book. My parents have been extremely supportive my entire life and I can never pay them back for all they have done for me. To my brothers and their families I would like to give my thanks for their support and enthusiasm of a book they will probably never read.

Outside of my family I must extend extreme thanks to Rafael Gorgal, fellow co-author and an outstanding man who pitched in whenever asked and always was there to lend a hand. A very special thank you to Andrew Rosen of ASR Data, another fellow co-author without whom we could not possibly cover the Macintosh system with such experience. Andy's SMART forensic system provided us with a commercial Linux alternative for our work.

To all of my old friends and co-workers I would like to say, Hi, how are you doing? Finally, to all of the people who read this book, I hope you walk away from this tome armed with forensic knowledge and practical techniques that you can put to work right away.

—*Dave*

I would like to thank my fellow authors for their tireless work and many long nights getting this book done. Thanks also to Arthur Dexter and Eric Tucker for keeping me honest with my writing.

Thanks to Neil Iscoe and Paul Ruiz for all the help; here's hoping that one day I have half the business acumen that you do.

Thanks to Fr. Patrick Johnson for all the sage advice and for reminding me of the importance of balance in life.

Thanks to Chris Sweeny, Jeff Gillette, and all of my teammates and brothers on the University of Texas Rugby Team. You taught me mental toughness, brotherhood, the value of perseverance, and how to never give up.

Thanks to Larry Leibrock and David Burns for introducing me to forensics and treating me so well while I was at the McCombs School of Business. And to every one of my computer science professors for showing me how much I still have to learn.

A huge thank you to Robert Groshon and Bradley O. Brauser, for believing in me all those years ago.

Finally, I would like to give another thank you to my family, my mother and father who gave me my first computer when I was seven, and my sister Renee.

—*Aaron*

"The excitement of learning separates youth from old age.
As long as you're learning you're not old."

—*Rosalyn S. Yalow*

INTRODUCTION

This is not an incident response handbook. It's about what happens after the incident response has taken place, the nights of prolonged investigation to find the truth. When we began writing this book, we had a fundamental tenet: Write a clear handbook for performing investigations of computer crime. There is a wealth of knowledge and resources out there for tracking down the hacker who has just broken into your server and changed your web page. That is not the focus of this book.

In our experience as investigators, we found that we were called on more often to locate documents and data that pointed to corporate malfeasance and violations of policy, or that broke the law. This included trolling through gigs upon gigs of e-mail, restoring data from old tapes, and finding ways to extract information out of seemingly defunct media. Time and time again we came across situations where evidence that could have been used to nail a suspect had to be thrown out because the person who collected and found the evidence did it in a haphazard or incorrect manner.

This book is for the first responders. The people who are on the front lines day in and day out, doing the best they can to investigate the various problems that a normal user base will cause. You never know when a violation will suddenly become a criminal act. We want to ensure that you have the proper toolkit to perform your investigations in a manner that is complete and defensible.

HOW THIS BOOK IS ORGANIZED

We have broken this book into five parts, reflective of the different stages of the investigation.

Preparing for an Incident

This section discusses how to develop a forensics process and set up the lab environment needed to conduct your investigation in an accurate and skillful manner. In addition, it lays the technical groundwork for the rest of the book.

Collecting the Evidence

These chapters teach you how to effectively find, capture, and prepare evidence for investigation. Additionally, we cover highlights of how the law applies to evidence collection.

Forensic Investigation Techniques

This section illustrates how to apply recovery techniques to investigations from the evidence you have collected across many platforms and scenarios found in the corporate setting. We introduce field-tested methods and techniques for recovering suspect activities.

Presenting Your Findings

The legal environment of technical forensics is the focus of this section. We discuss how you will interact with council, testify in court, and report on your findings. In many ways, this is the most important part of the forensics process.

Appendixes

We have placed a small library of supplementary materials, which over the years we have found to be useful, in the appendixes. This includes forms and checklists to use in the lab, case law that you can refer to, and a glossary of regularly used terms that you can use in your reports.

The Basic Building Blocks: Attacks and Countermeasures

This format should be very familiar to anyone who has read a *Hacking Exposed* book before. How we define attacks and countermeasures for forensics, however, is a bit different than in past books.

This Is an Attack Icon

In previous *Hacking Exposed* books, this icon was used to denote a type of attack that could be launched against your network or target. In this book, the attack icon relates to procedures, techniques, and concerns that threaten to compromise your investigation.

For instance, failing to properly image a hard drive is labeled an attack with a very high risk rating. This is because you are going to see it often; it is not difficult to create an image, and if when you are imaging you accidentally write to the disk, your whole investigation may be compromised, no matter what else you do correctly.

Popularity	*The frequency with which you will run across this attack or technique in an investigation; 1 being most rare, and 10 being widely seen.*
Simplicity	*The effort or degree of skill involved in creating an attack or technique; 1 being quite high, and 10 being little or involving no effort or skill.*
Impact	*The potential damage to an investigation if you miss this detail; 1 being trivial or no measurable damage, and 10 being certain loss of evidence or equivalent damage.*
Risk	***The preceding three values are averaged to give the overall risk rating, representing the risk to the investigation's success.***

This Is a Countermeasure Icon

In this book, the countermeasure icon represents the ways that you can ensure correct completion of the investigation for the attack. In our hard drive example, this would mean correctly hashing the drive and verifying the hash after you have taken the image.

Other Visual Aides

We have also made use of several other visual icons that help point out fine details or gotchas that are frequently overlooked.

ONLINE RESOURCES

Forensics is a constantly changing field. In addition, there are things outside the scope of the book that weren't included. We have created a web site that contains additional information, corrections for the book, and electronic versions of the things discussed in these pages. The URL is

     www.hackingexposedforensics.com

In addition, if you have any questions or comments for the authors, feel free to e-mail us @:

authors@hackingexposedforensics.com

We hope that you visit the web page to keep up-to-date with the content in the book and the other things we think are useful. E-mail us if you have any questions or comments; we'd love to hear from you.

A FINAL WORD TO OUR READERS

Thank you for taking the time to read this book. We have put countless hours and enormous effort into creating something we hope will be useful for you. Read this book all the way through, and then when you are done using it as a tutorial you can keep it around as a reference. Forensics is a detail-oriented job, and it is easy to get overwhelmed and overlook something. In addition, it is very easy to get in over your head. If an investigation goes far enough, you will end up against someone whose entire goal in life is to make you look bad; we like to call them the opposing attorneys. This book is a great place to start and learn, but don't be afraid to call in extra help if you have even the slightest inkling that it is needed. That being said, we hope you enjoy reading this book as much as we did writing it. Good luck in all your investigations.

—The Authors

PART I

PREPARING FOR AN INCIDENT

CASE STUDY: LAB PREPARATIONS

The service was a hit and very popular to the endless streams of new people coming to the city. Comfortable shoes are the norm for transportation here, and the Internet Café was gratefully received—at least until Charlie Blink arrived.

ACME Services is a large company operating in one of the largest cities in the world, offering Internet services to its patrons. In a flash, while walking on foot in premier shopping and touring districts, users of the Internet service could swoop in and check their bank accounts, read important e-mails, or spend countless hours surfing online. Charlie quickly saw the huge dollar potential of stealing the identities of these unsuspecting users. He installed key loggers on several computers to test his ability to steal a user's identity, open a line of credit at the user's bank, and cash it out.

Cashing Out

It was a success! Charlie and a small gang of helpers compromised more than 60 computers across dozens of locations, and unsuspecting users suffered hundreds of thousands in monetary damages—these people lost some serious cash.

It wasn't long before the U.S. Secret Service got involved and traced the source of the damages to Mr. Blink. After capturing the suspect, they further discovered that Charlie was taking advantage of ACME Services' computers, but they did not yet know how. The Secret Service notified ACME Services quietly to control any potential negative publicity for the publicly traded company. Acting as a silent partner, the Secret Service coordinated with ACME Services to bring in outside help.

In the meantime, the judge released Charlie on bail. The story wasn't over yet.

Preparing for a Forensics Operation

Before we start an investigation of any case, we have a thorough understanding of the forensics process, technical training, and proper lab preparation. These are critical to the success of an investigation. All the technicians assigned to our unit are required to have the necessary training and background to understand and conduct investigations. The training ensures that technicians avoid frequently made mistakes, such as turning on the computer to "check it out and see if anything important is in there."

Our team runs a secure lab and a formal case-management system. Before we started on the ACME case, we pretested all the tools in the lab and neatly tucked the portable hardware units into the flyaway kits. We were ready to go when the call came to us. Our case-management system lets us handle the case and organize the evidence as it is returned to the lab. We control a large number of systems, tracking where the systems go and assigning the systems unique numbers with the proper documentation attached. This enables us to compare notes quickly and understand similarities found in multiple computers.

Rapid Response

Our flyaway kit includes a fully portable system with write blockers and extra drive bays ready to copy data. We also carry a standard set of tools and hardware used for our investigations. The standard set helped immensely when we needed to re-create our working system onto five new computers to handle all the systems we had to image. Having the tools and paperwork ready beforehand was critical to the rapid response demanded by the customer, especially considering the number of computers we had to investigate.

Solid process controls, training, preparations, and case management allowed us to respond quickly and efficiently. Our success in this case depended on our investment in a deeper understanding of how case operations work and how we could get the system to tell us the information we needed to know.

CHAPTER 1

THE FORENSICS PROCESS

fo·ren·sics (fə-rĕn´sĭks, -zĭks) *n. (used with a sing. verb)* The use of science and technology to investigate and establish facts in criminal or civil courts of law.

Corporate espionage. Illicit images. Violations of corporate policy. Hacking attempts. Work in information technology for even a short amount of time and you will find yourself dealing with one of these situations. When an incident occurs, the inevitable first words from management will be "What happened?" Apply computer forensics correctly and you answer that question in a way that is technically, legally, and analytically sound. To meet this goal, a forensics investigator must combine time-tested forensic techniques, legal frameworks, and cutting-edge technology to determine the facts.

Forensics is, first and foremost, a legal process. Depending on the investigation, you must understand and apply a vast array of legal concepts and precedents, such as chain of custody, spoilage of evidence, and dealing with production of evidence in court. If this sounds daunting, that's because it is. If the crime is heinous enough, a lawyer will call on you to take the stand and testify about your investigation, your findings, and your qualifications as an investigator. If you do not perform the investigation with dedication to the process, technical details, and legal issues required, the facts that you uncover are useless. In the extreme, criminals get away, corporate secrets are leaked, and the investigator is held with a fiduciary responsibility for the mistakes made during the investigation. To put it in more concise terms: Be prepared. Have a process, understand what you know and what you don't know, and create a list of who to call when the investigation exceeds your knowledge of either the technical or legal issues.

TYPES OF INVESTIGATIONS

Determining the type of investigation you are conducting is vital in discerning the correct process to follow. Each type of investigation has its own set of pitfalls, and knowing the parameters for the investigation you are conducting will help you avoid them. For the purposes of this book, the types of investigations are divided into three main categories: internal, civil, and criminal.

 Internal

Popularity:	8
Simplicity:	6
Impact:	6
Risk Rating:	**7**

As an internal corporate investigator, you will be dealing primarily with internal investigations. This is the fastest and most covert of the three types of investigations. Typically, the company owns the resources that are the target of the analysis. This eliminates the need for subpoenas and discovery orders and allows the examiner to conduct the investigation in an expedient manner with full access to the relevant data. These investigations have an element of secrecy required, as the suspect is typically an active employee who is in violation of corporate policy. The simple knowledge that an investigation is occurring would be enough for the suspect to destroy evidence and potentially cause more harm. The technical process and procedures should be similar to those followed by the civil examiners, since the investigation may escalate to a civil one if the investigator finds corporate malfeasance.

Civil

Popularity:	10
Simplicity:	8
Impact:	7
Risk Rating:	8

A civil investigation is similar in form and function to an internal investigation. The main difference here is the fact that an opposing company owns the resources used in the investigation. This means that for every piece of data that you investigate, the court must issue a subpoena or discovery order. This can create problems for the investigator. If the judge becomes convinced that you do not need a certain piece of data to complete your investigation accurately, you must find a way to make do without that evidence. The spirit of the civil investigation lives and dies on the proceedings that occur in court, the skill of your counsel, and the personal styling of the judge assigned to the case. Because these cases typically involve two companies, the need for secrecy focuses on the mass media. Sometimes, however, companies can actually use the mass media as a leverage point in the court, which makes your investigation all the more important.

Criminal

Popularity:	8
Simplicity:	10
Impact:	10
Risk Rating:	10

These investigations are often for the highest stakes. The suspect's livelihood is on the line, and every aspect of the investigation is scrutinized and reworked multiple times. Time is typically not an issue. The investigation can last weeks, months, or even years. Accuracy is paramount, with attention to the process and documentation a close second. Know your process, know your tools, and above all know your limits. If you find yourself in the middle of a criminal investigation, pick up the phone and call the proper law enforcement authorities. Do not attempt to conduct these investigations in a vacuum. If you botch the investigation, justice is not served, and you are personally liable for the problems that caused the investigation to fail. These cases play out in the media, with the latest happenings of the court showing up on the 6 o'clock news. Credibility of the investigator is also at a premium, and if you don't have the proper credentials and background to testify properly on your findings, your credibility will be destroyed on the stand in a very public forum.

 NOTE The focus of this book is internal and civil cases. In the criminal world, even if you win the case, you can still damage your reputation simply by taking on the case. Do not take criminal forensic investigations lightly, and strongly consider leaving them to someone who is a career criminal forensics examiner.

 ## Determining the Type of Investigation

Knowing the type of case you are dealing with defines how you conduct your investigation. This determination is never as easy as it sounds. Cases can escalate in the blink of an eye. You don't want to get in a situation where evidence has to be thrown out because you took the situation too lightly and didn't fully think through what type of case you were dealing with. Until you are convinced otherwise, always treat a new case as a criminal one, and after your advising counsel has told you to stand down, you can then relax the standards. This simple guiding principle, although rarely followed, can save an investigator immeasurable grief down the line.

THE ROLE OF THE INVESTIGATOR

What makes a good computer forensics investigator? The ability to be creative in the discovery of evidence, to be rigorous in the application of a disciplined process, and to understand the legal issues that are involved every step of the way. However, other factors play into the equation, depending on the investigation's context. Stories of investigators who ruined or destroyed a case because of incompetence or arrogance are all too familiar. You must have a complete understanding of the risks you are taking on when accepting a case.

 ## Investigator Bias

Popularity:	7
Simplicity:	9
Impact:	8
Risk Rating:	**8**

The investigator must play the role of an unbiased third party. Think of it in terms of traditional forensic sciences. For example, if the scientist performing a blood test in a violent crime case is friends with the suspect, the results of the test are dubious at best. The same thing holds for computer forensics. As those who have been on the stand in this position will attest, you must be unbiased. If the opposing counsel can create the impression that you are biased, you will be embarrassed on the stand or in deposition.

Resolving Bias

Always practice full disclosure with your management and counsel. Discuss with them things that could be potential conflicts of interest. If you had dinner at the suspect's house two years ago, make sure they know about it. If the other side knows about it but your guys don't, you are in for a bad time during and after deposition. Don't be afraid to bring in a third-party firm or investigator who can conduct the investigation in an unbiased manner.

 ## Investigator Qualifications

Popularity:	6
Simplicity:	7
Impact:	9
Risk Rating:	7

The investigator must be qualified to perform the analysis in a skillful manner. For criminal investigations, the law enforcement examiners go through rigorous training seminars to become skilled in the art. Experts who have a track record in the industry and who have enough credentials to imply competency often conduct civil investigations. Commonly, IT administrators conduct internal investigations, or in the case of large-scale corporations, a special division of the company is employed. I have been a party to many dinners and outings where experienced investigators tell war stories about going against "newbies." These stories always end badly for the newbie. Don't be the subject of one of these stories. If you are not properly qualified and credentialed to perform the investigation, the court will throw out your findings and you will be in a world of hurt with your superiors.

 ## Investigator Use of Evidence

Popularity:	6
Simplicity:	7
Impact:	9
Risk Rating:	7

Evidence is a tricky thing. The best rule of thumb is that if you didn't empirically find the evidence through hands-on investigation, don't use it. Hearsay is not admissible in a court of law, and we all know what happens when you make assumptions. The best course of action is to treat every investigation as a blank slate with no prior knowledge. Go into an investigation with an open mind, and take the unsubstantiated words of others with a grain of salt. The tools and the processes exist for a reason; use them and trust them. The more that politics and personal agendas influence your analysis, the less credible your results become in court.

Investigator Liability

Popularity:	6
Simplicity:	7
Impact:	9
Risk Rating:	7

If you ignore the caveats and decide to conduct the investigation, you are financially and legally liable in the event it becomes a civil or criminal case and you are not doing a corporate investigation. In the best case, the courts throw out the analysis and a third party conducts another investigation. In civil cases, you may be liable for loss damages resulting from the destruction or inadmissibility of evidence. All those high-priced lawyers that your company is using to go after someone will soon be coming after you. In criminal cases, you can be tried for negligence and serve jail time.

 ### Being a Good Investigator

Know your limits, and don't be afraid to call in qualified professionals if the situation requires it. This may sound basic, but practice with your tools. Constantly revalidate your processes for handling evidence and test the results of your tools. You must be able to execute flawlessly when the time comes. This is a hard lesson that most rookie investigators learn in their first deposition when the opposing counsel's experts contest them. They leave the deposition with egos deflated, wishing that they had finished reading this book.

ELEMENTS OF A GOOD PROCESS

The task of a computer forensics investigator is difficult. It is one of the most adversarial occupations in information technology. You will have every aspect of your technical competency and methods scrutinized to their very core. As such, it is imperative that you use a deterministic, repeatable process that is clear, concise, and simple. Adherence to this process is the examiner's greatest asset. Deviate from it, and your investigation will be for naught. Having a defined, proven process means you show several elements:

- ▼ Cross-validation of findings
- ■ Proper evidence handling
- ■ Completeness of investigation
- ■ Management of archives
- ■ Technical competency
- ■ Explicit definition and justification for the process
- ■ Legal compliance
- ▲ Flexibility

This list will become your lifeline the day you either take the stand yourself or hand off the investigation to authorities who will pursue it further. These items are the difference between an effective, expedient investigation and playing around with a neat piece of software. Software is good, and while your friends may be impressed with your comprehensive knowledge of the latest in-vogue forensic tool, the opposing counsel, and more importantly the judge, will not.

Cross-Validation

Whenever possible, rely on more than one tool to back up your findings. Cross-validation is one of the key tools available to the forensic investigator. If you trust only one tool in your investigation, you live and die by that tool. If the opposing counsel can rip holes in the single tool you use, it doesn't matter how solid your investigative process is. A member of law enforcement once told me that he would assume that he could win cases based solely on the fact that the defense used a tool he knew had several holes. You can mitigate this type of situation by cross-validating findings with multiple toolsets.

Proper Evidence Handling

The forensic investigator must always be aware of the chain of custody of evidence after collection. It is vital that you show who had access to the evidence, what they did with it, and that no tampering with the evidence occurred. You must be able to show that the evidence you present in court is exactly the same as the evidence that existed at the time it was collected. Become familiar with the different cryptographic hashing functions, such as MD5 and SHA-1. These algorithms act like fingerprints, allowing you to show mathematically that the evidence is the same today as the day the investigator collected it. Also, always keep records of who accesses evidence, when they access the evidence, and what they do with it. This will help to refute evidence injection arguments that the opposing counsel may make during litigation. For your convenience, we have included a form for this in Appendix A of this book.

Completeness of Investigation

When conducting an investigation, a forensics investigator has to be able to show that he or she conducted the search for evidence in a complete manner. Lawyers hate new evidence brought up days before court time that they didn't know about. The clients they represent hate it even more when that new evidence causes them to lose the case. Know what you know and know what you don't know. Follow your counsel's direction on what evidence to look for and don't go outside the scope of that. But use a process that ensures that you will locate every piece and reference to that evidence. If you don't use a solid, tested process for evidence collection, analysis, and reporting, you will miss evidence.

Management of Archives

In the legal world, just because a judge has ruled does not mean the case is over. An investigator may be called on to rework a case months or years after the initial investigation. This makes it imperative always to ensure that proper archiving and case management is part of the process. If counsel comes back six months after a ruling asking you to rework a case for the appeal, you must be able to fulfill that request. This means proper document retention, data storage, and backup policies. As with your initial testimony, you will be required to show proper evidence handling and authenticity of the data. The last thing you want as a investigator is to subpoena the opposing counsel for an image of a hard drive because your process didn't include proper retention procedures.

Technical Competency

Have a complete technical understanding of everything you do. The surefire way to lose a case is to justify your actions by saying, "That's what the tool says to do." Challenge the assumptions that the tools make. If you do settle on a specific toolset, understand the tradeoffs that the developers made when designing the tool. Know the weaknesses and strengths of your toolset so you can stand by it when questioned. A prime example of this is the way that the novice investigator treats digital signatures. It is common for someone with a basic understanding of a cryptographic hash to make the statement that each dataset will create a unique hash. While this statement is marginally true, the "birthday attack" shows that this can be subverted. If you understand hashing and are familiar with the birthday attack, it is easy to address this subversion when questioned. If you don't understand these basics, you will be torn apart by the opposing expert.

 The birthday attack is based on the fact that if you continually change input datasets, the resulting hash will be the same alarmingly more often than one would expect. Its name is derived from the fact that with 23 people in a room, there is approximately a 50 percent chance that two of them share a birthday on the same day of the year.

Explicit Definition and Justification for the Process

Hardware malfunctions. Software crashes. You must conduct your investigation in a manner that allows you to retrace all your steps. You must follow a discrete and clear path while performing an investigation that is easily explainable to a judge and opposing counsel. If you end up questioned on your methodology and the line of thinking that led you to the results you are presenting, you have to justify yourself. Do this by showing the steps and walking others through the investigation. If, when questioned on your methods, you can't provide clear evidence that they were correct, the investigation was for naught.

Legal Compliance

Always ensure that your process conforms to the laws in the jurisdiction of the investigation. For an internal corporate investigation, ensure that it complies with the corporate policies set forth. The most technically creative and astute investigations are meaningless if they don't adhere to the legal rules of the case. Talk to the lawyers or the corporate higher-ups. Get feedback on how the investigation should proceed, the type of evidence desired, and where the legal or corporate policy landmines exist. Remember that at the end of the day, the role of the investigator is a supporting role in a much bigger play. Talk to the legal or corporate experts and don't perform the investigation in a vacuum.

Flexibility

Every investigation is different. Each has its own set of requirements and pitfalls. It is important that the process that you use to conduct investigations can cope with change. A common issue with rookie examiners is reliance on just one tool. If an investigation requires you to find evidence on technology not supported by the tool, your process is worthless. Make sure you design your process to cope with new technologies and requirements that may pop up as the investigation continues, and as you take on new investigations.

DEFINING A PROCESS

Now that we have discussed what makes a good forensic investigator and what are the elements of a sound process, let's define a process. The remainder of the chapter will focus on the process designed by Andrew Rosen, CEO of ASR Data; it's called the "6 A's." It is sound and has been tested in both legal and technical aspects. In addition, it is flexible enough to handle the diverse requirements that you may see as an investigator. The 6 A's are as follows:

- ▼ Assessment
- ■ Acquisition
- ■ Authentication
- ■ Analysis
- ■ Articulation
- ▲ Archival

When applied correctly, these steps can guide you to a complete and justifiable investigation. They have been tested in court time and time again, with years of refinement.

To understand the process as a whole, you must understand what each step in the methodology entails.

Assessment

This first phase of the process details what you do when presented with a case and need to determine a course of action. Five core steps guide you through the initial assessment phase:

1. **Determine Scope and Quantity of the Data**   This requires that you, as the investigator, work with the individuals requesting the examination to determine what the investigation will cover and approximately how much data the investigation will entail.

2. **Identify Repositories**   Before beginning an investigation but after determination of the scope, you must identify the location of data that could potentially hold evidence. This could be anything from personal computers to enterprise servers, PDAs, or cell phones. At this point, you need to determine whether you have the tools you need to complete the examination properly.

3. **Protect and Preserve**   Once you determine where the data to examine is stored, you must take steps to protect that data at all costs. If it can be shown that the data was modified outside normal business processes after the incident occurred, you will have problems justifying your findings. This preservation action must occur as quickly as feasible. As will be discussed in later chapters, accomplishing this depends on the circumstances of the investigation; no hard-and-fast rule applies to every case.

4. **Establish Chain of Custody**   After protecting the evidence, it is a legal requirement that chain of custody is established. As discussed earlier, this entails creating a record of who did what to the data when. The longer you wait to establish chain of custody, the more difficult it is to trace the findings back to the original data. You must be able to show that the data is unmodified and that every attempt to access and interpret it was logged.

5. **Preview the Data**   Only after the completion of steps 1 through 4 should you preview the data in a manner that guarantees it is not changed. This allows you to prepare for the Acquisition phase of the process, when you will create a forensic copy of the data for the purpose of investigation and interpretation. Be very careful to use only forensically approved tools, as standard interfaces such as Windows Explorer can cause inadvertent modifications to things such as file metadata.

Acquisition

This is the point at which you will actually acquire the data in a forensically sound manner for conducting the investigation. Detailed discussion of this phase occurs in later chapters. However, at a broad level, four core steps are involved in this phase of the process:

1. **Identify the Source Media**   Data is stored on media, and you need to know what type of data is stored and how to access it. While this step sounds obvious, some pitfalls can occur. This issue can be especially problematic when you are presented, for example, with 15-year-old tape backups and no one has a clue what format or media the tape is actually stored in. Creativity and ingenuity are paramount in such situations.

2. **Identify the Destination Media**   When making a forensic image of media, you want to copy the data onto media that is as similar to the source media as possible. If the source is a specific hard drive from a specific manufacturer, do everything you can to get the same one for imaging. Sometimes, as in the 15-year-old tape example, it's not possible to get identical media. In such a case, make sure you justify and document your media decision well and that the differences between the media didn't cause any problems or artifacts in imaging. This is a common method that opposing experts use to debunk each other. Be careful.

3. **Select Acquisition Parameters**   Establish the parameters required for proper imaging. The type of case and legal requirements placed upon the investigator will determine this. To use an old construction analogy, some jobs require a hammer and some require a screwdriver. Know what you are dealing with and act appropriately.

4. **Create the Image**. After you have determined the media and set your parameters, create the image. The image creation process needs to assure that it hasn't modified the data and that the image is complete. You must have metadata to accompany the image so that you can validate this process in the authentication phase.

Authentication

The purpose of this phase is to determine whether the image that you have created is identical to the original data. The reliable way to accomplish this is through metadata cryptographic hashes. Before you create the image, create a hash of the original data in its pristine state. Immediately after you create the image, create a hash of the image data. These two hashes must match; if they don't, you did something wrong and you will lose the case. It is also important that these hashes exist outside the data. If you place the hash inside the data to be imaged, you will be changing the original data and thus invalidating your image and your investigation. Also, ensure that the hashing algorithm you choose is sufficiently secure. A simple checksum is too easy to spoof for evidence verification. The two common algorithms used in this step are the MD5 and the SHA-1 algorithms. While the forensics community battles about which is better, at the end of the day as long as you can justify your usage of your flavor of choice, either will be OK to use in practice.

Analysis

After you have determined what data you need to examine and have forensically verified images of that data, you can begin analysis. This is the meat of the investigation. The entire second part of this book addresses this phase, so we discuss it only at a broad level here. The key thing to keep in mind whenever performing analysis is completeness. Always be sure that you have looked in every nook and cranny and that you haven't missed anything relevant. Lawyers hate it when opposing counsel finds new evidence that destroys your case. You should, too, as it will mean that you will probably never work for that lawyer again. Be complete and creative; unconventional thinking will help greatly in this phase.

Articulation

After you complete your investigation, you will probably have come up with evidence and information relevant to the case. Other people are interested in these findings, especially those paying your bill. This phase is discussed at length in the third part of the book. In general, just remember to keep it simple. As Andrew Rosen says, "A good analogy is worth a thousand words." To test how well you articulate your case, find the least technically competent member of your family and explain your findings to him or her. If you accomplish that goal successfully, you are ready to present the data to counsel. Lawyers are lawyers and CEOs are CEOs; if you find yourself having to describe the intricacies of the latest image format to them, you probably haven't distilled the findings sufficiently. For highly technical investigators, this can be the most difficult phase of the process, so tread with care.

Archival

After you have detailed your findings and the case has concluded, you must archive the data and findings because you may have to readdress the case in the future. The manner in which you go about this varies case to case. Ask yourself the following three questions to determine how to archive the data:

- ▼ **How Much?**   Some cases will require you to archive the complete images and datasets used in the investigation. For some cases, such as large-scale corporate cases, complete archival is either cost-prohibitive or impossible. Work with those who are directing the case to determine how much data and which datasets need archiving for the possibility of future issues.

- ■ **How Long?**   How long you need to keep the archives around depends again on the case. The lawyers or executives involved in the case will have knowledge of the process of wrapping up a case and the timeline for things such as appeals. Discuss this with them and create a plan that accommodates this timeline. Destroying evidence too soon after a case concludes can have disastrous consequences.

▲ **How Likely?**   Try to determine the likelihood that the case will be appealed or escalated. If it seems like an appeal is inevitable, archive as much as possible to prepare for the appeal. If it looks as though a case will be escalated, such as an internal investigation resulting in a wrongful termination suit, consider that as well. As with the previous two questions, look to counsel or the executive in charge of the case for guidance on this issue.

Once you have answered these questions, you are ready to design an archival solution for the case. The goal is to create a time capsule, a bundle that contains archived data, the proper documentation such as process checklists, chain of custody records, and the results and findings. Place this bundle in an environment-proof storage location. The last thing you need is to lose a case because a fire ruined your evidence. Archival details are covered in Chapter 4. With all things like this, a little prevention goes a long way.

Case Study: When Accounting Goes Bad

Now that we have outlined a process, let's look at a real-world example of why the process works and how valuable it is in the everyday life of an investigator.

The phone rings. It's the head of HR for a Fortune 500 company, and she says that they have a problem. It turns out that an employee in the accounting department is engaging in some illicit activities. Confidential balance sheets and forecasts have been finding their way to investors by way of his e-mail address. The company wants to get proof of what has been going on so they can verify that it was him and terminate if necessary and control the damage, and it needs forensic expertise.

Our investigator hops on the first plane to the company's corporate headquarters, with his standard toolkit in tow. When he arrives, he assesses the situation by sitting down with the head of HR and all relevant company executives. After a lengthy interview session, he determines that HR wants to conduct an internal investigation but prepare in case a wrongful termination suit is filed against the company. In addition, there may be criminal implications if the evidence determines insider trading was occurring. The investigator decides to treat this as a criminal case, just in case. Knowing the goal of the investigation, the examiner talks to the director of IT and finds where e-mail is stored, along with the suspect's private files. He then determines how this is stored and what will be required to pull images. Thankfully, the company is modern and pulling images of the data doesn't require exotic hardware. Imaging goes off without a hitch. Just to be sure, the investigator then authenticates his images before he leaves the company's headquarters to examine the results in his lab.

Once back in the comfort and controlled environment of his lab, the investigator begins his analysis. Right off the bat he locates the e-mails in which the suspect leaked corporate secrets. However, the investigator doesn't stop there. After further investigation, he discovers that the suspect was actually taking money in exchange for these confidential documents. After completing the rest of the analysis, he creates a report for his client. This report clearly articulates the findings, showing that the possibility of criminal acts definitely exists. The company thanks him for his exemplary work and says they are still trying to decide what to do. The investigator offers his recommendation that law enforcement be brought in and proceeds to archive the case.

One month later, the investigator gets another phone call. It turns out the company was afraid of corporate scandal affecting its stock share prices. This time, federal law enforcement is saying that the company had reported the incident and that the feds were taking over the case. Since the investigator had the case archived and thoroughly documented, he was able to hand it over to the authorities and they revalidated what he found. The authorities thanked him for his efforts and turned over the case to the district attorney for aggressive prosecution. The suspect was convicted of the crime and sentenced to prison time for defrauding the shareholders and the company.

CHAPTER 2

COMPUTER FUNDAMENTALS

As with any discipline, the key to employing effective computer forensics is a firm grasp and complete understanding of the fundamentals. Opposing counsel loves nothing more than to rip apart the credibility of an expert witness by playing "stump the chump" with obscure facts about storage media or operating system (OS) internals. For some, this chapter will be a crash course in the internal workings of computer technologies. For others, it will serve as a refresher course. Either way, this chapter offers a technical foundation to the rest of the book.

Before you can effectively complete investigations on any operating system, you must understand how a hard drive stores information and how the OS uses that hard drive. In addition, more exotic technologies such as flash memory and PDA RAM have their own sets of pratfalls. If you don't understand the fundamental concepts discussed in this chapter, you will not be able to complete a defensible investigation.

In addition, if you are called upon to perform a deposition or testify on the witness stand, this chapter will help serve as a crib sheet for testimony. A friend of mine was once asked, while on the stand, "What type of file system do floppy disks use in MS-DOS 6.0?" by opposing counsel to try to rattle him. The answer to this question is FAT12, and because he knew his stuff, he answered correctly. Floppy disks use a different file system than hard drives in the old DOS scheme. With all the point-and-click forensics tools available today, it is tempting to forgo learning details like this. However, this is a perfect example of how a complete understanding of the basics can protect you while under fire on the witness stand.

We wrote this chapter to serve as a reference. The night before you are scheduled to give testimony, dust off this book and reread this chapter. It will help prepare you for what is to come.

THE BOTTOM-UP VIEW OF A COMPUTER

As my "Introduction to Computing Science" professor once said, the essence of modern computing is abstracting complexity. The modern computer is much like the human body. Different modules each perform simple tasks; put them together in the right way, and amazingly complex tasks can be completed. A heart pumps blood. The lungs move air around. Eyes process light to create images. These are very basic tasks that work simultaneously to sustain life. Computers work in a similar way. A processor performs operations. A hard disk stores 1s and 0s. A video card converts those 1s and 0s to a signal a monitor can understand. Put them together and you get the computer and all the possibilities that go along with it. Figure 2-1 shows a modular illustration of a computer, from the application that balances your checkbook to the processor that crunches the numbers.

It's All Just 1s and 0s

1s and 0s seem simple enough, but these numbers are the building blocks for every computing technology and application in existence. Known as the *binary number system*, they

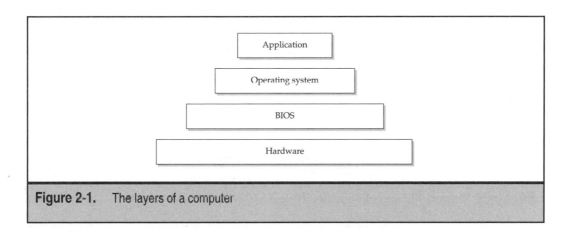

Figure 2-1.   The layers of a computer

are used in conjunction with transistors to create Boolean algebraic equations. The operations that these transistors can perform are AND, OR, NOT, and various combinations of those basic operators.

 To reduce the total number of transistors actually used, most processors today create all their operations with NAND gates as the basic building block. If you are interested in learning more, consult an elementary computer architecture book.

Once these operations are defined, you can take the 1s and 0s and create a combinatorial network that performs conventional math functions (addition, subtraction, and so on). Figure 2-2 shows how the Boolean operations combine to add two, 1-bit numbers (what is known as a *1-bit adder*).

After you have built an adder, you can use it and the Boolean operations to perform addition, subtraction, multiplication, and division. You can also hook the adders together to add 8-, 16-, or 32-bit numbers, as most modern processors do. In the race to have the fastest benchmark numbers on the market, computer builders have built specialized operations into computers that allow them to perform certain types of operations quickly. In fact, the staggering number of transistors on modern processors is a result of the need for specialized operations. While detailed descriptions of the complete modern processor is outside the scope of this book, the following table shows the number of transistors per chip to give you an idea of the complexity of these technologies.

Processor	Year Created	Number of Transistors
Intel 8080	1974	6000
Intel 80486	1989	1,200,000
Intel Pentium	1993	3,100,000
Intel Pentium IV	2000	42,000,000

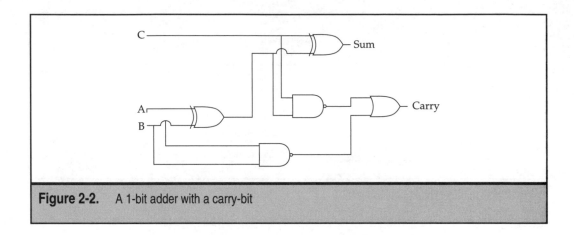

Figure 2-2. A 1-bit adder with a carry-bit

Learning from the Past: Giving Computers Memory

Now that we have the ability to perform mathematical operations on numbers, we need a way to load and store the results of these operations. This is where memory comes in. Computers use two basic types of memory: volatile and nonvolatile. Volatile memory is erased when the computer is turned off. Examples of this type of memory are main memory (RAM, or Random Access Memory) and cache memory. Nonvolatile memory is not erased when the computer is turned off. This is usually the secondary memory source, such as hard disks or flash memory. Figure 2-3 shows the interaction of the various types of memory and how they move information in a computer.

Volatile Memory

You can think of volatile memory as a scratch pad that the computer uses when evaluating data. The most fundamental unit of this type of memory is the *flip-flop*, shown in Figure 2-4. As the name suggests, a flip-flop can store a 1 or a 0 while the computer is on, and the computer can flip the stored value when it needs to store a different value.

If you hook together eight flip-flops, you can store an 8-bit number. In the common nomenclature, a series of these flip-flops is known as a *register*. By combining this with the adder described earlier, you can add two numbers and store the result for later use.

Registers hold a very small amount of data and are used only when the computer needs to store temporary values during multiple-step operations. For larger pieces of data, a second level of memory must be used, and this is where RAM comes in. RAM memory is outside the processor and can hold a very large amount of data while the computer is on. The downside to this type of memory, however, is the delay time the processor incurs when loading and storing data in RAM. Because of this lag time and the adverse effects on performance, most modern processors have what is known as a *cache*, which you can think of as an intermediate step between the registers and the main memory. It's slower than the registers but not nearly as slow as accessing main memory.

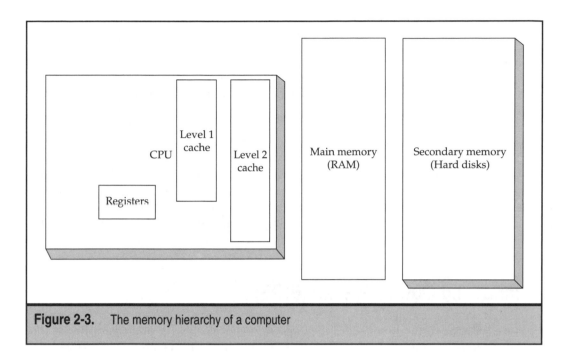

Figure 2-3.   The memory hierarchy of a computer

Nonvolatile Memory

Nonvolatile memory is used when data needs to be stored even if the computer is turned off. The most common type of media used in nonvolatile memory is magnetic media, such as a hard disk. The upside to magnetic media is that it can be purchased cheaply in comparison to volatile memory. The downside, however, is that it is incredibly slow in comparison. Magnetic media actually has moving parts: the typical hard drive has platters that spin

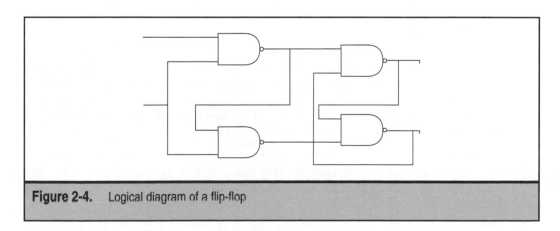

Figure 2-4.   Logical diagram of a flip-flop

around with a tiny magnetic head changing charges on the platter from positive to negative, which represent the binary 1s and 0s. Even though today's hard drives have been able to achieve mind-blowing speed, their inherent design prevents them from ever being as fast as volatile memory by an order of magnitude. Because of this speed difference, computers are designed to minimize the number of times that something has to be written out to this secondary memory.

However, since nonvolatile memory is so much cheaper than RAM, secondary memory is also often used as swap space for the processor. This presents a unique opportunity for the investigator, because you can go back through the hard drive, find the swap file, and take apart the memory of the computer to locate evidence that would otherwise be destroyed or obfuscated. The specific way to do this varies from operating system to operating system and is discussed in more detail in Chapters 6, 7, and 8. In fact, most of your time as an investigator will be spent going through nonvolatile memory. The different types are detailed later in this chapter; it's well worth your time to learn each type completely.

Basic Input and Output System (BIOS)

Now that we have created a processor and memory for the processor to use, we need to create a way for software to talk to the hardware and work with other peripherals. The BIOS provides simple methods for software to interact with hardware. When you first turn on the computer, the BIOS runs a series of self checks (called the *Power On Self Test*, or *POST*) and then turns control over to the operating system. An effective BIOS manages the allocation of resources (via interrupt requests, or IRQs, and direct memory access, or DMA) to the peripherals and handles basic security measures. Some of the more modern BIOS features are power management and digital rights management, or DRM. The BIOS provides only raw access to the resources; it does nothing to manage or allocate those resources for performance. Its function is strictly to act as the interface between the OS and the hardware.

The Operating System

The OS is by far the most complex piece of software on any given computer. It acts as the translation layer between the end-user applications and the BIOS or hardware. The OS manages the users, the memory, the applications, and the processor time on the computer. A well-written OS can breathe new life into an old computer, same as a poorly written one can bog down even the fastest of machines. As an investigator, I recommend that you spend time learning the mainstream OSs inside and out.

NOTE   Learning about an OS is not a trivial task. The latest version of Windows has more than 5 million lines of code. The file system, the swap space, and the memory map are all artifacts of the OS installed on the machine. We devote Chapters 6, 7, and 8 to discussions of various OSs.

The Applications

Applications are why you use a computer in the first place. They balance our checkbooks, allow us to browse the Internet, or entertain us with games, movies, or other activities. From a forensics perspective, it is beneficial for you to become familiar with the ins and outs of a few select applications. Understanding the way that office applications create and delete documents, how e-mail programs work, and how web browsers access the Internet will help you track down evidence that you can use in your investigation. Chapters 11 and 12 are dedicated to various applications that you will see again and again in your time as an investigator.

TYPES OF MEDIA

As discussed in the preceding section, investigations will focus primarily on the secondary memory area—hard disks, CD-ROMs, tape backups, and most other types of commonly used storage. Each of these types of media has its own nuances and pitfalls in an investigation. Let's look at the three most common types of media—magnetic, optical, and RAM—in detail.

Magnetic Media

You will spend the majority of your time dealing with magnetic media, including hard disks, floppy disks, and tape backups. Zip disks and other such large-capacity portable disks are just variations on the structure of the hard disk or floppy disk. The theory for all of these types is the same: Some kind of metal or magnetic surface holds a series of positive or negative magnetic charges. This series represents 1s or 0s, depending on the charge of the magnet. When data is changed on the media, the magnetic charge is changed. This means several things: First, when data is supposedly deleted, the charge is changed, but remnants from the old settings remain. This allows a highly skilled recovery service to go back and recreate the data on the media. Second, the media is open to being affected by external magnets. This means that your forensic lab procedures and storage policies must consider this, and you must be able to prove that this hasn't happened when dealing in a court of law.

Hard Disk Drives

Popularity:	10
Simplicity:	6
Impact:	10
Risk Rating:	**10**

If you learn the complete architecture for just one media type, make it the hard drive. Ninety percent of an investigator's time will be spent imaging, searching, or wiping hard drives, and none of these are as easy as they might seem. How do you know the image of a hard drive is an exact duplicate? What is slack space? What is your wiping procedure? Until you can answer these questions and fully justify your answers, don't even attempt an investigation. Let's break down the components of a hard drive and their interaction.

Physical Parts of the Hard Drive

Before we look at how data is stored on a hard drive, we need to talk a bit about the physical components of the drive. Hard drives are marvels of modern engineering. Imagine a plane traveling Mach 1 with an altitude of about 2 feet above the runway. This is the rough equivalent to what a hard drive does every time it spins up and reads or writes data. Figure 2-5 shows the parts of a hard drive.

Platters   Platters are the circular discs that actually store the data. A single hard drive will include multiple platters often made of some aluminum alloy, but newer drives use a glass or ceramic material. These platters are covered with a magnetic substrate so that

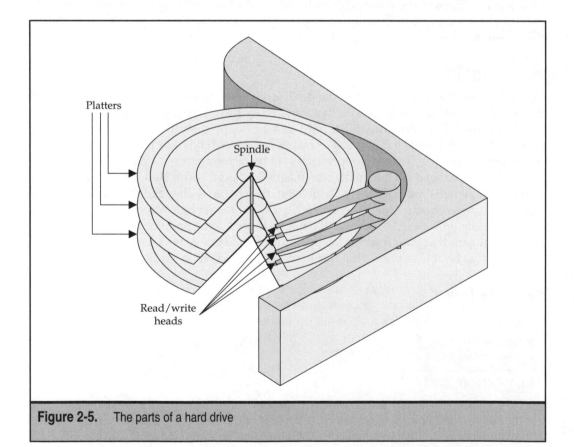

Figure 2-5.   The parts of a hard drive

they can hold a magnetic charge. Hard drive failures rarely occur within the platters. In fact, 9 times out of 10, if you send a drive off to a data recovery firm, they will take the drive apart and mount the platters in a new drive assembly to retrieve the data from them.

Read and Write Heads   Tiny magnetic read and write heads change and read the magnetic state on the platters. Think of these in the same way you think of a needle on an old LP record player or a laser on a CD-ROM player. In this case, the head is a copper coil that has charges pushed through it. This creates a magnetic field that can either read or write data. Because there are multiple platters, multiple heads are used. Typically, to optimize the usage of the platter, both the top and bottom of the platter's surface are used. For performance purposes and for better reliability, all the heads are hooked together and move in unison. This way, data can be read simultaneously from multiple platters. These are so compactly designed that they must be assembled in a clean room, because even a single stray particle can disrupt the head alignment.

Head Actuator   For many years, this was a major source of failure for hard drives. There are two types of head actuators: stepper motor and voice coil. Old hard drives (less that 100MB) used stepper motor actuators, which were nothing short of terrible: if you didn't park the heads before moving the drive, you broke it; if you didn't recalibrate the disk by formatting it after you cleared it, you broke the drive; if you used the hard drive too much, you broke it. Look at the thing wrong and you broke it! Over time, these actuators would "forget" where they were on the hard disk and you'd lose all your data.

On the opposite side of the equation are the voice coil actuators. These correct themselves if they get lost on the platter using *grey code*. In addition, they don't have to be parked before a hard drive is spun down.

    Grey codes are an alternative binary numbering system in which only 1 bit changes from one number to the next. Grey codes are particularly useful in mechanical encoders, since a slight change in position affects only 1 bit. Using a typical binary code, up to *n* bits could change, and slight misalignments between reading elements could cause wildly incorrect readings.

Spindle Motor   As you may have guessed, the spindle motor spins the platters. These motors are engineered to very strict standards, since they have to be able to maintain precise speeds and must not vibrate. These motors rotate at a constant rate (such as 3600, 7200, or 10,000 RPM). A feedback loop is set up inside the motor to ensure that it rotates at exactly the correct speed. On older hard drives, the motor was on the bottom of the drive, but now they are built into the hub of the platters to conserve space and allow for more platters in the drive.

Storing Data on the Hard Drive

Now that you have a grasp on what parts are inside the metal enclosure, let's focus on the platters and how they store the data. Modern hard drives hold a massive amount of information. Over the years, a structure has developed that optimizes the speed that this data is read off the drive. Figure 2-6 shows a cross-section of the platters.

A very logical and structured layout controls how data is stored on rotational magnetic media. Three basic units denote position of data on a hard disk: cylinder, sector, and track.

Cylinder   The cylinder came about when multiple platters were added to the hard drive assembly; the cylinder number corresponds to the platter that holds the data.

Sector   The name *sector* is derived from the mathematical term for a pie-shaped division of a circle (think of a triangle with one vertex at the center of the circle and two on the circle itself). This term was chosen because originally sectors were broken out in this shape on the physical disk. Each sector contains 512 bytes of user data and some extra bits for error

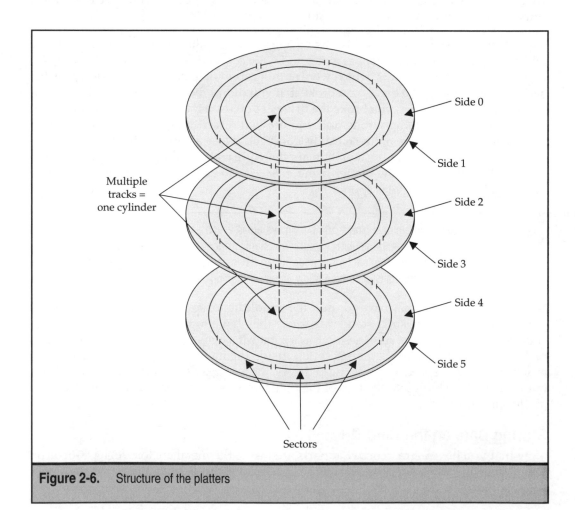

Figure 2-6.   Structure of the platters

correction and metadata. A sector is the "atomic unit" of a hard disk: it's the smallest unit of data that a hard disk can effectively read. On older hard disks, the actuator couldn't handle having different numbers of sectors for each track. Because of this, the shape of the sector was maintained and the density of the bits on the platter was lessened as you went to the edge of the disk. This changed with zone-density recording, where a variable number of sectors could be included per track. These sectors are rolled up into units known as *clusters* when a file system is placed on the disk—that will be discussed in more detail in the OS-specific chapters (Chapters 6, 7, and 8) when we talk about the different filesystems.

Track   Think about a photograph needle traveling around an LP. Now think about the concentric rings inside a tree. Tracks on a hard disk are laid out in the same fashion. These are the actual streams of data that are written to the hard drive.

Large Block Addressing (LBA)   Large Block Addressing is what happens when engineers guess about maximum limits—and guess wrong. LBA is a "hack" to get around the upper limit placed on drive size by the IDE bus system. Old IDE drives incurred a 504MB limit on how much data could be accessed. To get around this, hard-drive manufacturers figured out a way to "lie" to the BIOS about the size of the disk. Instead of addressing things by cylinder, sector, and head, only one value is used for sector number. This is similar to a phone number. The traditional system has a country code, area code, and then a local phone number. The LBA equivalent of this gives everyone in the world a local phone number without area code or country code. The reason this works is because it leaves the geometry translation to the drive itself (which isn't limited to 504MB), instead of allowing the BIOS or bus to do it.

Floppy Disks

Popularity:	6
Simplicity:	6
Impact:	10
Risk Rating:	7

Floppy disks are the eight-tracks of the computing world. Most people have used them and very few people have fond memories of the experience. These workhorses can be kicked, warped, melted, poked, and suffer any other number of abuses and they still keep going. These drives and associated media are similar in structure and form to the hard disk. As you can see in Figure 2-7, many of the same parts are used in both designs.

Just like the parts, the actual structure of the disk is similar to a one-platter hard disk. The platter is encased in either a hard or soft plastic cover that protects the storage disk inside. In the upper corner of the disk is a notch that can be set to write-protect the disk. The main difficulty you may have in a forensics investigation involving floppy disks is the formatting. OS and file system vendors created interesting ways to store more information on the disks

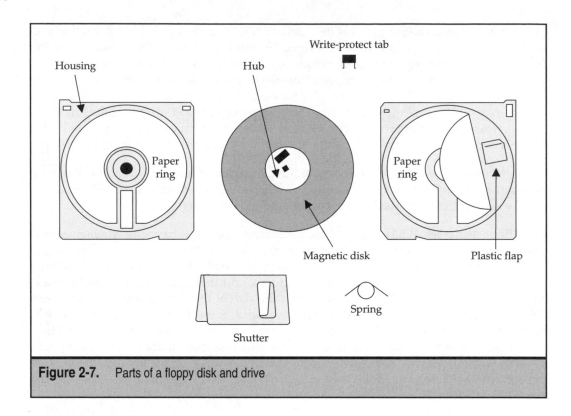

Figure 2-7.   Parts of a floppy disk and drive

than they could previously hold. The typical 3.5-inch disk would hold 1.44MB of data, but by using compression or extra sectors on the disk, an extra half meg of storage could be squeezed on. Woe be the investigator who has to figure out one of these cryptic methods of storing data on the disk. They are poorly documented and more than a few different ways are used to store on the disk, with no real identifying marks.

Working with Rotational Media

You will spend the majority of your time during investigations working with hard drives. Unfortunately, these are the trickiest of media to manage and investigate, and you'll encounter a ton of pitfalls when dealing with imaging, investigation, and documentation of such media. The long and short of it is this: Always use forensically designed and approved tools when you deal with disks. Some tools on the market claim to pull complete disk images, but fail to do so. Other programs claim to wipe drives completely, but don't. If you go up against an expert who is worth his or her salt, he or she will try to derail your investigation by placing bad data in end sectors and playing games with the media in general. Know the drives and layout inside and out. Use tools that you understand completely and know exactly how they work, and they'll do what you expect them to do.

Tape Backup Drives

Popularity:	6
Simplicity:	4
Impact:	8
Risk Rating:	8

While working in the server group of a large computer manufacturer, I learned the value of good, regular backups. It is rare these days to find a server that doesn't have some form of tape backup unit attached to it for data recovery purposes. Given the fact that data such as e-mail and office documents are normally centralized on these servers, you will probably be dealing with an investigation of a tape backup at some point in the future. Start crying now. The number of different hardware drive types, software packages that perform backups, and the percentage of backups that actually succeed make pulling evidence off a tape drive a dicey proposition at best. Let's look at two of the most common drive types: DAT and DLT.

Digital Audio Tape (DAT) Drives

DAT drives are among the most common of tape drives. They are more often referred to by their data recovery name, Digital Data Storage (DDS). As you can see from the following table, several generations of DDS drives exist, each with its own transfer rates and capacities.

Standard	Capacity	Transfer Rate
DDS	2GB	550 KBps
DDS-1	2GB	1.1 MBps
DDS-2	4GB	1.1 MBps
DDS-3	12GB	2.2 MBps
DDS-4	20GB	4.8 MBps

These drives were originally created for use in high-end audio applications, but after a few tweaks for robustness, they now work well for backups. They employ a helical scan technique that allows data to be tightly packed on the media, requiring less actual tape than traditional tape methods. As a tradeoff, however, they experience a lot of friction when writing to the tape. This causes the tape head to gain residue over time and can actually silently hamper the writing of data onto the tape. Also of note when you are dealing with these drives, keep in mind the difference between a DDS and a DAT. The DAT is held to a much lower standard of quality and manufacturing than the DDS. DATs can cause problems down the line with tape breakage and loss of data.

Digital Linear Tape (DLT) and Super DLT

As its name implies, the DLT technology relies on a linear recording method. The tape itself has either 128 or 208 total tracks. The capacities and transfer rates of the drives vary based on the generation and format of the DLT drive, as shown in the table.

Standard	Transfer Rate	Capacity
DLT2000	1.25 MBps	15GB
DLT4000	1.5 MBps	20GB
DLT7000	5 MBps	35GB
DLT8000	6 MBps	40GB
SDLT 220	11 MBps	110GB

These tracks are written in pairs along the entire length of the tape. The heads are then realigned, and two more tracks are written in the opposite direction. This process continues until the tape is full. The design of the DLT drive is a bit different because it has only one spindle in the tape itself. The other spindle is in the drive and the tape is wound back onto the cartridge upon ejection. This design is superior to DAT because it places less tension on the tape with less friction, and thus the drive requires less maintenance and has a lower failure rate. The super DLT is essentially the same technology, but it uses a combination of optics and magnetism (laser-guided magnetic recording, or LGMR) to increase the precision of the tape.

Multi-Loaders

Many times, the amount of data that needs to be backed up exceeds the capacity of a single tape. In such cases, multi-tape loader mechanisms are used. These can be anything from two-tape contraptions to advanced robotic arms that sling tapes around. From an investigator's standpoint, make sure you always find out not only what multi-loader was used, but also how the software stored data on the multiple tapes. Working with an archive created on a multi-loader is a tricky proposition and usually requires that you purchase hardware and software similar to what was used to create the archive. This gets expensive quickly, so make sure your contract has a clause stipulating that the client pays for materials.

⊖ Working with Tape Drives

Working with tape drives boils down to two simple questions: What type of tapes are being used, and what software created the archive? If you can easily answer these questions, you are home free, because you will be able to pull the archive off the tapes. Unfortunately, more often than not, you will be handed a pile of tapes created many years ago, before any of the current staff was employed. Someone will hand you a box, give you his or her best guess as to how it was created, and wish you good luck. Chapter 10 discusses in detail how to manage and investigate such situations.

Optical Media

I can still remember getting my first CD-ROM drive, eagerly awaiting what would happen when I saw my first full-motion video, roughly the size of a postage stamp with sound recorded in a tin can. I think it involved a growing plant. These days, optical media is everywhere in the forms of CD-ROM and DVD. With the widespread ability for users to burn their own discs, such media are finding their way into more and more court cases. Chances are you will deal with them either directly as evidence or as a transport mechanism for opposing counsel to give you evidence during discovery. It's important that you understand how these technologies work and how they can be manipulated.

 ## CD-ROM

Popularity:	6
Simplicity:	4
Impact:	8
Risk Rating:	**8**

The CD-ROM, shown in Figure 2-8, is the father of the optical revolution. These discs use a red laser as the read mechanism to extract data off the drive. Like hard disks,

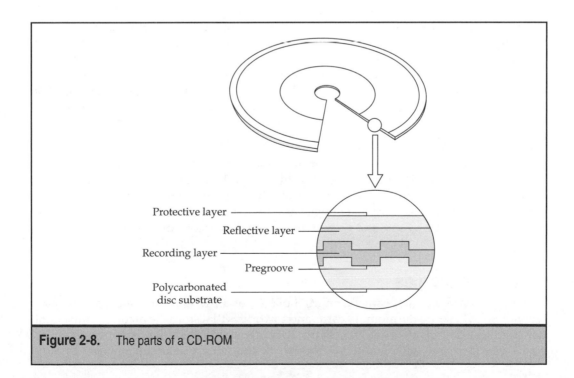

Figure 2-8.   The parts of a CD-ROM

CD-ROMs use high and low polarization to set the bits of data; however, CDs have reflective pits that represent the low bit. If the pit is nonexistent, the data is a 1; if the pit exists, it's a 0.

The laser mechanism actually detects how far into the disc the beam has gone and how it is refracted to determine whether the pit exists. This explains why getting a scratch or smudge on a disc renders it erroneous. The laser becomes "confused" as to the data and "punts." As density was the limiting factor on hard drives, laser wavelength is the limiting factor for capacity on these discs. Red is the largest of the visible spectrum, meaning that a red laser-based drive will be able to store the least amount of data. CD-ROMs have their own file system that is independent of the operating system. This is commonly referred to as the *Joliet file system*, and with certain parts of the disc populated, the disc can become bootable. The standard size for a CD-ROM disc is 650MB, but it can be written "outside of tolerance" to hold more data.

Digital Video Disc (DVD)

Popularity:	6
Simplicity:	4
Impact:	8
Risk Rating:	8

In function, DVDs are similar to CD-ROM technology with some tweaks. First, DVDs use a much more precise laser. Since the laser has a smaller wavelength, the data density is much greater, so the disc can hold more data. The entire DVD holds up to 4.8GB of data. The structure of a DVD is shown in Figure 2-9.

In addition, DVDs use a multilayer system that allows multiple discs to be overlaid onto one disc. The setup is much like the platters on a hard disk. The laser is focused on the layer holding the data being read, allowing it to pull data from only that layer.

Working with Optical Media

Working with optical media from a forensics standpoint is a bit easier than working with other types of media. The main reason for this is that the media is inherently read-only, which means you have to do much less work to show that the data on the disc hasn't been modified. Even so, make sure that you never work with originals, no matter how tempting it may be. Make a copy and archive the original in accordance with your evidence storage policy.

Memory Technologies

If you have used a digital camera, an MP3 player, or a PDA, you have used a memory technology. These are the memory cards and cartridges that store the pictures, music, and data for these devices. As you can imagine, they often become evidence in investigations, so it's a good idea to understand how they work and what you are up against.

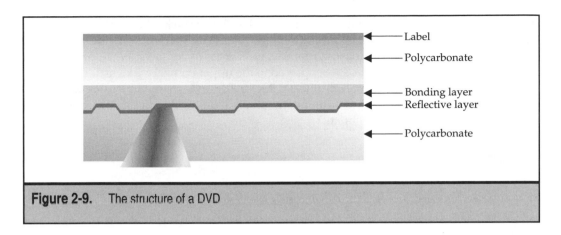

Figure 2-9.   The structure of a DVD

USB Flash Drives

Popularity:	6
Simplicity:	4
Impact:	8
Risk Rating:	8

USB flash drives are also known as *thumb drives*. They are the keychains, necklaces, and doodads that have become the gift of choice for people in the IT world. While a thorough explanation of how these drives work requires an electrical-engineering degree to understand, here is the digest version. Flash drives have no moving parts. Each bit is set by using a two-transistor cell, and the value is changed in each cell using a technique called *Fowler-Nordheim tunneling*. The memory bank then communicates with the computer using a controller and USB interface, much like a hard disk communicates over IDE or SCSI. The most important thing to remember about these drives is that most of them have a physical switch that forces a read-only mode. Use this whenever you are extracting data for investigation.

SmartMedia

Popularity:	4
Simplicity:	7
Impact:	6
Risk Rating:	5

Also known as the solid-state floppy-disk card (SSFDC), the SmartMedia card was developed by Toshiba. They range in capacity from 2MB to Multiple GB, with physical dimensions of 45 mm long, 37 mm wide, and less than 1 mm thick. These cards have a very small NAND electrically erasable programmable read-only memory (NAND EEPROM) sandwiched between a plastic base card and a gold plate of contacts. Write protection is performed using a small metallic sticker placed in the upper corner of the card. These cards write and erase data in very small chunks, in 256- to 512-byte increments. This allows for fast and reliable data transfer, but be aware that their size and design can create problems with ruggedness and they will break.

CompactFlash Cards

Popularity:	6
Simplicity:	5
Impact:	7
Risk Rating:	6

CompactFlash cards were developed by SanDisk in 1994. They are very similar in design and function to SmartMedia cards but vary in several ways. First, they are thicker, which increases the lifetime of the card in the real world. Second, they are not just dumb memory; they have a controller built into the card itself. The storage capacity varies from 8MB to Multiple GB and the controller can take the load off slower computers.

Sony Memory Sticks

Popularity:	6
Simplicity:	5
Impact:	7
Risk Rating:	6

Memory sticks are the beta tapes of the flash memory world. In fact, the memory stick was designed by the same company that brought us beta. Sony broke ranks with flash memory standards and created its own standard for its devices. The memory stick has a very distinctive form factor and color—it looks like a purple stick of gum. The first generation of the memory stick maxed out at 128MB, but later revs took the capacity up to 1GB. In addition, Sony introduced its Magic Gate technology, which placed Digital Rights Management (DRM) technology inside the stick itself. These memory sticks have a slider that denotes the read-only mode.

Working with Memory Technologies

From a forensics standpoint, the whole thing can be summed up in one word: *read-only*. Most of these technologies have a hardware-level read-only mode. Always, always use this stopgap to prevent modification of the data. Make sure it's a part of your methodology to do this even before inspecting the media. The other main problem with flash memory is getting an adequate reader. For the most part, this is an easy task, but you may end up obtaining some exotic or obsolete flash memory card that requires a reader that is not easily obtained. Learn what you are working with and how to set it to read-only as quickly as possible once you find out what you are going to be given. Also, sometimes pulling an accurate image from one of these devices can be a tricky process. Chapter 13 will cover this topic in more depth.

CHAPTER 3

FORENSIC LAB
ENVIRONMENT
PREPARATION

In this chapter, we discuss four components that work together to make your lab's output successful: the physical lab, forensic hosts, forensic tools, and case management. Each of these work in conjunction with the others to preserve, identify, and extract evidence:

▼ The lab's security, host computers, tools, and case management affect your forensic capabilities. Having the appropriate protections, documentation, storage mechanisms, room requirements, and environmental conditions aid the successful discovery and preservation of evidence.

■ Computer platforms used for forensic acquisition and analysis vary in usefulness and usability. They also vary from inexpensive homegrown platforms to extremely expensive, proprietary, prebuilt specialty machines.

■ Hardware and software tools used during the investigation can make or break your case. You need to understand what tools will yield the results you need for your case. Your decision to use open open-source or proprietary tools also plays a role in this discussion.

▲ Solid case-management practices provide the foundation for conducting and archiving the investigation.

THE ULTIMATE COMPUTER FORENSIC LAB

The very nature of this assertion should grab your attention, because it is impossible for us to know the particular circumstances you might face. How can we possibly know the best mix of equipment, policies, personnel, qualifications, and a myriad of other criteria that will produce the ultimate lab for your organization? The best forensic lab for you is a careful combination of cost and effectiveness. This chapter provides a short education on the best resources for a well-equipped lab as well as the pitfalls often found in home-grown forensic labs and how to counteract them. Keep in mind our focus is on the corporate lab, not those found in law enforcement or government arrangements.

What Is a Computer Forensic Laboratory?

The computer forensic laboratory houses the equipment and suspect media in a secure environment for day-to-day operations. There are a number of necessary components to consider when designing your lab. The physical lab size, placement, security controls, policies, and procedures vary depending on your organizational needs. Small companies that handle the occasional civil case may not need more than an office behind a locked door and an inexpensive, fireproof safe. A corporation that has tens of thousands of employees may have a substantial case load containing several dozen investigations each week. The differences here are obvious and include time, money, and resources necessary to sustain operations. You must design the right lab for your needs. Guidance Software has an excellent introduction to designing and building your lab, in which Lee Youngflesh aptly discusses how to start by defining your goals and objectives before you over or under engineer your lab and supporting resources. This document, "Developing a Forensic Response Unit," can be found at http://www.guidancesoftware.com/webinar/webinar_list.asp.

Forensic Lab Security

Ask yourself the following questions: How difficult would it be to compromise evidence in your lab? How many people have access to the lab? If a janitor came into your organization and visited late at night, would your evidence storage and processing facility be subject to compromise? Multiple attack vectors exist to destroy or alter evidence in your lab. As a computer forensics examiner, you should account for these in your lab environment. They present a direct threat to the preservation, or integrity, of your evidence. You must protect both physical and network access to your lab along with providing the appropriate environmental safeguards to protect the evidence.

Spoliation of Evidence Through Lab Network Access

Popularity:	3
Simplicity:	5
Impact:	10
Risk Rating:	6

The threat from curious and malicious crackers, hackers, and rogue employees grows because of the increased technical proficiency and curiosity of the workforce. A computer on an isolated network is protected from open access to hackers, viruses, and other malicious threats. If a trusted computer were placed on an open network without protection, the computer could not be trusted because it presents an opportunity for compromise. Protection from malicious network access is very important. Simply put, if the trusted platform is compromised over the network, the evidence findings may be in jeopardy. In the corporate environment, there is some initial level of protection. However, also consider isolating the corporate network from the forensic lab with an air gap (physical isolation) or at least a firewall (network isolation).

Granted, proper preservation procedures will document the authenticity of the evidence and therefore protect against the argument that the evidence was tampered with. However, lots of components must line up—the discovery of the evidence must be reproducible, the authenticity of the evidence must be verifiable, and the examiner must follow proper procedures and not take shortcuts. You do not want to find yourself in a deposition trying to explain why your lab network's security is careless and poor.

Spoliation of Evidence Through Lab Physical Access

Popularity:	9
Simplicity:	9
Impact:	10
Risk Rating:	9

Perhaps one of the easiest methods used to destroy or tamper with civil evidence is simply walking into a lab and taking it. Depending on circumstances, this may be easier than you think. Multiple books and self-proclaimed experts in the market discuss several methods for "social engineering" their way into a building to conduct malicious behavior. Unfortunately, in some cases, not even this bit of effort is required to compromise the sanctity of an organization's evidence. If a company doesn't take the time to place evidence in a secure location, how much credibility does that build for the company? What does this say about how well the company understands the value of critical evidence?

Spoliation of Evidence from Poor Environmental Safeguards

Popularity:	3
Simplicity:	10
Impact:	10
Risk Rating:	**9**

Fire, floods, and other disasters spell out a bad day in the lab, especially if no one has thought in advance about the risk mitigation of such disastrous events. A low rating represents the popularity, or likelihood, that this type of event will take place. However, note the rating for impact! Impact is a huge consideration in both a large corporate lab and a smaller company that desperately depends on the evidence findings.

Like insurance, nobody likes to pay for security, but should something happen—and it may—you need to be prepared. If you have not conducted a basic physical survey of your lab, you are needlessly jeopardizing your equipment, records, archives, storage, and any pending internal and external cases.

Protecting the Forensic Lab

The security stakes for the large corporation are possibly much higher than those for a small organization, and so is the expectation for lab controls and policies. However, small companies must still adhere to common sense and "best practices." A wealth of information is available about lab security, including the information in this chapter. Take the time and inventory the critical components needed for your lab. We will discuss some of these components in this chapter, but this is not meant to be an exhaustive review. The checklists provided in Appendix A will help you start checking your own lab.

Protecting the Forensic Lab's Network Access

The traditional school of thought is to isolate the examining computer completely from the network. However, some tools on the market are causing a shift in the way networks are used. These tools preview suspect computers prior to a formal examination in an effort to triage and determine the need for further investigation. An example of such a tool is EnCase Enterprise from Guidance Software, which allows a computer forensics examiner to examine a computer for documents, images, and other data (including volatile data) over the network without having to acquire the hard drive. (The advantages of a remote investigations tool are enormous and discussed in Chapter 5.) Consider the implications of leaving your analysis host on the network, unprotected, while examining evidence. It's an excellent practice to remove any doubt up front and affirm the integrity of your lab through carefully documented practices and formal lab policies regarding how your forensic hosts are used.

Using the Internet during an investigation is a powerful tool, and in several cases the Net has proved to be enormously beneficial in helping to understand a suspect's behaviors and interests. However, access the Internet on a separate, segmented network. Many professional labs use three separate computers:

▼ One for Internet access

■ One for administration

▲ One for evidence, testing, and training

Bottom line: Protect the integrity of your forensic lab from the rest of the corporate network. If possible, use a separate, standalone computer for Internet access during an investigation.

 ## Protecting the Forensic Lab's Physical Access to Evidence

The degree of security and access control required depends on the nature, sensitivity, and importance of the investigated evidence for your organization. If you are protecting information you believe may lead to a criminal investigation, you should increase the control of the material in question. Depending on the potential severity of the cases your organization will handle, you may be interested in the following types of access control considerations to help deter, detect, or defend possible asset compromise.

Remember also that there are multiple ways to skin a buffalo. The end result is that you want to minimize your risk. The following example illustrates this point.

Structural Design   Some time ago, a young office administrator received sexually suggestive e-mails from an anonymous e-mail address. After several weeks of receiving the e-mails, the offended office administrator began to suspect a fellow coworker in her group. The forensic examiner for the investigation covertly reviewed the suspect's drive and found remnants of web-based e-mail. The web-based e-mail clearly contained sexually explicit language directed toward the office administrator. When the examiner reported the findings to HR, the suspect was immediately called into the HR office, where HR staff were waiting on the examiner to print out the e-mail remnants. This should have been an easy task.

Unfortunately, the forensic examiner was locked out of the lab. The office held the critical evidence that HR needed to view so that they could settle the allegation of sexual harassment. Frustrated, the forensic examiner asked a coworker to look up the number of the manager who had the backup key for the office.

The coworker looked at the locked office door and said, "Young Grasshopper, go around the door, not through the door." A minute later, the investigator watched as the coworker climbed over the wall and dropped through the ceiling, landing on the office floor.

Structural design can be as complicated as erecting a concrete and steel bunker capable of withstanding category F5 tornadoes, or it may be as simple as mitigating the structural risk with locked containers and strict policies ensuring evidence is locked in a protected enclosure, such as a small safe, when the investigator is no longer working on the evidence. The perimeter walls of the forensic lab should not just partition the lab from the rest of the building, extending to just above the ceiling. They must extend all the way to the next floor deck. Otherwise, someone could easily climb over the wall into the forensic lab, as the above example illustrates. Again, multiple methods can be used for achieving the end result. If the walls cannot be extended, consider ways you can secure the ceiling entrance. For high-security forensic labs such as those you would expect from a consulting services organization or a large corporate environment, the room should be alarmed, and not with just contacts on the doors. Properly placed motion sensors will detect a door opening as well as a person climbing through the roof or over the wall. In both cases, the alarm signal could go to the onsite guard and police.

Locks, Doors, and Windows   Two components are necessary for creating effective lock-out controls. The first component is the physical lock, and the second component is controlling access to the authentication components to make the lock function. In simple terms, the door to your house has a "good enough" quality deadbolt that will keep out most criminals looking for a quick crime of opportunity. You control access to the authentication piece (the key) by allowing your children and spouse to have a key, but not your neighbors.

Locks for your forensic lab should be made of high-grade materials and specialized for high-security protection. Several types of locks on the market require multiple forms of authentication prior to operating. The authentication means vary as widely as requiring a special key, pin code, fingerprint, proximity badge, and other such methods. You must make the best decision based on the materials you control in your environment and the resources available to build out your lab. In short, your protection mechanisms need to be defensible as reasonable precautions used to protect the evidence and the lab under your control.

Additional considerations for doors and windows prevent them from getting easily bypassed. Doors should either hinge from the inside or have specialty hinges that prevent a person from removing the pin in the hinge and popping the door out. Windows and other glass should be too small for a person to fit.

Evidence Lockers   Evidence lockers provide additional protection beyond the physical barrier provided by the perimeter of the lab. With strict policy controls such as locking away original evidence at all times when an investigator is not in the lab, you help ensure that your evidence is protected from tampering and physical disaster. Large case processing facilities typically have a room within a room for holding and working on evidence; however, this is not practical in most resource-constrained corporate environments. An evidence locker can be as sophisticated as a keyless, multi-compartmentalized system used by some police agencies, or as simple as a locking, fireproof safe available at your local office supply store. (For some inexpensive solutions, check out Sentry safes online at http://www.sentrysafe.com.) An inexpensive safe that will accommodate several dozen hard drives costs about $200 to $300. More expensive safes can easily run in the tens of thousands of dollars.

The important message here is to protect your evidence. Standard backup procedures also apply. Whether your gig is investigating civil or criminal cases, you simply cannot afford to lose evidence. Take the time to find a secure method that works for you.

Policies and Procedures   In addition to obvious physical protections, remember policy and procedural requirements are necessary for controlling access to the lab. Access control lists (ACLs) determine who has access to the lab and who is allowed to escort others into the lab. Ideally, every entrance and exit to the lab contains a log that is initialed or signed by the people entering and exiting the lab. At a minimum, anyone not associated with the lab, as in not specifically listed on the ACL, should log his or her entrance, escort, date, time, and reason for entering the lab.

All of this tracking is especially true for evidence. Evidence must be traceable from the moment the media was confiscated to preserve the all-important chain of custody, as discussed in Chapter 1.

Protecting the Forensic Lab from Environmental Damage

Perhaps one of the worst ways to lose evidence is through an unforeseen natural disaster. Prepare up front and design protections into your lab in case of a potential problem.

Fire Protection   If your lab is located in a commercial facility, you should have automatic fire suppression. Take into account where the sprinkler or suppression agent dispensers are located, and plan accordingly. If you are using a locked enclosure with splash-proof vents, serious smoke damage will follow the fire as the smoke pours into the vents. For very little money, fireproof enclosures can protect your investments in specialized gear, licensed software, special operating system builds, and especially key evidence.

If you don't have experience with fire suppression or you don't know how to protect your assets, spend some time with your site's physical security manager or your local fire marshal. They are usually quite helpful and happy that you would bother to learn best practices in advance. Additionally, they will be able to look at your particular location and help determine any peculiarities you may have and need to solve.

Flooding   Like fire, if flooding occurs in your area, caused by leaks or something tipping off the fire-suppression system, you need to ensure that your critical evidence is properly protected. Look for an evidence safe that has a water-tight seal, and be mindful of water pipes running in the ceiling above your lab.

Temperature Control   Keep your equipment from overheating and prolong your equipment's life by using efficient ventilation and temperature control. Given the confined spaces in many labs and the heat produced by the equipment, this is a must.

Power Protection   Surge protectors and UPS should be a given by now. Protect your equipment from power surges caused by lightening with a good surge protector. Keep your equipment safe and running during power surges and outages with a solid UPS.

FORENSIC COMPUTERS

Once the lab is constructed—or in most cases, designated—the next step is to determine what kinds of cases the lab will handle and what resources are available to the department developing the forensic team.

Components of a Forensic Host

Host computers are the physical computer hardware and operating systems that host the forensic tools used by the examiner. The hardware will vary in scope and usage depending on the needs and budget of the examiner.

As a rule, examiners need lots of processing power. This isn't because they are power hungry, but because some forensic tools require lots of processing power. Recommended additional components include a large monitor, external drive bays, device adapters, and CD-R/DVD burners. The large monitor will help you view extensive data simultaneously. Adapters for USB, SCSI, FireWire, and flash media are recommended, and a fast burner will help you copy and archive data. Additionally, include ample storage for all the evidence and generous onboard memory to work with the data. Fast drives such as SATA and SCSI, ideally on a separate controller than the OS drive, are worth the investment. Consider external hard drives for large data acquisitions. Provide yourself the additional horsepower with a fast bus, fast RAM, and only the software necessary to carry out investigations. Use quality components when possible.

The operating system used will depend on the comfort level of the user, the tools used, and, in some cases, the budget of the examiner.

Wrong or Poorly Configured Hardware

Popularity:	6
Simplicity:	5
Impact:	8
Risk Rating:	7

The consequences of investigating a civil or criminal case with the wrong equipment sometimes only suffers you the time and ingenuity to overcome the shortfall. Other times, however, it may cost you the investigation. Learning that you need a SCSI adapter at 3:00 A.M. in Bumford, Texas, is a bad situation. Other bad circumstances include not having enough storage, memory, adaptors, and other necessary equipment for your organization's needs.

Understand Your Computer's Role

Forensic hosts can play multiple roles. In purist environments, the acquisitions computer is always separate from the analysis computer. However, most corporate environments currently use the same machine for acquisitions and analysis. Whatever the environment, prepare yourself before you need the gear. Buy the appropriate cables, readers, or accessories to interface with the hardware in your environment, and make certain that your analysis machine can handle the workload.

For many investigators, a small shuttle computer may suffice for a mobile unit, whereas others feel hampered by the single PCI slot and will carry a fully equipped mid-tower computer to an onsite call. Still other investigators prefer a laptop, and they can successfully triage, grab, and work with data effectively within those constraints. Keep an eye on the market, as new computers and form factors are coming out all the time.

Acquisition Units

Acquisition host computers need lots of drive storage. If you're short on funds, an older computer that's deemed inadequate for everyday use makes an excellent acquisition and duplication host. An internal removable drive bay or an external drive bay connected via FireWire or USB2.0 is recommended. Note that some old hardware write-blockers hook up only through a SCSI connection.

Analysis Units

Analysis host computers need lots of memory and processing power as they perform the brunt of the work with the forensic examiner on the machine. Because computer time is cheap and the examiner's time is not, it is a good idea to invest money in an excellent analysis host. This will maximize the examiner's time while minimizing frustration. If your organization has the funds, then multiple hosts may break up the investigation to get specific tasks completed quicker than serially feeding the tasks through the same host.

Also consider the surrounding environment, and ensure that the examiner has access to all the same software and equipment normally used in the environment. For example, if tapes are used in the environment, it makes sense to equip the investigator with the same access to hardware. Likewise, if the hardware used by the workforce supports certain high-end tools or software packages, the forensic investigator should have access to these types of tools or software packages.

Mobile Units

The forensic examiner might need to visit remote sites in your organization. A forensic services organization providing forensic acquisition and examination services at a customer's premises needs a highly mobile workstation. In addition, companies with multiple branch offices, manufacturing facilities, and storage facilities often need mobile workstations capable of performing onsite investigations.

Often, large corporations employ only a handful of trained forensic investigators. This small group of people is forced to travel, in some cases worldwide, to perform acquisitions (and sometimes investigations) onsite. A correctly built and configured mobile workstation is a tremendous asset to the investigator.

If this is your role, you will appreciate a smaller, more compact workstation than a full-sized desktop computer. A laptop can be configured to work well if only a few hosts need to be acquired or analyzed. If more than a few hosts need to be acquired, consider a mid-tower system with enough slots and ports to support all of your gear.

Hardware Components for a Mobile Investigator   The following components will help a mobile investigator:

▼   An internal or standalone external drive bay can offer plenty of storage. If you are going to use a laptop, consider using a laptop with a built-in FireWire. This allows you to use the available PCMCIA slot.

■   A hard, solid storage case built for traveling will protect your gear while you're on the move. Make certain the case locks or can accept a padlock.

■   A USB expansion card makes it effortless to add other components such as a printer or multi-card reader.

■   A wide array of adapters protects you from making last-minute trips.

■   A multi-card reader for different kinds of flash media can come in handy, especially if you are working covertly in a corporate environment.

■   Hardware write-blockers such as FASTBLOC by Intelligent Computer Solutions (ICS) prevent writing data accidentally to your source media during the acquisition phase.

■   The Paraben PDA Seizure Toolbox is a top-notch product for PDAs and cell phones. If you even remotely think you will face a personal digital assistant (PDA) during an investigation, the product is worth the money. Paraben also offers the ability to acquire cell phone data, and the company is constantly updating its products. Check out the latest updates on Paraben's web site at http://www.paraben-forensics.com.

▲   Hardware duplicating tools are sometimes useful, depending on what you want to accomplish. The Image MASSter Solo by Intelligent Computer Solutions (ICS) can duplicate data at gigabyte speeds, as can the Logicube, from www.logicubeforensics.com.

Depending on your established method and available tools, each situation might require a different acquisition technology.

The "Poor Man's Shop"

If your management has not allocated enough funds, or if it's a new group, you can save money by sharing hardware between the acquisitions workstation and the analysis workstation. Additionally, you can configure inexpensive hardware with open-source Linux and run freeware tools. Linux will run well on old hardware. The most important component in a "poor man's shop" is the technical competence of the examiner. Keep in mind you can always start out with limited tools and hardware and grow your abilities over time.

Commercially Available Hardware Systems

A number of commercial hardware systems are available. They are excellent if you can afford them but are not necessary to do the job. At the end of the day, the forensic computer spends most of its time waiting on the examiner to press the next key. If you get bored, graph the average CPU utilization during an investigation. That said, commercial systems can provide several benefits:

▼ Professional support is available for examiners, should you ever run into hardware problems.

■ Lots of horsepower helps handle large case loads and heavy data manipulation.

▲ Preconfigured computers are in many cases loaded and guaranteed to work with popular forensic software such as EnCase, SMART, or other tools.

The large drawback to commercial systems is that they are usually extremely expensive. They can cost tens of thousands of dollars with all the extras. Check out http://forensic-computers.com to see some prebuilt forensic computers.

Do-It-Yourself Hardware Systems

Do-it-yourself systems can be any size or shape and run any operating system you choose. Though not for the faint of heart, they are not difficult to build. Such hardware systems can save you a tremendous amount of money and offer you the flexibility you may need to buy exactly the components you want. With a little patience and knowledge, you can design and build a formidable lab machine. If you just want the design and not the build part, then check out some of the pre-built systems from DELL that may be loaded with everything you want. Hardware recommendations include the following:

▼ Extremely fast dual processor and front-side bus

■ Extra memory for heavy analysis work

■ Extra hard drive space for the operating system, programs, tools, and data output

■ Removable drive bay for quickly changing hard drives

■ Additional hard drive and controller to move acquired data, extracted information, or tools to a different hard drive from the OS

■ Drives should be fast SCSI or SATA hard drives on their own controller

■ A wide array of adapters

■ Excellent video card for large monitors and quickly reviewing hundreds of images

■ Multiple connections for FireWire and USB

■ Standalone external FireWire or USB drive enclosure that accepts IDE and laptop drives

■ SCSI connection if needed

■ Extra IDE controller(s) going to a hardware write-block device(s) of your choice (such as those made by Intelligent Computer Solutions, at http://www.icsforensic.com)

- Heavy-duty, fast printer
- Multi-card reader for different kinds of Flash memory
- Ultra-fast CD and DVD burners
- For some, a tape backup could also be a consideration
- ▲ Depending on your case load, a large file server on a local network to store media images while you work with them

Data Storage

Now that you have all of this data, how are you going to store it? Most forensic labs do not have the monetary resources to purchase large SAN or NAS systems, government agencies excluded. There are many corporations that are getting space on the SAN or NAS as a shared resource, and there are reasonably priced mini SAN's appearing on the market. If either of these options don't work for you, then you will have to get creative. To address this need, you have several options depending on how much you want to spend. For all of these options, it's assumed your storage needs are greater than the current largest IDE disk.

Cheapest Storage

The least expensive option is to create a large RAID set from a couple of internal RAID cards; these are now sold at most computer stores. We recommend making a hardware RAID for each card and then combining them with a software RAID 0 to allow the operating system to access the RAIDs as a single disk, giving you more storage. Other methods include using a couple of IDE drives with Windows 2000 software RAID or logical volumes across a number of physical disks.

Cheap Storage

The next step up would be an external IDE RAID. IDE drives are always less expensive than SCSI drives, but SCSI busses and drives are also faster. So these external RAID units allow you to take a set of IDE drives, anywhere between 2 and 15, and create a RAID disk that will be shown through the SCSI interface as a single disk to the operating system. These units can also be daisy chained. We use the Promise UltraTrack Series, found at http://www.promise.com, and can get up to 3.5 terabytes per 15 drive unit.

Not So Cheap Storage

Once you have outgrown multiple 3.5 terabyte boxes and need multiple servers to access a single set of data, you have outgrown most of the inexpensive solutions. At this point, you need to move to a NAS or SAN system, or to a distributed file system, such as GFS and OpenGFS for Linux and DFS for Windows. SAN systems are always more expensive than NAS systems. We would recommend the units from Equallogic, found at http://www.equallogic.com/, and BlueArc, found at http://www.bluearc.com. These units are not cheap; they typically cost at least $20,000, but they will allow you to grow your lab environment.

FORENSIC HARDWARE AND SOFTWARE TOOLS

This is almost a misnomer, because many so-called "forensic tools" were created for uses outside the forensics field. A forensic tool produces useful, reproducible, and verifiable results. Forensic tools can be broken into two large classes of tools: hardware and software.

Using Hardware Tools

Forensic hardware tools include every hardware element outside the traditional host, such as the specialized cables, write-blockers, drive-dupers, and other gear that allows forensic software tools to work. The forensic lab in your organization should be able to assess common digital storage devices rapidly. If your organization uses SCSI hard drives on production servers, you should have the ability to deal with SCSI drives. If you have other common storage mechanisms, consider whether it makes sense for you to include those capabilities in the lab.

A forensically sound write-blocker allows data to travel in one direction only, like a diode or check valve. One version, FASTBLOC, is detected automatically if you use EnCase. A note is added to the case log stating you used hardware write protection.

Another nice tool is the Image MASSter Solo 2 Forensic system, a hardware duplication device that will image a suspect's hard drive onto another hard drive. The target drive can hold multiple images from more than one suspect drive and can also be put into 640MB Linux-DD chucks for input into other programs. This device copies data at speeds close to 2GB/minute, depending on the source and destination hard drive spindle speed.

Using Software Tools

Software tools fall into many categories, depending on how you want to break them down. Some tools are multipurpose tools that can cover more than one scenario. EnCase, SMART, FTK, and TCT are all multipurpose tools. Something to definitely consider is the value of having and using a robust multipurpose tool. Consider a Swiss Army Knife. You want to have a tool that has all the blades you may ever need, even if you don't use them all at first.

Other tools are highly specialized, such as X-Ways WinHex. If you need a hex editor, WinHex is one of the best tools on the market. If you need to view e-mail, this is the wrong tool.

One frequently asked question is how to verify a tool for use in forensic investigations. Initiatives are underway at NIST to validate certain tools. Additionally, the Scientific Working Group on Digital Evidence (SWGDE) aims to provide guidelines for validation testing. You can find the latest SWGDE public documents, including the SWGDE Validation Guidelines, online at http://ncfs.org/swgde/documents.html.

Some of the tool categories we will cover in this book include the following:

▼ Acquisition tools
■ Data discovery tools
■ Internet history tools

- ■ Image viewers
- ■ E-mail viewers
- ■ Password-cracking tools
- ■ Open Source tools
- ■ Mobile device tools (PDA/cell phone)
- ▲ Large storage analysis tools

More than one tool can usually do the job, but depending on skill level, familiarity, and comfort, some tools are more effective for particular uses than others. The important result is that you can get your work done efficiently with verifiable and well-documented results.

CASE MANAGEMENT

You clear off your desk following the victory of completion of an investigation, and the phone rings. It's HR out of Boston, and they need you to answer some questions about the case you just completed. They are worried about a potential wrongful termination lawsuit. Now what? Where do you go from here? Where was that summary report? What happened to that hard drive? How was that information found? Case management is the practice of organizing, working with, and archiving information produced during an investigation.

Poor Case Management

Popularity:	7
Simplicity:	7
Impact:	9
Risk:	8

Unfortunately, many companies have extremely poor case management practices. When it comes to locating a file associated with a particular case, the difficulty and lack of controls can make the task nearly impossible. Ask many companies to locate the hard drive they had a couple of months ago, and good luck! You need those locked-away case findings if a terminated employee decides to file suit against your organization.

Effective Case Management

No matter the size or the number of investigations you handle, effective case management is essential to organizing your data and supporting documentation in a manner that is safe, preserved, and retrievable. Several important points to consider include the types of investigations you commonly encounter, the volume, and the number of people in your lab.

There are daily practices that can make your life easier. Use standardized forms for all of your tracking needs. This practice provides consistency in the lab and saves you time. Clearly label all hard drives, other media, and components you wish to store. They can be stored together however you wish as long as they are protected and organized. For example, you can place critical hard-drive originals used during the investigation inside anti-static wrapping and then inside manila envelopes. The envelopes fit nicely inside plastic containers or on a shelf in a fireproof safe.

In medium to large labs dealing with multiple ongoing investigations, it helps to have one individual and a backup responsible for case archival and retrieval to maintain consistency. This is an organizational decision based on your needs and resources. An experienced and efficient examiner can handle five to seven cases simultaneously. If you have more than four or five people on your team, then you want to consider seriously reassigning or hiring examiners to handle all of your case-management administration.

.COM

There are entire courses and disciplines involved in effective case management. If you have a large caseload and you don't have formal case-management procedures in place, you might want to research our web site, www.hackingexposedforensics.com, for more information and links to other sites.

THE FLYAWAY KIT

The following is a suggested list of additional equipment to include in a basic toolkit for use in offsite searches. Given that your circumstances may vary, use your best judgment when deciding what to take with you. Appendix A contains a detailed checklist you can copy.

Remember that you may need a small toolkit to dismantle the computer. Make sure you include assorted screwdrivers, pliers, wire snips, and a small flashlight in your flyaway kit. It can be frustrating after a long airplane getaway to a remote location to realize you don't have the right tools in your bag.

A digital camera with a date/time stamp ensures that you know exactly how the scene was laid out before you started your work. In covert collections, a digital camera will help you reposition the office papers, photos, and other personal items found on top of the computer you are investigating. In some cases, these images may help you remember something you forgot or bring attention to something you need to revisit.

Always carry a notepad to jot down information about who is in the room and what they have to say about the computer's usage. Also include notes on what is happening in the room, the date and time of incremental events, where everything is located, and details on how you are performing your search and seizure. An evidence or property log is great for recording details of computer and component makes, models, and serial numbers. Prepared forms will make sure you include everything in the rush or drudgery of responding.

Permanent markers and labels will help you tag components as they are removed. If you are removing and carrying a hard drive back to the lab, consider taking along appropriate protective means to carry the drive back safely to the office, such as anti-static bags and a small padded box. If you are traveling with only a few drives, hand-carry them on the plane if you do not have a sufficient protective enclosure for the drives. Most hard drives were not made for the rough handling they would surely get in the belly of the airplane storage area.

Copies of appropriate policies and procedures should be standard in your flyaway kits, including policies confirming your right to perform your job and standard procedures making sure you are thorough. Having these will help answer questions by workers who do not know you and have questions about what you are doing with the computers. A well-written checklist included with your procedures can be a blessing. Include a contact person at the local site to ensure you have access to resources. Additionally, you might digitally store or carry appropriate manuals for your own gear or the equipment you will encounter. Search-and-seizure guides or other notes may also help you respond to the incident.

BONUS: LINUX OR WINDOWS?

We leave the final verdict of which operating system to use up to you. In general, we suggest basing your decision on your organization's policy, types of investigations, resources, and your current OS understanding. We also recommend downloading and installing Linux for the experience. Take the time to kick around a few commands. If your department is short on funds, Linux is an excellent platform to use despite the initial learning curve.

On the flip side, Windows is easy to use, familiar, and has an excellent repository of tools available if you have the capital to acquire them.

Linux Benefits	Windows Benefits
Hardware devices are treated as files, which make imaging and MD5 verification easy.	Most users are familiar with it.
Supports multiple file systems.	Native environment for data in most investigations.
Supports read-only mode of files and volumes natively.	Some specialized tools run only on Windows.
Bootable Linux CDs such as FIRE or customized Knoppix versions are free and full of useful tools.	
Basic forensic utilities such as DD for imaging, file for file identification, and MD5 for verifying are all native to the OS.	
A fully usable Linux install can be done on a fast 486 computer.	
Linux Drawbacks	**Windows Drawbacks**
User must learn new platform.	Limited file system support.
Some specialized tools will run only on Windows.	Requires special boot disk or write-blocker.
	Licensing.

PART II

COLLECTING THE EVIDENCE

CASE STUDY: THE COLLECTIONS AGENCY

We received a phone call Thursday at 3 P.M. Then, at 5 P.M., we were notified that we were being deployed to New York City to meet with client personnel the next morning. Within that two-hour period, we were to gather up our personal items, such as clothes and other effects. We also had to bring along all of our paperwork and equipment packed and ready for the plane. Our advance preparations paid off, and we made it out on the last flight that night.

Preparations

With preparations in hand from Part I, we had our portable system in its air travel–safe container. We called it "The Heavy" because the box was plastered with multiple stickers warning would-be lifters how much the box weighed. The Heavy carried the imaging and preview systems, extra hard drives, write blockers, and other assorted parts. We also carried precompleted paperwork along with templates in case we needed to print more paperwork from our laptops. Waking up in New York that morning, we rushed to an 8 A.M. meeting with the client.

Revelations

At 10 A.M. Friday, after a two-hour meeting, what was supposed to be a simple, two-day operation revealed its true nature. Instead of the original and simple two-system collection for which our company deployed us, a larger pattern quickly emerged. Shortly after examining the first two systems, the controlled samples exposed the need to visit each of the systems across the company's network and throughout the city.

Collecting Evidence

The extent of the damage was clearly larger than anyone expected, and it was necessary for us to collect and image for preservation and analysis each of these computers. We began to collect systems throughout the city and visited 63 hard drives in four days.

We worked quietly and split the load between us and our corporate office. We kept systems we knew the suspect had used onsite in New York for immediate analysis and sent systems we knew were only affected but not used by the suspect to the lab for imaging. Once again, the preplanning from Part I allowed us to scale from three systems to more than ten systems working in parallel. Imaging continued around the clock. One of our portable systems was used so much and jarred so hard during acquisitions that the fan broke off in transit and the processor overheated to the point that the chip cracked.

The goal was to analyze the impact of the situation and preserve relevant data to minimize the legal risk to the client and client's duty to preserve. Moreover, we needed to identify the potential ongoing damage from the suspect. Life was about to get interesting.

CHAPTER 4

FORENSICALLY
SOUND
EVIDENCE
COLLECTION

E vidence collection is the most important part of the investigation of any incident, and it's even more important if the evidence will find its way into a court of law. No matter how good your analysis, how thorough your procedures, or how strong your chain of custody, if you cannot prove to the court that you collected your evidence in a forensically sound matter, all your hard work won't hold up and will be wasted.

In this chapter, we discuss several types of collections, also called *acquisitions* or *imaging* (short for forensic imaging), scenarios that might play out in your day-to-day investigative duties. We cover the most common scenario, collecting evidence from a single system, and discuss some common mistakes that are made while collecting evidence. Other types of imaging are covered throughout the rest of the book.

COLLECTING EVIDENCE FROM A SINGLE SYSTEM

Popularity:	10
Simplicity:	8
Impact:	10
Risk Rating:	**9**

A *single system* in this context can include any type of *x*86-based system, such as desktop and laptop computers and possibly lower-end servers. I say *possibly* because in most cases a higher-end server may contain a RAID set, which is discussed in detail in Chapter 10. A single system may include IDE (Integrated Device Electronics) or SCSI (Small Computer System Interface) drives and may have a wide assortment of peripherals attached to it; in this section, we focus on collecting evidence from IDE or SCSI hard drives.

Typically during an investigation, you should power down any system that you are about to acquire and boot it into a safe operating system environment or remove the hard drive(s) and attach the drive(s) to some sort of hardware-based write blockers and to your own forensic system. However, at times you may want to keep the system powered on and acquire the information from the active memory, but that is outside the scope of this section and should not be attempted by anyone who does not feel confident enough in his or her procedures to defend his or her actions in court.

After reading the previous chapters, you should have a good understanding of the basic tools and issues that exist in the forensics process. You can now use that knowledge to go through the process of collecting evidence from a single system. While we attempt to cover the most popular tools in use today, more are available, and there is no reason why any particular tool or technology that is documented to conform to your forensic needs could not be used in this generic framework.

We use the terms *suspect system* and *forensic system* to distinguish between the system from which you are collecting data and the system on which you will be performing your forensic analysis, respectively.

Step 1: Power Down the Suspect System

Powering down the suspect system allows you to state on the record and in your documentation that you've established a time and date upon which no other modifications will occur in the system. It is important that you are able to prove that nothing you do in the course of your collection, analysis, and reporting modifies the original evidence. If you cannot prove this, your findings will be dismissed. Use the Chain of Custody form found in Appendix A and note the time and date of this action.

 Never rely on the power buttons on the front panel of a computer case to power off a system, as many systems today by default will go into stand-by mode when these buttons are pressed. Instead, remove the power cord from the system and wait until the power supply fan stops spinning to continue. If LEDs on the motherboard stay lit after shutdown, they should turn off in about 20 seconds.

Step 2: Remove the Drive(s) from the Suspect System

Look inside the system to determine what drive(s) exist and remove them, even if they are not currently attached to any cabling. Then use the Chain of Custody form found in Appendix A and fill in the fields described in Table 4-1. You will typically want to document one sheet per drive you have removed.

Depending on your level of comfort in reliably describing and re-creating the technology present in the suspect system, you may want to take photographs of all of the drive connections, cable connections to the case, and general work area for future use. Photos, however, are not required for admittance into court. Whether or not you choose to take pictures is up to your discretion, as well as your company's policies regarding investigations. (See also the sidebar "Legal Brief: Admissibility of Images," later in this chapter.)

Field	Description
Manufacturer	The manufacturer of the drive removed, as found on the drive label
Model	The model of the drive removed, as found on the drive label
SN	The unique serial number of the drive itself, as found on the drive label
Evidence Description	The full name of the suspect and the type of drive technology you are dealing with: Parallel ATA (IDE)/SCSI/Serial ATA (IDE)

Table 4-1. Drive Information Fields for Chain of Custody Form in Appendix A

You can also leave the drives in the system and acquire them with some forensically safe boot disks. We do not recommend this, however, until you have experience with the tools and the time to test them.

Step 3: Check for Other Media

At this point, the drives are removed and the system is powered off; you now need to look in the floppy drive, zip drive, and any other drive that does not require power to function and is located on the system to see whether any storage media is still located in the drive. This media should be considered evidence and handled as such. Remove all of the media found in the system (at least the media you can remove when the drives are powered down) and fill out the Chain of Custody form for each piece of media removed from the suspect system.

Also, if you have the authority and right to search the suspect's work area, you should check all drawers, folders, cabinets, and suitcases in the area for evidence.

 You should always check corporate policies before attempting to search a suspect's work area, as this could be an area of potential liability for you and your employer.

Step 4: Record BIOS Information

At this point, the drives are removed and you have identified and removed the media in the system. You can now safely boot up the system to check the BIOS information.

In the Chain of Custody form, enter information about the BIOS of the system; you can typically access this information by pressing ESC, DEL, or F8 during the initial boot screen, but this varies radically depending on the system manufacturer, so always try to search the system manufacturer's web site ahead of time to determine how to access this information. Once you've accessed the BIOS information, you need to record the system time and date in the Chain of Custody form. The BIOS time is important because it can radically differ from the actual time and time zone set for the geographical area in which you are located. If the BIOS time is different, you need to note this and then adjust the times of any files you recover from the image in order to determine the actual time and date they were created, accessed, or modified.

Now that power has been restored to the system, eject all media contained in drives that cannot be operated without power (such as some CD-ROMs and DVD-ROMs) and remove them. Then, fill out a separate Chain of Custody form for each of the items removed. If you forget to eject the CD-ROM before powering it down, do not worry, because most CD-ROMs can be opened by sticking the end of a paper clip in the tiny hole near the eject button.

Step 5: Forensically Image the Drive

At this point, your steps stop being generic to any system. Here, we go into specifics about tools and technologies used in the imaging process; if you want to emulate this process with tools and technologies not discussed here, do so with caution and only after reading all of the procedures described here to identify similar feature sets you'll need to enable.

Modifying Original Evidence

Popularity:	10
Simplicity:	10
Impact:	10
Risk Rating:	**10**

Be warned that the next steps lead you into the most risky part of your endeavor (other than carpal tunnel from filling out all of the documentation): actual access to the original evidence drive(s). Any time you access the original media, you must take precautions to avoid writing to it. How easy is it to write to the drive accidentally? Consider the following possibilities, which each add information to the drive:

▼ Booting up the suspect system in Windows with the drive still in it

■ Using an unmodified DOS boot disk

■ Mounting the drive read/write in Linux

■ Booting up the forensic system in Windows with the original drive attached to it

■ Plugging in the original drive with a USB/FireWire hard drive enclosure in Windows

▲ Choosing the wrong drive to write to when collecting evidence

If any of these scenarios play out, you could be facing disaster. You may write to the original evidence and change a large amount of system times that you need to rely on in the analysis phase. This could lead to unverifiable evidence and your suspect walking away—unless you have a good attorney or established repeatable processes and you have created a well-documented investigation. (You did do that, right?)

Legal Brief: The Chain of Custody

What does *chain of custody* mean? The chain of custody is a document (this document can be found in Appendix A) that details who has had possession and access, thus custody, of the evidence. The chain of custody is not unique to computer forensics; in fact, it exists for any criminal investigation for which evidence of some type is collected. The chain of custody provides proof that the evidence you have collected during an investigation has not been accessed by anyone else since you collected it, and it provides proof, via documentation, that no one else could have changed the evidence without your knowledge. This is especially important in cases for which you have only an image of a suspect's system and not the original drive to refer to.

Countermeasure: Procedures and Tools for Preventing Modification

If you use any of the following tools or procedures, you will have created a verifiable image of a suspect system—and kept yourself out of trouble.

Step 5a: Wipe Image Drives Before Using Them

Before you use a drive to store an image, you should always use some kind of wiping software to clean the drive of any previous evidence. The wiping process allows you to state to a court that any evidence found in your investigation came from the forensic image and is not a remnant of any other evidence collected and stored on the drive. This is accomplished by overwriting every sector on the drive; what data is used to overwrite the drive with varies from vendor to vendor. The most basic tools allow you to overwrite a single character sequence, while the most advanced tools use U.S. Department of Defense (DOD) guidelines for random sequences of multiple writes to the disk before finishing. (More information about DOD guidelines for disk sanitizing can be found at http://www.dss.mil/isec/chapter8.htm.)

In most cases, a single wipe using a single-character sequence will suffice, and that is demonstrated next.

Note that you do not have to wipe a drive in order to use any of the imaging tools we cover in this book. The reason you do not have to wipe the drive is that our tools create a file(s) that contains the image of the drive instead of duplicating sector by sector the contents of the drive. If, however, you previously stored extracted evidence, notes, or personal data on this drive, it is still good practice to wipe it as any opposing attorney may request access to it in the future.

Wipe a Drive Using EnCase   Encase provides a wiping as a standard feature of the software. The limitation with the wipe that Encase is capable of is that it can only write a static set of data out to the drive. This means that if you follow the example in this chapter, the drive will contain '00' for every sector on the disk. Please remember that if you choose to re-create this sector, the tools covered in this book cannot recover the data you have wiped.

1. Hook up to your system the image drive you want to wipe. In this case, you don't need to be concerned about modifying the contents of the disk, since you are about to overwrite all of it.

2. Load EnCase in Windows. When wiping using EnCase, the licensed version is not needed; in this case, you can use EnCase in unlicensed or acquisition mode.

3. In EnCase, choose Tools | Wipe Drive.

4. In the Wipe Drive dialog box, shown here, make sure that Local Devices is selected under Source. Leave the defaults under Include, and then click Next.

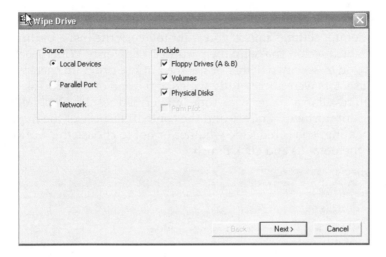

5. You are presented with a list of available drives to overwrite. Notice that the drive you booted from is not available; this prevents you from accidentally overwriting your system drive. (Older versions of EnCase did allow you to overwrite your system drive, so be careful and know your software.) Select the drive you want to wipe and click Next.

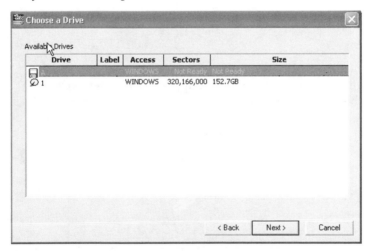

6. The next window, seen in the following illustration, shows wiping options. The Wipe Char entry represents the character that will be written to all the sectors of the disk; you can leave this set at the default 00. The start and stop sectors

are set automatically by EnCase and should be correct, so you can leave these at the default settings unless you want to overwrite just a partition and you know which sectors make up the partition. The Verify Wiped Sectors check box allows you to specify whether or not the EnCase program checks to determine that all sectors were successfully wiped at the end of the process; checking this box will result in a longer wipe time but verified results. Depending on your level of comfort with EnCase and the contentiousness of the matter you are investigating, you can decide whether or not to choose this option. For now, accept the defaults and click Finish.

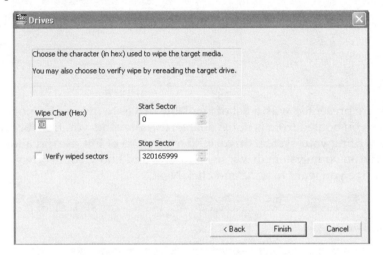

7. You are prompted to type **YES** in uppercase letters to verify that you want to wipe this drive. Then click Yes.

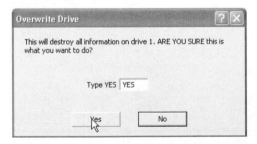

8. The drive then wipes the disk; you can click the bottom left progress bar to discover how much time remains in the wiping process. Upon completion of the wiping process, a summary message box, shown next, pops up to let you know that drive wiping has completed successfully.

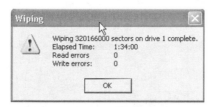

Note that while Encase is capable of wiping the drive, it does not claim to be a full wiping utility. As such, it will not wipe the last cylinder on the drive itself. This is normally not an issue. If, however, this becomes an issue for you, then use one of the other wiping tools we mention in this book; we recommend wiping with Linux, as described below.

Wipe a Drive with Linux   Windows and EnCase are not the only operating system and tool that you can use to wipe a drive. Using Linux, you can wipe a drive using the standard distribution tool dd using the following command:

```
dd if=/dev/random of=/dev/<image drive>
```

Where *image drive* is the device to write to, such as hda1 or sda1.

The command would read random values from the virtual device /dev/random and then write them to the drive specified, from the beginning of the drive until the end.

Step 5b: Forensically Image the Drive with an EnCase DOS Boot Disk

Here you'll create an EnCase DOS boot disk using the EnCase program. If you do not have an image for the Encase DOS boot disk, you can download them. Guidance Software offers boot disks that you can download at http://www.guidancesoftware.com/support/downloads.shtm (under the drivers section).

1. Choose Tools | Create Boot Disk in EnCase and follow the prompts.

2. Power down the system.

3. Re-attach the suspect drive to the system.

NOTE When acquiring evidence in DOS, you may find that the types of connections that you can read from are very limited. Most DOS USB and FireWire drivers use too much memory for DOS acquires and tend to use only the local IDE or SCSI drive connections. We do not need to worry about writing to the suspect drive at boot time, though, because the modified DOS boot disk prevents writing to the drive without unlocking the drive in the EnCase software. This means that using an EnCase DOS boot disk, instead of acquiring a drive in Windows, saves us the cost of acquiring a write-blocker for these types of acquisitions.

4. Boot up the system using the EnCase DOS boot disk; depending on the version of EnCase you're using, you will either go directly into EnCase for DOS or to the command prompt. At the command prompt, enter **en** and press RETURN.

5. You should see the EnCase DOS Version interface.

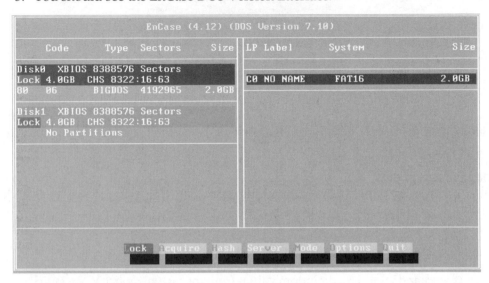

Unlock the disk to which you will be writing the image of the suspect drive by highlighting Lock, pressing ENTER, and choosing the disk drive to unlock (in this case, we're unlocking Disk1, as shown here.

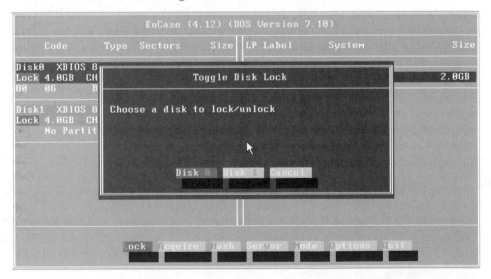

6. Your screen should now look like the following illustration, with the suspect drive (Disk1) shown as locked and the drive to which you want to write the image (Disk0) unlocked.

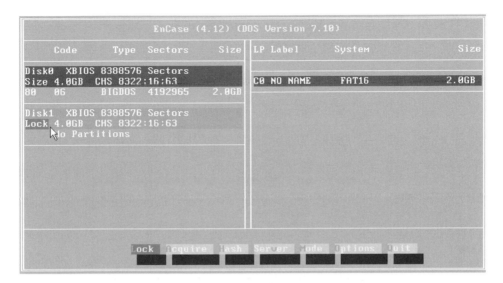

7. Select Acquire and choose the suspect drive (Drive1). You can move between options by pressing the TAB key. After you have selected the suspect drive, press ENTER.

8. Provide the path to the directory on the image drive where you want the image of the suspect drive to be written to and the name of the image file, and then press ENTER. Before you choose OK, make sure that the drive you are writing to is FAT16 or FAT32, as DOS cannot read from or write to drives of other file systems. You must also make sure that enough free space is available on the destination drive to hold the image. The image will always be about 2K larger than the suspect drive for case-specific information EnCase stores in the file, so never try to image a suspect drive to another drive of the same or a smaller size without using compression.

9. Type in a case number for your image. Use a unique number for each case you work on to help you keep track of your evidence. In this case, type **he** for hacking exposed, as shown here. Then choose OK.

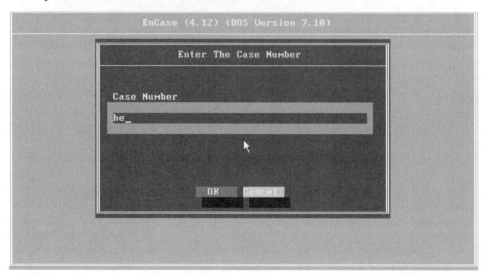

10. Type in the examiner's name. Choose OK.

11. Now enter the evidence number and choose OK. Like the case number, this needs to be unique, except here it needs to be unique only for the case. Since this is our first image in the *he* case, assign it evidence number 0. The next image created in this case would be evidence number 1, then evidence number 2, and so on.

NOTE If you are working with another person, make sure you divvy up your evidence numbers early on, because you cannot change them inside the image file after you have created the image. This approach only works with small cases. When you work at larger cases, you should look into implementing the case management techniques we talk about in Chapter 3.

12. Enter a description of the case. Normally, you would type in the name of the suspect or any other identifying information about the system. This information will be displayed in place of a name within EnCase when you analyze the system later. Choose OK.

13. Enter the correct time according to the investigator, in case the system BIOS shows an incorrect time set; you must make sure your image creation time reflects the true time as the investigator knows it. If the BIOS time is correct, accept it and choose OK, as shown next.

14. Enter any other notes about the system. Enter the serial number of the hard drive and any other notes that might be handy to know later.

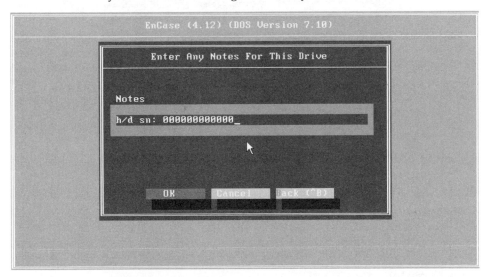

15. Now you must decide whether or not to compress the image. If speed is your primary concern, you probably should not compress the image at this point, as this can take a bit longer. However, if you have the time, you should choose Yes to compress the drive so you can fit more images on a single image drive.

16. Next, you're asked whether you want to make an MD5 hash of the drive; you should always choose Yes. Creating the MD5 hash and storing it in the image file is what lets the EnCase evidence file authenticate and thus verify itself in future accesses. It also allows you to testify to the fact that the image of the suspect drive has not changed during the course of your investigation.

17. Choose whether you want to set a password on the image. This is a good idea if for no other reason than to prevent other parties from getting bored and reviewing evidence files, or more seriously, if you are concerned about external parties or unauthorized individuals viewing the evidence. Choose OK when you're done, and you'll be asked to reenter the password to confirm it.

18. When you are asked for the number of sectors to acquire, you should normally accept the default value and choose OK.

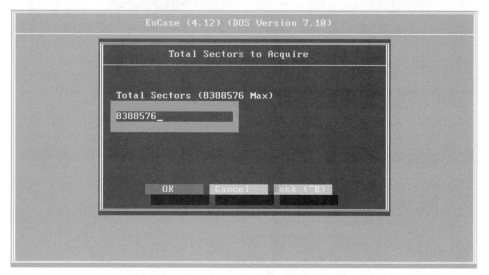

19. Now choose the maximum size that a single segment of the image file should consume. The image will be broken up among multiple files that will span the contents of the suspect drive. The size of those pieces will determine how you can move them around. The default of 640MB is good, as it supports the size of the smallest recordable CD. We recommend using the 640MB size. Choose OK.

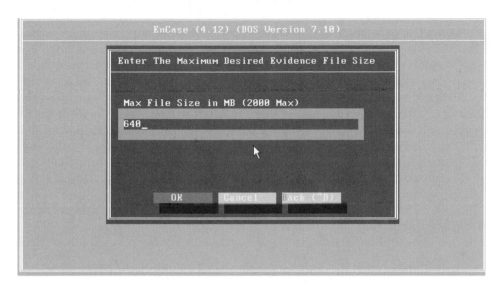

20. A status bar on the bottom of the screen appears with an estimate of the time remaining, as shown next. Review all of the information you have entered, as it is summarized here for you. If you see any incorrect information, cancel the imaging now by restarting the system; then restart this process from the beginning. Once you have created the image, you cannot change the information you entered.

```
                      EnCase (4.12) (DOS Version 7.10)

User Input
-------------------------------------------------------
   Drive            1
   CaseNumber       he
   Examiner         David Cowen
   EvidenceNumber   0
   Alias            Hacking Exposed Forensics Test Image
   Notes            h/d sn: 000000000000
   OutputPath       c:\he1.E01
   Compression      Y
   ZeroPadding      1




Acquiring Hacking Exposed Forensics Test Image
```

21. After you have successfully completed the imaging, power off the system, remove the image drive, and place it and the suspect drives in static-proof bags.

Image the Drive Using the Fastbloc Hardware Write-Blocker and EnCase   Imaging systems outside of DOS allows you to take advantage of memory ranges beyond 640K and the ability to write to NTFS drives. However, imaging systems in operating systems such as Windows requires that you take extra precautions. Specifically, you need a hardware-level write-blocker. Upon attaching a new piece of media to a Windows system, Windows will automatically attempt to write some system level data to the drive. Allowing this to happen would defeat all the work you've put into your forensics effort up to that point. Using a hardware write-blocker in line between the system and the suspect drive allows you to be able to state to the court without a doubt that you prevented any modification of the original evidence during your imaging. Hardware write-blockers work by preventing a write command from ever reaching the drive itself; instead, it returns a true value to the operating system and does not pass on the command. This physically prevents your system from ever modifying your evidence.

You can image the drive using a Fastbloc write-blocker by following these steps:

1. Attach the suspect drive to the Fastbloc hardware write-blocker.

2. Attach the Fastbloc hardware to your imaging system.

3. Load EnCase.

4. Click Acquire.

5. You are prompted to choose the source of the data, as shown here. In this case, leave the defaults as they are; we are going to image a local drive attached to the Fastbloc device. (In Chapter 8, we cover acquiring drives over networks.) Leave the Include check boxes set to their defaults. Click Next.

6. Select the drive you will be imaging. The Fastbloc device has been identified with the label "GSI FastBloc," as shown here. Select that drive. Note that you select the icon for the physical disk and not the volume E. The physical disk gives you a complete image of the drive, while the volume E would give you an image of only one logical partition. You should always choose to image the physical disk to reduce the risk of missing data.

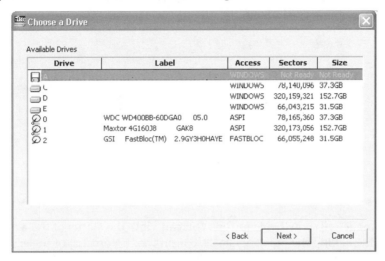

7. At the Identification screen, you'll notice that you're required to supply the same information you supplied for the EnCase DOS version, but here the fields are all on one screen. Fill out all fields as shown here and click OK.

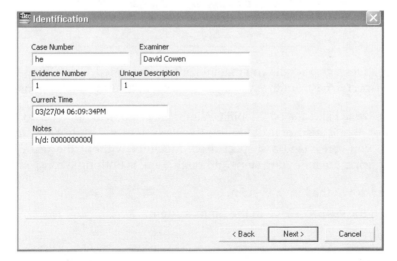

8. In the Output File screen, choose the options shown in the following illustration. Make sure you set the Evidence File Path to your image drive, and then click Finish.

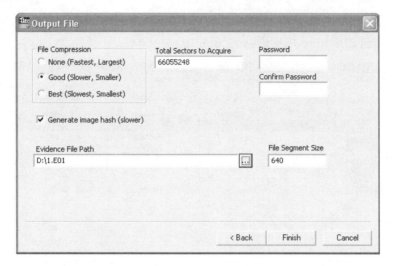

9. The image will now be acquired. You can view the status of the acquisition by double-clicking the blinking status bar on the bottom left of the screen. You can also cancel imaging from this dialog box:

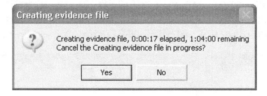

10. After a message box tells you that imaging is completed, click OK and then remove the suspect drive from the system and place it in an anti-static bag for storage.

Image the Drive Using Linux and dd   Unlike Windows, Linux will not write to any device attached to it, nor does it attempt to determine the file system and mount any device attached to it. Instead, you can image a suspect drive in Linux without the use of a hardware write-blocker using the following steps, although there is nothing wrong with using one:

1. Power down the Linux system.
2. Attach the suspect drive to the Linux system.

3. Power up the Linux system.

4. Determine the device name of the suspect drive. You can normally do this by inspecting the messages log or viewing /proc/partitions.

5. Run the following command to image the device:

```
dd if =/dev/<suspect drive> of=</some dir/imagename>
```

This creates a single file that is an image of the entire physical disk of the suspect drive. Here *suspect drive* represents the device name of the suspect drive, such as /dev/sda or /dev/hdb, and */some dir/imagename* is the full path and name of the file that you want the image to be written to.

6. Create an MD5 hash of the drive using the following commands:

```
md5sum </some dir/imagename>
```

and then

```
md5sum /dev/<suspect drive>
```

Compare the results to verify that the image is complete.

7. Power down the Linux system and place the suspect drive in an anti-static bag for storage.

Image the Drive Using SMART   SMART is the only commercial Linux forensic suite available today. SMART, written by ASRdata and found at http://www.asrdata.com, is a forensic suite that is capable of all of the common forensic tasks of other products such as EnCase. In addition, SMART gives you the power of the Linux operating system. When an image is accessed through SMART, it can be mounted as a local file system and browsed and searched with all of the open source tools available to the investigator. Here's how you image a drive in SMART:

1. Power down the Linux system.

2. Attach the suspect drive to the Linux system.

3. Power up the Linux system.

4. Load SMART.

5. Choose the device you want to acquire; then right-click it and choose Acquire.

6. In the Acquire window, select the number of copies of the device you want to make and the hashing algorithm you would like to use. As shown next, one copy will be made using the MD5 hashing algorithm.

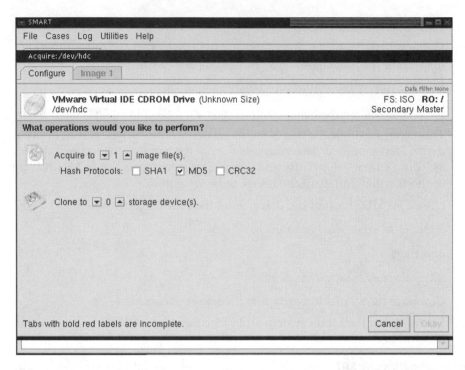

7. Click the Image 1 tab and type in the name of the image and its description.

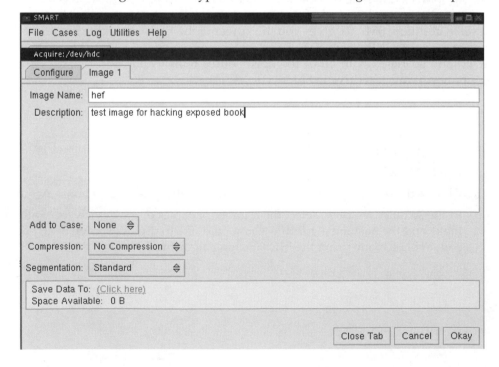

8. Click the area next to Save Data To and choose the directory where this data should be stored, as shown next. Click Okay and the imaging begins.

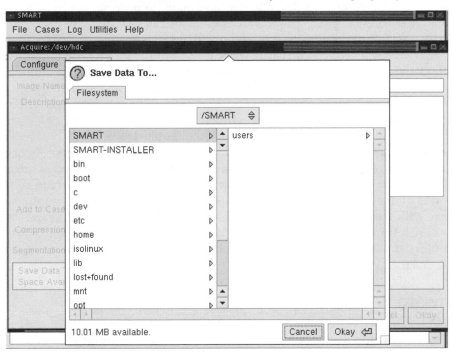

Step 6: Record Cryptographic Hashes

You have now successfully created images of your suspect media. You now need to record the cryptographic hashes created by your imaging programs. A *cryptographic hash* is any mathematical function that can take in a varying length of data to create a fixed length output that mathematically represents the entire data set in such a way that it is statistically infeasible that two different data sets could ever have the same result. Typically, we use MD5, an acronym for Message Digest 5, as our cryptographic hash function, since it is an industry standard within the forensic world.

This is a very important step. The MD5 hash that is created will allow you to demonstrate that not only does the image you have created have an exact one-for-one correspondence with the original suspect drive, but that any analysis that you perform has not modified the image in any way and thus represents the same data that would have been extracted from the original suspect drive. If one bit of the contents of the drive is changed, the MD5 hash will be different.

Step 7: Bag and Tag

Now that you have completed the collection and imaging process, you need to label the drive that your forensic image has been written to and store it in a safe place. Although you can use any type of labeling, we recommend that you use some kind of peel-and-stick preprinted drive label so you can easily work with your image drives without worrying about the labels falling off. For a safe storage place, we recommend at a minimum that you place the drive in an anti-static bag. The bagged and tagged image drive should then be stored in a location with no access to unauthorized personnel. Specifically, you must be able to testify to the fact that the image drive was placed in some kind of locked room, filing cabinet, or drawer to which only you and other authorized individuals have access.

The suspect drive at this point may or may not be bagged and tagged for remote storage, depending upon your scenario. A properly validated image drive will stand as original evidence in a court of law, so the suspect drive becomes a supplemental source of verification and recovery if the image drive(s) were to fail. While we recommend that you store the suspect drive with the image drive, on many occasions this may not be possible, and the actual drive will be returned back into operation in the suspect system. We would like to reiterate at this point that you should avoid using the original drive in the future and only access the forensic image.

Move Forward

Now that you have created your image(s) and documented your evidence, you can move forward with the next part of your investigation, the analysis—that is, of course, if you are lucky enough to have a case that involved only one system. Otherwise, you will have a lot more evidence to collect and systems to work with. Forensics is a *science*, and with such a strong word comes a lot of paperwork. If you are the type of person who cannot stay organized enough to keep up with this paperwork, you may want to hand the case over to someone who can. Repeatable processes are what will stand up in court and are the things that you should consider implementing as quickly as possibly.

Unverifiable Images

Popularity:	10
Simplicity:	10
Impact:	10
Risk Rating:	**10**

Now that you have an image and a hash of an image, do you have any way of putting these two together? Hopefully, your answer is yes. If no, you just created an image of a system which will be difficult to use as evidence. According to the federal rules of evidence, an image must have some kind of automated mechanism that allows for a duplicate to be shown to be an exact copy of the original. In the computer forensics world, this usually comes down to some kind of hash, typically MD5, and a mechanism that allows for continuous self-validation of the evidence you create. By *self-validation*, we mean that within the contents of the image it can be seen and proven that the image has not been modified without referring back to the original suspect media.

Legal Brief: Admissibility of Images

Are images admissible in court? Absolutely—if they conform to the federal rules of evidence. The federal rules of evidence have three major provisions that relate directly to forensic images of systems. Those rules, shown in the following table, set the groundwork for the courts' acceptance of forensic images of systems that have some sort of automated mechanism to validate contents, thus proving it an exact duplicate of the original.

Rule	Explanation
Rule 1001(4): Definitions	Duplicate. A "duplicate" is a counterpart produced by the same impression as the original, or from the same matrix, or by means of photography, including enlargements and miniatures, or by mechanical or electronic rerecording, or by chemical reproduction, or by other equivalent techniques which accurately reproduces the original.
Rule 1002: Requirement of Original	To prove the content of a writing, recording, or photograph, the original writing, recording, or photograph is required, except as otherwise provided in these rules or by Act of Congress.
Rule 1003: Admissibility of Duplicates	A duplicate is admissible to the same extent as an original unless (1) a genuine question is raised as to the authenticity of the original or (2) in the circumstances it would be unfair to admit the duplicate in lieu of the original.

Countermeasure: Image Verification

You can verify an image in a number of ways, but depending on the tool you used to create the image, you may be limited to one.

Verifying an Image with EnCase

If you have added an Image to an EnCase case, it will automatically begin verifying your image. However, you can manually verify the image after acquiring it from within the acquisition or unlicensed version using the following steps:

1. Load EnCase.
2. Choose Tools | Verify Single Evidence File.
3. Choose the icon of the evidence file you want to verify and click Open.
4. The verification status will appear on the bottom left of the EnCase window. The verification should show 0 errors. The verification is now completed.

Verifying a Raw Image

If you have a raw image created with a tool like dd, you can still verify the image. Retrieve the previously documented hash that you created when you first created the dd image, and then run the following command in Linux:

```
md5sum "image file"
```

The md5sum should be the same as the hash you created earlier.

COMMON MISTAKES IN EVIDENCE COLLECTION

There are several common mistakes that examiners make in evidence collection. Some are technical and others are procedural. Reading this section will alert you to what investigators have learned are easily avoidable pitfalls. We hope that you can avoid the mistakes of others by following the advice in this section.

When Not to Create an Image

Popularity:	10
Simplicity:	10
Impact:	10
Risk Rating:	**10**

There are times when you should not create an image. If you are in a situation where the opposing side has requested evidence from a system, for example, you may be providing your opponents with too much information by giving them a forensic image of a system. Always stop and analyze the particular situation before imaging a system.

Discuss the Case with Legal Counsel

If you work for a company, meet with the company's inside counsel; if you work for yourself, call and meet with your attorney. Creating a forensic image means having a large amount of evidence that is readily available to opposing parties. Make sure that your attorney understands what you are being asked to do and understands the risks. Often, a collection of relevant files on the system is all that is needed.

 ## System Downtime

Popularity:	7
Simplicity:	10
Impact:	7
Risk Rating:	8

Most people are not familiar with computer forensic processes, and they will not understand that a system will have to be down for some time while the system is imaged. On average, a DOS acquire images at about 10GB an hour, without compression. In an EnCase acquire in Windows, you can expect 20GB an hour, without compression. Compressing during acquisition is actually slower in DOS than acquiring without compression. Acquiring with compression in Windows can be fast if your processor is at least a Pentium 4 or equivalent. Linux acquires are faster than either, as they do not have the overhead of the evidence file creation that EnCase brings, but Linux imaging is still a lengthy process.

 ## Communicate with Clients

Make sure that you communicate with your client(s), and make sure that the client, internally or externally, tells you how large the drive is and what type of system it is attached to. This way, you can respond to the client with an estimate of the downtime depending on the acquisition methodology for the system. It could be that you decide to do the image at night or that the user will use another system while you image his or her system. There are some mission-critical systems, though, that cannot be taken offline. In these cases, you have to go to the judge and opposing counsel to attempt to work out an arrangement to produce backups of the live system. The best way to prevent unnecessary conflicts is to communicate as much information about the process as you can without divulging any sensitive information.

CHAPTER 5

REMOTE
INVESTIGATIONS
AND
COLLECTIONS

In today's business climate, corporations face an array of security issues on a daily basis, including wrongful termination lawsuits, e-discovery requests, employee performance issues, whistle-blower investigations, intellectual property theft, and employee harassment issues. In addition, new government regulations hold organizations to updated standards for securing and responding to incidents in their environments. These types of challenges are forcing current forensic approaches to evolve because traditional forensic investigative techniques cannot meet the increasing demand. Not only has the forensic practitioner's workload increased, but they also have to deal with global logistics, extremely large data sets, increased network complexity, workplace privacy, legal issues, and unrealistic time frames in which to perform their investigations.

This chapter discusses a number of approaches and tools designed for the changing investigative landscape. Moreover, this chapter touches on many of the technical, legal, and organizational challenges that come with utilizing some of these newer investigative methods.

PRIVACY ISSUES

Before carrying out any type of remote investigation or collection, ensure that the appropriate end user policies are in place. In performing an investigation, you must consider the issue of "reasonable expectation of privacy" and how the corporate culture may affect your remote investigation. Many organizations don't want their employees to feel as if they are being watched continually because it lowers morale. Therefore, you must employ effective controls and methods to protect the corporation and its employees.

⬤ Pitfall: Violating Private-Sector Workplace Privacy

Popularity:	5
Simplicity:	8
Impact:	9
Risk Rating:	7

If an employer does not have a clearly defined policy related to an employee's expectation of privacy or an *Acceptable Use Policy (AUP)* when an individual logs on to a company-owned computer or network, the employee may claim a reasonable expectation of privacy.

The courts generally look at two areas when evaluating workplace searches:

▼ The employer's justification for conducting the search

▲ The employee's reasonable expectation of privacy

Companies with poorly defined policies and procedures expose themselves to liability. Employees may be able to claim that their expectation of privacy was reasonable and their rights violated.

Countermeasure: Correctly Written Acceptable Use Policies

It is critical that an AUP be written and implemented effectively. The AUP must indicate to a user that any private, non-business-related activities are at the user's own risk and with no expectation of privacy. Employers should consider obtaining a signed document from each employee that acknowledges receipt and understanding of the corporate policies and procedures. This may help to strengthen an employer's position should an employee challenge the expectation of privacy issue.

In the sections that follow we are going to discuss two major types of remote forensic capabilities: remote investigations and remote collections. First, a remote *investigation* is the practice of actually performing the investigation, such as keyword searching and file hashing on the remote machine. Second, a remote *collection* is the practice of actually going across the network to take a forensic image of the remote machine for preservation and future examination purposes.

REMOTE INVESTIGATIONS

A remote investigation is the practice of actually performing the investigation on a remote machine. In most cases, you want to investigate the machine before actually carrying out the remote collection. That way you can verify the presence of suspect artifacts on the remote machine before carrying out a collection.

One of the biggest challenges facing forensic investigators is how to access and investigate the suspect media prior to carrying out any level of forensic collection. It is still considered acceptable practice to acquire the machine's image and then begin your analysis. However, these traditional approaches in which you collect evidence before analyzing it, make it almost impossible to carry out large-scale legal discovery and fraud cases without devoting considerable resources and disrupting business. This can be both costly and time consuming, especially if the machines are located in a number of remote offices. There are several relatively new tools, however, that enable investigators to forensically analyze a network computer without having to travel to the computer's location and bring it offline to acquire its hard drive.

With the remote investigative capabilities available today, the forensic examiner can, from a secure location, carry out many of the standard investigative tasks discussed in other chapters—examining file signatures, performing keyword searches and file hashing, viewing deleted files and images, copying files to the examiner workstation, and generating reports of suspect information.

CAUTION To carry out a remote investigation, the investigator needs to configure and deploy the appropriate software in advance. The tools discussed next have at least an examiner component that resides on the investigator's machine and an agent component that resides on the target machine that will be investigated. In the case of EnCase Enterprise, a third component is required for authentication purposes.

Real-World Example for Remote Investigations

The ABC Company is based in Denver, Colorado, with an office in Newark, New Jersey. The company has a small IT support staff in its Newark office, but for the most part, the core IT investigative team is located in Denver. During routine patch maintenance of the workstations in the Newark office, one of the IT support personnel discovered explicit pornographic material on two machines assigned to two different employees. He notified his supervisor immediately, who in turn notified the Denver office.

Let's consider a few issues. First, the IT staff in the Newark office has no idea how to collect digital evidence. Second, staffers do not know whether both employees are involved or whether their computer system has been compromised. Third, they do not want to falsely accuse anyone of wrongdoing, nor do they want anyone to know about the investigation or that the systems are being reviewed.

Without the use of remote-investigation capabilities, someone from the Denver office would have to travel to the New Jersey office to image the involved systems and then travel back to Denver to perform the analysis. A roundtrip flight from Denver to New Jersey takes time, and airfare is not cheap. Of course, another approach may be to talk an IT person through properly removing the hard drive and packaging it for shipping. In either case, the investigation will be delayed.

With a remote-investigation tool, the Denver-based examiner can remotely connect to the suspect systems in New Jersey and investigate further. This negates the need for travel, keeps expenses down, saves time, and maintains the covert nature of the investigation—all of which are important considerations, especially if the employee discovers that he's been had and starts to destroy the material before anyone arrives on-site.

Remote Investigation Tools

Two remote forensic analysis tools are EnCase Enterprise Edition and ProDiscover. The breadth of analysis varies depending on the technology used to carry out the remote investigation. Of the two tools discussed here, EnCase Enterprise is the most robust, secure, and the first commercial tool available for remote investigation. No matter which tool you use, ensure that the appropriate security controls are in place.

 You should test and deploy the remote investigative technology in your environment well in advance of actual usage. The last thing you want to be doing is deploying agents to machines that you should be examining immediately.

Remote Analysis with EnCase

To perform remote analysis with EnCase, follow these steps:

1. Log on to EnCase Enterprise Edition from the examiner machine, as shown here.

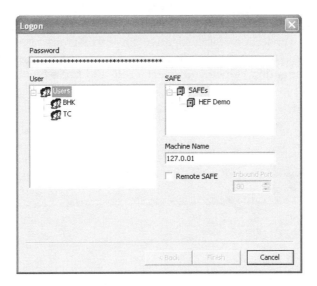

2. Select Network from the View drop-down list.

3. Create a new node using an IP address or hostname within the network view. Press OK.

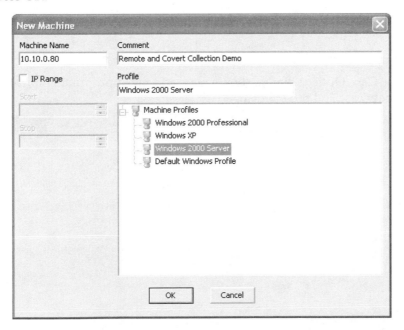

4. Then press the New button, which will create a new case to work from.

5. As shown next, a new window will appear where you select the appropriate security role. (EnCase uses granular role-based permissioning, which enables an organization to clearly define what actions the examiner can perform and to

whom. Roles are defined by the administrator during setup of EnCase Enterprise. The roles are a collection of investigative powers that are granted to an authorized examiner. Each examiner must be assigned a role before they can carry out any type of investigation.) Once you select a role and press Next, the New Case dialog will appear.

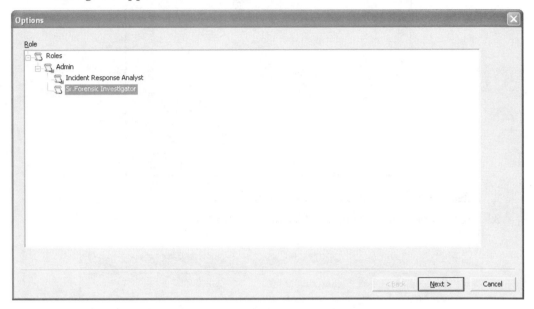

6. In the Case Options dialog, shown next, add the appropriate information for the new case and press Finish.

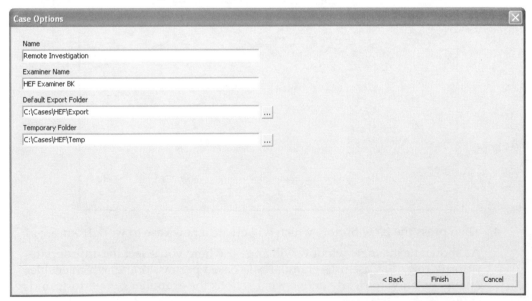

7. Press the Add Device button, as shown here.

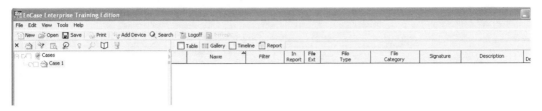

8. In the new dialog that appears, shown in Figure 5-1, select the appropriate node under the Enterprise section and press Next.

EnCase will display both physical drives and logical partitions or volumes. In most cases, you will want to select and acquire the *physical* drive. As shown in Figure 5-2, there are two entries. The second entry indicates that the target system has one physical drive (drive 0) with 4,194,304 total sectors. The top entry indicates a single logical partition (Volume C) with 4,192,901 total sectors. Make your selection and press Next.

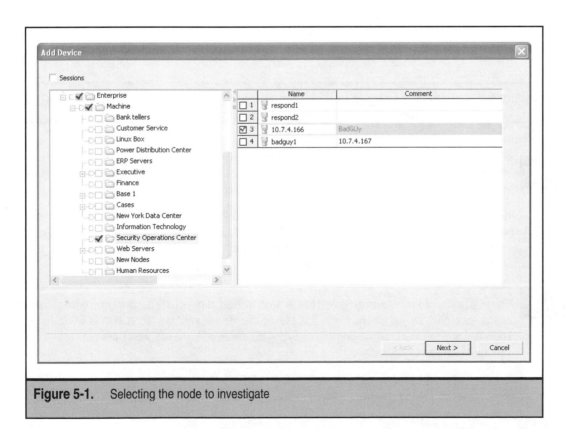

Figure 5-1. Selecting the node to investigate

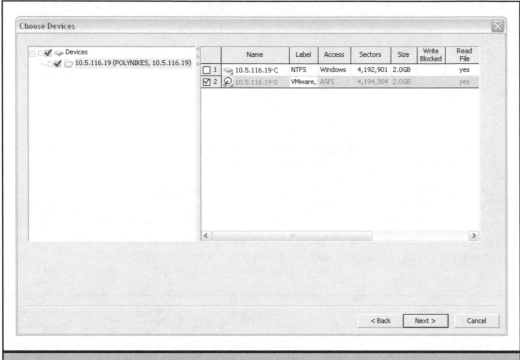

Figure 5-2.   Selecting the physical drive or logical partition

NOTE   When you preview a computer's hard drive across the network remotely, you are viewing all of the data in a read-only forensic fashion without having to copy the entire drive contents before analyzing.

Once you've finished previewing the drive, as shown in Figure 5-3, you can perform a full forensic investigation of the remote system by analyzing the registry, carrying out keyword searches, performing file signaturing and hashing, carving data from the unallocated space, copying out deleted files, and many more operations.

NOTE   The true power of a remote investigation tool is clear. Instead of physically acquiring the drive to carry out forensic analysis you can do it with just a few clicks. The user of the target system would never know that an examiner is previewing and analyzing his machine. In the real world, this remote and covert approach can be invaluable.

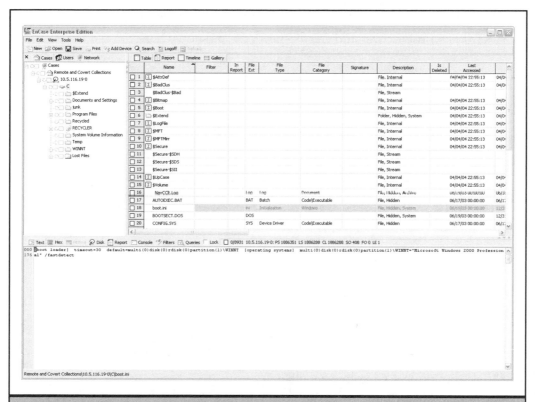

Figure 5-3. Remote system hard drive preview

Remote Analysis with ProDiscover

Before beginning your analysis, keep in mind that ProDiscover does not have encryption enabled by default, which means all analysis and collection traffic will be transferred in the clear if not enabled. In addition, ProDiscover has no user permissioning system in place to prevent unauthorized examiners from carrying out investigations. Make sure the remote investigative technology deployed by your organization has been thoroughly tested and approved by the security organization.

To perform a remote analysis with ProDiscover, follow these steps:

1. Launch ProDiscover and create a new case, as shown here.

2. Select Connect To from the toolbar.

3. In the pop-up window that appears, enter the hostname or IP address of the target machine, and then press the Connect button. You will then have access to the remote file system.

Once connected you can carry out a forensic investigation of the remote system by viewing images and performing keyword search and file hashing.

CAUTION As is the case with all forensic tools, training is critical to ensuring that the tool is used properly and that you understand how the technology works. You may have to defend your use of the tool and process if it becomes a material issue in a civil or criminal proceeding.

Failing to Keep an Investigation Covert

Popularity:	5
Simplicity:	7
Impact:	10
Risk Rating:	**9**

Depending on the sensitivity of the case and the people involved, the ability to carry out a covert forensic investigation from a safe location is critical. The ability to investigate a machine remotely means you no longer need to acquire the machine in the middle of the night (typically referred to as a *black bag job*) or escort the suspect away from their machine, causing a commotion among their coworkers. Some of the scenarios and issues that endanger a covert investigation include the following:

▼ Somebody discovers who is involved in the investigation and notifies other coconspirators, damaging the investigation.

■ The subject discovers they are being investigated and destroys the evidence.

■ The subject discovers they are being investigated, and when other coworkers find out, it destroys employee morale.

▲ The subject discovers the investigation is taking place and modifies any inappropriate behavior, such as ceasing to perform fraudulent transactions.

Properly Performing Covert Investigations

Both EnCase and ProDiscover give you the ability to carry out covert examinations without the subject discovering they are actively being investigated. This capability is a key aspect of these technologies and if used correctly can determine the success or failure of the investigation. The following techniques and actions can help you ensure the success of a covert investigation:

▼ Minimize the number of simultaneous operations to keep system resource usage down. For example, don't perform a keyword search, file signature analysis, and hash analysis all at the same time.

■ Give the remote investigative agent an operating system–friendly name such as *svchost.exe* and run it from the system directory.

■ If your organization uses personal firewalls, make sure a standard policy is in place to allow inbound connections from the examiner machine. Otherwise, the subject could be alerted by the firewall that somebody is trying to connect.

■ Ensure the remote investigative agent does not leave any events in the event logs because many savvy users check them regularly.

■ Minimize the number of people who know about the investigation to reduce the risk of the subject finding out accidentally or intentionally that they are being investigated.

■ To keep from alerting the subject, try to use an agent that runs as a system service each time the machine is started. That way, you aren't required to connect to the remote machine and start the service before beginning the examination.

■ For sensitive cases, carry out the investigation during the evening when the suspect is most likely not at their machine.

- ■ Time the investigation for periods when the subject expects a lot of hard drive activity, such as during regular antivirus scans or recent security vulnerability announcements.

- ■ Search only the data that is relevant to the case. For instance, if you are looking for documents, narrow the search to specific areas and data types.

- ■ Determine if the target machine is a laptop or desktop machine. If the suspect is using a laptop, sustained hard drive activity can alert them to the investigation.

- ▲ Be patient and don't rush the investigation; if necessary, break it into different phases.

⊖ Protecting Against Covert Investigations

Now that we have discussed how to successfully carry out a covert investigation, let's talk about how to protect yourself from getting investigated. Under normal circumstances, you won't know you are being investigated covertly. There are, however, a number of methods that you can use to protect yourself. Depending on your organization and skill level, these methods can be used individually or in conjunction with each other.

- ▼ Install and configure a personal firewall to block any defined unauthorized network connections. If the firewall is in place, it will keep the remote investigator from connecting to your host workstation.

- ■ Cover your tracks using disk wiping or privacy tools. Keep in mind that this approach is risky if company policy states explicitly that these types of tools are unauthorized.

- ■ Encrypt any relevant information and keep encrypted volumes open only while using them. Otherwise a remote analysis tool can analyze the unencrypted volumes.

- ■ Know your trusted running processes in Task Manager; the remote investigative agent runs as a process and can be identified by looking in Task Manager. Both EnCase and ProDiscover have the ability to rename their agent process.

- ▲ Turn your machine off or disconnect it from the network to prevent the investigator from analyzing the machine.

REMOTE COLLECTIONS

Remote collections are changing the manner in which forensic investigators, compliance officers, human resource personnel, and other forensic practitioners are conducting computer and network-based investigations. By remote collection, we mean acquiring a computer hard drive across the network in a forensically sound manner without having to be within physical proximity of the target media. Previously, we discussed remote investigations, which typically happen before you carry out a remote collection. In almost all cases, using remote tools like EnCase Enterprise and ProDiscover, you will first check for relevant artifacts and then carry out a collection if necessary. In Chapter 4, we covered methods and procedures for examining the evidence on-site. It's clear from the previous discussion in "Remote Investigations," that being able to investigate a system remotely without acquiring it first dramatically changes the way traditional investigations are carried out. In the event you need to acquire the machine for preservation or authentication purposes, you can accomplish this across the network using remote collection tools. The creation of these tools has reduced and simplified many of the challenges of collecting forensically sound evidence. You no longer have to travel to the target location, power down the machine (and potentially disrupt the business), or crack the computer case to collect media.

There are times when performing a remote collection is the only option. Here are a few examples:

▼ When you need to acquire a revenue generating production server that can't be brought offline for any reason.

■ When dealing with a large RAID server with many drives and complex configuration, in which case acquiring each individual drive and reassembling for analysis is an unreasonable option.

■ If the machine is in a hostile environment, going onsite could be potentially dangerous.

▲ When critical evidence will be lost between the time an investigation is deemed necessary, and when the investigator can gain physical access to the computer.

CAUTION   To carry out a remote collection, the investigator needs to configure and deploy the appropriate software in advance. The tools discussed next have at least an examiner component that resides on the investigator's machine and an agent component that resides on the target machine. In the case of EnCase Enterprise, a third component is required for authentication purposes.

Remote Collection Tools

As discussed previously, two commercial remote collection tools currently on the market are EnCase Enterprise Edition and ProDiscover, EnCase Enterprise being the most robust, secure, and first commercial tool available for this type of remote collection. The collection options available to the examiner vary depending on the technology used to carry out the remote collection. No matter which tool you use, make sure the appropriate security controls are in place and that the tool works well over various network types, such as slower WAN (wide area network) connections.

CAUTION   These remote collection tools can cause serous network problems if used incorrectly. It's important to understand your network environment and plan accordingly. Unlike the remote analysis process that only brings a subset of the drive data across the network to the examiner, the acquisition process, in essence, brings the entire contents of the hard drive across the network. It's important to understand that acquiring hard drive contents across a network is the same as copying a very large file, but in this case you're copying a forensic image. The amount of time it takes to collect a drive is typically a function of the available bandwidth and target machine resources and the amount of data on the remote machine's hard drive.

Remote Collections with EnCase

To perform remote collection with EnCase, follow these steps:

1. Log on to EnCase Enterprise Edition from the examiner machine.

2. Select Network from the View drop-down list.

3. Create a new node using an IP address or hostname within the network view and press OK.

4. Then press the New button to create a new case.

5. Select the appropriate security role from the new window that appears. (The roles are described previously in "Remote Analysis with EnCase.") Highlight the appropriate role and press Next.

6. In the Case Options dialog, enter the appropriate information for the new case, as shown here, and press Finish.

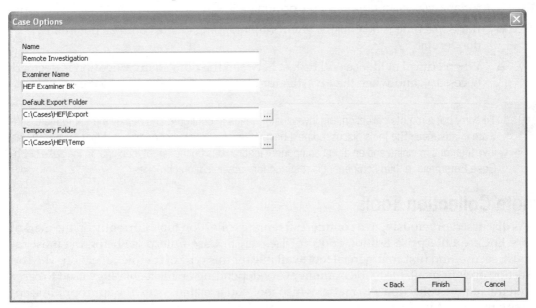

There are a number of different methodologies available for structuring your case information. It's important to follow your organization's policy and procedures or what you learned from a forensic training program.

7. Press the Add Device button and select the node you are planning to acquire under the Enterprise section. Press Next.

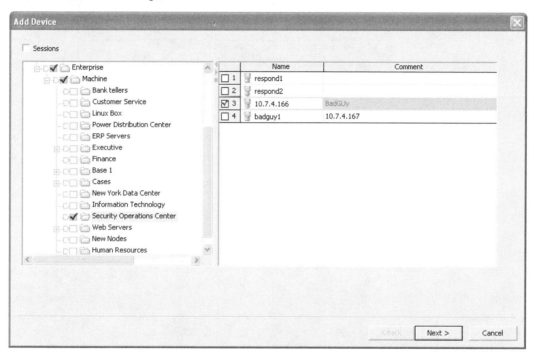

EnCase will display both physical drives and logical partitions or volumes. In most cases, you will want to select and acquire the *physical* drive. As shown earlier in Figure 5-2, there are two entries. The second entry indicates that the target system has one physical drive (drive 0) with 4,194,304 total sectors. The top entry indicates a single logical partition (Volume C) with 4,192,901 total sectors.

NOTE EnCase also has the option to collect the hard drive without previewing first. This enables the examiner to begin a collection without having to read the file system first. To begin collecting without previewing first, right-click the Read File System box and invert the selection as shown in the following illustration.

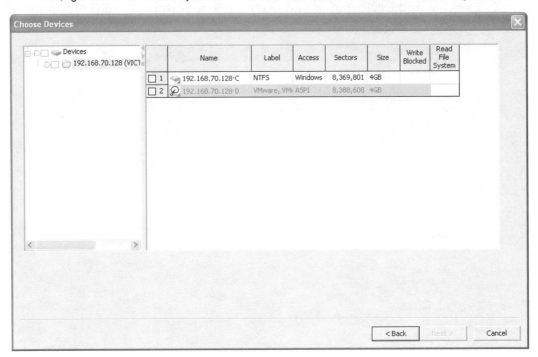

8. Make your selection and press Next.

9. After the preview is complete, highlight the physical or logical volume within EnCase that you plan to acquire. If you only selected the logical drive in the previous step, the only option available is to acquire the logical volume.

10. Press the Acquire button and the After Acquisition dialog box, shown here, will appear. If you simply want to acquire the drive, select the Do Not Add radio button and press Next.

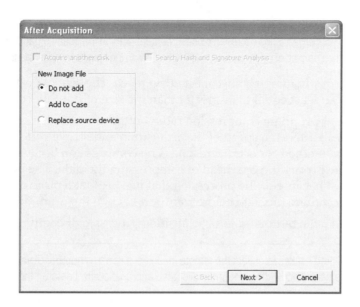

11. The Options window will appear. Enter all the relevant evidence and case information.

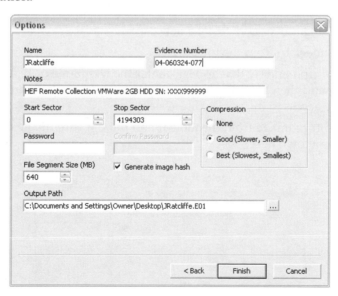

NOTE   As you develop your organization's forensic procedures, keep in mind that many organizations stick to a common format for their naming of evidence files, one that ties in with their overall case management methodology.

12. Select the destination for the collected evidence. The size of destination location should be at least equal to or greater than the size of the collected hard drive.

13. Select the appropriate compression radio button. The compression method selected will affect the speed of the acquisition and size of collected evidence. The fastest method for acquiring data is no compression because it does not require the processing overhead of compressing the data. The best method is the slowest because of the processing that needs to take place on the remote node to compress the data before transport back to the examiner workstation.

14. Press the Finish button and the acquisition process will begin.

NOTE   The amount of time it takes to collect the remote machine is tied to a number of variables such as overall available network bandwidth, amount of allocated and unallocated data on the drive, and available host resources.

Remote Collection with ProDiscover

To perform a remote collection with ProDiscover, follow these steps:

1. Launch ProDiscover and create a new case.

2. Select Connect To from the toolbar.

3. In the pop-up window that appears, enter the hostname or IP address of target machine, and then press the Connect button, as shown in Figure 5-4. You will then have access to the remote file system.

4. Select Capture Image from the toolbar and the Capture Image dialog box will appear, as shown here.

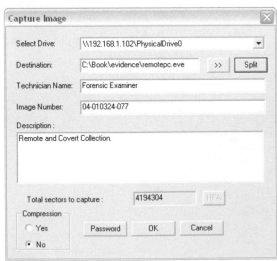

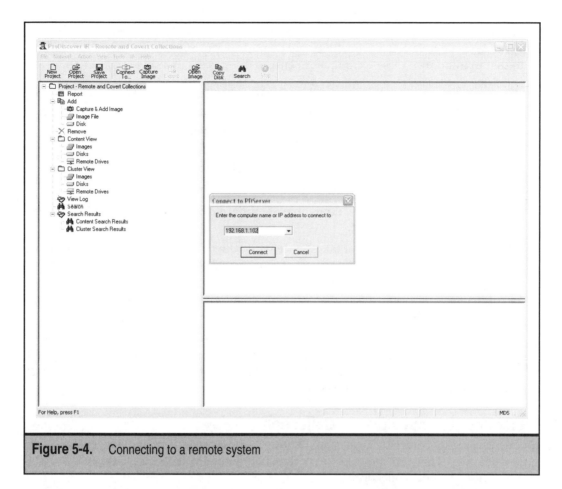

Figure 5-4.   Connecting to a remote system

5. Specify which device you want to acquire from the drop-down list.

6. Enter the appropriate evidence and case information.

7. Select a destination for the evidence.

8. Start the acquisition process by pressing OK.

Carrying Out a Successful Covert Collection

Popularity:	8
Simplicity:	8
Impact:	9
Risk Rating:	7

Covert, or secret, collections occur without the knowledge of the target or others—their existence is deliberately kept hidden. Covert acquisitions are possible but not in all cases, especially during business hours. Unlike doing remote analysis, remote collections poten-tially cause sustained hard drive activity and degrade performance on the remote machine. With that in mind, use these techniques to ensure the success of a covert collection:

▼ Perform remote collections in the evening when users are not at their machines.

■ Make sure company policy and culture require users to leave their machines on at all times as part of standard maintenance procedures.

■ Collect when the subject expects a lot of hard drive activity, such as during regular antivirus scans or recent security vulnerability announcements.

■ Acquire only the media you need to support the investigation.

■ Avoid acquiring laptops, if possible; their hard drives are slower and increased disk activity is apparent.

■ Time your collection so it takes place when the subject is going to be away from their desk for an extended period of time. Schedule an offsite meeting during the day and require laptops be left in the office.

▲ Whenever possible, acquire the machine using a high-speed network connection; it will take much less time to acquire than it will on a slow WAN link.

CAUTION   If the machine is shut down during the acquisition process, you must start the acquisition over again. In some cases, this may add many hours to the collection process, but most likely, not nearly as many as would going on site with needed equipment.

Protecting Against a Covert Collection

If you are a savvy computer user, you'll know, in most cases, if your system is being ac-quired covertly. There are, however, a number of methods you can use to protect yourself and identify a remote collection:

▼ Pay attention to increased and persistent hard drive activity at odd times.

■ Identify and stop the remote agent's system process in Task Manager. You will be able to stop the process only with appropriate admin credentials.

■ Use a personal firewall to block the inbound connection from the collection tool.

■ Pay attention to overall performance degradation, such as when copying a very large file to another machine.

■ Connect to your internal network through a VPN connection whenever possible; this hampers the collection process severely because of the slower network connection.

▲ Be a good corporate citizen and don't do anything against corporate policy.

Challenging the Authenticity of Network-Collected Evidence

The process of collecting evidence across the network is, in essence, similar to the process of acquiring the evidence while physically connected to the media. There are, however, a number of differences that can cause problems, depending on the audience and the approach taken to collect the evidence. Collecting evidence across the network is still a fairly new concept in regards to traditional forensic collection techniques. Although it's not a very widespread technique, it is growing in popularity as more and more organizations adopt technologies with remote collection capabilities.

Beyond the relative newness of the approach, there are a few other challenges. Successfully using remote collection tools does require an understanding of multiple operating systems and network environments. Two of the biggest challenges arising from network collections are being unable to authenticate the original acquisition data and legacy forensic policy and procedures.

Protecting Against Attacks to Network-Collected Evidence

Although collecting evidence across the network poses a number of challenges, there have been a number of cases in which evidence collected across the network has been used successfully for litigation purposes both in the corporate and law enforcement arenas. In addition, there are also a number of methods to overcome the challenges.

▼ Ensure that all investigators are highly trained and understand exactly what is going on during the collection process.

■ Work from a defined repeatable procedure. In many cases, cross examiners will go after the investigator's process not necessarily the technology.

■ When you've completed collecting the media from across the network, have a trusted person on the remote end preserve the machine so it can be added into the formal evidence collection process.

▲ Do your best to tie the collected evidence to the correct machine.

The Data Is Changing   In order to perform a remote network collection, the machine must be powered on and running. With the machine running, the data on the hard drive is, for the most part, changing constantly as the user or applications function normally.

NOTE   Applications such as EnCase Forensic Edition allow an investigator to acquire a machine via a crossover cable, which could be considered a network collection. In order to carry out of this type of collection, the investigator must be in close proximity and have physical access to the target machine. In the context of this chapter, we are only talking about *remote* network collections.

Court Use of Network-Collected Evidence

Computer data retrieved in a network environment in the regular course of business has been successfully admitted into evidence in many cases, as reported in various decisions.[1] In addition, hundreds of law enforcement agencies, corporations, and government entities use network-collected evidence regularly.

[1] See, eg., *United States v. Moore*, 923 F.2d 910, 915 (1st Cir. 1991); *United States v. Briscoe*, 896 F.2d 1476, 1494 (7th Cir. 1990); *People v. Lugashi*, 205 Cal.App.3d 632 (1988); *Positive Software Solutions, Inc. v. New Century Mortgage*, 2003 WL 21000002 (N.D. Tex. 2003)

When you begin a network collection, the tool typically starts collecting at the first sector of the media and keeps going until the last one unless otherwise specified. When the acquisition is complete, the examiner or the tool will generate an MD5 hash of the acquired data to authenticate it. In many cases, that MD5 hash is used so another examiner can compare the acquisition of the original media to your acquired version of the media. In the case of a network collection, you can't collect the media from a running system and expect to get the same MD5 hash as the original since the hard drive data will have changed due to normal operations when it is collected a second time. Forensically sound evidence collection is discussed in Chapter 4.

Policy and Procedures   The second issue arising from network collections is dealing with existing policy and procedures. Depending on the maturity of the organization, it might take some time to adopt new polices around acquiring media via a network collection mechanism versus the traditional method of physically connecting to the media in order to acquire it and take the original media with you.

CAUTION   Remote network collections are growing in acceptance; however, it's a good idea to keep your legal group involved so they can support you in the event a matter does arise and the evidence is needed for litigation purposes.

ENCRYPTED VOLUMES OR DRIVES

A challenge faced by many forensic examiners is dealing with encrypted data. In some cases, subjects will use encryption technology for both legitimate and/or illegitimate purposes. Regardless, investigating encrypted data is typically difficult and a sometimes impossible problem to overcome.

With network-enabled analysis and collection tools like EnCase Enterprise, it's now possible to overcome some of the challenges presented by encrypted volumes. Many encryption technologies make it easy to store and retrieve data from encrypted volumes of various sizes by mounting them as logical volumes on the host machine. For example, as shown in Figure 5-5, a mounted Stealth volume disk shows up as a logical drive on the host OS (we named the volume for demonstration purposes).

NOTE   ProDiscover cannot do mounted encrypted volumes.

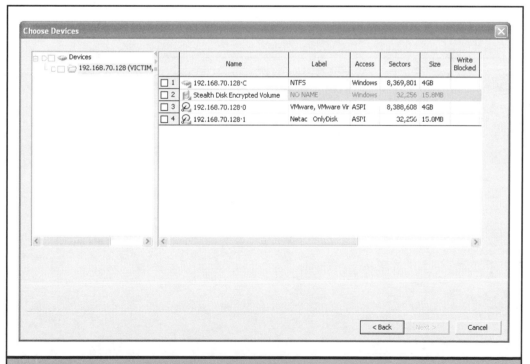

Figure 5-5.   Selecting the mounted encrypted volume

When the encrypted volume is unmounted, you can no longer select it for investigation or collection. See Figure 5-6.

By investigating the volume that hosts the encrypted volume, you can most likely find the encrypted file by its extension. In Figure 5-7, you can see the file called HEF Volume.sdv. When we examine the specific file within EnCase, we see all the data is encrypted.

If the subject has their encrypted drive mounted, it's a fairly trivial task to analyze and acquire a remote machine's mounted encrypted volumes. Follow the same process described previously in the sections on investigating and collecting remote systems. You'll increase the odds of catching a person with their encrypted drives mounted by

▼ Checking the last access times on the encrypted volume, which gives you an idea of when they last used the volume.

▲ Understanding the characteristics of the encryption program. Find out if it mounts the volumes on startup and if there is auto unmount feature.

NOTE   During an investigation, look for encrypted files on the hard drive. Find one that is the same size as one of the mounted logical volumes on the remote machine, and it is a good indication the mounted volume is the encrypted one.

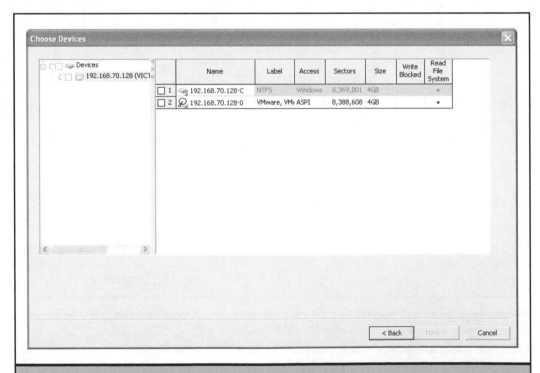

Figure 5-6.   Same machine with un-mounted encrypted volume

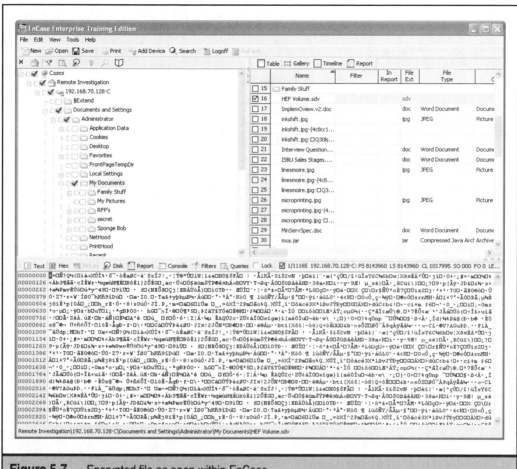

Figure 5-7.   Encrypted file as seen within EnCase

USB THUMB DRIVES

Another challenge faced by many forensic examiners is dealing with external media such as USB thumb drives and FireWire IDE drives. These technologies are a great convenience but also a gigantic risk for corporations if not managed properly. Back in the day, it was pretty tough to smuggle lots of data out on floppy disks or on paper without drawing attention. In addition, you couldn't burn a CD on most corporate computers so walking data out on CD was not as common. Now that external storage is readily available and easy to use, corporations find their intellectual property walking out of the office on a regular basis through thumb drives.

In the past, if you suspected an employee of stealing intellectual property or keeping inappropriate material on a thumb drive, it was quite difficult to view the contents of the USB device. And it was almost impossible to do in a way that didn't modify any of the time data stamps on the external media. With remote analysis and collection tools, you can now analyze and collect these external storage devices covertly.

 A good way to find out if a person has been using a USB device is to check the registry. Go to HKEY_ LOCAL_MACHINE\SYSTEM\CurrentControlSet\Enum\USBSTOR to find out what types of devices have been plugged into the system.

In Figure 5-8, you see a machine with a USB storage device plugged in and initialized properly. These devices show up just like any other volume on the remote machine. At this point, you can connect to the volume and carry out a forensic investigation or remote collection without the suspect knowing.

 There are USB thumb drives with a safety feature that hides part of the drive's available storage. When doing a investigation that includes a USB thumb drive, keep in mind it could be a secure USB device and you may not be seeing all the data. The best thing to do is to first identify the manufacture of the device and then identify if it is indeed a secure USB Device.

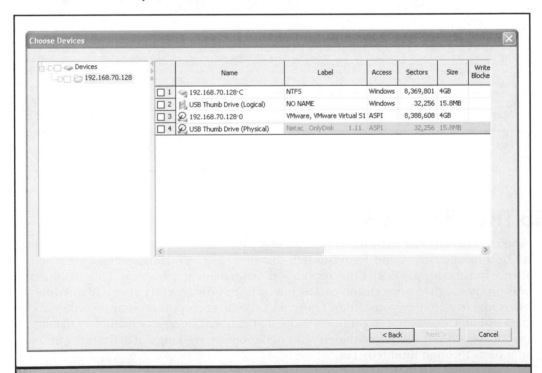

Figure 5-8.   Selecting Physical or Logical volume of USB thumb drive within EnCase Enterprise

PART III

FORENSIC INVESTIGATION TECHNIQUES

CASE STUDY: ANALYZING THE DATA

ACME Services was greatly concerned. There was no way of knowing before the investigation began how long Charlie Blink had been compromising banking accounts, and how he was getting the information. They knew at this point that Charlie was using keylogging software. However, they didn't know the scope of his crimes.

Digging for Clues

Digging under the cover of the hard disk images, the real fun began. It wasn't long before the examination revealed the specific tools the suspect used. The analysis also exposed the web sites the suspect was visiting, including information on defeating the security settings on the computers he was using in manufacturer forums. We discovered that Charlie was working with a small gang to install a stealth keylogging program on computers, and he would manually visit the computers looking for bank account information. Later, Charlie's methodology and behavior became an indicator used to search other images quickly for subsequent activity, including the use of web-based e-mail he was using to deliver the logged keystrokes to himself. Charlie had written programs to allow him to sift through the keyloggers data quickly, finding only entries where people were logging into banks. With his routine close to automated, he enlisted the help of some friends to help pick his crop. The recovered keystroke logs' date and time stamps helped investigators tie the video surveillance cameras to the user at the computer, further providing evidence that the person leading this ring was in fact Charlie. Moreover, he had been capturing account information for more than two years in downtown New York City.

We're Not Done. Yet.

Remember that in the meantime, the judge released Charlie on bail, and, as a dog returns to its vomit, so a fool repeats his folly. The story wasn't over. Our team wrote countermeasures to traverse the network and search for new instances of the keylogging executable. The software resurfaced on ACME Services' computers shortly after Mr. Blink was released on bail. Subsequent coordination with the video surveillance cameras clearly showed Charlie was at it again. Using a downloaded cracking tool, l0phtcrack, on one computer, Charlie discovered the new administrator password and installed the keylogging software with administrative rights on several others. When we put a stop to the keylogging software, he shifted to hardware keyloggers. These physically hide in the back of the computer, sitting between the keyboard connection and the PS-2 connector. There was no way for software to discover these, but our continued investigation into the browsing habits and recovery of deleted files tipped us off as to what the suspect was trying to learn and how to get ahead of him by putting in preventative measures he had not researched.

Finally

After the careful examinations and thorough researching, we had enough evidence for the U.S. Attorney's Office to approach the judge and place Charlie Blink behind bars.

CHAPTER 6

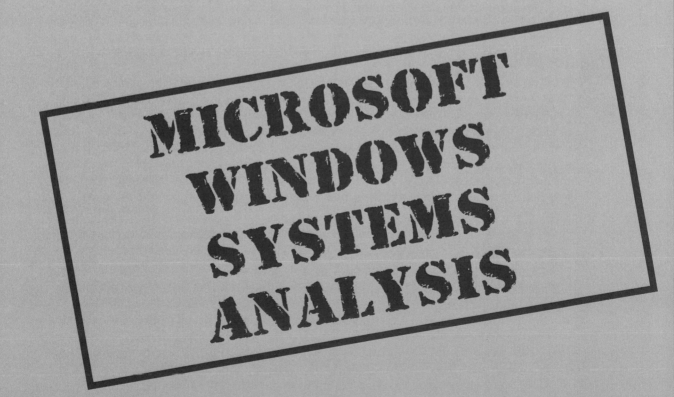

MICROSOFT
WINDOWS
SYSTEMS
ANALYSIS

The Microsoft Windows operating system contains an ample amount of opportunities for forensic recovery of deleted documents, user activities, and system artifacts. This chapter focuses on common tasks the forensic examiner will perform in an investigation of a Windows system, and specifically the file systems that it writes our evidence to. For each task, we will discuss the data you can expect to recover and the tools you can use to recover it. Each task is meant to stand on its own, so you can refer to this book as a reference when you are performing your investigation.

 This chapter does not offer an exclusive list of all possible forensic techniques for Windows operating and file systems, so this should not be your only source for forensic techniques.

WINDOWS FILE SYSTEMS

The Windows operating system has had two generations of file systems available to its users. The first file system, FAT (File Allocation Table), was used in earlier versions of the Windows/MS-DOS system and grew from a 12-bit file system called FAT12 to a 32-bit file system called FAT32. The second file system, NTFS, was introduced with Windows NT. Table 6-1 shows the Windows versions and the default file system present in each.

Master Boot Record

The first block of a drive is known as the MBR, or Master Boot Record. This record tells the BIOS where on the disk it should go next to continue booting the system. The MBR will point either to a boot loader that allows you to choose between installed operating systems or to the operating system on a partition. Most operating systems make use of the MBR, and all file systems we cover in this book are accessed through the MBR. The MBR points to partitions on the disk and for each partition on the disk, there is a *partition table* that informs the operating system of what type of file system is contained within it. If the partition table gets deleted, which can occur when someone deletes a partition with the fdisk utility, the partition still remains.

FAT File System

The FAT file system was used in MS-DOS and Windows 98 and earlier versions. FAT came in three flavors—FAT12, FAT16, and FAT32—according to the amount of space that the file system could address and thus access in each partition. After Windows 98, some Windows server versions had their boot partitions formatted in FAT and data partitions formatted in NTFS to allow for easy system recovery, since most boot disks cannot access NTFS file systems. Another offshoot introduced in Windows 95 was VFAT (Virtual File Allocation Table), which gave Windows the ability to use filenames longer than eight characters.

Common among all the FAT file systems is its structure on the physical disk. By knowing this structure, you can examine a disk and determine whether a FAT file system

Windows Version	Default File System	Practical Maximum Size	Notes
MS-DOS	FAT12	8MB	Disks could be formatted FAT12, 16, 32
Windows 3.1	FAT16	4GB	Disks could be formatted FAT12, 16, 32
Windows 95	FAT16	4GB	Disks could be formatted FAT12, 16, 32
Windows 98	FAT32	32GB	Disks could be formatted FAT12, 16, 32
Windows NT 3.5	NTFS	256TB	Disks could be formatted FAT or NTFS
Windows NT 4	NTFS	256TB	Disks could be formatted FAT or NTFS
Windows 2000	NTFS	256TB	Disks could be formatted FAT or NTFS
Windows XP	NTFS	256TB	Disks could be formatted FAT or NTFS

Table 6-1. Default file systems for Windows

existed on it and whether files and directories can be recovered from it, and you can possibly recover a deleted FAT partition. The FAT structure begins with the *boot block*. A hard drive is laid out in a logical form for the BIOS to access. Figure 6-1 shows an example of how this physical disk layout looks in EnCase.

In the FAT file system, the FAT table describes clusters that are free for use and those that are occupied and indicates whether they are linked to another cluster, which cluster to go to next, and which clusters are bad, if any. Note that the FAT table does not contain filenames; attributes; modified, accessed, and created (MAC) times; or any other data about the file. The FAT table simply informs the operating system of which clusters are free for use. The actual filenames, attributes, and MAC times are stored in the directory entries. Directory entries are stored just like files on the disk but are linked to the FAT table and noted as special case, directory entries. These directories are linked from a parent directory, meaning that the directory layout is not defined in the FAT table but rather is found as you traverse linked directories. The exception is the root directory, which is a special file whose space is allocated at the time of the file system creation, or formatting, if you will. By accessing the root directory, you can access files and directories that are

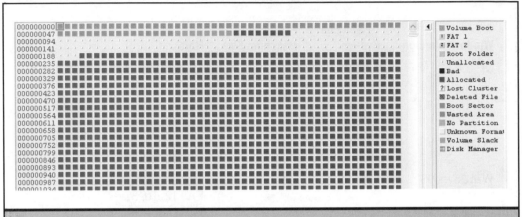

Figure 6-1. Hard drive layout in EnCase

linked to it. The directory contains the first cluster of a file or a directory that you want to access; you can then follow that chain of clusters to read the data from it.

Because all FAT directories are written to the disk the same way as files, you can recover FAT directories as well as files. This is useful when portions of the disk have been overwritten or are physically damaged. You can recover a FAT directory entry and from that point determine what files were within it and their MAC times. If the clusters to which the directory links still contain those files, you can then access them as well.

NOTE   A FAT directory is just a directory, except that it exists on a FAT file system.

You can recover a deleted FAT partition by finding the first sector of the partition and using your forensic tools to reconstruct it. For a FAT partition, the first sector, or the volume boot sector, of the file system will begin with ëXⱭMSDOS or ëRⱭMSWIN4.1 and end with hex characters 55 AA. For FAT32, a backup of the volume boot sector also is present, so if the volume boot sector is overwritten or physically damaged you can still recover the partition.

Recover FAT Partitions in EnCase

Here's how you can recover FAT partitions using EnCase:

1. Load your image in EnCase.
2. Create a new keyword: **MSWIN4.1**
3. Search the image for the keyword you just created.
4. View the hits in the disk view.

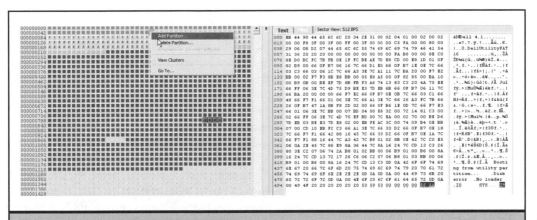

Figure 6-2. Adding a FAT partition in Encase

5. If the last four hexadecimal characters of the sector are 55 AA, right-click the sector in the disk view and choose Add Partition, as shown in Figure 6-2.

6. In the Add Partition dialog box, accept the defaults and click OK, as shown in Figure 6-3.

Recover FAT Partitions in SMART

1. To recover FAT partitions using ASR Data's SMART, simply load your image into SMART. The program will scan the image and find the partitions itself.

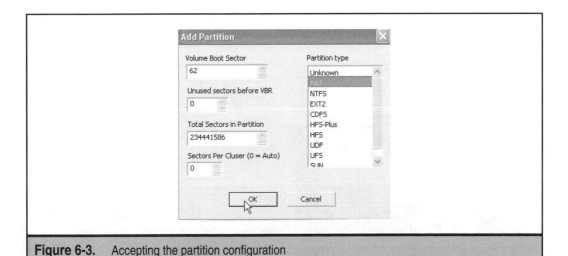

Figure 6-3. Accepting the partition configuration

NTFS

The NTFS file system, present in Windows NT and later versions, is a much more robust file system than FAT, as it allows for a multiple user environment with file-level permissions and ownership and much more security. Instead of using a FAT table, NTFS uses a MFT, or Master File Table, to keep track of the contents of the partition. For each entry in the MFT, a filename, attributes, and MAC time are stored, and many other attributes accessed by the system are stored when a user accesses a file. The list of available clusters exists in a special inode called $BITMAP, which stores that information. One entry is made for every cluster on the disk, and a value indicates whether the cluster is free.

Like FAT32, NTFS keeps a backup of its file records in a backup MFT. So if the MFT is overwritten or physically damaged, the backup can be read and you can still re-create the drive. However, you can no longer easily recover directories, as you can in FAT. Just as in FAT, an NTFS partition can be recovered if the partition entry is deleted. You will often encounter a system that has had its partition table wiped or the MFT quick-formatted. When this occurs, the backup MFT should still be in place, and you should still be able to recover the original data. The NTFS partition lies on the disk, just like FAT. In NTFS, the volume boot sector begins with ëRⵁNTFS and ends with the hex characters 55 AA.

Recover NTFS Partitions in EnCase

To recover NTFS partitions in EnCase, follow these instructions:

1. Create a new keyword: **NTFS**

2. Search the image for the keyword you just created.

3. View the hits in the disk view.

4. If the last four hex characters of the sector are 55 AA, right-click the sector in the disk view and choose Add Partition, as shown in Figure 6-4.

5. In the Add Partition dialog box, accept the defaults and click OK, as shown in Figure 6-5.

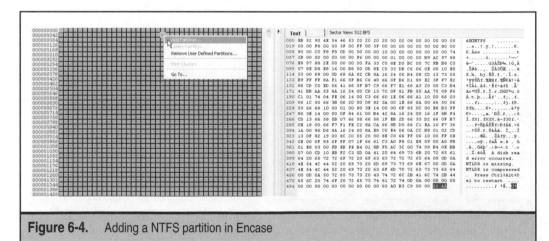

Figure 6-4. Adding a NTFS partition in Encase

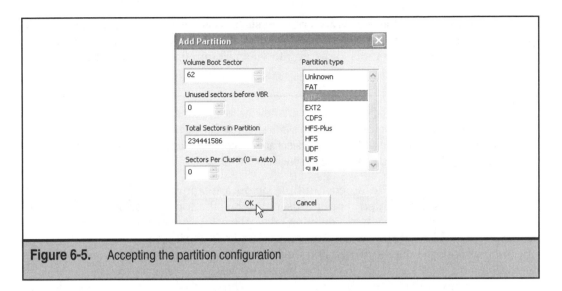

Figure 6-5.   Accepting the partition configuration

Recover NTFS Partitions in SMART

To recover NTFS partitions using SMART, load your image into SMART, which will scan the image and find the file system itself.

RECOVERING DELETED FILES

Popularity:	*10*
Simplicity:	*10*
Impact:	*10*
Risk Rating:	*10*

One of the most common tasks requested in any investigation is to find and recover the files that have been deleted from the system. This will often be a prime indicator of what the suspect was trying to hide if you find mass deletions before your imaging occurred.

Legal Briefs

If you are involved in a lawsuit, the judge may put forward a protective order, which allows the judge to state that nothing should be removed on identified systems. Protective orders are common in suits where electronic evidence is identified early in the case. With a protective order in place, there are real sanctions that can be put in place for even attempting to remove data from the system. If you are working on a system that is under a protection order, you should check to see when the last file was deleted to determine whether that order was violated.

Recovering deleted files with modern forensic tools is not an overly complex task, depending on the time frame between when the files were deleted and when they are being recovered. Most recovery tools allow you to view, examine, and recover many deleted items on a system.

NOTE This note is especially for those unfamiliar with how the file system works. When we use the term *Deleted items* here we are not referring to items in the Recycle Bin. Rather, it refers to files that have been marked as deleted or inactive by the file system and are no longer accessible to the user or the operating system, but that are still referenced through the FAT or MFT.

When file systems are designed, multiple factors are examined to determine what features should be implemented. For end-user systems, the top two priorities are usually speed and throughput. So when a deletion takes place, the software designer has two options: overwrite the data that existed on the disk and remove it from the disk, or mark it in the main allocation table as unused and move onto the next operation. Almost all file system designers choose the second option, because it takes less time to process. As a result, the data remains and only the pointer to it is lost. The good news for the forensic investigator is that we can recovery possibly years' worth of deleted data because of this design.

Every file system marks a file as deleted in different ways. In Windows FAT file systems, the first character in the filename is marked with special hex characters E5h, which are displayed as _. These characters tell the operating system that the file is no longer in active use and that the clusters it occupies are available for reuse, as shown in Figure 6-6. In NTFS, the operating system will change an entry in the MFT to reflect this deletion. Specifically, when a user deletes a file, the operating system clears the IN_USE flag from the file's entry in the MFT.

Forensic tools automatically scan the MFT and FAT tables to show you the file system that exists on an image; locating any files that have been marked as deleted is part of that scan. The deleted filename, its attributes, and its data will continue to exist until it is overwritten in part or in total while other actions are saved to disk. How soon overwriting occurs depends on three factors: the size of the disk, how far into the disk data has been written to, and how often large amounts of data are written to the disk. You may wonder why the size and location of data on the disk is important; since a disk allows for random access, why would we care about linear access? While it is true that you can access any part of the disk at any time, continually doing so takes time. Causing the user to wait for processing is considered bad, so designers try to eliminate this from occurring.

		File Name	Short Name	File Ext	Description	Is Deleted	Is Bookmarked	Last Accessed	Last Written
☐	1	⊘ _ET.BAT	_ET.BAT	BAT	File, Deleted, Archive	•			02/20/02 10:39:44AM

Figure 6-6. Deleted FAT file with E5h character

This means that the operating system will attempt to write data out in a linear stream so that it can be read faster. If it cannot find a free cluster in its current position, it will skip forward in the disk to another free area.

Over time, the data deletions that occur cause *fragmentation* of the disk. This is why Windows comes with a defragment utility (defrag) that scans the disks for the unallocated space left by deleted files and tries to put the still active files on the disk in a more linear form. However, until that defrag utility is run, the deleted data remains in its pristine state unless it is overwritten by a file that would fit in the space left behind. Even though a file is overwritten, fragments of the file may still exist and the file's name and MAC times may still exist in the MFT or FAT. We discuss recovering file fragments later in the chapter. When the end of the disk is reached, data can no longer be written out in a linear fashion, so the operating system looks for locations to place new data. This might help you understand the three factors that make deleted files available for longer periods of time:

▼ **Disk Size**   The larger the disk, the longer it will take for the operating system to reach the end of the disk and then go back to overwrite deleted files.

■ **Disk Position**   If the operating system is storing data at the beginning of the disk, it will take longer to reach the end of the disk; if the storage occurs further down the storage line, it will reach the end more quickly.

▲ **Disk Activity**   The more data is written to the disk, the faster it will affect the other two factors.

Deleted Files

Popularity:	*10*
Simplicity:	*10*
Impact:	*10*
Risk Rating:	*10*

Deleting files is something that everyone knows how to do. If you as an investigator do not review the deleted files in a system, you could be missing out on important evidence, placing your investigation at risk of losing valuable information.

Recovering Deleted Files

When we talk about recovering deleted files, we are talking about taking a file that we know was marked as deleted or inactive in the file system and exporting that data out of the forensic environment for review with the application that created it. Although many tools can help you recover deleted files from a hard drive you directly attach to your system, forensic images require that sophisticated forensic tools be used to examine images. Most forensic software tools include built-in features for recovering deleted files. Let's look at the steps you'll need to make each tool recover deleted files. Because the recovery process is the same for both FAT and NTFS file systems, they are treated as equals for the processes described here. If you were not using a modern forensic utility, the procedure could be much more manual and involve many more steps.

Recovering Deleted Files in EnCase

Here's how to use EnCase to recover deleted files:

1. Load your image into EnCase.

2. Choose a deleted file (as identified in the Description column) and right-click the filename.

3. In the context menu, select Copy/Unerase, as shown in Figure 6-7.

4. Choose the Highlighted File option; for FAT file systems, you will pick the character to replace the first character with, which defaults to _. Remember that we lost the original character when the operating system replaced it with _. Then click Next.

5. In the following dialog box, choose Logical File Only or Entire Physical File. Then click next.

6. Indicate where you want to save the file and click Finish.

The file is now recovered and stored in the location you indicated in step 6.

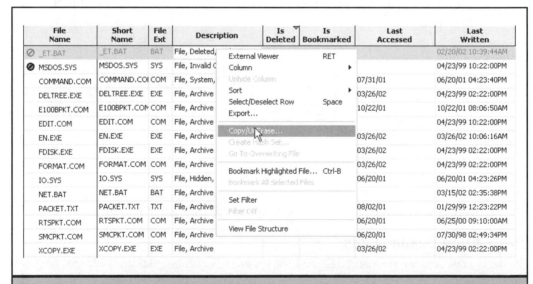

Figure 6-7.   Selecting a file to recover in EnCase

Recovering Deleted Files in SMART

To recover a deleted file in SMART:

1. Load your image into SMART.
2. In the active case menu, right-click the partition in which you are interested.
3. Choose Filesystem | SMART | Study.
4. When the study completes, click File List.
5. Select a deleted file. A red *X* in the file icon next to the filename marks these files as deleted.
6. Right-click the deleted filename and choose Export Files, as shown in Figure 6-8.
7. Click Save Data To and choose where you want to store the data.
8. Click Export Files.

The file is now recovered at the location you selected in step 7.

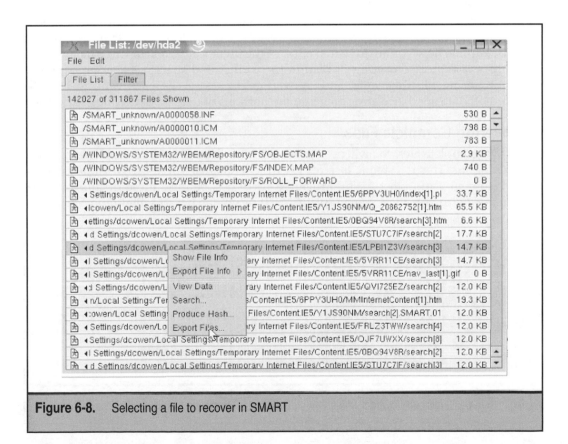

Figure 6-8.   Selecting a file to recover in SMART

Unallocated Data

Popularity:	10
Simplicity:	10
Impact:	10
Risk Rating:	**10**

After the file entry has been overwritten in FAT or NTFS, the clusters that contained the file's data become part of the *unallocated space*. The unallocated space is the group of clusters not in active use by any file; data within this space could have come from any file including the pagefile, and its file system MAC times are gone for good because you can no longer match the files contents to its entry in the MFT or FAT. Good evidence often exists in unallocated space, and not taking the time to find it means you could risk missing valuable data. Figure 6-9 shows how allocated and unallocated space looks on the disk.

Recovering Unallocated Data

Since the unallocated space has no structure, you cannot expect an automated tool to show you a list of all of the files within it. Instead, you must decide what you are looking for to determine how you are to search or parse the unallocated space. Three major methods can be used for recovering data from the unallocated space: recovering complete files, recovering file fragments, and recovering slack space. As we venture into the unallocated data space, we also come into the portions of deleted data called *slack space*.

Recovering Complete Files

To recover complete files, you will need to know the header and footer for each file type you are looking for. This is a simple task for HTML documents, Microsoft Word documents, PDF documents, and other major structured file types, because these documents have well-defined structures that contain plain ASCII or unique hexadecimal representations.

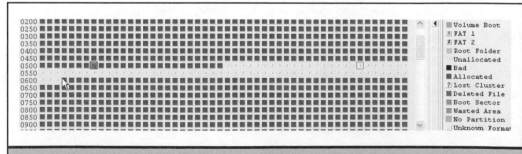

Figure 6-9. Viewing allocated and unallocated space on a disk

These lead to results with few false positives. This process lends itself to automation, and most recovery tools provide some ability to perform an automated recovery of complete files in the unallocated space.

Recovering Complete Files in EnCase   Using EnCase, you can either use EnScript or manually choose portions of unallocated space to export out of the image and back on to your local hard drive.

When using EnScript, you can either choose to write your own script or go to Guidance Software's web site and choose an EnScript script from the EnScript library.

Here's how to run an EnScript to recover complete files:

1. Load your image into EnCase.
2. Depending on the EnCase version, do one of the following:
   - In version 3, click the EnScript button.
   - In version 4, click View Scripts.
3. Select the appropriate EnScript script you want to run, we recommend File Finder.
4. Click Run.

 Recovering files manually is covered in the sections "Recovering File Fragments in EnCase" and "Recovering File Fragments in SMART," a bit later in the chapter.

Recovering Complete Files in SMART   In SMART, it is easier to use the extended features of the searching interface to automatically write out any complete files it finds. Here's how:

1. Load the image in SMART.
2. Right-click the image and choose Search.
3. Right-click the empty space where search terms are stored, and do one of the following:
   - Choose one of the file types from the Term Library to have SMART automatically fill in the header and footer of the document you are looking for.
   - Choose Add New Term and define your own header and footer.
4. Click Auto-Export.
5. Choose where you want to save files by typing in a prefix and extension, as shown in Figure 6-10.
6. Click Search, and as the search runs, the files will be recovered and stored in the location you defined in step 5.

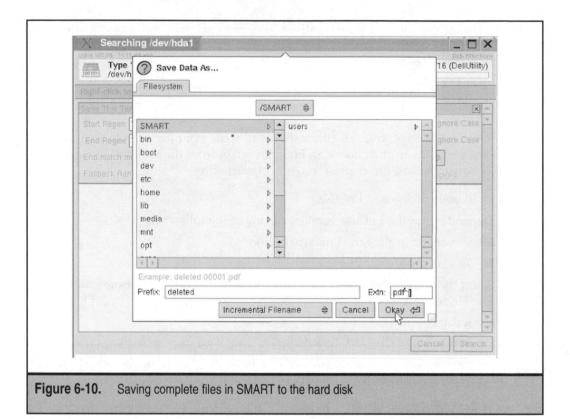

Figure 6-10.   Saving complete files in SMART to the hard disk

Searching for Relevant Data in the Unallocated Space

You will need to search the entire disk to locate all relevant documents, logs, e-mails, and more in most of your cases. At times, though, you may want to find relevant data only in the unallocated space. To do so, you would search the unallocated space for keywords. This part of the process can be difficult, because it's a manual process; no automated method is used to let the tool know in what context or file type the relevant data you are looking for exists. You will have to locate what appears to be relevant data and then export it out of the tool of your choice to go about reconstructing it for review.

Recovering File Fragments in EnCase   To manually recover files in EnCase:

1. Create a new keyword, which will be the unique part of the header you are looking for.

2. Search for that keyword across the physical disk.

3. Review the hits and highlight the complete portions of the document that you would like to export out of EnCase.

4. Right-click the highlighted text and choose Export, as shown in Figure 6-11.

5. In the Export View dialog box, choose the name of the file and the directory to write it to and click OK, as shown in Figure 6-12.

The fragment now exists in the directory you chose.

Recovering File Fragments in SMART   To manually recover files in SMART:

1. Load your image in SMART.

2. Right-click Search.

3. Right-click the empty area in the Search box and choose Add New Term.

4. Enter the header of the type of document you are looking for.

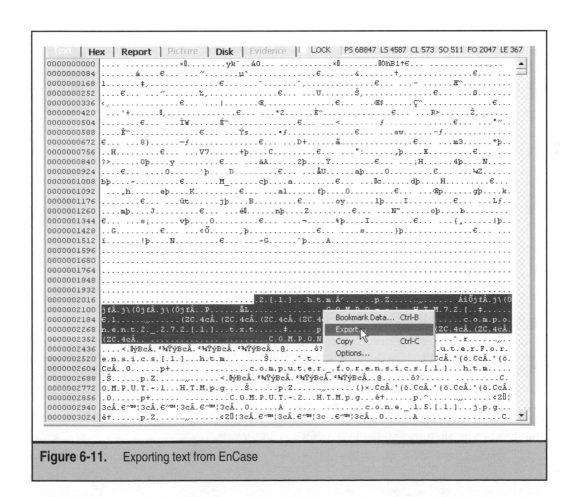

Figure 6-11.   Exporting text from EnCase

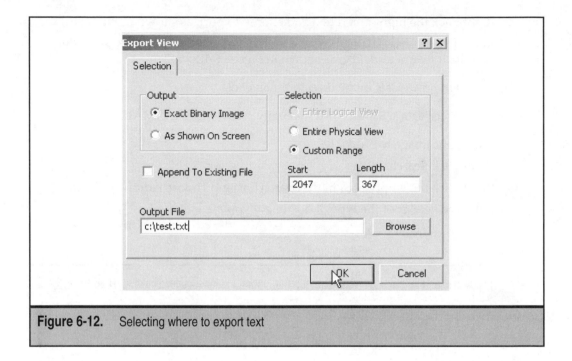

Figure 6-12.   Selecting where to export text

5. Search the image.

6. Right-click a hit from the search and choose View Hit.

7. Highlight the text you would like to view and right-click it.

8. Choose Selected Data | Export Data, as shown in Figure 6-13.

9. Click Save Data To and indicate where you want to save the data.

10. Click Export.

The data now exists in the directory you chose in step 9.

Parsing the Unallocated Space

Tools such as AccessData's Forensic Tool Kit allow an investigator to take an entire image and try to identify all of the documents in the file system, including the unallocated space. If you want to search the entire disk many times over, tools like AccessData provide the ability to build a full-text index. Full-text indexing allows you to build a binary tree–based dictionary of all the words that exist in an image and lets you search the entire image for those words in seconds. For more information on full-text indexing and more tools that can accomplish this task, please refer to Chapter 10.

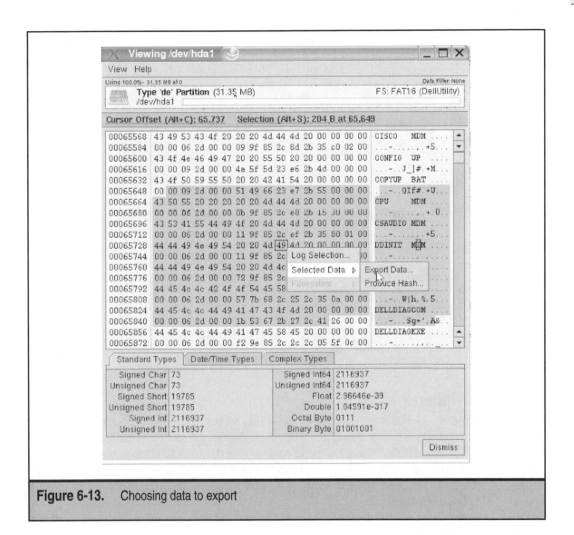

Figure 6-13. Choosing data to export

Limitations

Although data recovery methods mean that recovery is possible, there are limitations to recovering deleted data. Not every system will produce results. This can be caused by a number of reasons:

▼ The system is newer and the user's data was copied to it, leaving the forensic remnants you are looking for on the older disk. When a file system is restored to another disk using a utility such as ghost, it does not by default bring the deleted files or unallocated space with it.

■ A new hard drive could have been purchased and the data was copied to it.

■   The system could have been reinstalled, meaning that the file allocation tables would have been overwritten and only the unallocated space would contain the deleted data you are looking for. This prevents you from recovering all of the deleted documents.

▲   The user could have constantly run defragmentation tools. This would cause the earliest deleted data to be overwritten more quickly. This prevents you from recovering all of the deleted documents.

 Drive-Wiping

Popularity:	7
Simplicity:	8
Impact:	10
Risk Rating:	8

Another scenario, drive-wiping, involves overwriting every bit of the disk. Some tools in the market , such as PGP Wipe and BCWipe, allow a user to wipe out only the deleted and unallocated portions of the disk. This type of wiping will eliminate most of the deleted and forensic data you are trying to recover. For a detailed review of wiping and all of the types of wiping you will encounter, please reference Chapter 9.

 Detecting Wiping

Detecting when a disk has been wiped can be a manual task. You must check the image to determine to what date the deleted files extend back and examine the unallocated space to see what data lies within it. Most wiping tools allow the user to choose the pattern that is used to write to the disk. Some tools will turn the entire unallocated space into 0's or the alphabet. Most modern wipers will employ a more randomized scheme usually following the DOD specifications for secure wiping. If actual recoverable text cannot be viewed in the unallocated space, and if the sectors tend to look exactly the same, you can be pretty sure that wiping has occurred.

In such a case, you should search the disk for wiping tools and review the user's Internet history for accesses to web sites that discuss or provide wiping tools as well as the program files directory and the registry. Many partial wiping tools are available today that advertise themselves as "system cleaners" or "Internet evidence eliminators." These tools follow the same methodologies but are often not as thorough as a full disk wipe, as they are designed to target only certain files or locations and generally leave some evidence behind. While many evidence eliminator packages exist, with more coming out every day, most of them share the same trait of any application that they do not totally remove themselves upon being uninstalled. Finding them should be a matter of reviewing the programs installed on the system and reviewing the recently deleted files if your image was created soon after the program was uninstalled. Because the existence of a wiper is against policy at many companies today, you should check the relevant companies' policies if you locate one.

WINDOWS ARTIFACTS

Popularity:	10
Simplicity:	10
Impact:	10
Risk Rating:	**10**

In the process of using Windows, many files are created, deleted, modified, and accessed. Some of these patterns or specific types of changes are unique enough to allow us to say without doubt that a certain action has taken place. If you fail to determine whether or not these artifacts exist, you can wind up making incorrect conclusions or not being able to support your case argument. Windows artifacts often become key points in your investigations and often lead to the identification of key evidence. This is not a comprehensive list of artifacts that can be covered in a windows system, so make sure to research other artifacts as your perform your own investigations.

Emptying the Recycle Bin

Popularity:	10
Simplicity:	10
Impact:	10
Risk Rating:	**10**

Most users empty the Recycle Bin often. Sometimes the files will wind up in the unallocated space, including much of the useful data you are hoping to find, such as the filename or where on the disk the file was stored.

Recovering INFO Records

Upon entering the Recycle Bin, a, INFO record (INFO2 for Windows 95 and later) is created for each file. The INFO record contains the path, full filename, and the time when the file was deleted. Even after the Recycle Bin has been emptied, you can search for these INFO records to find all of the files that have been put in the bin. This is useful in cases where certain named documents are alleged to have been misappropriated.

Recovering INFO Records in EnCase

Use the Info Record Finder EnScript that comes by default with EnCase to recover records. Here's how to run an EnScript to recover INFO records:

1. Load your image into EnCase.
2. Depending on the EnCase version, do one of the following:
   - In version 3, click the EnScript button.
   - In version 4, click View Scripts.
3. Select the Info Record Finder script.
4. Click Run.

The results will be in your bookmarks.

Recovering INFO Records in SMART

In SMART, you must create a custom search term in the term library. You would do so by adding the hex string

```
05 00 00 00 00 00 00 00 00 00 00 00 20 03
```

The hex string will match the header of any INFO2 record, which will contain one entry for every file placed in the Recycle Bin.

Recovering Data from the Pagefile

Popularity:	10
Simplicity:	10
Impact:	10
Risk Rating:	**10**

The data that is created from processes that are active in memory does not exist in a structured file. For instance, examples of data that are created by a running program include the data created from copying a file from a floppy disk or a CD-ROM, or data from loading a document from a removable hard drive. Instead of creating a structured file to store the data, it resides in memory. However, part of the recommended procedures for imaging from Chapter 4 is to pull the power plug from the system and thus clear the memory of that data.

 ### Understanding What Lies in the Page File

The *page file*, called pagefile.sys in the file system, is a single file used by the system as additional memory. Within this single file is a free-form block of data much like the unallocated space, except that it holds data that was written to it as a form of secondary memory, called *virtual* memory. Virtual memory can be thought of as a block of specialized unallocated space that has no structure. Not only is the data unstructured, but much of it is actually raw data that we typically cannot reconstruct. We call this raw data *binary* data. With experience and effective keywords, you can begin to determine what possibly could have created the data you see within it and begin to identify things such as chat sessions, e-mails, and web pages.

Understanding the purpose of the page file is important, as many of the searches you perform in your investigation may show hits in it. Being able to view these hits and understand how they might have been created will help you determine whether a hit is something that came from a file access or whether it is a file that is being loaded into memory.

Here's an example of reconstruction of a page file that recovered the properties of an SSL certificate from a web site that was visited:

```
"ldap:///CN=cert.io.fiosinc.com,CN=cert,CN=CDP,CN=Public%20Key%20Services,
CN=Services,CN=Configuration,DC=fiosinc,DC=com?certificateRevocationList?
base?objectclass=cRLDistributionPoint0@ >
```

Here's an example of the recovery of the name of a document opened in Microsoft Word:

```
SourceURL:file:///C:\Documents%20and%20Settings\dcowen\My%20Documents\
personal\book\forensics%20exposed\Content\chapter6\chapter6.doc"
```

Printer Spools

Popularity:	10
Simplicity:	10
Impact:	10
Risk Rating:	**10**

Printing involves a spooling process that delays the sending of data to a printer. Print spooling is accomplished through creating temporary files that contain data to be printed and sufficient information to complete the print job. The two methods used to spool printing are RAW and EMF. Many times, documents that were deleted or accessed on external media will still exist in the printer spool.

Recovering Printed Documents

The spool that Windows created is stored in a file in the Windows system folder, which varies on the version of Windows you are using: \system32\spool\printers. The files that end with the extension .SPL are the image files—normally .EMF, a Windows graphic file format—that are being created. In Windows 95/98, you will find a .SPL file and a matching .SHD file that gives the name of the printer used, the name of the document, and the location of the temporary file that contains the image. If you find a printer spool, you can view its contents by loading it into a application that supports EMF.

In Windows 2000, you must search the disk for a file that has this header, in hexadecimal notation:

```
\x01\x00\x00\x00\x18\x17\x00
or
\x01\x00\x00\x00\xC4\x36\x00
```

In Windows XP, you must search the disk for a file that has this header, in hexadecimal notation:

```
\x01\x00\x00\x00\x5C\x01\x00
```

NOTE If you are looking for printer spools on an NTFS file system, you may be out of luck. NTFS can create temporary files that are never committed to the disk and will not exist for later recovery.

 ## LNK Files

Popularity:	10
Simplicity:	10
Impact:	10
Risk Rating:	**10**

For every document opened on a Windows 95 and later system, a LNK, or link file, will be created. This file contains the path of the file and the type of storage on which it existed, such as hard drives, network drives, or floppy drives. It also contains the file's MAC times as well as having MAC times of its own showing when the LNK file was created. When you're trying to re-create a suspect's dealings with a document, as you would do when a suspect is accused of stealing a document, not reviewing LNK files can mean that you miss valuable evidence. An example of this is when a suspect accesses documents that were stored on external USB drives or on a CD-ROM. In these cases, the only evidence left that shows where these files existed and how they were accessed is in the LNK file.

Recovering LNK Files

You will find LNK files in the active file system through its extension, *.LNK*. Recovering all deleted LNK files in the unallocated space can be accomplished by searching the physical disk for the occurrence of the hex value 4C 00 00 00; this may turn up a large amount of false positive hits, however. Instead, it's better to search for the name of the file that is in question. Remember that the LNK files contain the filename in either ASCII or Unicode, depending on the version of Windows, so make sure you are searching for both encodings. In addition, most forensic tools today provide libraries and scripts to find LNK files in the unallocated space for you; try these utilities first.

> **NOTE** ASCII is an 8-bit computer representation of a character that almost all computing systems can easily represent and write. Unicode is an extended character set that can use 16 bits to represent a single character. Windows now uses Unicode at the system level, so some Windows files created by the operating system may exist in Unicode instead of ASCII.

> **NOTE** For a thorough review of LNK file information, check out "The Windows Shortcut File Format" at http://www.i2s-lab.com/Papers/The_Windows_Shortcut_File_Format.pdf.

 ## Identifying the Windows Version

Popularity:	10
Simplicity:	10
Impact:	8
Risk Rating:	**8**

In many investigations, you may find it necessary to learn which version of Windows is running on a suspect's system, because many version-specific features and forensic remnants exist in Windows that can be properly viewed only when the version is known. Making conclusions on Windows artifacts without knowing the version of Windows can lead to mistakes.

⊖ How to Identify the Windows Version

Identifying the Windows version involves examining the structure of the Windows directory and looking for the system's registry.

Version	Directory Path
Windows 98	\windows\system.dat
Windows NT	\winnt\system32\config\system
Windows XP	\windows\system32\config\system

 ## System Times

Popularity:	10
Simplicity:	10
Impact:	7
Risk Rating:	**7**

Discovering the last time a suspect has shut down a system can be important in some cases. Specifically, if a suspect alleges not to have used the system during a specific period, or, in some cases, if a suspect is alleging that a system was in fact in active use, this information can help make a case. Checking system times can also help identify whether anyone else logged into the system after the suspect shut it down, or if an administrator or someone else tampered with the evidence. Trusting a suspect's word implicitly is not as reliable as checking out the system yourself.

Determining the Last Time a System Was Shut Down

In Windows 2000 and XP, you can determine the last time the system was shut down by viewing the last written time of the registry hive key $\$\$\$PROTO.HIV$.

For Windows 98 and earlier versions, you must rely on your own ability to determine whether the last dates of files being written to on the disk are feasible. This is a reliability issue, however, as file dates can be changed.

Determining the First Time a User Logged in

You can determine the first time a user logged into a system by viewing the creation date of the user's directory.

Version	User Directories
Windows 95	\windows\profiles
Windows 98	\windows\profiles
Windows NT 4.0	\documents and settings\
Windows 2000	\documents and settings\
Windows XP	\documents and settings\

Determining the Last Time a User Logged Out

In Windows NT 4.0 and later, you can determine the last time a user logged out by viewing the modification date of the ntuser.dat file in the user's documents and settings directory.

Office Document Metadata

Popularity:	10
Simplicity:	10
Impact:	10
Risk Rating:	10

While Office is not part of Windows, it is the most common document creation application for users. Whenever an Office document is created, certain attributes and hidden data fields are placed in the document automatically. Many times, a suspect will delete a stolen Office document, and your ability to prove certain arguments, such as when or by whom it was created, can only be proven by data stored within the document itself.

Discovering the Properties of Deleted Office Documents

If you are able to recover an entire Office 97 or later document from the unallocated space, you can load the document into the Office application and view its properties. Or, if your forensic application supports it, such as EnCase, you can view the metadata within your forensic environment. Otherwise, if you can only recover a fragment of the original document, you will need to have access to utilities such as the OLE/COM Object Viewer from Microsoft to view the properties of the COM objects that the Office document contained. You will not always be able to recover the metadata from a fragment, but many times you will.

You can download the OLE/COM Object Viewer from http://www.microsoft.com/com/resources/oleview.asp.

 ## Discovering the MAC Address of the System that Wrote a Word Document

Loading a Word document for any version of Office 97 and later (up to, but not including, Office XP) into a text editor that is not Word will show you the raw binary data in the document. Search that document for the keyword PID_GUID, and after some other data appears, you will see a bracket-enclosed piece of Unicode text:

```
{ 1 0 4 A 8 A 2 2 - 6 2 3 B - 1 1 D 4 - 8 8 D D - 0 0 D 0 B 7 1 B 0 4 C 4 }
```

The string 0 0 D 0 B 7 1 B 0 4 C 4 is the MAC (Media Access Control) or the hardware address MAC assigned to an Ethernet card. The Ethernet MAC is important to us because it allows us to tie the creation of a document to a particular user's system. This is powerful evidence in showing that a user was involved or directly responsible for some activity.

 ## Dr. Watson

Popularity:	10
Simplicity:	10
Impact:	6
Risk Rating:	8

Whenever a program crashes in Windows NT, 2000, or XP, the error handler called Dr. Watson creates a memory dump of the current system. If your case has at issue events that would have existed only in memory while the user experienced a crash, finding these files could provide valuable evidence.

 ## Recovering a Memory Dump

A file called user.dmp, if it exists, is a dump of the physical memory on the system. Before you can work with the file, it must first be converted, since it has null characters in between each character in the file. Once these null characters are removed, you can search the file to find any of the data you would hope to find in memory, such as Internet history, viewed file contents, opened files, and accessed processes.

Determining Programs a User Has Run (Windows XP Only)

Popularity:	10
Simplicity:	10
Impact:	8
Risk Rating:	8

When a user executes a program or accesses certain types of files in Windows XP, a built-in Windows function documents his or her actions. Often, when tools such as wipers, encryption programs, and other so-called anti-forensic tools are used, you will want to identify those tools. In an XP system, where actions taken or programs executed are of relevance in a case, you should always check for User Assist keys.

User Assist

User Assist is a new feature in Windows XP that is not well documented or well understood by the public. It is like a built-in spyware tool that cannot be disabled in XP, and it captures the actions of a user until someone or something removes the entries from the registry. User Assist entries are encrypted, however, but luckily for us investigators, they are encrypted with ROT 13! The following shows an example of what a User Assist entry looks like encoded:

```
HRZR_EHACNGU:P:\CEBTEN~1\ZVPEBF~2\Bssvpr10\BHGYBBX.RKR
```

And here's a decoded User Assist key:

```
UEME_RUNPATH:C:\PROGRA~1\MICROS~2\Office10\OUTLOOK.EXE
```

User Assist keys can be found in the registry under

```
HKEY_CURRENT_USER->
     Software->
          Microsoft->
               Windows-    CurrentVersion->
                           Explorer->
                                UserAssist
```

In this registry key, you will find two subkeys, and within these are programs and web pages that the user has executed or visited. To recover User Assist entries from the unallocated space, search for HRZR_, which is a static entry in all User Assist entries.

 For more information about User Assist, read "Yet Another Method Windows Uses to Log Your Computer Activity" at http://www.utdallas.edu/~jeremy.bryan.smith/articles/explorer_spy.txt. For a simple ROT 13 decoder, visit http://tools.geht.net/rot13.html. In addition, many forensic tools have the ability to view or search for ROT13 within their environment.

CHAPTER 7

LINUX ANALYSIS

Within the past five years, Linux has become the second most popular operating system, behind the Microsoft Windows platform. Linux users love its stability and the "close to the metal" feel they get from using it. The majority of scripted hacks and vulnerabilities are written to run under Linux, which means as an investigator you may spend a lot of time unwinding attacks that script kiddies and sophisticated hackers alike were trying to launch. Luckily, Linux is copiously documented and you can easily find references on common attacks and procedures hackers use as well as how they try to cover their tracks. The other edge of the sword, however, is that a criminal can easily modify the OS to hide data, implement trap doors, and launch other kernel-space operations that are very difficult to unwind. Add to this the hundreds of arcane commands that exist, just waiting to be trojaned, and you can see why an investigation of a Linux system can be a daunting task.

THE LINUX FILE SYSTEM (EXT2 AND EXT3)

Much like Windows uses NTFS and FAT, Linux has its own file system structure. For older versions of Linux, you will find the data is stored on an ext2 format partition. Newer versions use ext3, which is functionally identical to ext2 with the addition of journaling (more on that later in the section "ext3 Structure"). As a practical matter, an ext file system also exists, but it's so old that it was deprecated about the time that Minux became Linux and is very rare to find in use today. You may also run across other more exotic file systems, such as the encrypted file system, and those will be covered in more detail in Chapter 9. For now, we will focus on the ext2, ext3, and the Linux swap formats.

ext2 Structure

The layout of ext2 is heavily based upon UNIX file system concepts. The disk is broken up into partitions that are subsections of the disk. These partitions are then further broken up into groups, which are nothing more than partitions of the partition, and they help to break up the clustering. Each group contains a superblock, a group descriptor, a block bitmap, an inode bitmap, an inode table, and finally data blocks, in that order.

Superblock

The *superblock* is the block that stores all the metadata about the file system. Each group has its own superblock, and a master superblock stores the data about the entire file system. This block is vital to system operation since it is read when the file system is mounted. If this block becomes corrupted, the file system will no longer mount. If you think a system's superblock has been knocked out, you can re-create it, since the Ext2fs stores a copy of the superblock in each group. When you run Ext2fschk, it checks for superblock consistency and repairs it if necessary.

CAUTION Some versions of Linux, such as those that run on 68K platforms, use a byte-swapped file system to compensate for little-endian versus big-endian formats. Make sure you are aware of the type of platform you are working with.

Group Descriptors

The *group descriptor*, as its name suggests, contains information about the group. Within the group descriptor is the table of inodes and the allocation bitmaps for inodes and data blocks. This allocation bitmap is of huge importance to the investigator, since it tells the file system which blocks are used and which aren't. When a file is deleted, the allocation bitmap changes the state of the blocks used by the file to *unallocated*. This does not mean that the data in the blocks has been deleted. You can use the blocks along with the inode table to reconstruct a file that has supposedly been removed from the disk.

Inodes and File Structure

Files are represented by inodes, and directories are simple files that contain a list of entries and pointers to the files that can be found in said directory. To understand the inode structure, think about it like a hierarchical chart. Each inode points to a set of data blocks that contain the data in the file. Fifteen pointers to data blocks are inside each inode. If you do the math on that, you will quickly see that this is not a sufficient number of blocks for any reasonably sized file. Thus, only 13 blocks are used to hold data. If the file is bigger than 13 blocks, then the 14th block is used to hold a pointer to a new "indirect block" that gives 13 more slots. If that still isn't enough, the 15th block is used to point to a "doubly indirect block" that stores pointers to other blocks that themselves have 15 slots. You can see how this gets confusing fast. Look at Figure 7-1 to clarify the picture and see how the inodes link together in ext2.

If you do any substantive work at all with file recovery under Linux, understanding this inode structure inside and out is a must. Later, when we talk about recovering data in this chapter, we will look at how to use inodes to recover previously deleted files. As a aside, the linked structure of this system has some significant performance increases as well. Since the smaller files are so close to the inode root in the hierarchy, they are accessed more quickly than the larger files. As the following table shows, the majority of files on a disk are small enough to fit into this category.

File Size (bytes)	0–768	769–1.5K	1.5–3K	3–6K	6–12K	12K and up
Occurrence (%)	38.3	19.8	14.2	9.4	7.1	10.1
Cumulative (%)	38.3	58.1	72.3	81.7	89.8	99.9

As you may have guessed, the ext2 file system has inodes flying around all over the place. To consolidate all of this into one logical data structure, the inode table was created.

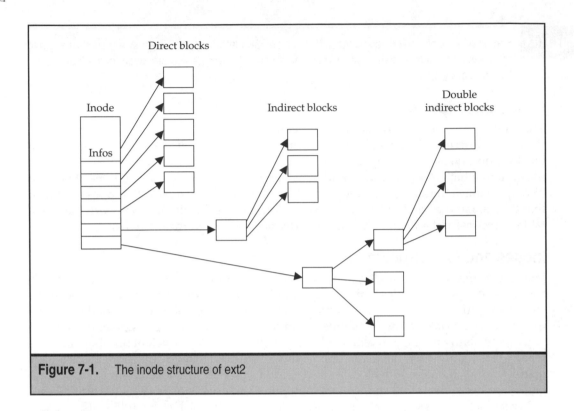

Figure 7-1.   The inode structure of ext2

Directories

Using a system in which the end user would have to refer to files by their inode number would be near impossible for the user. (Think about your daughter trying to access her school paper, named 15332. Good luck remembering that.) As such, we need a way to tie a filename to an inode number. Enter the directory. As stated earlier, directories are nothing more than files that store pointers to the files contained in the directory. To clarify, take a look at Figure 7-2.

A special directory on the ext2 is /, the root directory, located at the top of the hierarchy. So that the hierarchy can be found when the system is rebooted and the file system remounted, the root directory node is stored in a constant location, namely the second inode. From this directory entry, the entire file system can be re-created. A subdirectory is nothing more than a link to the file that contains the directory entry for said subdirectory. Two special entries exist in each directory, . (a dot) and .. (two dots). These are the identity and previous pointers, respectively, and they are created when the directory is created and cannot be deleted.

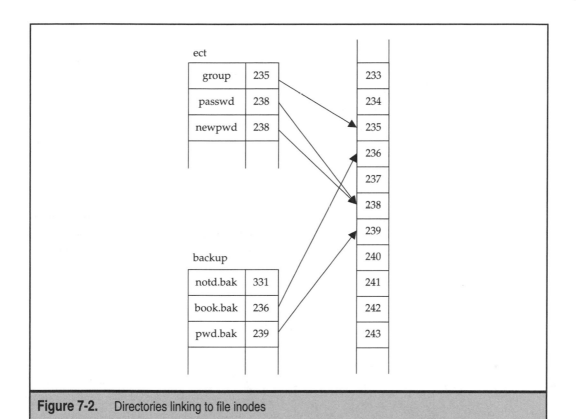

Figure 7-2.   Directories linking to file inodes

ext3 Structure

The ext3 is commonly referred to as "ext2 + journaling." *Journaling* is a concept by which you protect the structure of the files by changing the read/write process on the disk into an atomic transaction. This means that either all the data gets written to disk or none of it does. The majority of file system failures occur when a disk crashes mid-write and loses half of the information that it was writing to disk. To prevent this, a journaling OS uses an atomic write and has the file system first write to a buffer, or journal. Once in the journal, a transaction flag is set, which says the disk is in mid-write. After all the data has been successfully written to the disk, the transaction flag is cleared and the data is wiped from the journal. If something should happen mid-write, the next time the file system mounts, the system will see the transaction flag and recommit all the data in the journal, assuming that something happened in the process. This is important from a forensics standpoint: you should always check the journal to see whether something that was supposed to be written wasn't written. Conversely, by mounting one of these journaled file systems, you *will* change the disk, and any hashes you made of the disk will no longer be valid.

Linux Swap

Linux supports swap in two forms: either as a swap file or as a swap partition. If it is stored as a partition, the kernel uses the disk blocks to act as additional memory blocks for program usage (a memory paging system, to be semantically correct). This format is nothing more than an array of blocks. While this was never meant to be human-readable, it can be accessed with raw search tools that can search for keywords and binary sequences in the blocks themselves. This can be useful in memory and file-reconstruction.

LINUX ANALYSIS

Now that you have looked at the file system Linux uses, you can start doing some real investigation of user activity and tracking malicious activity. Now that you have the theory, let's look at a real file system and how that theory translates into usage. We are going to use both SMART and an open source set of command-line tools (TCT), which when used together can perform a fairly comprehensive internal investigation and can act as a cross validation. The open source tools require an image which is dd compatible, meaning that it is a noncompressed, byte-for-byte copy of the partition. As with any investigation, always use some sort of case management tool such as SMART, and hash, hash, hash.

Finding File System Signatures

Popularity:	6
Simplicity:	8
Impact:	10
Risk Rating:	9

You may run into situations where the disk appears to have been cleared of the partition table in an effort to destroy evidence. If you look at the disk with an editor and see that good information is still on the disk, chances are you can recover the data by finding the partition signatures and reconstructing the disk. Some tools can do this for you, but to complete the task in a forensically sound manner, use a tool like SMART to find the signatures and reconstruct them yourself. Remember that in ext2/ext3 everything is based upon the superblock, so if you can find that, you can reconstruct the whole file system.

NOTE   You can use several good utilities to find the partition information, such as findsuper and PartitionMagic. For further information, check out the Linux Documentation Project and its ext2fs undeletion how to's (http://www.tldp.org/HOWTO/Ext2fs-Undeletion.html), keeping in mind that they are not meant to be forensic tutorials.

The signature that you are looking for is 0xef53. Realize that you will get a bunch of false positives to go along with the true superblock. Also realize that backup copies of the superblock are stored all over the file system, so if the primary one is gone, you can still re-create it from a backup.

Locating and Recovering Deleted Files

Popularity:	6
Simplicity:	8
Impact:	10
Risk Rating:	9

The first thing that a suspect will do when she thinks she is in trouble is delete incriminating evidence. Searching for and recovering deleted files is a vital part of an investigation with Linux. The first place to start is the inode table, which is like a lookup table for the file system. When a file is deleted, it's respective inodes are marked as deleted and set as available for overwriting. If you can get to them before they are overwritten, you can reconstruct the files. If you want to use open source tools, the TASK toolkit has several command-line tools that can help. The tool fls can find files that have been deleted and help you get their inodes. Once you have the inodes, you use ICAT to pull out the file from the inode, if it still exists.

Recovering Files with SMART

SMART has great tools for performing analysis on ext2/ext3 file systems. It supports searching through unallocated space and finding deleted files. To find deleted files, mount the image read-only in SMART. Then right-click the image and choose Filesystem | SMART | Study. This will analyze the file system and find the deleted files.

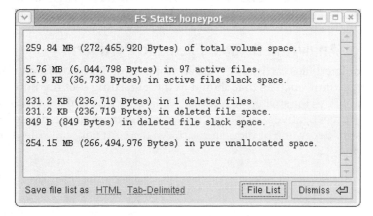

After the Study has completed, you can then choose Filesystem | SMART and look at the file list, as shown here. You can right-click the Filter tab and add a filter for active or deleted files from the drop-down box. Select Deleted and click the Apply button at the bottom of the window.

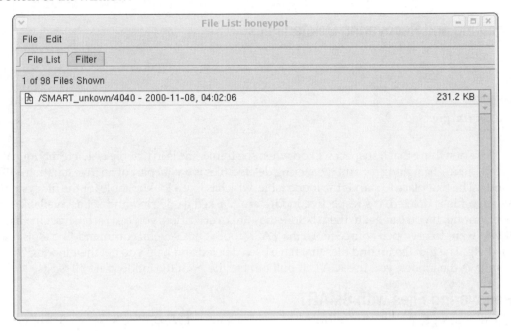

You can right-click the individual files and view them as text or graphics, hash them, and create reports for them. You can also export the file out so you can do further analysis on it if desired. If you do this, make sure you hash when you export and hash during your analysis to show that the file hasn't been changed.

Guidelines for Analyzing Deleted Files and Partitions

Working with deleted files can be a very tricky thing. Even if you do find information that you think is important, such as that shown in the preceding section, how do you know whether it actually ties the suspect to a crime? Make sure that you are thorough when doing this type of investigative work. Find and investigate all of the deleted files, and be prepared to justify every one of them in court. All the conventional rules for forensic investigation apply.

Differences Between Linux Distributions

Popularity:	10
Simplicity:	9
Impact:	2
Risk Rating:	5

It's difficult these days to throw a rock and not hit two different Linux distributions. While they are all based upon the same Linux core, the supporting programs and file locations can vary widely. Once you determine what version of Linux the computer was running, you can adjust your investigation accordingly. The first place to look is in the /etc directory. Typically, you'll find a file such as redhat-release, debian-release, or redhat-version in this directory, which will indicate both the distribution and version of the install. Another file to check is the /etc/issue file, as most distributions place their information in this logon banner. Realize that these files are non-authoritative and act only as a marker that points you in the right direction, not to a definitive answer.

If the answer cannot be found in one of these files, try looking in /var/log/dmesg or /var/log/messages. This is the startup log for the OS, and the distribution will typically announce itself in these logs. In addition, these files are not as obvious as those in /etc, and less sophisticated users will not be able to sanitize them easily. Once you know the distribution, you can make some inferences about the type of user that you are dealing with.

Red Hat/Fedora Linux   This is the most popular Linux distribution and typically the choice of those who are new to Linux. New programs are installed using the binary RPM (Red Hat Package Manager) distribution system, and a record of every program installed on the machine appears in the RPM database. Mandrake Linux is very similar in form and function to Red Hat.

Gentoo Linux   This distribution has made a lot of waves as of late. The interesting thing about Gentoo is that everything is compiled for the machine on which is it being installed; nothing is done from a binary package. This can lead to epic installation times. The package manager for Gentoo is called portage/emerge and acts similar to the BSD (Berkeley Software Distribution) ports system.

SUSE Linux   SUSE recently was acquired by Novell, and the company is in the process of porting all of its networking products to it. This means you may end up doing investigation on SUSE if you ever have to investigate a Novell network. The package manager for SUSE is YAST and has capabilities similar to Redhat's RPM system.

Debian Linux Debian has traditionally been more of a developer's distribution. It has one of the best package management tools, APT, and the default installation is geared toward development tools and testing.

 ## The Importance of Determining the Distribution

Each distribution has its own way of tracking and auditing user activity and system events. If you don't correctly identify which distribution is used early on, you will end up in the best case chasing your tail for unnecessary hours, and in the worst case missing evidence that can turn the outcome of a case. Spend the time to identify what you are dealing with and document your findings accordingly.

 ## Tracking User Activity

Popularity:	8
Simplicity:	8
Impact:	8
Risk Rating:	8

The command interpreters for Linux are much more advanced than those used by Windows. From a forensics standpoint, this is a very good thing, because the two most popular interpreters, tcsh and BASH, leave audit trails for you to access that outline every command the user has run. Several other files are also unique to each shell that contain information we want to examine.

BASH

BASH is what you will most commonly run into on Linux systems. On the Linux platform, it is arguably the most advanced of the shells, with elaborate scripts and startup files that can do everything from give you the weather at the command prompt to color code your prompt based on machine name. The following table takes a look at the files that BASH uses and the purpose of each file. They can be found in the user's home directory.

Filename	Purpose
.bash_profile	Stores the commands that are run automatically when the shell is started. Commonly references a global file in the /etc/skel directory, so check that out.
.bash_history	The audit trail of the commands the user has run. The format is one command to a line with no time/date stamps.
.bash_logout	Like .bash_profile, the set of commands that are run when the shell exits. Many Linux installs ship with a global file in the /etc/skel directory.
.bashrc	Serves the same purpose as .bash_profile.

Tcsh

In our experience, tcsh is the shell of choice for people who learned on a platform other than Linux. The semantics are about the same between BASH and tcsh, with even the filenames being similar.

Filename	Purpose
.history	The audit trail of the commands the user has run. The format is one command to a line with no time/date stamps.
.logout/csh.logout	Like .bash_profile, the set of commands that are run when the shell exits. Many Linux installs ship with a global file in the /etc directory.
.tcshrc/.cshrc	Stores the commands that are run automatically when the shell is started. Commonly this references a global file in the /etc directory, so check that out.

Investigation Using Shells

Now that you have a frame of reference for the files we will be looking at, let's look at the common ways that suspects try to subvert this system. The most common way is by simple deletion. If you go to the user's directory and these files aren't stored there, that should be a red flag. Either the suspect is using a shell from the 1980s, or he deleted the files. Time to fire up the deleted file recovery tool of choice and go to work. You will also commonly see that the suspect has created a link from the history file into the /dev/null special file. This is the kernel's version of a black hole. Things go in and nothing comes out. If you find this, you can do a check to determine whether you can get the prelinked file, but you may end up just trying to find another audit trail to follow.

Printer Activity

Popularity:	8
Simplicity:	8
Impact:	7
Risk Rating:	7

Determining what was printed can be extremely useful in espionage and IP cases. Linux has very stout printer auditing, derived from the older UNIX LPR daemons. If the distribution is newer, instead of using LPR, the CUPS daemon is used. LPR keeps a log in the /var/log directory named lpr.log and keeps the printer spools in /var/spool. Look at these files to determine who printed what and when. If you determine that CUPS is installed, look in the directory /var/log/cups for the log files. In addition, if you can't find the logs, check in the /etc directory for the configuration files to see whether the logging has been moved.

Finding Printed Documents

It's important that you locate both what was printed and who printed it. This can also serve as a tool for timeline reconstruction and as proof that a file was deleted. If you see that a file was printed and you can no longer find it in the file system, you now have a place to start when searching through deleted space.

Mounting an Image

Popularity:	10
Simplicity:	8
Impact:	6
Risk Rating:	7

Using the mount command and the loop kernel module, you can mount drive images in Linux. This will allow you to work with the drive as a live file system. To do this, run this command:

```
[root@dhcppc3 mnt]# mount -r -o loop <image> <mount dir>
```

After this command is run, you can access the drive just as you would any other disk and run your favorite searching tools. The -r option requires some explanation—it forces the OS to mount the image as read-only. Never mount a forensic image where you can write to it. And always hash before you mount it and after you unmount it to show that you made no modifications to the data while it was mounted.

Searching Unallocated Space with Lazarus

Popularity:	10
Simplicity:	8
Impact:	6
Risk Rating:	7

The Coroner's Toolkit (TCT) has a very useful tool called lazarus that attempts to re-create files from unallocated and deleted space. Be warned that this is not a fast process by any means. Simple extraction can take from hours to days, depending on the size, and the investigative time involved is also a consideration. Typically, you will want to run a tool such as unrm before you use lazarus, as unrm will extract only the deleted portions and significantly reduce the work lazarus has to do. Lazarus will then attempt to break the data into file types and blocks, and if you specify the -h option, it will actually create HTML that you can use to navigate around. Let's look at an example:

```
[root@dhcppc3 blocks]# unrm ../image.dd > output
[root@dhcppc3 test]# lazarus -h ../output
```

Running these commands creates the following files,

```
-rw-r--r--   1 root    root        206 May 22 22:36 output.frame.html
-rw-r--r--   1 root    root        158 May 22 22:39 output.html
-rw-r--r--   1 root    root       1472 May 22 22:36 output.menu.html
```

along with several subdirectories with the data files referenced in the HTML. If you take a look at the menu that lazarus creates, you'll see that it attempts to classify and color code the recovered data by file type.

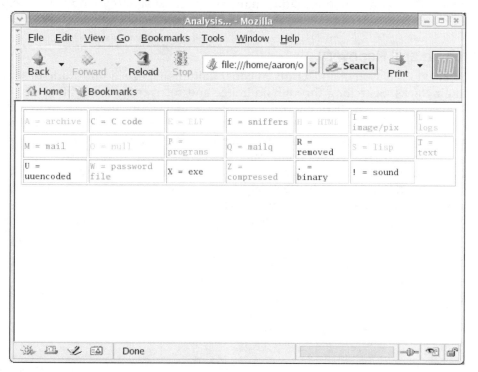

Analyzing the Swap Space

Popularity:	8
Simplicity:	8
Impact:	9
Risk Rating:	8

When the OS runs out of space in RAM, it will use the swap partition to store data temporarily. This can be a source of evidence and should always be examined when you are performing a Linux investigation. Pull the image of the swap partition in the same manner used to pull the other drive images. Once you have done that, you can treat it like a binary file. Remember that the Linux swap structure consists only of data blocks that represent blocks in memory that have been swapped out. Anything that can be stored in memory can end up in the swap file, including passwords, text files that were opened using editors, pictures, and so on. The downside to this structure is that you will very rarely find an entire file. Most of the time, since the blocks are not going to be allocated sequentially and nothing is tying the blocks together like an inode, you won't be able to pull an entire file. When you find information in the swap, make sure that you always explain what it is and how it fits into the context, and you should be OK.

 ## Searching and Recovery

The ext2/ext3 file system and Linux in general offer suspects a multitude of ways to hide their tracks. Searching through an image and recovering the evidence is a very time-consuming and meticulous process. Always make sure that you approach this process in a methodical manner that is consistent with your process. Also, good search techniques can really speed up your investigation time. You will commonly find yourself going through gigabytes of unallocated or deleted space with little to no structure. This is the type of situation in which false positives can become your worst enemy. Take the time to learn how to search effectively, because it will save you a ton of time in the long run. Appendix D is a good place to start.

CHAPTER 8

MACINTOSH
ANALYSIS

Y ou're in an airport lounge. A few people are working on their laptops. Nobody is talking, just working. Someone takes out a Macintosh. The next thing you know, another Mac user asks her, "How do you like Jaguar?" and the two strike up a conversation. There's just something different about a Macintosh and perhaps the people who use them.

You can conduct a forensic examination of a Macintosh in a number of ways. As for the "best" way, that's a matter of opinion. From an analysis standpoint, you can look at data from a Mac using a Mac or any other platform. You'll learn about the pros and cons to each approach in this chapter.

One of the more valuable resources for a deeper understanding of the Mac OS is the Apple Developer Community. Despite its many differences when compared to other operating systems, the Mac OS is just another OS and HFS is just another volume format when it comes down to it. The mantra "it's all just ones and zeros" is a good chant to remember if you are tasked with examining a Macintosh for the first time.

THE EVOLUTION OF THE MAC OS

As with Microsoft Windows, Apple's operating and file systems have undergone a relentless and driving evolution. The major versions of the Mac OS (7, 8, 9, and X) have been increasingly more complex than earlier versions and introduced many changes in the fundamental behavior of the operating system. Mac OS X exemplifies this with the many differences between versions 10.1, 10.2, and 10.3. The recent focus on the need for trustworthy computing, security concerns, and other initiatives and continued integration of the OS and the Internet has precipitated a paradigm shift not only of consumer awareness but fundamental OS design as well.

Know Your Operating System

Popularity:	7
Simplicity:	7
Impact:	9
Risk:	8

Even a slight difference in the OS version, patch level, or update versus a "fresh install" can have a profound effect on the way your computer works, where and what data is stored, and the format of that data. Try this simple exercise at home:

1. Running Microsoft Windows XP, press CTRL-ALT-DEL to open the Task Manager window.

2. Click the Processes tab.

3. Start at the first item and ask yourself what it is and what it does. Also ask yourself how it may change the default behavior of the system and when it may not operate as intended. Repeat this process for each and every item in the list.

Remember that in court, questions like "Isn't it possible that…?" are fair game. Understanding your operating system is imperative. Since the chain is never stronger than the weakest link, an unknown process running on a proprietary and undocumented system does not avail you much and weakens your case. Clearly, you must be smart about how you approach, implement, and articulate your process and methodology in conducting a forensic investigation. Reducing the number of unknowns is a smart practice and a necessary part of your job.

 ## It's Still Just 1s and 0s

From a technical standpoint, quite a few aspects of the Macintosh OS makes it different from Windows or other operating systems. But let's review the similarities first, and then discuss the differences. Evidence collected from a Macintosh is no different than evidence collected from a PC, a Cray Supercomputer, or any other computer. It is digital evidence and is likely to exist in the same basic format and on the same types of media as any other digital evidence. The important concepts and attributes, such as chain of custody, quantifiable assurance of integrity, and preservation of best evidence, will still apply.

A Disk Is a Disk

Modern Macintosh computers use Enhanced Integrated Drive Electronics/Advanced Technology Attachment (EIDE/ATA) hard disk drives, just like most $x86$ personal computers. Although Apple has historically "branded" its OEM (original equipment manufacturer) hard disk drives, branding is an issue only when running the Apple OS and utilities. While many versions of Apple disk utilities will work only on Apple-branded drives, for the most part, Macs use an EIDE hard disk drive and would work just fine if placed into a WinTel-based (Windows + Intel) personal computer. The branding is based on the controller firmware and serves to identify Apple "authorized" hard disk drives. Older Macs used SCSI drives, which are also branded.

Image Is Everything

Disk drives from an Apple computer can be removed and duplicated in any of the ways that work with disks from PCs: hardware duplication, software duplication, cloning—after all, it's just another EIDE disk at the device layer. If you didn't want to disassemble a laptop and remove the hard drive (and really, who does?), you could boot the Macintosh into FireWire disk mode. Most Macs that have onboard FireWire (IEEE1394) allow you to hold down the T key during the boot process and place the computer into FireWire disk mode. When in this mode, the computer presents the internal primary master device as a FireWire device, similar to a Maxtor or other external IEEE1394 hard disk drive. You can connect the Mac to another machine via the FireWire cable and image, view, and search.

Alternatively, you could create a bootable CD-ROM designed to bring the system up to a minimal state and image via the NIC card.

Regardless of whether you use hardware or software, you should end up with, among other things, a bit image copy—a device clone or a segmented image that resides on a file system. Either way, you're ready to start looking at the data and answering some questions.

 Never boot a Macintosh that contains evidence unless you know exactly what you are doing. The "normal" boot process *will* change data.

LOOKING AT A MAC DISK OR IMAGE

As with other rotating magnetic media, Macs have a partition map that points to various partitions on the drive. *Partitions* are logically contiguous ranges of sectors. *Sectors* are 512 bytes of sector data with a handful of device data. Just as with WinTel architectures, logical sector 0 of the device contains critical information you need to know.

To help you better understand the Mac partitioning scheme, let's review a Windows Master Boot Record (MBR) and partition map, both located in logical sector 0 of the device.

A Windows MBR contains boot code, disk geometry information, and four buckets for primary partitions. Primary partitions can point to extended partitions, which give you four more buckets. Partitions within extended partitions may be conceptualized as belonging to the parent partition, which in turn belongs to the device. The device contains everything and describes how the disk is laid out right up front. As a result of enforcing the concept of cylinder boundary alignment, a lot of space is wasted.

The Apple partitioning scheme is actually more straightforward and in many respects, easier to understand than Windows. The first logical sector of the device is the Device Descriptor Map (DDM), which contains a signature byte, just like Windows. Instead of *0x55AA* at the end of the sector, the Mac uses *0x4552ER* (ER is for Eric Rosenthal, an early developer) at the start of the sector. Other than some basic information like the sector size, number of blocks, and pointers to the drivers, not much shows up here, and what is here is most useful when booting, not viewing.

The Apple Partition Map

The *partition map* describes the partitions on the device, where they are located, how big they are, and what type of partition they are. The partition map is *self-referencing*, meaning that it counts itself as a partition.

Before we go looking at raw data, it is a good time to mention another thing that makes Macs different: "endian-ness." WinTel machine architecture is *little-endian*, which means that the least significant bits are at the front end of the word (lower in memory/on disk). The Mac, on the other hand, is a *big-endian* architecture, meaning that the most significant bits are at the front end.

Take the decimal value *4660* for example. On a PC, we would see that represented in hex as *0x3412*, and on a Mac we would read that as *0x1234*. It's easier than it sounds once you get the hang of it. (A Chinese friend once told me the same thing about reading Hebrew from back to front, right to left.)

If you look at the first 16 bytes (the top line) of the partition map entry in Figure 8-1, you see the first two bytes (0x504d) are the partition map signature bytes. The next two bytes are null (0x0000). Then a DWORD (double word—4 bytes) of 0x00000007 appears. This is the number of blocks (sectors) in the partition map, including the partition map entry you are looking at. This tells you that six partition entries follow the entry you are looking at, or seven in all. The next DWORD is 0x00000001. This is the starting sector of this partition. Remember that your DDM was at 0, so this one starts at 1. The next DWORD is 0x0000003f. This tells you that the partition whose entry you are looking at is 63 sectors long. In this case, it is the partition map itself that is 63 sectors. That gives you much more flexibility than the four primary slots you get in DOS/Windows. If you look at the next sector in the partition map, you see the information shown in Figure 8-2.

This partition starts at sector 0x40 (64 in decimal). This make sense because the previous partition started at 0 and was 63 sectors long. You can also see that the partition is 0x36 (54 in decimal) sectors long. If you have figured out that the next partition should start at 0x76 (118 in decimal), then you've got the hang of it.

The ability to identify and interpret partitions and their contents is important for several reasons. Some data protection/encryption products utilize data stored in non-file system partitions, but for the most part, you will be primarily interested in the partition or partitions that contain the file system. These are identified by a partition type of Apple_HFS.

NOTE Offsets in the partition map are absolute (device offsets). In the next discussion, the file system offsets are relative to the start of the partition that contains the file system.

Trees and Nodes

A quick review of File Allocation Table (FAT)-based file systems will remind you that the file system has a *root* from which everything on the file system can be referenced via a *fully qualified path*. *Directories* are simply file entries that have a directory attribute set. File entries contain a pointer to a starting block and a length. Directory entries point to subdirectories.

```
Offset     0  1  2  3  4  5  6  7   8  9 10 11 12 13 14 15
00000000  50 4D 00 00 00 00 00 07  00 00 00 01 00 00 00 3F   PM...........?
00000016  41 70 70 6C 65 00 00 00  00 00 00 00 00 00 00 00   Apple...........
00000032  00 00 00 00 00 00 00 00  00 00 00 00 00 00 00 00   ................
00000048  41 70 70 6C 65 5F 70 61  72 74 69 74 69 6F 6E 5F   Apple_partition_
00000064  6D 61 70 00 00 00 00 00  00 00 00 00 00 00 00 00   map.............
00000080  00 00 00 00 00 00 00 3F  00 00 00 00 00 00 00 00   .......?........
00000096  00 00 00 00 00 00 00 00  00 00 00 00 00 00 00 00   ................
```

Figure 8-1. Raw data view of an Apple partition map entry

```
Offset      0  1  2  3  4  5  6  7    8  9 10 11 12 13 14 15
00000000   50 4D 00 00 00 00 00 07   00 00 00 40 00 00 00 36   PM........@...6
00000016   4D 61 63 69 6E 74 6F 73   68 00 00 00 00 00 00 00   Macintosh.......
00000032   00 00 00 00 00 00 00 00   00 00 00 00 00 00 00 00   ................
00000048   41 70 70 6C 65 5F 44 72   69 76 65 72 5F 41 54 41   Apple_Driver_ATA
00000064   00 00 00 00 00 00 00 00   00 00 00 00 00 00 00 00   ................
00000080   00 00 00 00 00 00 00 36   00 00 07 7F 00 00 00 00   .......6....I....
00000096   00 00 00 00 00 00 00 00   00 00 00 00 00 00 00 00   ................
```

Figure 8-2.   Raw data view of ATA driver partition map entry

The FAT is an array of pointers. The values in the FAT are either pointers to clusters, EOF markers (that say "I am the last cluster in this chain"), or perhaps BAD, as in blocks that are mapped out by diagnostic programs.

It should be no surprise that the Macintosh file system is completely different. For one thing, no FAT is used in the Hierarchical File System (HFS and HFS+). The job of keeping track of the allocation blocks (clusters) allocated to a file is performed by two balanced (or binary) *trees*, the Catalog B-tree and the Extents B-tree. The Catalog B-tree tracks the blocks associated with a file and the first few fragments of the file. If the file is very fragmented, the Extents B-tree tracks the file fragments.

The tree analogy is an extension of the notion that everything grows from the root. Trees are made up of *nodes*, logical groupings of information that are internal to the file system and contain records. *Records* contain data or pointers to data.

Different types of nodes appear on the tree: header nodes, index nodes, and leaf nodes. The leaf nodes give us information about files—their names, access times, and other attributes. Nodes are pointed to and/or linked together and may be conceptualized as layers. The header node is at the top, and underneath that are index nodes. Index nodes may point to other levels of index nodes or to leaf nodes.

You could say that the root node is at the top of the tree, at level 0. The root node contains pointers to B-tree header nodes, which in turn point to index nodes. Index nodes can point to other index nodes or to leaf nodes. The more files, folders, and stuff you have in your file system, the more levels you will have between the root node and the leaf nodes. In general, nodes that exist on the same level point to one another. These are FLINKS (forward links) and BLINKS (backward links), which are shown in Figure 8-3.

Unique Sequential File Identifiers

Every file system object in an HFS file system is assigned a unique, sequential FILE ID number when it is created. For a forensic examiner, this information is very useful, as the file with FILE ID 100 was created in the file system after the file with FILE ID 99, regardless of any date or time stamp information. The FILE ID attribute is relative to the file system you

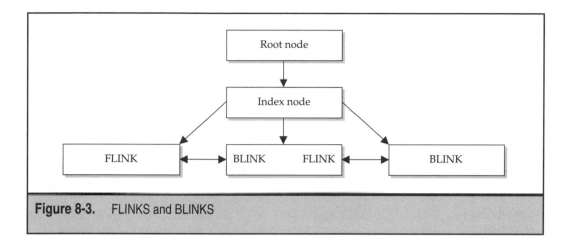

Figure 8-3. FLINKS and BLINKS

are examining. FILE ID numbers do *not* "go along with the file" when it is copied, downloaded, decompressed, and so on. The FILE ID number is one of the things that the HFS file system uses when organizing the B-tree.

DELETED FILES

On a FAT32 file system, files are "deleted" by replacing the first character of the file name with the hex byte E5. The file's clusters are flagged as "available," and the E5 entry in the directory still contains the (munged) name, attribute flags, date and time stamps, and logical size. On an NTFS system, the entry is "un-indexed" from the MFT. This is closer to what happens on an HFS or HFS+ volume. Let's take a look at a Catalog B-tree leaf node containing file records (the lowest level of the tree), shown in Figure 8-4.

Looking at the B-tree data, you can see filenames in plaintext, as well as information that you can identify as type and creator codes:

```
\x00 ulong    fLink    Forward link to next node on this level
\x04 ulong    bLink    Backwards link to previous node
\x08 uchar    nodeType FF=leaf node, 00=index node
              01=B-tree Header node, 02=2nd VBM
\x09 char     level    level of this node (1=leaf)
\x0A uint     numRecs  Number of records in this node
```

So looking at the first 12 bytes in Figure 8-4, you see that

▼ The forward link is 00 00 04 60 (Node 1120).

■ The backward link is 00 00 04 5c (Node 1116).

■ The node type is FF for a leaf node.

■ The leaf node is at level 01 of the tree.

▲ Three records are contained in this node.

The three records in the example are leaf node entries for the files

▼ Windows 98.img

■ Wipe Info

▲ wrap.gif

So what happens if you delete the file Wipe Info? What changes would you observe in the node you are looking at? For one thing, offset \x0A (the number of records) would be decreased to 2. Slightly less obvious, the file records are arranged alphabetically within the node. Therefore, if you deleted the second file, Wipe Info in this example, the third entry would pop up in the stack of records tracked by the node. Think of it as the stack of plates at your favorite all-you-can-eat place. If you take the top plate off the stack, the second plate now becomes the first plate, and every plate underneath it shifts up the queue by one.

If you take the second plate off the stack, the first plate is still the first plate, but the second plate used to be the third plate. What this means to you is that the second entry (Wipe Info) is overwritten by the third entry (now the second entry). You would see that only two

Offset	0	1	2	3	4	5	6	7	8	9	10	11	12	13	14	15	
00000000	00	00	04	60	00	00	04	5C	FF	01	00	03	00	00	14	00	...`....\ÿ.......
00000016	00	00	0C	A2	0E	57	69	6E	64	6F	77	73	20	39	38	2E	...¢.Windows 98.
00000032	69	6D	67	00	02	00	00	00	72	6F	68	64	64	64	73	6B	img.....rohdddsk
00000048	80	00	00	00	00	00	00	00	00	00	00	0D	4D	00	00	00	▌...........M...
00000064	00	00	00	00	00	00	00	00	00	00	02	14	00	06	9E	00	...............▌
00000080	B4	37	A4	D4	B4	37	A4	D4	00	00	00	00	00	00	00	00	´7¤Ô´7¤Ô........
00000096	00	00	00	00	00	00	00	00	00	00	00	00	00	00	00	00	....
00000112	00	00	00	00	00	00	00	00	00	00	13	A7	00	01	00	00	...........§....
00000128	00	00	00	00	00	00	00	00	00	00	0F	00	00	00	0C	A2	...............¢
00000144	09	57	69	70	65	20	49	6E	66	6F	02	00	00	00	41	50	.Wipe Info....AP
00000160	50	4C	50	4E	77	69	80	00	00	00	00	00	00	00	00	00	PLPNwi▌.........
00000176	0D	4E	00	00	00	00	00	00	00	00	00	00	00	00	00	00	.N..............
00000192	02	06	00	06	9E	00	B4	9A	BB	D6	B4	9A	BB	D6	00	00	....▌.´▌»Ö´▌»Ö..
00000208	00	00	00	00	00	00	00	00	00	00	00	00	00	00	00	00	....
00000224	00	00	00	00	00	00	00	00	00	00	00	00	00	00	00	00	....
00000240	13	A8	00	01	00	00	00	00	00	00	00	00	00	00	00	00	.¨..............
00000256	0E	00	00	00	0C	A2	08	77	72	61	70	2E	67	69	66	00	.....¢.wrap.gif.
00000272	02	00	00	00	47	49	46	66	4A	56	57	52	80	00	00	00	....GIFfJVWR▌...
00000288	00	00	00	00	00	00	0D	4F	00	00	00	00	00	00	00	00	.......O........
00000304	00	00	00	00	00	00	02	DE	00	06	9E	00	B3	E5	92	9A	.......Þ..▌.³å'▌
00000320	B3	E5	92	9A	00	00	00	00	00	00	00	00	00	00	00	00	³å'▌............
00000336	00	00	00	00	00	00	00	00	00	00	00	00	00	00	00	00	....

Figure 8-4. Tree leaf node data

records were indexed in the node, Windows 98.img and wrap.gif, and you would see the original third entry as well as the "new" second entry. It might look like Figure 8-5.

However, not all is lost. Although the leaf node entry may be physically overwritten, other instances of the node data may still exist in unallocated space, in index nodes and nodes that have been removed from the tree at a higher level. If all of the files in a node are deleted because their common parent (directory) has been deleted, it is not unusual to see "pruned" nodes with all of the records intact.

Within each file entry in the B-tree are numerous bit fields, pointers, keys, and data values that include important things like creation and modification dates, file ID numbers, locations for the data blocks that make up the file, and things like an icon's location and color. Apple's developer support and documentation are fairly comprehensive regarding these structures. The Apple Developer Tech Note 1150 and the reference "Inside Macintosh: Files" are great places to start digging deeper. To see this tech note, take a look at http://developer.apple.com/technotes/tn/pdf/tn1150.pdf.

Recovering Deleted Files

If you are interested in recovering deleted files from an HFS or HFS+ file system, you can go about it in two primary ways. The first way is to aggregate the unallocated space and concatenate it, essentially creating one data stream comprising sequential (although not

```
Offset       0  1  2  3  4  5  6  7   8  9 10 11 12 13 14 15
00000000    00 00 04 60 00 00 04 5C  FF 01 00 03 00 00 14 00    ...`...\ÿ......
00000016    00 00 0C A2 0E 57 69 6E  64 6F 77 73 20 39 38 2E    ...¢.Windows 98.
00000032    69 6D 67 00 02 00 00 00  72 6F 68 64 64 64 73 6B    img.....rohdddsk
00000048    80 00 00 00 00 00 00 00  00 00 00 0D 4D 00 00 00    ¦...........M...
00000064    00 00 00 00 00 00 00 00  00 00 02 14 00 06 9E 00    ...............¦
00000080    B4 37 A4 D4 B4 37 A4 D4  00 00 00 00 00 00 00 00    ´7¤Ô´7¤Ô........
00000096    00 00 00 00 00 00 00 00  00 00 00 00 00 00 00 00    ................
00000112    00 00 00 00 00 00 00 00  00 00 13 A7 00 01 00 00    ...........§....
00000128    00 00 00 00 00 00 00 00  00 00 0F 00 00 00 0C A2    ...............¢
00000144    0E 00 00 00 0C A2 08 77  72 61 70 2E 67 69 66 00    .....¢.wrap.gif.
00000160    02 00 00 00 47 49 46 66  4A 56 57 52 80 00 00 00    ....GIFfJVWR¦...
00000176    00 00 00 00 00 00 0D 4F  00 00 00 00 00 00 00 00    .......O........
00000192    00 00 00 00 00 00 02 DE  00 06 9E 00 B3 E5 92 9A    .......Þ..¦.³å'¦
00000208    B3 E5 92 9A 00 00 00 00  00 00 00 00 00 00 00 00    ³å'¦............
00000224    00 00 00 00 00 00 00 00  00 00 00 00 00 00 00 00    ................
00000240    13 A8 00 01 00 00 00 00  00 00 00 00 00 00 00 00    .¨..............
00000256    0E 00 00 00 0C A2 08 77  72 61 70 2E 67 69 66 00    .....¢.wrap.gif.
00000272    02 00 00 00 47 49 46 66  4A 56 57 52 80 00 00 00    ....GIFfJVWR¦...
00000288    00 00 00 00 00 00 0D 4F  00 00 00 00 00 00 00 00    .......O........
00000304    00 00 00 00 00 00 02 DE  00 06 9E 00 B3 E5 92 9A    .......Þ..¦.³å'¦
00000320    B3 E5 92 9A 00 00 00 00  00 00 00 00 00 00 00 00    ³å'¦............
00000336    00 00 00 00 00 00 00 00  00 00 00 00 00 00 00 00    ................
```

Figure 8-5.   B-tree leaf node data showing node slack

contiguous) unallocated clusters. This is relatively easy to do if you just invert (Boolean NOT) the bitmap that tells you which clusters are allocated and which ones are not. The second method of data recovery involves identifying file system metadata and mapping those entries to unallocated areas of the volume.

NOTE   Newer versions of the Mac OS allow files to be "shredded" or physically overwritten with the rm – P option. If you see this in the bash_history file, it is safe to assume the locations referenced by the file at the time of its deletion have been overwritten.

Concatenating Unallocated Space

This method gives you everything marked as unallocated. No file system information is directly associated with the data—it's just a blob of data. This type of data is great if you are trying to recover data such as graphics, text, and other simple data formats. Fragmentation is eliminated, so if a deleted file were fragmented by an active file's allocation, the data taken together would be contiguous.

Large Ranges of Null or Other Wasted Space

Popularity:	7
Simplicity:	6
Impact:	8
Risk:	7

The aggregate of the unallocated space often consists of very large ranges of null or other wasted space. This can be a formatting pattern, a null, or some other repeating pattern. Depending on what you are looking for, filtering the blob can have many benefits. First, most grep implementations are line-based, so if you grep a blob of 2GB of null, grep will likely exhaust memory trying to buffer the first line. Since no line (just null) exists, memory is needlessly exhausted.

If you are looking for HTML or plain text, you don't really need to know about nulls, and a side benefit is that if your term exists as a UTF-encoded term, stripping the nulls allows you to find it without the need for a Unicode search term. If you think about RFC822 headers, URLs, e-mail addresses, contact information, log entries, and other simple data types, you realize that you really need to concern yourself only with printable ASCII characters. Filtering the unallocated space (depending on what you are looking for) saves storage, time, effort, memory, and aggravation. This is called "normalizing" the data that you are working with. If the hex character \xFF doesn't appear in what you are looking for, then why copy and search it?

Normalize Data

You have several friends here to help you—tr is your friend, strings is your friend, and SMART is your friend. Preprocessing (normalizing) the data before searching it for simple data constructs (when done correctly) allows more data to be searched fast using less memory and storage. Why wouldn't you do this?

While this is great for data recovery, you aren't helping much in a forensic analysis if all you can say is that the data exists in unallocated space. You want to be able to identify file attributes (name, date and time stamps, original location, and other info). For that, you need to use the second method of data recovery.

Scavenging for Unindexed Files and Pruned Nodes

Scavenging allocated leaf nodes for unindexed files and scavenging unallocated space for "pruned" index and leaf nodes is probably the best practical way to identify file system metadata and map those entries to unallocated areas of the volume.

Searching Unallocated Space for File Entries in Leaf Nodes

You could search unallocated space for file entries in leaf nodes. This presumes that you know what you are looking for, as in a filename or attribute data. When you don't have that, though, you need to search for the places that are likely to have what you want to find: leaf nodes in the B-tree. You could use a search term like this:

```
\xff\x01\x00
```

This expression means "Since I don't know about the fLink and bLink, match any two double words (8 bytes) that are followed by \xff (leaf node), followed by \x01 (leaf level), followed by \x00 (index node)." You will probably never see a node with more than 255 descriptors in it. Of course, it helps if you know *what* you are looking for *and where* you are most likely to find it.

 The searched term \xff\x01\x00 is pretty loose and will likely generate hundreds, if not thousands of false hits. Since you know that the data you are searching for is node header data, and you know it's offset within the node, you can search for hits that exhibit sector boundary alignment. Since all file system constructs are based on a sector, this will reduce your hits to those most likely to be responsive and independent of cluster or node size.

Whew. Let's take a moment and review. We've discussed devices, partitions, file systems, trees, and nodes—just scratching the surface of each. It's all important stuff, but way beyond the scope of this (or any single) chapter. Just like stacking matching bowls, you can see how these things relate to each other, as shown in Figure 8-6.

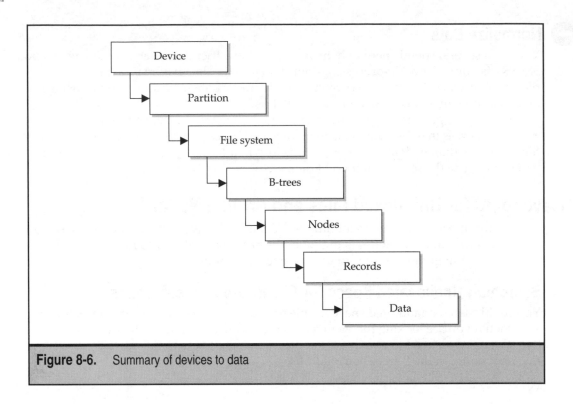

Figure 8-6. Summary of devices to data

A CLOSER LOOK AT MACINTOSH FILES

Now that we've taken a brief look at the file system structure, let's take a closer look at the files themselves. One of the things that makes Macintosh files unique is the *resource fork*. Nowadays, file systems are more extensible and attributes can often be easily added, but it wasn't always this way. The Macintosh HFS filing system was one of the, if not the first, file systems to embrace the concept of a file comprising multiple streams of data. This is commonplace now in NTFS, but the concept's origins can be traced back to the Macintosh (as can the mouse, windows, task bars, and a great many other computer interface elements we see every day).

Archives

Relatively few major advances have occurred in compression technology lately. Compression algorithms are mature and reasonably well standardized. Years ago, StuffIt was the dominant Macintosh compression technology. With the Mac's interoperability enhancements, Mac-centric compression algorithms such as BinHex have fallen by the wayside in favor of zip, gzip, and tarball formats. This trend seems to be accelerating now that the Mac has more POSIX underpinnings.

Date and Time Stamps

The Mac never really had a Y2K crisis. At worst, it faces a year 2040 crisis. Over the years, the Mac OS and ROMs have used different "time zero" references and have stored date and time stamps in different formats. The original date and time utilities (introduced with the original Macintosh 128K computer in 1984) used a long word to store seconds, starting at January 1, 1904. This approach allows the correct representation of dates up to 6:28:15 A.M. on February 6, 2040. The current date and time utilities, documented in *Inside Macintosh: Operating System Utilities*, use a 64-bit signed value, which covers dates from 30,081 B.C. to 29,940 A.D.

E-mail

In stark contrast to the Windows experience, e-mail has remained much easier to analyze on Macintosh machines. Although PST files can be created and used to store e-mail on Macs, the native format for non-Microsoft MUAs (Mail User Agents) e-mail stores are plaintext. Remember that mail may exist in a wide variety of formats, including cached web pages (Yahoo!, hotmail, and so on), PST files, mdir, mbox, and others.

The e-mail accounts for the Mac built-in mail client Mail are stored in /Users/*<user>*/ Library/Mail. The files named mbox contain the actual plaintext e-mail data, rfc822 data, and attachments. Attachments may be compressed in a variety of formats, including TAR, ZIP, GZ, BZ2, and graphics are typically encoded using base64 or UU-encoding. Programs like SMART may be used to carve individual messages and attachments automatically from mbox and newsgroup files.

/Users/*<user>*/Library/Caches/ contains recently cached images, movies, or other data viewed by Mail.app and Safari.app. The mail folder contains many subfolders (labeled 00–15) that appear to be recursive (of depth 3), but it is actually using a hash table (a programming technique used for efficiency). The Safari folder is the same, except it is of depth 2. The MS Internet cache is contained in a standard .waf file.

Graphics

The Mac has been known as a graphically intense machine since its introduction and still enjoys a stronghold in prepress, layout, and graphic design. Contemporary Macintosh operating systems support a myriad of graphics formats, although most often we see the "standard" graphics file formats (GIF and JPEG), particularly when they come from the Internet. The "endian-ness" of the processor doesn't affect the data format of the files. This is to say that even though memory and words are represented backward on a big-endian system, a GIF header will still be laid down on the disk in the same way, whether it is written to a FAT32 or HFS+ file system.

Web Browsing

Form follows function. Web browsing artifacts are similar to those found in the WinTel world. This is largely due to the standards in place for the various protocols that make the Internet work. HTTP is still a stateless protocol, cookies are still cookies, and HTML is still HTML (in fact, this is far truer on the Mac compared to the Microsoft HTML implementation).

/Users/<*user*>/Library/Safari contains the history files and bookmarks for the user. Also included is a folder of thumbnails named Icons. In Safari, when some web sites are viewed, a thumbnail is displayed next to the URL that is relevant to the web site being viewed (for example, Google uses its *g* logo, CNN uses *cnn* in red on a white background).

/Users/<*user*>/Library/Cookies contains cookies of recently viewed web sites. The cookies are stored in XML format. For more information about reviewing web activity, see Chapter 12.

Resources

Resources are common objects whose templates are already defined elsewhere. A file's resource fork (stream) can contain anything but is supposed to contain data and customizations of common objects that are unique to the file. A good example is language localization: a program is written once, and all the dialog boxes have their text and buttons in English. To localize the program, all you need to do is edit the resources (the words displayed in menu bars, dialog boxes, and so on), so instead of being labeled *No*, the button would say *Nyet* (*No* in Russian) without having to recompile or rewrite the actual executable code.

Virtual Memory

Most every OS (and many applications) use a backing store, virtual memory, swap file (or slice or partition), or some other method of caching memory to disk. As with other forensic investigations, these artifacts may contain a wealth of pertinent information. Preprocessing or normalizing the data prior to searching for simple data constructs can save you time, disk memory, and storage.

The swap files are located in /var/vm. This is where passwords temporarily stored in memory could be written to disk.

System Log and Other System Files

/var/log/ contains a wealth of information and is an extremely important file. Some of the information it contains includes serial numbers of removable media (thumb drives, smart media, and so on) and some names of mounted media like CDs and floppies.

/var/log/daily.out contains snapshots of mounted volume names and the dates they were mounted, as well as the used disk space on each of the mounted volumes.

/var/spool/cups contains files that hold information about documents recently printed. This includes the name of the document printed and the user who printed it.

/Library/Receipts is a folder containing system information about updates. This is useful in detecting whether a user had the latest system patches or security updates installed.

/Users/<user>/.bash_history contains recent terminal commands issued by the user. Look for rm -P commands, which means the user intentionally attempted to wipe data from a drive.

The var/vm folder contains another folder named app_profile. The files here that end with _names contain the names of applications that were recently opened. The files ending with _data contain temporary information useful to the applications in the _name documents.

/private/var/root/.bash_history contains recent terminal commands issued by the administrator. If this file exists, the user is probably familiar with Linux and should be considered to have at least an intermediate knowledge of OS X.

/Users/<user>/Library/Preferences/ contain preference files of programs installed on the computer. Even deleted programs will still have their preference files left behind if the program generated one. Inside the preferences folder are the following:

▼ com.apple.Preview.plist contains a list of recently viewed pictures and PDF documents.

▲ QuickTimeFavorites contains a list of recently viewed movies and the disk location of the movies.

/Users/<user>/Library/Logs/DiskUtility.log contains information about disks recently mounted using DiskUtility as well as disks erased or burned by this application.

MAC AS A FORENSICS PLATFORM

If you have the luxury (budget) of getting a Mac, use it as a "base camp" for some exploration. A great way to start is to wipe a drive with null (this verifies the media as well as facilitates tighter compression); install the Mac OS of your choice; go through the initial first boot process using documented information for username, Internet settings, preferences, and so on; and then make a compressed image of the drive. This way, you can always return to a known state quickly and easily.

If you are using a Macintosh as your forensic platform of choice, you can minimize the possibility of an "Oops!" Whenever possible, use a hardware write-blocking device. Although not essential with a properly configured forensic acquisition and analysis platform and a well-trained examiner, you can think of write-blockers as airbags for your investigation. You wear a seatbelt, keep your eyes on the road, and hope to never see your airbag. You protect yourself by disabling automount and understanding the system configuration and behavior.

The Mac has been able to mount disk and file system images for quite some time. Numerous utilities let you mount images of CD-ROMs and many other types of file systems. Be aware that these files may contain a complete file system with many files, as well as their own slack space, deleted files, unallocated space, and directory structures. Type and creator codes of DIMG, DDSK, VMK, and IMG should be looked at very carefully, as should any very large file. Virtual PC provides hardware emulation and may mount and create disk images, as can Apple's Disk Copy.

Images of HFS, HFS+, many of the FAT flavors, and several other file systems may be mounted to this system for analysis. Setting the permissions of the underlying image file(s) to read-only should prevent any modifications to the data contained within the image. It is a common practice to embed the CRC or MD5SUM of the data into the image file's resource fork. This allows authentication information about the image to be integrated into the image without affecting the data (fork) of the image file.

CHAPTER 9

DEFEATING ANTI-FORENSIC TECHNIQUES

An *anti-forensic technique* is any intentional or accidental changing of data that can obscure the data, encrypt it, or hide it from forensic tools. Very few anti-forensic techniques work the way a suspect might expect. Most suspects believe that by following the techniques illustrated in this chapter and in other publications that they can hide their tracks. Trying to do so often only has the effect of enabling the investigator to know where to look for evidence. An investigator's success can be strengthened more by a suspect's lack of knowledge on how the evidence he or she is trying to hide truly exists on the system than by his or her not trying to hide the evidence at all.

Most forensic examination tools used today tend not to trust data or view it in the same ways they did when computer forensics was a new field. For example, earlier versions of open source forensic tools could miss files and data due to logical coding errors. Most of the concepts discussed by most anti-forensic articles and covered in this chapter won't affect modern tools, but you should still be aware of them because you could be expected to know this information in court. Plus, if you design or create your own forensic tools, you'll need to be aware of these issues.

OBSCURITY METHODS

An *obscurity method* is a method by which someone tries to obscure the true nature or meaning of some data, typically by changing its name or its contents. For our purposes, the term refers to a case in which someone has intentionally or accidentally changed the name or contents of a file, resulting in a file that will either be misinterpreted or disregarded in subsequent forensic analysis.

File Extension Renaming

Popularity:	5
Simplicity:	10
Impact:	5
Risk Rating:	**6**

Of the types of obscurity methods encountered today, the most common and easiest to detect is file extension renaming. File extension renaming can entail either renaming the entire filename or just the file extension to obscure what program can access it. Although you can now detect file renaming using a variety of automated techniques, you should be aware of its impact on your investigation, especially if you do not have time to run these tools, though you should in any investigation. If you are conducting an investigation and are asked to review documents of only a certain type, renamed files could cause you to overlook evidence contained in them.

File Signaturing

File signaturing is a technique that allows you to determine what application has been used to create a file without regard to the file extension or name. File signaturing compares some unique aspect of the file, typically the header and footer of the file, to a database of signatures that relate to an extension. A *signature* in this case means a unique portion of data that exists in a certain file type that indicates what program can access it. For instance, a GIF image file always contains *GIF8* in the header of the file. Several tools can be used to determine a file's signature for you, and some of them are built into forensic tools.

 Renaming a filename or extension does not modify its contents, so file renaming or signaturing would not prevent a search from finding relevant data.

File Command

The UNIX `file` command will return the type of file according to its database of signatures. The database that `file` uses is called *magic* and is typically found in Linux under /usr/share. The most appealing feature of `file` is that the database is a plaintext file with standard delimiters. This allows the investigator to create and customize file signatures for investigations; thus, the database will grow as the investigator's cases do. To execute `file`, you would use the following:

```
# file top.jpg
top.jpg: JPEG image data, JFIF standard 1.02, aspect ratio, 100 x 100
```

As you can see, this execution of the `file` command on a JPEG image file returned information that not only tells you that the file is an image, but also provides the aspect ratio and the size of the image in pixels. Here, for example, we rename the file as *nothing.here* and rerun the `file` command, and the following occurs:

```
# mv top.jpg nothing.here
# file nothing.here
nothing.here: JPEG image data, JFIF standard 1.02, aspect ratio, 100 x 100
```

The name of the file had no bearing on the `file` command's ability to detect its true type. The `file` command is also available for Windows as part of the Cygwin package, which is found at http://www.cygwin.com.

EnCase

EnCase has the ability to detect file types and carry out file signature analysis to detect modified file types. After you load an image into EnCase, you can choose to validate the signatures on all of the files in the image when searching. To do so, open the Search dialog box by clicking the search icon and choose Verify File Signatures, as shown in Figure 9-1.

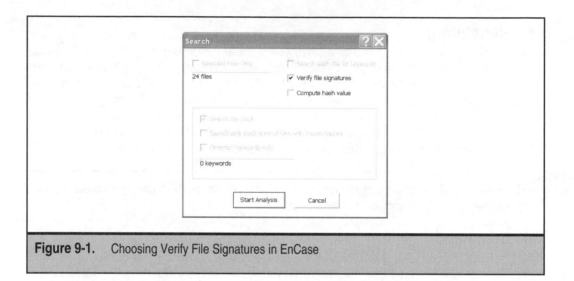

Figure 9-1. Choosing Verify File Signatures in EnCase

After the search is completed, the Signature column in the EnCase interface will be updated, as shown in Figure 9-2. If a file did not match its signature, this column would either read that it was mismatched or display the actual name of the file type, as shown in Figure 9-3.

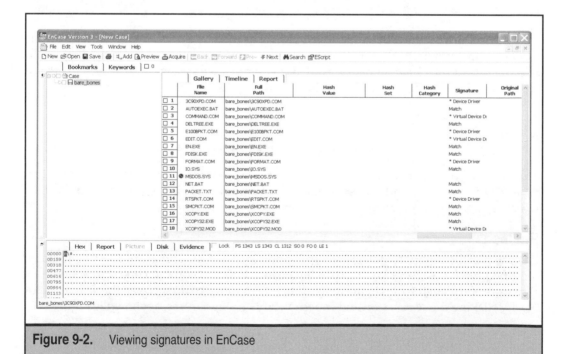

Figure 9-2. Viewing signatures in EnCase

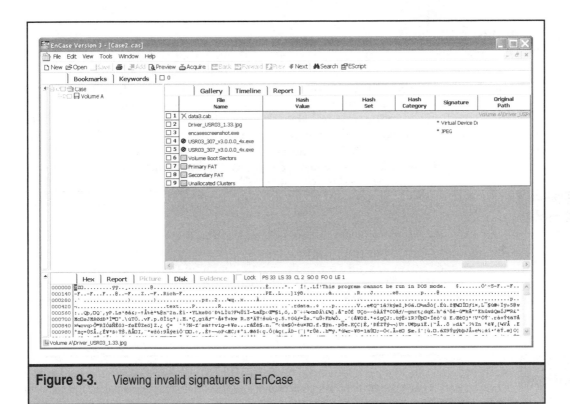

Figure 9-3.   Viewing invalid signatures in EnCase

Encoding Methods

Popularity:	5
Simplicity:	10
Impact:	10
Risk Rating:	8

Encoding means that a file's contents are changed in some way that can be easily reversed. Many times, a simple encoding mechanism called ROT-13 is used (ROT means *rotational* and *13* means the characters are rotated 13 times). If someone were to run ROT-13, the algorithm would take each character provided and replace it with a character 13 values in front of it. So, for example, an *A* would be replaced with an *N* (*B* starts the count as element 1). However, if you were to perform a search across encoded data, the search would not find the relevant data, as the expression the search was looking for would not decode ROT-13 without being instructed to do so.

Detecting Encoding

To detect that some kind of encoding has been used, such as ROT-13, you would need to rely on file signaturing if the original extension remained on the filename. However, ROT-13 and similar algorithms do not leave behind any standard signature, and no simple tool exists to detect its presence automatically. This doesn't mean, however, that detecting encoding cannot be accomplished. If a statistical analysis of the data were to occur with a ROT-13 decoder, and the data was compared against the distribution of the English language, the distribution should be shown to be uniformly off by 13 places. ROT-13 is especially popular for obscuring data contained in Windows registry keys.

NOTE   You can find ROT-13 decoders by searching for them on the Internet.

Although this method has not been proven scientifically, we have found that if back-slashes (\) or colons (:) or any other non-alphabetic characters appear in a file, a ROT-13 decoder can help you sort it out. ROT-13 will rotate and replace alphabetic characters only; spaces, slashes, colons, and any other non-alphabetic symbols remain as is in the file after decoding. Although this will not help you in automatically decoding the data while searching across a disk, once you've found such data, you can subsequently search it.

NOTE   Most people who are trying to hide data do not use ROT-13; ROT-13 is most commonly used to hide movie spoilers on web pages and newsgroup postings. However, Microsoft also has a long-standing "affair" with ROT-13, so you should never assume that a ROT-13 decoder won't be of help.

 ## Compression Methods

Popularity:	10
Simplicity:	10
Impact:	10
Risk Rating:	**10**

Compression allows a files contents to be reduced in size for storage and transmission. Compression algorithms analyze files to determine how the size of the file as it is stored can be reduced. This reduction is performed by analyzing the frequency of data in the file and applying an algorithm such as deflate, gzip, or the PKZIP and WinZip. It is not diffi-cult to detect compressed files; however, most forensic tools do not permit direct access to compressed files during a search without some kind of prior interaction.

Accessing Compressed Files

Forensic tools provide a couple of options that can help you search within compressed data. We have to handle compressed data differently in order to search and analyze its contents. Compressed data cannot be searched or analyzed within the forensic tool successfully without virtually uncompressing the data for searching. FTK and EnCase both allow you to perform searches using this functionality. SMART and other systems require that you export these files out of the image, decompress them, and then search across them using separate tools.

Accessing Compressed Files with FTK

By default, the AccessData Forensic Toolkit, or FTK, opens and adds to its index the contents of any compressed files it finds on the image. In fact, if you are working with another forensic tool, such as SMART, that does not support the ability to virtually uncompress the files within the image, you can export that data for import into FTK as it will allow you to perform searches.

Accessing Compressed Files with EnCase

Within EnCase, you can choose to mount a compressed file, as shown in Figure 9-4. *Mounting* here means that you are viewing the internal files within the compressed files.

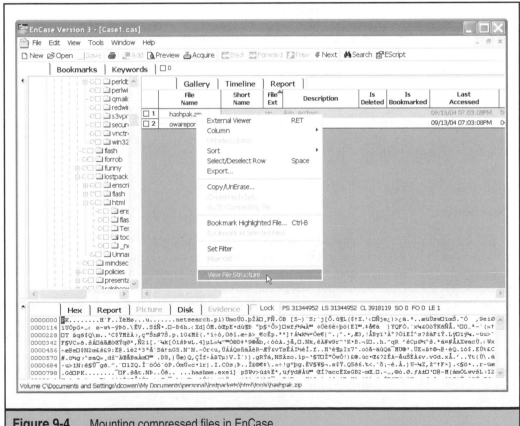

Figure 9-4.   Mounting compressed files in EnCase

By mounting the compressed files, EnCase's search function will be able to search through the files normally.

NTFS Alternate Data Streams

Popularity:	10
Simplicity:	10
Impact:	10
Risk Rating:	**10**

On of the more popular topics that people like to bring up at anti-forensic talks is *alternate data streams*. An alternate data stream is a secondary set of data that is attached to a single file within a NTFS file system. An alternate data stream is invisible to someone viewing the file through a Windows interface, such as Windows Explorer.

Searching Alternate Data Streams

Most modern forensic tools have the ability to display alternate data streams. Specifically, FTK, EnCase, The Sleuth Kit, and SMART all detect alternate data streams and display them to the user when an NTFS image is provided. Even so, the presence of an alternate data stream does not prevent any tool that searches the physical disk from finding the data within the alternate data stream. What an alternate data stream does prevent is detecting its existence on the disk without a utility that can view its structure.

Slack Space

Popularity:	10
Simplicity:	10
Impact:	3
Risk Rating:	**7**

Slack space is a remnant of data that exists within a sector of data that has been overwritten. Specifically, slack space is the area of the sector that was not fully overwritten by a recent write to disk. Remember that sectors are fixed in their size, so if you wrote 3K of data to a 64K sector, the remaining 61K of data would not be reused. Instead, this unused sector space would still contain whatever data was written to it previously. Figure 9-5 shows a conceptual drawing of how slack space exists on the disk. While slack space is not a problem for any forensic tool that examines the physical disk itself, it is a problem if you are attempting to search a disk. If you were to search a disk using non-forensic utilities, you would miss all of the data in the slack space, while a forensic utility would allow you to see what is stored in the slack space and even allow you to confine searches to it.

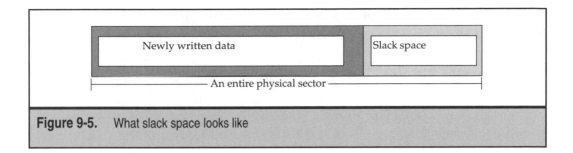

Figure 9-5.   What slack space looks like

Searching Slack Space

The answer to this dilemma is simply not to use standard search utilities in forensic investigations. By this we mean do attempt to search evidence using non-forensic tools and expect to re-create the data you would find using a forensic tool. All modern forensic tools examine the entire disk during searches and imaging, and as such always capture and review the slack space.

PRIVACY MEASURES

Some of the recognized anti-forensic techniques are legitimate attempts to protect the privacy of the individual. Of course, this does not help us in our forensic examination of a system, so we need to be able to identify and access that protected information. In this section, we will address problems and solutions concerning privacy software, such as encryption, steganography, evidence eliminators, and disk wiping. We are not concerned here with spyware removers, pop-up blockers, or anti-spam tools, because these tools are meant to protect the privacy of information leaving a computer. We are interested in the privacy software that either protects or erases the data that exists on the disk.

Encryption

Only one true anti-forensic method will defeat forensic analysis of data other than wiping, and that is encryption. However, even encryption has its weaknesses depending on the type used. For data to be encrypted, it must first exist on the disk in its unencrypted form—normally. I say *normally* because it is possible for someone to download a document in memory and encrypt it in memory before the data even touches the disk, although this is very rare except in the cases of e-mail. Instead, most people choose to encrypt a file that already exists on a disk. This means the data could still be stored at three locations: in the original file on the disk if it is still present, in the contents of the deleted file in the unallocated and slack space, and in the original file in the swap or pagefile.

This section covers the two dominant types of encryption: symmetric and asymmetric. Note that technical detail on how encryption works and the methodologies behind it are beyond the scope of this book. What we will cover is how to identify the encrypted data and what tools you can use to break it.

Symmetric Key Encryption

Popularity:	5
Simplicity:	5
Impact:	10
Risk Rating:	**6**

Symmetric key encryption, in the most basic of terms, means that a symmetric key has been used to encrypt data: in other words, the same encryption key is used to encrypt and decrypt the data. Symmetric key encryption is only as strong as its key length and its ability to keep others from finding out the key itself. If data is encrypted with a symmetric key, you will not be able to analyze or search its contents directly, and you will have to find some other method of identifying and accessing the data. In fact, you cannot determine if data was encrypted with a symmetric algorithm unless you've identified it as such.

 ## Identifying and Accessing Symmetric Key Encryption

You can identify symmetric key–encrypted files in two ways: either the file has an extension that is used by an encryption program to identify its files, or you will use a process known as *entropy testing*. Entropy testing is a process by which the randomness of the distribution of data within a file can be tested. The specific randomness can then be compared against a table of known algorithm randomness to identify whether a known algorithm has been used. This works well for all publicly known and documented encryption algorithms, because you can use them to document their randomness scale. However, if your suspect is using a new or non-public algorithm, an entropy test will not be able to identify the type of encryption used.

Identifying Symmetric Key Encryption with FTK

When any data is brought into FTK, you can run an entropy test on the data to determine whether it could be encrypted with a known algorithm. The entropy test option screen, as shown in Figure 9-6, is displayed when evidence is added to FTK. After FTK has completed its indexing and analysis, encrypted files may be identified for you.

Accessing Symmetric Key with the Password Recovery Toolkit

Accessing the symmetric key–encrypted data requires a tool that not only supports the algorithm but also provides the ability to do brute-force searching for the key. Although the original tool could be scripted against a list of keys of your own creation, several tools are available today to help you crack these encrypted files, such as AccessData's Password Recovery Toolkit. While this is the not only tool available, we have had success with it in the past.

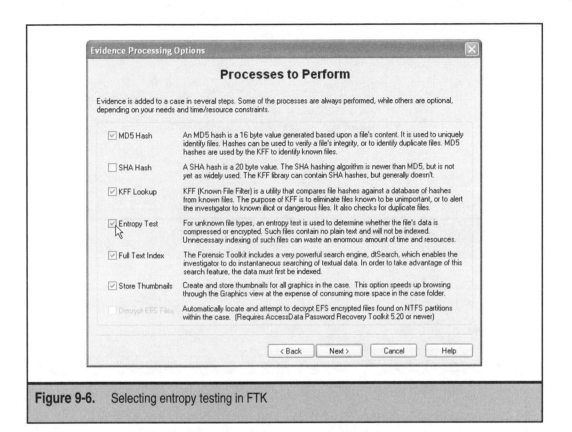

Figure 9-6. Selecting entropy testing in FTK

Here's how to crack a file with the Password Recovery Toolkit:

1. Load the application.

2. From the main menu, click the Select Files button, as shown in Figure 9-7.

3. Select the files that have passwords you want to crack. You will then see a status screen, as shown in Figure 9-8.g

4. After the password has been discovered, you will be notified, as shown in Figure 9-9. You can then click the Open File button; for some types of files, you will still have to enter the password to view the file in its application.

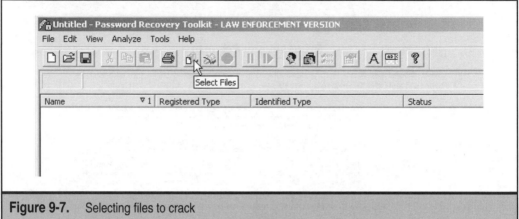

Figure 9-7. Selecting files to crack

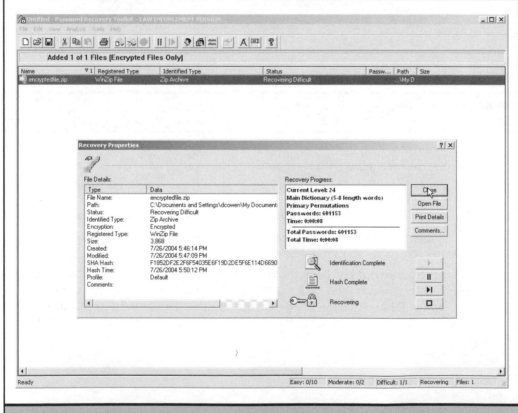

Figure 9-8. Viewing the status screen

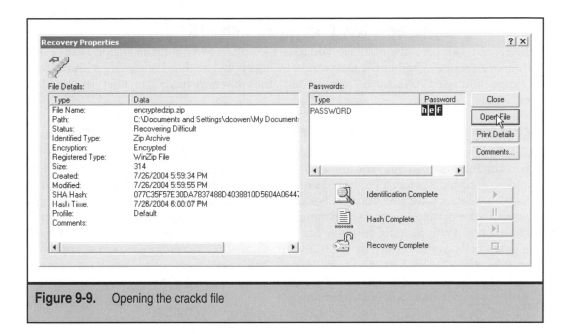

Figure 9-9. Opening the crackd file

Asymmetric Key Encryption

Popularity:	8
Simplicity:	8
Impact:	10
Risk Rating:	**9**

Asymmetric key encryption, in the most basic of terms, means that you have used asymmetric keys to encrypt data—in other words, one encryption key was used to encrypt and another was used to decrypt the data. Asymmetric key encryption is stronger than symmetric encryption because not only does the length of the key protect it, but the private key that is used to decrypt the data must be found before the data can be accessed. Having the public key—the key that is used to encrypt the data—will not allow you to access the original data. If data is encrypted with an asymmetric key, you will not be able to analyze or search the data contents; instead, you will have to find some other method of identifying and accessing the data.

Identifying and Accessing Asymmetric Key Encryption

You can identify asymmetric key encrypted files in two ways: either the file will have an extension that is used by an encryption program to identify its files, such as .pgp, or you will have to use entropy testing, as discussed previously.

Identifying Asymmetric Key Encryption with FTK

When any data is brought into FTK, you have the option of running an entropy test on the data to determine whether the data could be encrypted with a known algorithm. Once FTK has completed its indexing and analysis, files that may have been encrypted will be identified.

Accessing the Asymmetric Key with the Password Recovery Toolkit

Accessing the asymmetric key–encrypted data requires a tool that not only supports the algorithm but also provides the ability to brute-force the key. Although the original tool could be scripted against a list of keys of your own creation, ready-made tools, such as AccessData's Password Recovery Toolkit, are available to help you. You should understand, though, that most asymmetric algorithms may require years of run time in order to determine the key. With a strong key, this can even become hundreds of years. We can crack the passwords in the same way we did with symmetric encryption, except asymmetric keys take much, much longer to crack. AccessData's documentation states it may take as long as 254 days to crack an asymmetric key, so before you try this method, be sure that you cannot recover data in any other way.

Here's how to crack a file with the Password Recovery Toolkit:

1. Load the application.

2. In the main menu, click the Select Files button (see Figure 9-7).

3. Then, select the files whose password you would like to crack. You'll see a status screen.

4. After the password has been discovered, you will be notified. You can then click the Open File button and use the password to view the file in its associated application.

The General Solution to Encryption

If you run into encryption during a forensics examination, a simple and general solution is at hand: ask the suspect to supply the encryption key and the method by which he or she encrypted the data. Although this sounds simplistic and too good to be true, it often works. If you already have someone's data and he or she refuses to give up the encryption key, you can ask the court to order the person to produce the encryption key and the method used to encrypt the data. The person can, of course, refuse, but that will result in a contempt of court charge. The person will then be placed in a holding cell or have fines placed against him or her until the information is produced. This is how law enforcement normally deals with encryption.

Steganography

Popularity:	3
Simplicity:	5
Impact:	10
Risk Rating:	6

   Steganography is the ability to hide data inside another file. Using the steganography tools available today, suspects can even hide data inside JPEGs and audio files. When a sophisticated suspect is being investigated and remnants of a steganography tool exist, it would be bad practice for you not to attempt to discover the existence of any hidden data.

⊖ Detecting Steganography

Currently, we have used only one open-source tool to detect steganography with reliable results. Stegdetect, found at http://www.outguess.org/detection.php, allows you to inspect JPEG files for hidden data. Although other products are emerging on the market to deal with this problem, we have not used them so we cannot recommend them. The main commercial application that exists, Steg Suite by Wetstone, http://www.wetstonetech.com, is part of that list. In addition to these techniques, you can also search the system to determine if steganography programs have been installed. However, we have yet to encounter steganography in a case to date, and it's hard to say when it will become a common forensics issue. Until then, though, keeping a steganography detection tool in your toolkit will allow you to do a more thorough analysis when it is demanded.

Wiping

Popularity:	10
Simplicity:	10
Impact:	10
Risk Rating:	10

   Wiping is a real problem when it's done correctly. It can be accomplished in many different ways, as you will see, but it shares some common aspects. For example, any data that has been truly wiped from the disk has been overwritten at least one time. Using the software tools that exist today, you cannot access any data that has been overwritten. However, you can recover the data using an electron microscope to find the previous state of all the electrons on the disk, thus restoring the wiped information. Unfortunately, very few of us will ever have access to an electron microscope to analyze our disks, and even fewer of us will have access to an application that can then extract the data we want to recover. If you happen to work for a government agency with the resources and capacity to use an electron microscope, you can recover and record the previous states of the electrons across the disk, but this is an expensive and labor-intensive process and not one you should expect to occur in any case. You can determine if wiping tools have been installed by reviewing the programs that exist and have existed on the disk, but you cannot bring that wiped data back.

Wiping a File

Popularity:	10
Simplicity:	10
Impact:	10
Risk Rating:	**10**

File wiping, also called *secure deletion*, is the most popular method and involves the removal of a file's data from the disk. File wiping will, in fact, overwrite the contents of the file as it existed on the disk, and upon completion of the wiping process that data is considered unrecoverable.

Recovering Remnants of Wiped Files

As stated, no silver bullet brings back this data. To recover a file that has been wiped, you can look at several places to determine whether at least parts and backups of previous copies of the file still exist. As a file is accessed, portions of it will be stored in various areas of the disk. You can look in the following locations for files that have been wiped:

▼ The pagefile or swap space if it was loaded into memory

■ The MFT or FAT table to determine the file existed

■ The NTFS journal if the data existed on an NTFS partition

■ The slack space and unallocated space if it existed previously on the disk

▲ Any backups of the system

None of these solutions are bullet proof, but they can work. If you know part of the contents of a file, searching the physical disk for those contents could locate the file in any of these locations.

Wiping the Slack Space

Popularity:	10
Simplicity:	10
Impact:	10
Risk Rating:	**10**

Wiping the slack space is being used in some of the more popular wipers. As discussed earlier, the slack space contains data from a file that was previously partially overwritten. Remember that slack space is simply unused space at the end of a fixed sector size, so a disk can be wiped of its slack space without modifying any of the data that is in use on the disk. When the slack space is wiped, the existing data is overwritten and can no longer be recovered.

Recovering Remnants of Files Stored in the Slack Space

To recover any files that existed in the slack space that has been wiped, you can look in several places to determine whether the copies or backups of the data exist. As a file is accessed, portions of it will remain in areas of the disk. You can look in the following locations for data that was in the slack space that has been wiped:

▼ The pagefile or swap space if it was loaded into memory

■ The MFT or FAT table to determine the file existed

■ The NTFS journal if the data existed on an NTFS partition

▲ Any backups of the system

Again, none of these solutions are bullet proof. If you know part of the contents of a file, searching the physical disk for those contents could locate the data. Remember that data that existed in the slack space was already previously deleted, so the likelihood of recovery is low.

Wiping the Unallocated Space

Popularity:	7
Simplicity:	10
Impact:	10
Risk Rating:	9

Wiping the unallocated space takes a long time to do. Although unallocated space wipers are available, it can take an entire day to wipe the space. This is good news for us, because we rarely see a disk that has had its unallocated space wiped clean. However, if the unallocated space is wiped, the wiped data cannot be recovered.

Recovering Remnants of Data in the Unallocated Space

You can never fully recover the data that was stored in the unallocated space from the active portion of the disk because the unallocated space is too large. However, you can look in several places to determine whether some portion, copy, or backup of the data still exists:

▼ The NTFS journal if the data existed on an NTFS partition

■ The MFT or FAT table to determine the file existed

▲ Any backups of the system

If you know part of the contents of a file, searching the physical disk for those contents might locate the file in any of these locations. Remember that data that existed in the unallocated space was deleted previously, so the likelihood of recovery is low. Notice that we did not include the pagefile or swap space in our list of locations. This is because most wiping tools that wipe the unallocated space also overwrite the pagefile or swap space by filling the memory of the system. This will not *always* be the case, however, so make sure to check the pagefile and swap space as well.

Wiping a Disk

Popularity:	5
Simplicity:	7
Impact:	10
Risk Rating:	7

Of the available options for wiping, none is more detrimental to your investigation than a full disk wipe, which overwrites the entire physical disk. While it is obvious when the entire disk has been wiped, there is no way to recover the data.

Recovering Remnants of Data from Wiped Disks

Even though you cannot recover data that has been wiped from the disk, you can and should look for backups of the system itself. However, if you have received this disk in the course of a court investigation, you can have the judge either file sanctions against the person who has done this or order the person to produce any other data that may exist.

The filing for sanctions is important because it applies only if someone knowingly destroys evidence from any system that has been identified with a *protective order*—a document that a judge signs that states any evidence that exists on a system may not be deleted and must be preserved. Whether or not a preservation order exists, a judge will likely order an opposing party to do further production of evidence if you can prove that some of the data provided was wiped. Also, many companies have policies that prevent using wipers on their property. As such, you should work with the company to determine if any such policies apply to this employee.

CHAPTER 10

ENTERPRISE
STORAGE
ANALYSIS

Y ou can apply most of the tools and techniques covered so far in this book to any type of investigation. Despite their growing scope and complexity, most investigations scale well with the tools provided in other chapters. However, when you're forced to deal with terabytes of data with technology that was not designed for easy access from the desktop PC or laptop, you have to reevaluate your situation. This chapter defines how to deal with RAIDs (redundant array of inexpensive disks), SANs (storage area networks), tapes, and the large and expansive datasets that you will gather when dealing with a large investigation.

Many of the techniques discussed in this chapter also apply to electronic discovery. Electronic discovery relates to the collection, processing, review, and production of electronic documents in a lawsuit. Large datasets and wide ranges of types of systems are the rule and not the exception in electronic discovery.

THE ENTERPRISE DATA UNIVERSE

Popularity:	10
Simplicity:	5
Impact:	10
Risk Rating:	**8**

First, let's define the *enterprise environment*. In this book, the enterprise environment means all of the systems, servers, and data that make up a company's computing system. Most sets of data that are included in an enterprise scenario include *x*86-based servers (any operating system), non-*x*86 based servers, NAS (Network-Attached Storage) systems, SAN systems, servers with RAIDs, tapes (lots of them), and hundreds to thousands of desktops and laptops. This list does not even include the portable devices now popular, such as PDAs, cell phones, and thumb drives, but those devices are covered in other chapters. Dealing with all of this data requires that you use tools that are made to handle searches of large quantities of data, so full-text indexing is also discussed here.

Working with RAID

Popularity:	10
Simplicity:	10
Impact:	10
Risk Rating:	**10**

RAID sets can be created by hardware or software such that either the hardware-based RAID controller creates and maintains the RAID set or the software does. A RAID allows several disks to be viewed as a single disk to the operating system. A RAID can pose a huge problem to an unprepared examiner, and most systems that use RAID are on server systems. This means the data on RAIDs is typically valuable and the risk of modifying the raid system can be quite harmful to its owner as they would loose access to all of their data.

RAIDs, unless configured as RAID 1, will write data across all the disks that make up the RAID set. This means that you will have to image each disk in the RAID and keep the system powered down before you can allow the owner to have access to his or her data again. SAN and NAS systems, which are covered next, both utilize RAID.

Acquiring a RAID

Acquiring a RAID is similar to imaging other types of media except that you need to be able to write down the disk's original sequence in the drive bays. If possible, you should also get the RAID configuration's settings stored either within the hardware card or the operating system. The system owner should be able to provide this information to you.

 Once you have acquired the RAID set, you can either reassemble it in Windows with Guidance Software's EnCase or within Linux using the raidtools set. It is difficult to replicate the hardware environment of the original RAID set. Additionally, the re-creation using the original hardware could possibly overwrite the restored images in the process of initializing the RAID, resulting in high costs and potential failure.

Rebuilding RAIDs in EnCase

To rebuild a RAID in EnCase, you must select all of the RAID disks' images that you have created in EnCase when adding evidence to the case. EnCase will "automagically" recognize individual images that are part of a RAID set and then attempt to reconstruct the RAID. The newly reconstructed RAID will then appear to you as a single disk.

Rebuilding RAIDs in Linux

To rebuild a RAID in Linux, you must have each of the images created with the dd utility. Once you have these images, you must mount them with the local loopback using the following command:

```
mount -o loop,ro /path/to/image /path/where/to/mount
```

where -o loop is for local loopback and ro is for read-only. If the mount was successful, you will have a read-only version of the image that will be treated as a disk on the Linux system. This means that you can use the raidtools program that comes with Linux to rebuild the RAID array. Since the RAID images are marked as read-only, you do not have to worry about raidtools or any other RAID toolkit overwriting or changing the image.

WORKING WITH NAS SYSTEMS

Popularity:	10
Simplicity:	10
Impact:	10
Risk Rating:	**10**

NAS systems are normally singular units that provide a large data volume as a single disk or a set of shares to a network. NAS systems can be as small as 200GB but are quite capable of growing up to several terabytes in size.

CAUTION If you do not *have* to image a NAS system forensically, do *not* do it. Request a backup tape set instead.

Acquiring NAS

Unless the NAS you are working with supports iSCSI (Internet SCSI), you cannot make a direct connection to the NAS to create a true and correct image. Instead, you must shut down the NAS system and image each drive. This is not something to be taken lightly, as you could have the NAS system shut down for an entire day. Make sure that you plan ahead, and give the NAS owner time to prepare for the downtime.

WORKING WITH SAN SYSTEMS

Popularity:	10
Simplicity:	10
Impact:	10
Risk Rating:	**10**

SAN can be a potential nightmare to you in the field. A SAN is either a single system or a set of systems interconnected on a dedicated network, normally fiber, to create large sets of disks that can be either assigned to specific servers or shared among multiple servers. A single SAN disk can span terabytes of data, which will quickly exceed the capacity of any single drive you put in front of it. Removing disks from a live SAN may cause the SAN to lose its index to data and cause the SAN owner to lose the data. So, if possible, do not remove the disks from the SAN itself.

CAUTION If you do not *have* to image a SAN system forensically, do not do it. Request a backup tape set instead.

Acquiring a SAN System

If you are required to make an image of a SAN network, you will need to gather some facts by asking the following questions:

▼ What type of network is connecting the SAN to the systems using it?

■ On that network, are any ports free on the switch (fiber switch or Ethernet switch for iSCSI)?

▲ What type of adapter cards will you need? (Fiber adapter cards are not sold in stores, so make sure to ask this question ahead of time.)

Next you need to do some research. Your best bet in creating an image of a dataset this large would be to bring a RAID set of your own in which to store all of this data. The only way to mount multi-terabyte volumes and acquire terabytes of data with high throughput—and without ever modifying the evidence—is to use a Linux system. If you use Windows to do this, the first thing Windows will do is touch—write to—the SAN disk. And, as you know, *modifying evidence is always a bad idea*.

Which distribution of Linux you choose to use depends on the adapter card you must install. Red Hat offers good support for adapter cards and is probably the best solution. Next, on most networks, the operational staff will have to add your system to its SAN so that you can do your job. Then you will have access to the SAN disks you need to image.

 Make sure that any other system that could have access to the SAN is *shut down*; otherwise, the data can be modified as you collect it.

After you have done all of this, your adapter card will give mappings to SAN disks as SCSI devices. Use dd as you normally would, or use SMART. Hashing and verification will take some time, so plan on at least a day to do this.

 Many things can go wrong. We do not recommend that you attempt to image a SAN disk unless you are comfortable with the situation and are able to test all of your equipment beforehand. Remember that you don't want to harm what could be a million-dollar system.

WORKING WITH TAPES

Tapes, specifically backup tapes, come in a wide variety of flavors and have changed a great deal in the last decade. In fact, if you are given a tape that was written to more than five years ago, you may not be able to find a drive to read it. Tapes are slow and prone to breakage. Additionally, tapes are written with proprietary software in proprietary formats, and usually large sets make up a single backup. If you are doing any type of long-term work with an enterprise, you will encounter tapes. Your ability to work with those tapes and show competence doing so is important.

The current dominant tape formats, as of the year 2004, are digital linear tape (DLT) and linear tape-open (LTO). Many other formats, including 8mm, 4mm, quarter-inch cartridge (QIC), 16-track, and 32-track, among others, come in a large variety of formats themselves—including advanced intelligent tape (AIT); Exabyte; IBM 3840; DLT 3000, 4000, 6000, 7000; SDLT1 and SDLT2; LTO1 and LTO2; DDS-1, 2, 3, and 4; StorageTek, and more. You could spend a very large amount of time and money trying to prepare to handle every type of tape media that exists. Instead, if you understand the basics of how tapes operate and how to interact with them, you will be well served in your efforts to deal with them.

If you receive more than 20 tapes to examine, you should look into getting a tape robot, also called an *autoloader*. It used to be that any type of tape robot was expensive and required large, complicated systems to work with, but this is no longer the case; the dot-com bust and the rapid change of tape technologies has created a large market for refurbished and used, low-priced tape robots. Most tape robots, and hopefully all tape robots you are required to handle, support a SCSI connection to your system. With the fall in prices of tape robots and the wide availability of SCSI components, a desktop system can quickly be adapted to handle any tape production. Your only concern, then, becomes how to store all of this data, a topic that is covered in Chapter 3.

Tapes have some inherit qualities that make forensic analysis easier: Almost all tapes have a write protect tab, meaning that upon setting the tab in the proper direction (this varies per tape), your drive will be unable to write to it. This is not a unique ability, but it means that you do not have to worry about tape write-blockers or modifying evidence on a tape while reading it. Before loading any tape, you should make sure to check the write-protect tab and set it properly.

Reading Tapes

Popularity:	10
Simplicity:	8
Impact:	10
Risk Rating:	**9**

When you are handed a tape, ask the following questions:

▼ Where did the tape come from?

■ Who wrote the tape?

■ What software wrote it?

▲ What type of drive wrote this tape?

While the model number on the tape can answer most of your drive-related questions, many times you cannot discover what software wrote the tape or even what is stored on it. If you cannot even determine what software wrote the data, let alone what is on the tape, the evidence becomes worthless and you cannot defend against its production to another party in a lawsuit. If this occurs, the opposing party can request to be given the tapes themselves in an attempt to access the data. The act of doing so can be seen as a "waiver of privilege." See Chapter 15 for details of privilege and evidence production.

 ## Identifying Tapes

We have found it possible and beneficial to access the tape from its *raw device*—the actual path to the tape drive itself. This method lets you read data directly from the tape without having to use any translation or interpretation software in the middle. This can be done on Windows and UNIX systems.

Accessing Raw Tapes on Windows

Before accessing the raw tape drive in Windows, you should first install Cygwin, a free UNIX emulation environment for Windows, which is found at http://www.cygwin.com/. UNIX utilities such as dd, covered in Chapter 4, were made to access tape devices and read the data out in blocks. Other utilities, such as type and more, will try to send the tape device control signals that it does not support, and your attempts to access the information will fail.

A plus side to accessing raw tape devices in Windows is that the Windows drivers automatically detect the block sizes of the tapes and any other tape-level settings, so you do not have to spend your time trying out different options.

After you have installed Cygwin, you can access the tape device by executing the following command:

```
dd if=/dev/st0 | less
```

Cygwin maps the standard Linux location of st0 or "standard tape 0" to the Windows physical, raw device \\.Tape0. This is the actual location the operating system uses to access the tape drive. The number at the end of st and Tape will grow to reflect each drive you attach to your system—so st1 = tape 1, st2 = tape 2, and so on. When the command has been successfully executed, abort it after the first screen of data has passed.

You may optionally choose to write out the data to a file by executing the following:

```
dd if=/dev/st0 > tape0
```

This command will write the tape's data out to a file called tape0. You are looking for data typically located in the first five lines of the file or screen. Most backup software identifies itself here with lines such as *arcserve*, *netbackup*, *tar*, and so on.

You can see a listing of all of the tape drives remapped for you by typing the following command:

```
mount
```

Accessing Raw Tapes on UNIX

Accessing the raw tape device under UNIX is actually the same as doing it in Windows using Cygwin. You will use the same dd command with both operating systems.

However, if you receive errors, you will have to attempt to guess the block size used to write to the tape. The easiest remedy to try is the following dd command:

```
dd if=/dev/st0 bs=0 > tape0
```

Setting bs, or block size, to 0 tells dd to detect the block size automatically. This usually solves the problem, but if it does not, you will need to install and use the MTX toolkit (available at http://mtx.badtux.net/) to check the status of the tape drive. The MTX toolkit allows you to control attached tape robots manually and access tape devices at the raw SCSI level. Because no single solution to this problem exists, our recommendation would be to start at bs=64 and work your way up in powers of two.

Commercial Tools for Accessing Tapes

The only commercial tool for identifying and accessing tapes that we have used with good results is eMag Solutions' Media Merge for PC (MM/PC), available at http://www.emaglink.com/MMPC.htm. MM/PC is one of few specialized tools available for accessing tapes in their raw form. This tool attempts to detect their format automatically and has the capability to read, extract, and—for some formats—catalog the contents of tapes without the original backup software that wrote the tapes.

MM/PC will also allow you to view the contents of a tape within a GUI environment. With the MM/PC environment, you can see the ASCII and hex values of the data on the tape and skip through the file records on the tape to view the type of data within it. MM/PC also offers a "forensic option" that allows you, if MM/PC supports the format, to inventory and capture the data on the tape without restoring the tape itself.

Preserving Tapes

Popularity:	10
Simplicity:	10
Impact:	10
Risk Rating:	10

You might think that a tape cannot be imaged, but this is not true. Using the dd tool, you can take an exact image of any tape that your tape drives can read. Imaging tapes can be useful when a tape has been reused multiple times in a backup. If older data on the tape was not overwritten—if the new backup did not completely overwrite the old—the older data can be restored by imaging the tape.

Imaging Tapes

The dd command can be used to image an entire tape, including every block that is readable on the tape. To do so, use the following command:

```
dd if=/dev/nst0 bs=0 conv=noerror >> tape0.image
```

Note that nst0 is used instead of st0. The device nst0 means "non-rewinding." When you access st0, it will automatically rewind the tape before processing your request. Using nst0, you can continue to read into the tape with every consecutive execution of dd. To ensure that you have a complete image of the tape, you must execute the dd command multiple times to guarantee that you have hit the end of the tape and not just a blank file marker. A good rule of thumb is five end of tape error messages.

Note that this command is the same on Windows or UNIX systems.

Creating Too Much Evidence

Popularity:	10
Simplicity:	10
Impact:	10
Risk Rating:	**10**

One of the major misconceptions that exists when collecting large amount of systems and data is that forensic imaging is the only option available to you. Another larger and more damaging misconception is that forensic imaging is something that should be applied broadly and across any potentially relevant system.

Truth is, if you are collecting a large amount of data from a large number of systems, it is usually in support of some kind of legal action at the request of the court. When you are doing anything in support of a legal action, you have to be aware of the ramifications of your decisions in court. In a nutshell, creating too much evidence is almost as bad as not preserving any at all. Let me explain: When you create a forensic image without either a court order or the specific understanding that the system involved contains some amount of relevancy to the case, you remove several of the protections that your legal counsel depends on.

Specifically, you have lost your client's counsel most of his or her argument for "overly burdensome requests" that protects your client from having to spend exorbitant amounts of money to provide evidence to the court. For example, suppose you were approached in either an internal or external capacity to collect data from 100 users. If you decided on your own, without a request from counsel or the court, to incur the expense of creating forensic images of all 100 users' machines, you have basically cost your client unnecessary money, time, and possibly important defense tactics. If the opposing counsel were aware of the images' existence (and such information is normally discovered during depositions), the opposing counsel could make a motion for the court to order their production. Because your side would incur no additional costs in creating the images in response to the order, your counsel would have lost a major tactic in defending his or her side from overly broad evidence productions. (Evidence productions are discussed in detail in Chapter 15.)

Live-File Collections

A *live file collection* is a fancy way of saying that you are copying, while preserving the MAC times of active files, to a central location for preservation, review, and production to opposing counsel. The MAC times of active files include Modification, Access, and Creation or

Change, depending on the operating system. *Active* files are known to the operating system and are not marked for deletion.

This obviously is not a technically difficult problem but is, however, a logistical and organizational problem. You need to discover where the relevant data exists, which users are relevant, which departments are relevant, which servers they use, and other similar information. After you have defined the scope of where your data lies, you need to deploy a tool that users can run to collect their own data or one that can access their systems over the network to allow the data to be copied.

Collecting Live Data from Windows Systems

Two tools that we have used to collect data in this fashion are Pixelab's XXCopy, found at http://www.xxcopy.com, and Microsoft's RoboCopy, available in the Windows resource kits. Pixelab provides a free version of XXCopy, while RoboCopy is only available as a free tool within the resource kit.

Preserving Files with XXCopy

XXCopy is a DOS-based tool that takes a large variety of command-line parameters for a wide range of results. We recommend the following syntax:

```
C:\xxcopy c: z: /s /h /tca /tcc /tcw
```

This would tell XXCopy to copy all of the files including all subdirectories, /s, and all hidden files, /h, from the c: drive to the z: drive. The switches /tca, /tcc, and /tcw tell XXCopy to preserve the access, creation, and modification times of the files. It does so by taking the original times from the source files and applying them to the destination files.

Preserving Files with Microsoft RoboCopy

RoboCopy, short for Robust File and Folder Copy, in the most recent version by default will preserve all of the modification, access, and creation times. The syntax for executing it is as follows:

```
C:\robocopy c: z: /s
```

This tells RoboCopy to copy all files from the c: drive to the z: drive for all subdirectories in C:.

FULL-TEXT INDEXING

When you encounter large datasets (such as those greater than 300 gigabytes), you may find yourself with a "needle in the haystack problem." The search features of most of the forensic and system tools we have discussed so far are not designed for continuous searches against large amounts of data. What you need is a way to take all of the data, which in some environments can grow to terabytes in size, and place it in some kind of search tree. The exact type of tree structure used varies by vendor.

Binary Search Trees

A binary search tree is a structure that allows your system to store dataset information in two "subtrees," one left and one right. Data is sorted by key into one of the subtrees, and the key is used to determine in which subtree the search should continue. The search process continues to divide the information into two parts, narrowing the search to one part in sequence, until the sought item is found. The binary search tree enables you to search terabytes of data in seconds instead of hours or days.

The overall benefit is that you can search through any dataset of any size, the worst case being log base 2 n times, where n is the size of your data. This means that instead of searching through 500 gigabytes of data sequentially, you can find the specific words that make up your search in 39 steps, and you can search through 5 terabytes of data in 43 steps!

Compare this to the steps required to perform multiple sequential searches through the dataset: assuming we are examining 64k-byte blocks from a drive, it would take 7,812,500 steps to search 500 gigabytes of data completely and 78,125,000 steps to search through 5 terabytes of data completely. While the indexer must also perform these steps initially, for each subsequent search of the data it would only have to perform the log base 2 n searches.

This means you can search terabytes of data in seconds. Now you can perform all the searches requested without suggesting it will take a year and you'll call them when you're done. The general rule we follow is that if you plan to search the data only once, perform a linear search; if you plan to search it more than once, create a full text index using a binary search tree.

Missing Data When Indexing

Popularity:	10
Simplicity:	10
Impact:	10
Risk Rating:	**10**

As is often the case, you pay a price when using additional functionality, and in the case of indexing, the price is encoded files. When indexing, you must first create a *full-text index* of all of the data. This means that the indexer, the program that creates the index, must be able to distinguish words from your data to be included in the binary tree. While this is not a problem for source code, basic e-mail, and text files, it *is* a problem for Office documents, e-mail attachments, e-mail container files (such as Microsoft Outlook PST files), and any other file that is not made up of plain ASCII characters. You need to use an indexing program that will convert these file types for you, or you will have to convert the file types yourself. We will cover both types of indexing.

Glimpse

Glimpse is a free full-text indexing program that is packaged with a search interface called WebGlimpse, available at http://www.webglimpse.org/. Glimpse will give you incredibly advanced indexing options such as merging indexes, appending and deleting files from indexes, and even regular expressions against indexed data. WebGlimpse even offers free and low-cost options for support. However, what Glimpse does not do is automatically convert files for you. Glimpse expects that the files fed to the program will be in ASCII text form.

The WebGlimpse package addresses the file-conversion challenge with a user-customizable listing of programs to call to convert your files. The WebGlimpse web site even provides links and instructions on how to convert the most popular file formats that their users encounter. Adding file types and finding conversion utilities as well as testing their accuracy are up to you. Glimpse is not for the novice user, but with some experience and work, you'll find that Glimpse is a great free indexing system that will make quick work of your data searches.

WebGlimpse acts like a familiar web search engine to search the data. In fact, WebGlimpse was primarily created to allow for indexed searches of web sites. The search interface will allow you to select and search across your indexes and will highlight the hits in an abstract of the file on the web page that it returns. Anyone with a web browser can access the WebGlimpse interface and multiple users can search it at once. Also, Glimpse supports the ability to search the index directly from the command line, making for some great automation possibilities. Glimpse code must be compiled, but it can be compiled in either Linux or through Cygwin in Windows.

 ## dtSearch

dtSearch leads the market of mid-range cost indexing systems and can be found at http://www.dtsearch.com. dtSearch has several configurations of its indexing system, including just the dtSearch engine for implementation into other products. dtSearch has support for the most popular data formats such as PST files, Office documents, and zip files and will create a full-text index of the data.

dtSearch allows you to search your indexes via a GUI. You pick the index you would like to search, enter in keywords, and then dtSearch will generate a list of files that match your query. Selecting a file will bring up a preview of it with the search strings highlighted within. dtSearch does not have a command-line interface and is available for Windows only. Another product they offer, called the dtSearch engine, does support Linux as well as Windows.

 ## AccessData's Forensic Toolkit

AccessData's FTK, found at http://www.accessdata.com, makes use of the dtSearch indexing engine. In addition to the standard file types supported by dtSearch, FTK offers internal conversions. FTK also allows you to index whole images: just feed FTK an image from Guidance Software's EnCase, ASR Data's SMART, or a dd image, and it will build a full-text index of all of the files and the unallocated space. When you are dealing with a large case, this can be a very useful feature that will quickly pay back its cost.

FTK allows you to search indexes through its GUI. You pick the index you want to search, enter in keywords, and FTK will generate a list of files that match your query. Selecting a file will bring up a preview of it with the search strings highlighted within them. FTK does not have a command-line interface and is available for Windows only.

⊖ Paraben's Text Searcher

Paraben's Text Searcher, found at http://www.paraben-forensics.com, also makes use of the dtSearch indexing engine. Text Searcher allows you to search your indexes through its GUI. You pick the index you would like to search, enter in keywords, and Text Searcher will generate a list of files that match your query. Selecting a file will open a preview of it with the search strings highlighted within. Text Searcher does not have a command-line interface and is available for Windows only.

⊖ Verity

Verity, found at http://www.verity.com, is the 500-pound gorilla of indexers. Verity's product line of engines and enterprise-ready indexing systems do not come cheap but can handle the largest and most complex situations. Verity's product line is not a simple desktop-driven application that can be installed in an hour. Rather, the company's server systems require configuration and customization to create the results you desire. You may find few situations that demand a system as intensive as Verity, but in the event that you do, it is well worth the cost.

MAIL SERVERS

When dealing with the types of data and systems we describe in this chapter, it is only a matter of time before you have to deal with mail servers. Mail clients have data files designed to be accessed and have open interfaces to them, such as PST and NSF, with well-documented APIs and tools for using them. Mail servers, on the other hand, are designed to be accessed only by their own systems. Microsoft Exchange, Lotus Domino Mail Server (with Lotus Notes), Novell GroupWise, Netscape iPlanet, and others all contain proprietary methods for storing and accessing e-mail stored on the mail server.

💣 Microsoft Exchange

Popularity:	10
Simplicity:	10
Impact:	10
Risk Rating:	10

Exchange servers keep their e-mail data in a file called priv.edb. The .edb, or exchange database format, is a Microsoft database with no known published structure. If you have the time, you can access the Microsoft Developers Network documents, located at http://msdn.microsoft.com, and try to reverse-engineer a solution yourself, but chances are you do not have that kind of time. Being able to search the .edb directly allows you to pull relevant e-mails from the current system and any backup of the system that may relate to your investigation.

Kroll-Ontrack PowerControls

Kroll Ontrack's product PowerControls, available at http://www.ontrack.com/powercontrols/, is an excellent tool for accessing, searching, and extracting e-mails from an .edb. Not only will PowerControls allow you to access an .edb on the disk, but a licensed version of the software will also allow you to extract .edb files directly from tapes written by Veritas NetBackup, Veritas Backup Exec, Computer Associates Brightstor ARCserve, Legato NetWorker, and NT Backup, the free backup utility that has come with Windows server since Windows NT. PowerControls does the job well, while it is a bit more expensive than the other options. PowerControls has two limitations in the enterprise environment, the lack of automation capabilities and the inability to control tape robots while using the extract .edb tape tool in the Extraction Wizards.

Paraben's Network E-mail Examiner

On the commercial but lower cost end comes Paraben's Network E-mail Examiner, or NEMX, available at http://www.paraben-forensics.com. NEMX will allow you to access, search, and extract messages from an .edb. However, NEMX does not give you the tape-restoration abilities that are found in PowerControls. NEMX, like PowerControls, does not provide for any automation ability.

Aelita Recovery Manager for Exchange

Quest Software's Aelita Recovery Manager for Exchange, found at http://wm.quest.com/, offers additional functionality that other tools in the market do not offer. While Aelita Recovery Manager for Exchange, here after referred to a ARME, allows you to access, search, and extract messages from an .edb, it also allows the software to act as a virtual exchange server. Why is this useful? If you are restoring exchange servers from a set of tapes, which is typically the case when you are asked to do this type of work, you can point the backup software at the system with ARME installed and running in emulation mode. In emulation mode, ARME will take the restored data as if it were an exchange server and write it to an .edb locally, where you can extract the messages. If you are dealing with a software package that will not allow you to restore an exchange agent–based backup without restoring it to an exchange server, the emulation mode is immensely useful. Additionally, you can interoperate with the native backup software and take advantage of its abilities to use tape robots in automating the restoration using emulation capabilities.

Microsoft Exchange Server

The final option you have is to install a new Microsoft Exchange Server, at http://www.microsoft.com/exchange/default.mspx, on a Windows server system. (MS Exchange will not install on Windows XP.) You can then re-create the configuration to emulate the name and domain of the original server. In doing so, you can either restore messages to the Exchange system using the backup software or you can have it access a restored .edb by loading the Exchange Server in what is called *recovery mode*. Recovery mode allows the Exchange Server to start up and access the .edb as it would normally, allowing you access to the messages within it. Exchange does not provide the ability to search across the text of mail in the mailboxes, so you will have to export out each user's mailbox into a PST and search it afterward to determine whether it contains the evidence you're looking for. You can, however, search by sender, recipient, and date. This is by far the least preferred solution, and unless you have licenses for Exchange already, this is also likely the most expensive option.

Lotus Domino Mail Server and Lotus Notes

Popularity:	6
Simplicity:	10
Impact:	10
Risk Rating:	8

IBM's Lotus Notes mail client has a corresponding mail server named Domino. Lotus Notes client and server both store their data in NSF, or Notes Storage Facility, files. Lotus supports *real encryption*—the Lotus server and client use public key encryption algorithms that cannot be easily broken. Thankfully for us, the option to use encryption is not the default configuration. If you encounter an encrypted NSF, you should inform your client that the encrypted data might not be recoverable.

Network E-mail Examiner

NEMX will allow you to access, search, and extract messages from an NSF. NEMX, as stated in the Exchange section, does not provide for any automation ability.

Domino Server

Your only other option is either to automate the Lotus Domino Mail Server through Lotus script or install a new Domino server and configure it as a recovery server to access the existing NSF.

Novell GroupWise

Popularity:	4
Simplicity:	10
Impact:	10
Risk Rating:	8

Novell's GroupWise mail server has been around for quite some time. However, there has never been an easy way to recover data from its local e-mail database. GroupWise is a closed architecture that by default stores all e-mail on the GroupWise server and allows you to archive e-mail off it to a local system. However, be aware that some systems are configured to delete e-mail messages automatically after a certain number of days, so make sure to examine the GroupWise server configuration before waiting to capture data.

 UniAccess

One of the few tools available to convert GroupWise data is UniAccess, available from Com Axis at http://www.comaxis.com. UniAccess will allow the conversion of GroupWise data to a number of different formats so you can access the e-mail in one of the other tools we have covered in this book, such as AccessData's FTK. While UniAccess can connect to a GroupWise server to do the conversion, the GroupWise server must exist first for it to work. So in either case you are stuck installing a GroupWise server and recovering the previous mail database.

GroupWise

Many investigators are unhappy when they hear that GroupWise is involved in a case, because few tools are available to access e-mail data directly. Good news may be in the future as Novell is placing the GroupWise suite on the Linux platform. With the support of the Linux community, it may only be a matter of time before new tools are created to solve these problems. Until that day arrives, though, you will have to install a new GroupWise server and configure it to recover the existing mail database to extract the messages.

Sun's iPlanet

Popularity:	5
Simplicity:	10
Impact:	10
Risk Rating:	8

Sun's iPlanet mail server is a UNIX-based mail system that shows its origins in its mail storage. The iPlanet system stores each individual message in a RFC-822 complaint e-mail format within a hive-like directory structure named after the user. This makes your life much easier as you do not have to worry about dealing with proprietary databases for accessing the messages.

Searching RFC-822 and Decoding MIME

To access e-mail and attachments in an iPlanet server, you will need some tools that can search RFC-822 and decode MIME. Paraben's E-mail Examiner and AccessData's FTK will allow you to do this. Using any search utility, you can access the text of the e-mails. For MIME encoding, you can also combine some open-source tools such as MUnpack to extract the attachments for further searching.

CHAPTER 11

E-MAIL
ANALYSIS

According to the global market intelligence and advisory firm IDC, by the year 2006, users will send 60 billion e-mails each day. Nearly half of these e-mails will contain personal information. E-mail is one of the fastest growing forms of communication and one of the most common means for transferring information about people, places, and activities. People will continue to use e-mail and the Internet to conduct business, whether legitimate or not.

This chapter discusses tools and techniques used to reconstruct client and web-based e-mail activities from the perspective of the local hard drive. (Enterprise server investigations are covered in Chapter 10.) Although a single chapter can't cover every tool and technique available today, we do cover mainstream e-mail investigative techniques applicable for use in a corporate environment.

This chapter breaks up content into client-based and web-based e-mail. *Client-based* e-mail refers to programs installed on the client for reading e-mail, such as Outlook Express, Outlook, and generic UNIX readers. *Web-based* e-mail refers to online e-mail resources such as Yahoo!, Hotmail, and Excite that are usually accessed through a browser.

Three key interesting components of an e-mail include the e-mail headers, body text, and attachments. Additionally, other items useful to investigators may include message flags, certificates, or requested receipts for delivering or opening an e-mail.

FINDING E-MAIL ARTIFACTS

In the scenarios that follow, programs and techniques used to view e-mail data and extract relevant artifacts are discussed. If available, we discuss how to use professional products such as Paraben's E-mail Examiner, OutIndex, Guidance Software's EnCase, and Access Data's Forensic Toolkit. Other methods include using the native e-mail client or various tricks to get around simple controls. Remember that multiple tools and methods are available for searching and analyzing this data. Choose the tools and methods that best fit your needs.

Client- and web-based e-mail readers share much in common. Both can have e-mail headers, proofs of receipt, attachments, and more. Both generally follow the same rules as outlined in the RFCs (requests for comments). However, some differences are worth exploring, including the viewing methods, location of the evidence, and how easy it is to access and recover the evidence. We will get into more of this in each of the following sections.

CLIENT-BASED E-MAIL

Popularity:	10
Simplicity:	10
Impact:	8
Risk Rating:	9

Client-based e-mail includes programs such as Outlook and Outlook Express. Client e-mail is typically stored on the hard drive in an e-mail archive. This is important, as it increases the likelihood that you will find the information you need. Client-based e-mail is typically easier to work with than Internet-hosted mail in corporate environments because the e-mail exists on a company-owned asset. In the case of client-based e-mail, typically both the incoming and outgoing e-mails are recorded; this is not always the case for Internet-hosted mail.

An important point for overloaded corporate investigators is ease of access to the mail server. Investigators will have access either to the e-mail on the suspect's computer or the company-owned servers. Either way, this is much easier than demanding e-mail from an externally hosted e-mail provider. In many cases, the latter choice is not practical. (E-mail server investigations are covered in Chapter 10.)

Microsoft Outlook PST

Popularity:	10
Simplicity:	10
Impact:	8
Risk Rating:	9

Outlook, installed with the Microsoft Office suite, is the most popular e-mail client used in large corporations. It is also one of the most popular e-mail archive formats encountered in corporate investigations.

 PST (Microsoft Outlook) Examination Tools

The most well-known tools for reading Outlook files are Paraben's E-mail Examiner, Guidance Software's EnCase, Access Data's FTK, and Microsoft Outlook. For the open-source advocates, a great tool is included in the libPST package.

Paraben's E-mail Examiner works by using a PST converter to translate the contents of the PST file into a generic UNIX mailbox format. The text file is then easily read and searched by E-mail Examiner. Paraben's product supports a large number of e-mail formats and is very fast in converting the PSTs.

You can use EnCase by Guidance Software to open and search the contents of the PST directly. EnCase lets you use the same tool for e-mail that you use for locating other artifacts on the drive.

 If you have EnCase and haven't updated your version from 3.x, you need to do so. The newer versions have much better e-mail support.

Forensics Toolkit (FTK) by Access Data is yet another tool capable of searching through multiple mail files such as Outlook, Outlook Express, America Online (AOL), Netscape, Yahoo!, Earthlink, Eudora, Hotmail, and MSN e-mail.

The open-source tool, readPST, from the libPST package, is a project of SourceForge headed by Dave Smith. When you're done using readPST, you can use UniAccess to convert UNIX mail back into PST and other formats.

Examining Outlook Artifacts

Table 11-1 provides a helpful list of MS Outlook data and configuration files. Some of the folders have hidden attributes. You can change the Windows Explorer view to show hidden files by choosing Tools | Folder Options | View | Show Hidden Files And Folders.

Data and Configuration Files	Location
Outlook data files (.PST)	*drive*:\Documents and Settings\<*user*>\ Local Settings\Application Data\ Microsoft\Outlook
Offline Folders file (.OST)	*drive*:\Documents and Settings\<*user*>\ Local Settings\Application Data\ Microsoft\Outlook
Personal Address Book (.PAB)	*drive*:\Documents and Settings\<*user*>\ Local Settings\Application Data\ Microsoft\Outlook
Offline Address Books (.OAB)	*drive*:\Documents and Settings\<*user*>\ Local Settings\Application Data\ Microsoft\Outlook

Table 11-1. Summary of Microsoft Outlook Data Configuration Files

Data and Configuration Files	Location
Outlook contacts nicknames (.NK2)	*drive*:\Documents and Settings*<user>*\ Application Data\Microsoft\Outlook
Rules (.RWZ)	*drive*:\Documents and Settings*<user>*\ Application Data\Microsoft\Outlook Note: If you use the rules import or export feature, the default location for .RWZ files is *drive*:\Documents and Settings*<user>*\ My Documents
Signatures (.RTF, .TXT, .HTM)	*drive*:\Documents and Settings*<user>*\ Application Data\Microsoft\Signatures
Dictionary (.DIC)	*drive*:\Documents and Settings*<user>*\ Application Data\Microsoft\Proof
Message (.MSG, .HTM, .RTF)	*drive*:\Documents and Settings*<user>*\ My Documents

Table 11-1.   Summary of Microsoft Outlook Data Configuration Files *(continued)*

Examining Artifacts with E-mail Examiner

E-mail Examiner (available at http://www.paraben-forensics.com/examiner.html) simplifies the complexity of the PST mail store by converting it into a generic mailbox format. Because of this simplicity, the search capabilities are excellent. E-mail Examiner runs in a Windows environment and supports a wide variety of mail formats. Support for MS Outlook .PST files is available through Paraben's PST Converter, which is distributed with E-mail Examiner. This is similar to the conversion process used when converting AOL files.

Begin the conversion process by starting the PST Converter. Choose File | Import PST Files to open the PST Converter dialog box shown in Figure 11-1. If you do not see this command on the File menu, go to Program Files\Paraben Corporation\E-mail Examiner, and double-click pstconv.exe.

When the PST Converter dialog box opens, select the PST files to convert into a generic format by clicking Add Files. Carefully select the destination directory, and then begin the conversion process by clicking Convert. When the process is completed (it may take some time for large PST files), the files will automatically appear in E-mail Examiner.

If you used the pstconv.exe utility and you need to open the e-mail later, choose File | Open Mailbox. Select Files Of Type "Generic mail [*.*]" and find the folder in which you previously chose to store the converted files. When this is completed, you will find the e-mail located in the E-mail Examiner window, as shown in Figure 11-2.

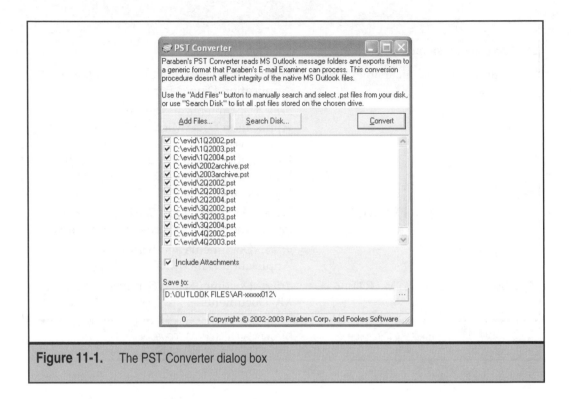

Figure 11-1.   The PST Converter dialog box

If you typically have a large caseload with PST files, consider Paraben's text searcher, which is capable of searching through unique file types such as Outlook PST, PDF, and more.

Be aware that the searching options are robust and will require some learning to take advantage of all the features. Numerous options are available, and just about every view and feature is customizable to some degree. Ready reports are available for quickly producing statistical data based on variables such as word count and e-mail domains used. Options exist for extracting the attachments as well as extracting e-mails into EML and generic mailbox formats. Additional quick-reporting features of interest include the ability to extract all e-mail addresses and all originating servers into a single file.

Examining Artifacts with EnCase

For the expert, EnCase's view of a PST and its MAPI objects proves valuable. Add the filtering, enscript, and searching capabilities to this mix, and you have a powerful tool.

After collecting the evidence relevant to your case, consider using the readily available filters for locating different types of mail files. Simply select Filters in the bottom pane and double-click the filter you would like to use. At this point, you can choose to mount and view the files within EnCase, or you can export them for use in other programs you prefer.

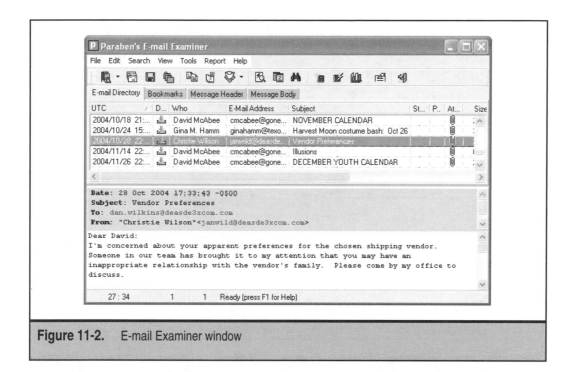

Figure 11-2.   E-mail Examiner window

It's important to remember that a PST is a binary file structure that is not interpreted correctly without mounting the file inside of EnCase. Do this by right-clicking your PST of interest and selecting View File Structure. Then the regular searching features inside EnCase will work on the file.

Figure 11-3 illustrates the selection for viewing the file structure and the filters available for quickly accessing PST files in your evidence. More features are available in the newer versions of EnCase, which continues to improve the experience with PST files.

Examining Artifacts with FTK

FTK is an excellent all-around tool for investigating e-mail files. Principle among its strongest features is the ability to create a full text index of large files. While this is time-consuming up front, the amount of time you will save in large investigations is enormous. A good rule of thumb is that if you are going to search a file only one time, you don't necessarily have to index the file. If you are going to search the file more than five times, you need to consider the value of indexing the files. If you are going to search the file more than ten times, we would hope that you have indexed it already.

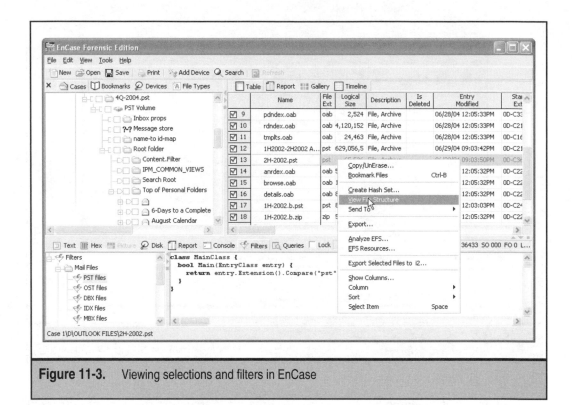

Figure 11-3. Viewing selections and filters in EnCase

An advantage to using FTK is its ability to read PST and OST archives directly by accessing internal structures. The result is that e-mails are automatically indexed during the import process, making them easy to search quickly, especially across multiple mail stores. Keep in mind that FTK can also take EnCase images directly and create a full text index of the entire file. Figure 11-4 shows an example of the interface. Because there is no need to break down the PST, the e-mail is readily accessible right after you get the evidence imported.

Examining Artifacts with Outlook

If no other tools are available, you can use Microsoft Outlook to import and view PSTs. To do this, install and start Microsoft Outlook. When the prompt to create another mailbox appears, select No, and then Continue.

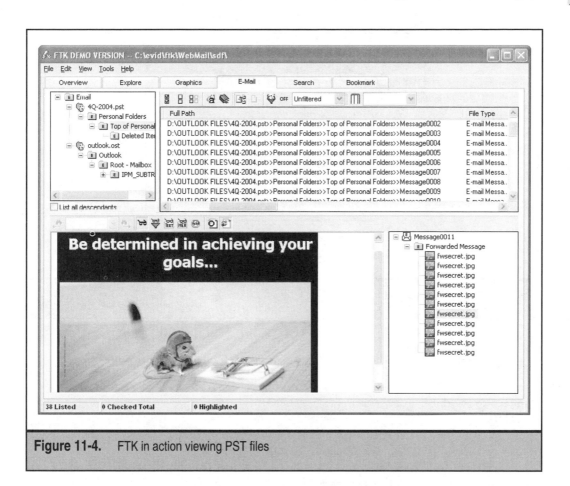

Figure 11-4. FTK in action viewing PST files

When Outlook opens, choose File | Data File Management | Add. Select the correct file type and follow the prompts, as shown in Figure 11-5. When you're done, you can use the familiar Outlook interface to search the PST as you would normally search any mail through Outlook.

Examining Artifacts with ReadPST (LibPST Package)

ReadPST is a program made available as part of the libPST package, which is available from SourceForge at http://sourceforge.net/projects/ol2mbox/. Downloading the libPST package and extracting it will place the contents of the package in the libpst directory on your hard drive. Enter that directory and execute the `make` command.

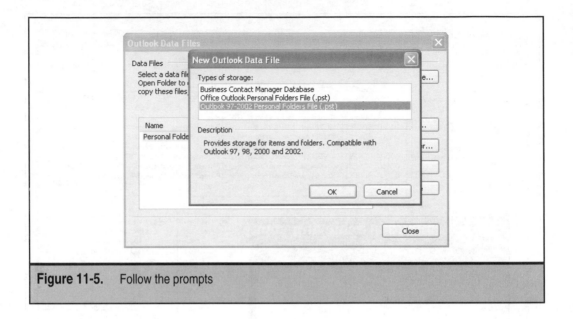

Figure 11-5. Follow the prompts

You can then execute the readPST program with the following options:

```
ReadPST v0.3.4 implementing LibPST v0.3.4
Usage: ./readpst [OPTIONS] {PST FILENAME}
OPTIONS:
        -h      - Help. This screen
        -k      - KMail. Output in kmail format
        -o      - Output Dir. Directory to write files to002
                  CWD is changed *after* opening pst file
        -r      - Recursive. Output in a recursive format
        -V      - Version. Display program version
        -w      - Overwrite any output mbox files
```

ReadPST will the convert the PST into RFC-compliant UNIX mail. You can access the extracted mail and attachments with any standard UNIX mail client. For example, to convert a PST into KDE mail format you would execute this command:

```
./readpst -k mypst.pst
```

Microsoft Outlook Express

Popularity:	6
Simplicity:	10
Impact:	8
Risk Rating:	8

Outlook Express is a common e-mail and Internet news client. It is installed by default on a Windows-based operating system with Internet Explorer. Because it is readily available, some users choose to use it as their default e-mail client. Therefore, the forensic investigator must be prepared to reconstruct the e-mail generated from this program. Table 11-2 shows common data file locations.

DBX (Outlook Express) Examination Tools

A number of tools are capable of reading the Outlook Express DBX files, including the tools listed previously. The steps for importing and examining the data are nearly identical to those used with PST files in the "PST (Microsoft Outlook) Examination Tools" section with a few noted differences, which are outlined here.

Examining Artifacts with E-mail Examiner

E-mail Examiner reads Outlook Express files directly, and the same conversion process used for PSTs is not necessary for DBX files. You can import DBX files directly into E-mail Examiner, as shown in Figure 11-6.

Operating System	Location of Outlook Express Mail Storage
Windows 2000/XP/2003	C:\Documents and Settings*<local username>*\ Local Settings\Application Data\Identities\ *<unique lengthy string>*\ Microsoft\Outlook Express\
Windows NT	C:\winnt\profiles*<local username>*\Local Settings\ Application Data\Identities*<unique lengthy string>*\ Microsoft\Outlook Express\
Windows 95/98/Me	C:\Windows\Application Data\Identities\ *<unique lengthy string>*\Microsoft\Outlook Express\

Table 11-2. Summary of Mail Locations for Outlook Express

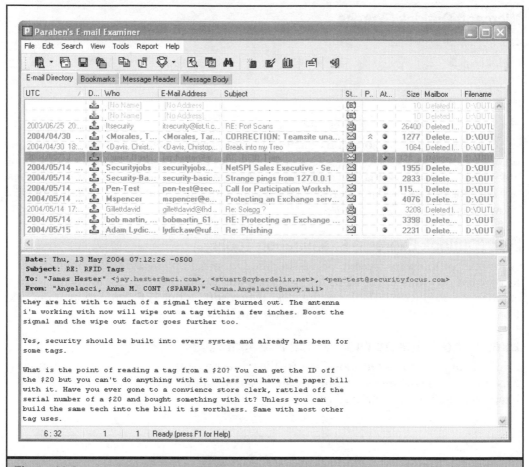

Figure 11-6.   Using Paraben's E-mail Examiner to examine Outlook Express e-mail

Examining Artifacts with EnCase

EnCase still requires that you right-click the files and use the command View File Structure. However, afterwards there are filters and other search tools available to help you with the investigation. In Figure 11-7, we are looking at the deleted e-mail folder for the suspect. Notice that the e-mail is broken out under Deleted Items.dbx and listed as individual files named by subject of the e-mail. You can view the file contents by clicking the file.

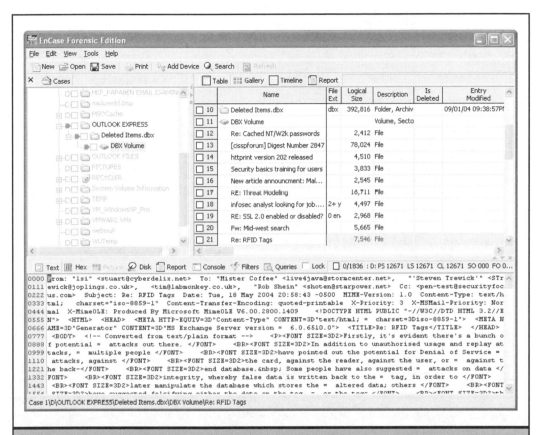

Figure 11-7.   Viewing Outlook Express E-mail with Guidance Software's EnCase

Examining Artifacts with FTK

FTK's operational look and feel is the same for DBX files as it is for PST files. The index and search features are helpful across multiple and large e-mail data containers. Figure 11-8 illustrates how FTK handles Outlook Express e-mail.

Examining Artifacts Using Outlook Express

Importing files into Outlook Express is similar to importing data files into Microsoft Outlook. It is assumed that you understand how to perform this task on your own.

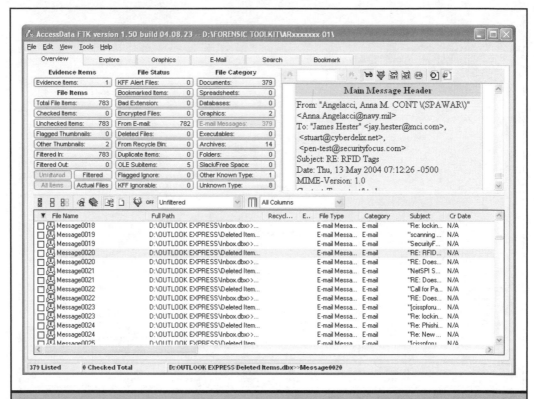

Figure 11-8.   Viewing Outlook Express E-mail with Access Data's Forensic Toolkit

Using readDBX

Like its sister program libPST, libDBX contains a program called readDBX. This program, like readPST, allows an examiner to extract the contents of a DBX file into a RFC-compliant UNIX mail format. LibDBX can be found at http://sourceforge.net/projects/ol2mbox/. Downloading the libDBX package and extracting it will place the contents of the package in the libDBX directory. Enter that directory and execute the make command.

You can then execute the readDBX program with the following options:

```
readdbx - Extract emails from MS Outlook Express 5.0 DBX files into mbox format.
File is taken from stdin unless -f is specified.
Output emails are written to stdout unless -o is specified

Usage: readdbx [OPTIONS]
Options:
        -h              display this help and exit
        -V              output version information and exit
```

```
-f "file"      input DBX file
-o "file"      file to write mbox format to
-q             don't display extra information
```

ReadDBX will convert the DBX into RFC-compliant UNIX mail. You can access the extracted mail and attachments with any standard UNIX mail client. For example, to convert a PST into UNIX mail format you would execute this command:

```
./readdbx -f mydbx.dbx -o mydbx
```

UNIX E-mail

Popularity:	8
Simplicity:	8
Impact:	8
Risk Rating:	8

UNIX mail is commonly used in many organizations, especially among engineering-oriented groups that are accustomed to using Linux and UNIX. With the increasing popularity and ease of use of the Linux desktop, the statistical likelihood of encountering UNIX e-mail is growing.

UNIX Examination Tools

UNIX e-mail, unlike most Windows formats, does not normally contain binary information. Instead, the UNIX e-mail format follows and extends the RFCs and writes out its data as plain ASCII text. Attachments in UNIX mail, however, are encoded with MIME encoding, typically BASE64. This means that while you can search through the text of any e-mail with any standard search tool, you cannot search through the attachments without decoding all of the MIME information. Multiple variations of UNIX mail are available—such as KMail, Vm, and RMail—but they all share the same common characteristics.

Examining Artifacts with E-mail Examiner

E-mail Examiner reads UNIX mail files directly. You can import UNIX mail files directly into E-mail Examiner by choosing File | Open Mailbox and selecting the e-mail store. Another method of importing UNIX e-mail is to drag and drop it on the program window. The net result and view is the same as in the previous examples using Outlook and Outlook Express.

Examining Artifacts with EnCase

EnCase allows you to search through the text of any e-mail, but you cannot search through the attachments without decoding all of the MIME information.

Examining Artifacts with FTK

FTK's operational look and feel is the same again for UNIX mail files as it is for other types of mail files. The indexing and searching features are still advantageous across multiple and large e-mail data containers.

Examining Artifacts with Grep

One of the beauties of UNIX e-mail is how easy it is to use regular grep expressions to search the mail store, because it's a simple text file. Regular grep expressions and searching techniques are covered in Appendix D of this book.

Netscape Navigator and Mozilla

Popularity:	5
Simplicity:	8
Impact:	8
Risk Rating:	7

Netscape Navigator and Mozilla are installed by default by their associated browser installations. These clients are not as popular as MS Outlook or UNIX, but they do exist in a number of organizations.

Netscape Navigator and Mozilla Examination Tools

Netscape Navigator and Mozilla have their own extensions of UNIX mail. Similar to UNIX mail, the Netscape and Mozilla files that constitute the e-mail folders are stored in a directory. All of the tools applicable to UNIX mail are applicable in the same way to Netscape Navigator and Mozilla. If you are dealing with these types of mail stores, review the previous section, "UNIX Examination Tools."

America Online

Popularity:	4
Simplicity:	9
Impact:	9
Risk Rating:	7

AOL is not typically used in corporate environments, but it is popular enough to cover here. If AOL is discovered, the impact can be quite high, because people are more likely to use this for their personal e-mail and let their guard down. Employees are more cautious with their work e-mail than with their play e-mail. It's also quite possible that workers will take their laptops home and check their AOL home accounts using their work machines.

It is important in this section to differentiate among AOL mail that remains on the AOL server, AOL mail archived on the local machine, and AOL mail that is accessed through a browser. In the following cases, we discuss the investigation of AOL's client storage archive.

AOL Examination Tools

America Online uses a proprietary format, and only a few tools can read AOL's PFC files. Three tools discussed briefly here are E-mail Examiner, EnCase, and FTK. Another tool we do not discuss is Hot Pepper Technology's E-mail Detective (http://www.hotpepperinc .com/EMD.html).

Examining Artifacts Using E-mail Examiner

Similar to the same process used by AOL for examining PST files, E-mail Examiner first converts AOL mail files into a generic mailbox format. Begin the conversion process by starting the AOL Converter, shown in Figure 11-9. Choose File | Import AOL Files in E-mail Examiner. Choose the command to open the AOL Converter dialog box. If you do not see this command under the File menu, go to Program Files\Paraben Corporation\ E-mail Examiner and double-click AOLConverter.exe.

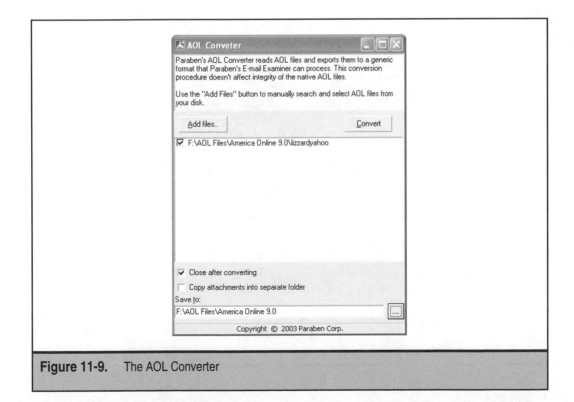

Figure 11-9. The AOL Converter

When the AOL Converter dialog box opens, select the AOL files to convert into a generic format by clicking Add Files. Finally, carefully select the destination directory, and then begin the conversion process by clicking Convert. When the process is completed (it may take some time for large AOL formats), you can view the e-mails in E-mail Examiner. Choose File | Open All E-mails. Select Mailbox type Generic mail (UNIX/mbox) and find the folder where you chose to output the files when you converted them. When this is completed, you will find the e-mail located in the E-mail Examiner window, as shown in Figure 11-10.

As with dealing with any other format using Paraben's tool, numerous options and ready reports are available. You can also extract e-mails into EML and generic mailbox formats.

Examining Artifacts Using EnCase

You may use EnCase if you want to find the e-mail archives in their default location using the provided enscript Initialize Case. However, EnCase does not currently have the ability to decode the archive. If you are not using the scripts now, you can take advantage of a lot of additional functionality inside EnCase by choosing View | Scripts.

You should be aware of several limitations here. First, the initialize script searches only for the files in specific locations. Second, you need to export the files and use a third-party tool for analysis.

NOTE Rather than using EnCase, we recommend that you use E-mail Examiner or FTK.

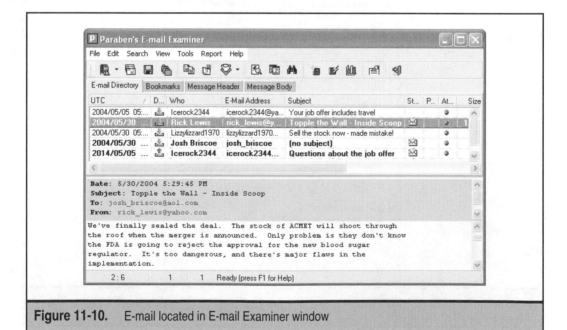

Figure 11-10. E-mail located in E-mail Examiner window

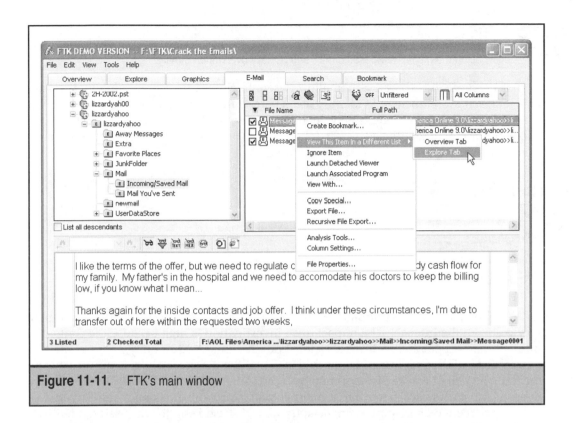

Figure 11-11. FTK's main window

Examining Artifacts Using FTK

FTK's operational look and feel (Figure 11-11) holds the same continuity for AOL mail archives as it does for other types of mail archives. FTK is an easy-to-use tool that decodes the mail archive seamlessly, retrieving e-mail and other items of interest, such as the user's marked Favorites.

Often, multiple mail types appear on a corporate user's computer. The ability of FTK to search, locate, and import multiple mail formats seamlessly is an asset. If you have a user with an Outlook PST and an AOL account, FTK does an excellent job of retrieving data across the different formats.

WEB-BASED E-MAIL

Web-based e-mail such as Yahoo! and Hotmail challenges investigators to find the e-mail on the computer, reconstruct activity, and identify users in ways that are different from client-based e-mail. Depending on the web mail service, where the e-mail is stored, how it is stored, and other factors, you may find nothing, the entire e-mail, or an e-mail remnant.

NOTE E-mail remnants are stored on a drive found on the media during analysis. Examples include previously deleted e-mails, web-based e-mail, and partially overwritten e-mails.

For example, web-based e-mail allows users to choose their own e-mail addresses. This makes it more difficult to identify users than with typical corporate e-mail systems. An address that doesn't definitely identify a user, such as Barney8237@yahoo.com, makes it difficult to identify a suspect. John.Smith@somecompany.com pretty much nails a user's identity.

Internet-Hosted Mail

Popularity:	8
Simplicity:	9
Impact:	7
Risk Rating:	8

Web-hosted e-mail is popular because a number of companies provide free e-mail services from the Internet. The impact to an investigation is high because the content of Internet mail is personal and reveals a lot about the user. Additionally, Internet mail requires credentials, providing further evidence that the user was at the computer during the time the e-mail was read—assuming you can somehow tie the User ID to the suspect. Even so, most users still believe that Internet mail is private and cannot be recovered.

In one recent case involving financial fraud, web-based e-mail was used to identify a single user from more than 200 workers who had shared access to a computer. The user was logging into his e-mail account to delete possible evidence. Using EnCase and a few scripts, we culled the web mail into a readable format. The result was a quick confession and subsequent dismissal.

It takes time and energy to get e-mail logs, attachments, and e-mails from hosted e-mail service providers. In some cases, this effort is definitely warranted. In others, or when you are searching for leads in a case, you will find additional methods useful for recovering cached e-mail. This isn't a perfect world, and at times these methods will not work. For example, if the suspect is using a privacy-friendly browser, you may have to resort to other evidence or consult the web e-mail hosting company to gather the necessary evidence.

NOTE Today's browsers are increasingly more secure than their predecessors. Users are demanding privacy features and paying a premium for the luxury. Unfortunately, this creates a challenge for the investigator. For example, one browser encrypts the cache with Blowfish Encryption, does not use the registry, and does not use index.dat files. If that's not bad enough, all of the session data is securely wiped during and after the session is completed. When this occurs, you have moved from a technical problem to a people problem. You must now either confront your suspect to recover encryption keys or request subpoenas against the e-mail provider to allow you to view the suspect's e-mail logs.

Yahoo! E-mail

Popularity:	8
Simplicity:	10
Impact:	9
Risk Rating:	9

We know that end users are more likely to use web-hosted e-mail for personal business because they feel it's safer. Because of Yahoo!'s popularity and host of services, Yahoo! web mail is common among end users as a way to handle personal business. The interface is simple, and with Yahoo!'s 100MB free space, there is plenty of room to store information.

Yahoo! Examination Tools

These techniques target recovering e-mails from the Internet cache. You can apply the same techniques to other Yahoo! services to recover information from Yahoo! Groups and other locales by re-creating the suspected event and studying the output.

Some key filenames of interest for Yahoo!-related mail include those beginning with *ShowFolder*, *ShowLetter*, *Compose*, and *Attachments*. They include the rendered HTML that was on the screen. It is possible to add the .HTM extension to these files and view them in your browser as the user would have seen them. However, in some cases you may have to remove the script that redirects you to the login page. The script exists to determine whether the session is still active. If this is the case, you can remove the script by editing the file in your chosen text editor.

ShowFolder   The ShowFolder file lists all of the suspect's folders on the left side of the screen when viewed in a web page. The body of the page contains e-mail subject lines with the alias of the person who sent the messages, message dates, and the sizes of the e-mails. This is a quick way to view the type of e-mail the user typically receives.

ShowLetter   The ShowLetter files contain the opened e-mail as seen by the user. Remember that the files are not binary or encoded files, and you can search them for strings using any tool you wish.

Compose   The Compose files contain the e-mail to which the user is replying before any modification is done by the user. Additionally, another Compose file is present when the e-mail is sent as a confirmation that the e-mail was sent. This file contains the username and the name of the intended recipients. Look for the information immediately following the hidden values:

```
input type=hidden name=<field name> value=
```

This is true for TO, CC, BCC, Subject, and 40 to 60 other fields, depending on the message. What's amazing, however, is that the entire text of the message is held as a hidden field. Look for the text following

```
input type=hidden name=Body value=
```

In this particular sample, it looks something like this:

```
<input type=hidden name=Body value="&lt;DIV&gt;
&lt;DIV&gt;
&lt;DIV&gt;You&#39;re nuts!  There&#39;s no way we can get away with
this!  I&#39;m not going to join you in selling weapons
```

Attachments   The Attachments file contains the name of any attachments and the person or group of people for which the e-mail was intended. This file also contains all the same information as the compose field.

Examining Yahoo E-mail Artifacts Using EnCase

EnCase does an excellent job of locating specific strings and ordering files. The search capabilities allow you to find files and e-mail remnants, but it will take time on large volumes. To find Yahoo! files, use the following grep expression for your search. You can export your findings or use an external viewer if you have one.

```
window.open\(\"http:\/\/mail.yahoo.com\", \"_top\"
```

One of the strengths of EnCase is the ease of ordering every file in the system by date, regardless of where the file resides in the hierarchical folder structure. We have used this feature to tie other computer-related events into a cohesive timeline rather quickly.

Examining Yahoo E-mail Artifacts Using FTK

FTK is by far the fastest tool for searching through e-mail files. After acquiring and adding your evidence to FTK, select the Overview tab and then click the Documents button under File Category, as shown in Figure 11-12. FTK is smart enough to recognize these documents as HTML files and will render them as the suspect saw them on his or her computer. In the bottom pane, you can browse through documents until you find something of interest.

Remember, however, that much of the text does not show up here, but is actually in the source of the message as a hidden field. Right-click documents and use the viewer of your choice to see whether more information is contained in the source of the file.

Also remember the powerful indexed searching. If you are looking for something specific enough, you should start with those search terms and try to find corresponding e-mail messages.

Examining Yahoo E-mail Artifacts Using Open-Source Tools

Essentially, once you have the suspect's hard drive, you can find the location of the temporary Internet files. From there, carve out and manipulate the files of interest with the

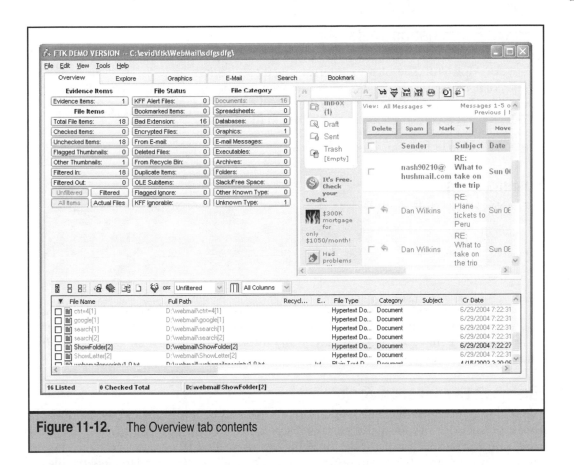

Figure 11-12.   The Overview tab contents

tools you're most comfortable using. This works because the files are not encoded. You can use any tool you wish on the files, such as grep or strings.

Hotmail E-mail

Popularity:	8
Simplicity:	10
Impact:	9
Risk Rating:	9

Hotmail has chosen to expand its mail store to 250MB for personal, free e-mail. As the popularity of this hosted service has grown, so has the use of Hotmail on corporate assets. Again, because of the usually personal nature of web-hosted e-mail, the impact and subsequent risk rating is high.

Hotmail Examination Tools

The tools and methods are the same as those of other types of e-mail, but the files are different for Hotmail. The files of interest are those beginning with *Hotmail*, *doaddress*, *getmsg*, *compose*, and *calendar*. When you're viewing the files in FTK, they will render as obviously Hotmail files and will have the e-mail data in the viewing window.

Here is a search expression to find Hotmail files:

```
/cgi-bin/dasp/E?N?/?hotmail_+#+.css\
```

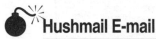 **Hushmail E-mail**

Popularity:	4
Simplicity:	7
Impact:	9
Risk Rating:	7

Although it is still used less often than Yahoo! or Hotmail, Hushmail is growing in popularity. People value their privacy. Employees using Hushmail for personal communications may believe no one can gather any information about their e-mail activities. These employees tend to risk more in their communications.

 Hushmail Examination Tools

What employees usually don't know is that Hushmail never promises client-side security, only security in transit and storage. Depending on how you want to approach the case, you can search for the individual files or use a low-level search for the specific strings. The files are titled beginning with *showMessagePane*. If you try to view the files as HTML files, you will miss most of the information that is buried in the message source.

To dig into the files or search for e-mail remnants, search for the e-mail field you want to find in this format:

```
hushAppletFrame.message.<e-mail field>
```

Figure 11-13 is a screenshot of EnCase being used to find the message inside the file by searching for hushAppletFrame.message and looking for the large splash of highlighted files. This allowed us to clue into the message body and other details rather quickly.

The following is from the source of an e-mail using Hushmail and helps illustrate the fields. Notice that the message body is located in the source, but if you render this in a browser, you will miss this information.

```
hushAppletFrame.message.from = "George Henderson
\<rockondude1999@yahoo.com\>";
hushAppletFrame.message.replyto
= "George Henderson \<rockondude1999@yahoo.com\>";
```

```
hushAppletFrame.message.to = "Dan Wilkins \<danwilkins1970@hotmail.com\>,
nash90210@hushmail.com";
hushAppletFrame.message.cc = "";
hushAppletFrame.message.bcc = "";
hushAppletFrame.message.date = "Sun, 27 Jun 2004 18:34:59 -0700";
hushAppletFrame.message.subject
= "RE: What to take on the trip";
hushAppletFrame.message.hushEncryption
= "";
hushAppletFrame.message.hushKeyblock
= "";
hushAppletFrame.message.body
"Yes - do that.\r\n\r\nDan Wilkins \<danwilkins1970@hotmail.com\>
wrote:Yeah, I agree. This too much money and too easy.
```

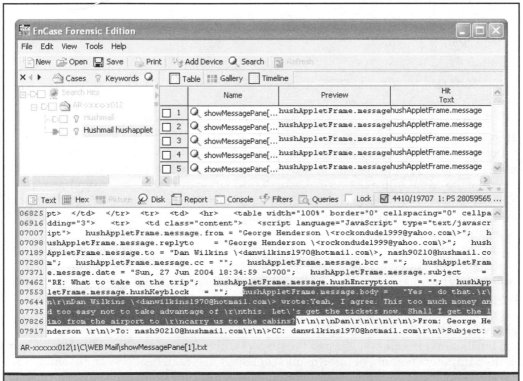

Figure 11-13.   EnCase finding a message inside a file

INVESTIGATING E-MAIL HEADERS

E-mail headers contain general information including the e-mail addresses of who apparently authored the e-mail and the recipient of the e-mail. E-mail headers also contain routing information from the point of origin to the final destination. The servers assemble this information en route to the final destination and attach it to the top of the e-mail. Sometimes, depending on the client used and the e-mail servers, the information contained in the headers helps the examiner trace the origin of the e-mail back to the sender's computer or Internet connection. Other information found in headers includes the type of e-mail client used, the e-mail gateway used, and the names of e-mail attachments. This information is helpful to investigators because it helps tell the full story of what happened or points to other areas to investigate. The headers are constructed more or less uniformly across web-hosted and client-based e-mail.

 E-mail Headers

Popularity:	10
Simplicity:	10
Impact:	5
Risk Rating:	8

The popularity and simplicity values of e-mail headers are high because e-mail programs automatically generate e-mail headers as part of RFC 8-22. Despite the ability to spoof e-mail headers, they are typically accurate in civil cases where it matters (spam aside). The impact to an investigation depends on the nature of the investigation. If e-mail is part of the crime, you must verify header information during your fact-finding routine. E-mail headers have influenced investigations by identifying the originating source of information, the type of computer the suspect may be using, and the completeness of a seizure, among other things.

In one recent example, federal authorities investigated a young man for creating an automatic key generator for a well-known piece of software. The expensive software suite normally sold for hundreds of thousands of US dollars, but the suspect advertised a key generator on his web site for only $10. As part of the seizure, the authorities took the user's work computer and his home computers. The suspect verified that the authorities had seized all of the home computers.

Further investigation suggested the suspect withheld evidence from the legal seizure of his computers because of information contained in e-mail headers. The examiner discovered e-mails on the work asset sent from the user's home network. The e-mail headers contained information about an e-mail client program that was not on any of the computers seized from his home. The net result? The suspect must have used another computer from his home network to send e-mail, and this meant the suspect may have lied about the completeness of the seizure.

When the authorities confronted the suspect because of this find, he caved in and quickly confessed that he had one more computer in the house. This computer had the hard evidence that nailed him.

Examine E-mail Headers

E-mail headers reveal key information about the suspect's computer, the client used, and sometimes the approximate geographic location of the originating e-mail. When you find the e-mail headers, copy and paste them into your logs or text document of choice for easy viewing. This isn't to say that e-mail headers are completely trustworthy, because they can be spoofed. The only authoritative information included in a header is what is inserted by the routing servers. Now let's take a look at some e-mail headers.

E-mail Header Components

A typical e-mail header might look something like this:

```
From root  Mon Jan  6 04:02:16 2003
Return-Path: <root@fw>
Received: (from root@localhost)
        by fw (8.11.6/8.11.6) id h06A2FZ01645
        for root; Mon, 6 Jan 2003 04:02:15 -0600
Date: Mon, 6 Jan 2003 04:02:15 -0600
From: root <root@fw>
Message-Id: <200301061002.h06A2FZ01645@fw>
To: root@fw
Subject: LogWatch for fw
X-IMAPbase: 1010645096 1016
Status: RO
X-Status:
X-Keywords:
X-UID: 819.
```

From: "From:", with a colon, identifies the sender of the message. Unfortunately, this is the easiest component to forge and hence the most unreliable.

From   "From", without a colon, is distinctly different from the From: line in the mail user interface and is not actually part of the e-mail header. This line is often inserted by mail servers upon receiving the mail. This is especially common for UNIX mailers, which use this line to separate messages in a mail folder. This line can also be forged, but not always.

Reply-To: or Return-Path: This line contains the e-mail address for sending replies. This is an easy component to forge and is often not in the headers. In the world of spam, this line is helpful. This field is usually legitimate because spammers want to make money off their e-mail orders.

Sender: or X-Sender   The way this is supposed to work is that mail software inserts this line if the user modifies the From: line. However, most of the mailers ignore this rule, so this line is rarely present.

Message-ID: This is a unique string assigned by the mail system when the mail is created. This is more difficult to forge than the From line, but not impossible.

Received: These are the most reliable lines in the header and can be quite useful in identifying date/time approximations and geographic locations. They form a list of all sites through which the message traveled en route to the recipient. They are forgeable up to the point the message is inserted into the Internet on its way to the recipient. After this, they are authoritative and accurate.

Received: lines are added to the top of the headers as they pass through the mail servers. Therefore, they are read from bottom to top beginning with the server that first handled the e-mail and ending with the server that delivered it to the final recipient. The last (bottom) nonforged Received: line shows the likely starting point for the e-mail.

One easy way to identify fake Received: lines includes using nslookup to identify the purported sender. In the following illustration, mail.yahoo-store.com does not match the given IP address of 64.70.43.79, and instead reveals the message came from mx1.real-coupons.com. Some mail servers will do the reverse lookup for you, as illustrated here:

```
Received: from mail.yahoo-store.com (HELO mx1.real-coupons.com) (64.70.43.79)
by mta291.mail.scd.yahoo.com with SMTP; Tue, 25 May 2004 17:24:13 -0700
```

Other obvious things to check are the time stamps and IP addresses. If the time stamps between successive servers show a negative time, one of them is likely forged. The headers are also likely forged if the IP address contains a number greater than 255 or is an internal address such as 10.x.x.x, 192.169.x.x, 172.16.x.x, or 127.x.x.x.

E-mail Header Locations

E-mail header locations for popular mail programs are provided in Table 11-3. If you are working with another mainstream product or an esoteric mail reader, take a look at http://www.spamcop.net for information on how to find the e-mail headers.

E-mail Client	Location of E-mail Headers
Outlook	Open message and choose View	Options. Headers are in Internet Headers box.
Outlook Express	Select message and press CTRL-F3.
Pine	Press H to view headers. If they are not enabled, go to main menu, press (S)etup, then (C)onfig. Scroll down several lines to Enable-Full-Header-Cmd. Press ENTER. Press (E)xit and (Y)es to save changes. Then press H to display headers.
Netscape Navigator/ Communicator	Click yellow triangle to right of brief message headers to display full headers.
America Online Client	Open e-mail. Find Sent From The Internet (Details). Click Details.
Yahoo!	Open e-mail. Click Full Headers.
Hotmail	From main mail page, choose Options	Mail Display Settings. Select Advanced under Message Headers. Click OK and choose Mail tab to read e-mail with full headers displayed.

Table 11-3.   Header Locations for Popular Mail Programs

CHAPTER 12

TRACKING USER ACTIVITY

The majority of your time during a forensics investigation will be spent reconstructing and tracing the actions that a suspect has taken. This can include what web pages the suspect visited, what documents he created, and other data he may have modified. Finding this evidence is only the first step in the process, however. You must be able to tie that evidence back to the suspect. What good is an incriminating Word document if you can't prove who wrote it?

Especially in the field of digital forensics, proving who was sitting at the keyboard and where documents came from is a nontrivial task. Think back to the news reports of e-mail viruses running rampant. Most of these viruses took advantage of the Office macro language to spread automatically across the Internet. When the writers were caught, it was usually because authorities found some distinctive fingerprint in the code that pointed them to the suspect. For Office files, as will be discussed later in the chapter, this could be a MAC address, a unique identifier, or a timeline reconstructed from metadata. For web browsers, this involves investigating the history and using the cache files and cookies to reconstruct where a suspect went on the Internet and what he did while visiting those sites. The purpose of this chapter is to show you how to perform this digital sleuthing in a way that will stand up in court.

MICROSOFT OFFICE FORENSICS

Office has become ubiquitous in today's modern business world. As such, investigators frequently have to investigate incidents that involve Word documents. This can be trickier than it initially sounds. How do you prove that the suspect wrote the content in the document? How can you tie that document to a specific computer? What methods exist to subvert the Word user-tracking facilities and how can you tell when someone has tried to subvert tracking? With a bit of sound investigation and a couple of tricks, you can pull a surprising amount of information from Word documents, Excel spreadsheets, and other Office applications that can give you a clear picture of the timeline of events.

Since the release of Office 97, Microsoft Office has been notorious for storing a wealth of sensitive information about who authored the document. For example, if you are lucky enough to have a document that was modified with Track Changes turned on, you can pull a wealth of data out of the document. The file stores who made modifications and all the content that was ever included in the document, even if it was deleted, plus information about the filenames and to whom the document was e-mailed. This can be incredibly useful in the process of re-creating a timeline.

NOTE   Microsoft has released a utility called rdhtool.exe for Office 2003 that strips Office documents of all of this metadata. If you stumble onto a document that has no metadata at all, this tool may have been used to cover someone's tracks or as a matter of practice. Take this information in context and make note of the omission in your report.

E-mail Review

Popularity:	8
Simplicity:	6
Impact:	7
Risk Rating:	7

This first appeared in Office 2002 and can be incredibly useful in tying a specific user to a document. When you e-mail a document for review, you may see a dialog box like this when you open the document again:

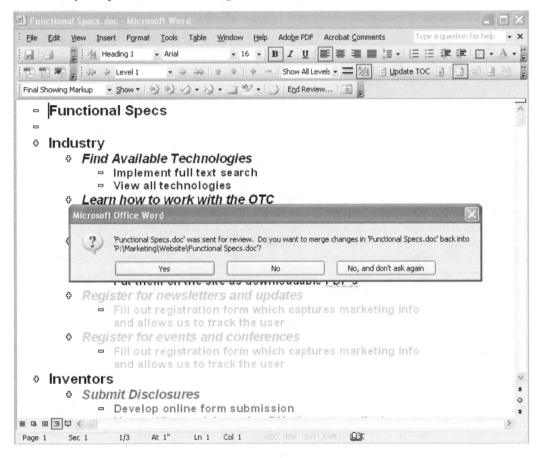

The sequence of events that causes this dialog to appear can provide some very important forensic data. Let's examine this process in detail. When you send an Office document for review in Outlook, several custom properties tags are placed into the metadata of the file. We show the five most important of these tags in the following table.

Tag Name	Format of Tag	Description
_TentativeReviewCycleID	Number	The unique ID of the revision of the document
_ReviewCycleID	Number	Often the same as _TentativeReviewCycleID, also a unique ID
_EmailSubject	Text	The subject of the e-mail message in which the document was sent
_AuthorEmail	Text	The e-mail address of the person who sent the document
_AuthorEmailDisplayName	Text	The display name (what shows up in Outlook) for the e-mail address

To view this data in any Office application, choose File | Properties, and then click the Custom tab. You will see a Properties dialog similar to that shown in Figure 12-1. As the figure shows, the information contained in these custom tags is incredibly useful for tying a user to a document.

Let's turn our attention for a second to the tag _ReviewCycleID. As you can see from Figure 12-1, this is a number that appears to be some kind of identifier. In fact, it's the number that Office uses to determine whether it needs to merge changes back into an original document. So the next natural question is, Where does Office store the ID number outside the document for comparison? Actually, an old .ini-style file is placed in the user's Application Data folder, which stores all this information. The file is placed in *<User's Documents and Settings DIR>*\Application Data\Microsoft\Office. The file, depending on the version of Office, can be named either Adhoc.rcd or Review.rcd. Let's take a look at a snippet of the Review.rcd created for our file:

```
[DocSlots]
NextDoc=29
Doc22=3839962597
Doc24=1518299362
Doc26=1030839747
Doc28=4246392232

...
[4246392232]
Path=C:\Documents and Settings\Aaron Philipp\Desktop\Forensics Exposed\
Chapter 12 data\figure 2.doc
Slot=Doc28
Url=file:///C:\Documents%20and%20Settings\Aaron%20Philipp\Desktop\
Forensics%20Exposed\Chapter%2012%20data\figure%202.doc
```

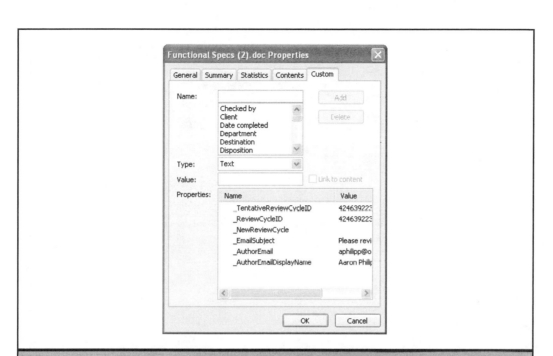

Figure 12-1.   The custom tags that Outlook adds to an Office document

Recall from Figure 12-1 that the `_ReviewCycleID` property value for our document was 4246392232. As you can see in the snippet from Review.rcd, an entry for this document shows that it was in fact e-mailed from this machine by username Aaron Philipp. Not only that, but the e-mail address (property value `_AuthorEmail`) from which it was sent and the subject of the e-mail (property value `_EmailSubject`) are also displayed, so you should be able to go back through the Exchange server and dig up the message itself.

Recovering Undo Information

Popularity:	8
Simplicity:	6
Impact:	7
Risk Rating:	7

If a Word document is saved with Quick Save turned on, you can extract the undo information from the document. Look at the document shown in Figure 12-2. It seems to contain only one sentence.

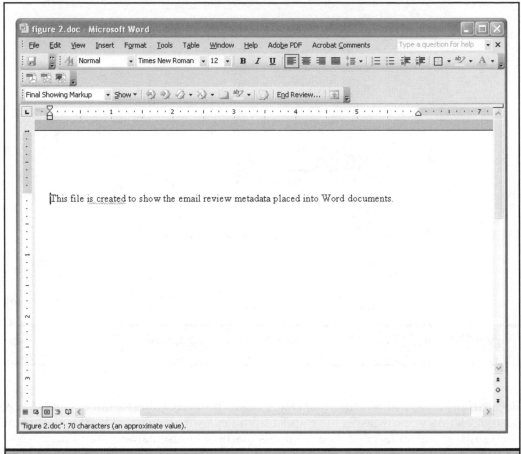

Figure 12-2.   A Word document that has been modified and quick saved

First off, the thing to understand here is why Quick Save exists. When a document gets big, it can be very time-consuming to save the document, tying up resources and basically slowing down the whole show. With Office's Auto Save feature, saving can become distracting and time-consuming while you are working. So Quick Save was created to save documents quickly and painlessly with minimum disruption to the user. The way that it does this is by not making changes to the body of the document; rather, it appends the changes, and information about where the changes appear goes at the end of the document. Once a certain file size is exceeded, the save goes back, incorporates all the changes into the main body of the document, and shrinks the file size back down. From a forensic investigation standpoint, this can be a great thing because data that a user *thinks* is deleted actually still exists in the document.

Let's go back to our example. If you open the file in a binary editor (I recommend XEmacs for non-forensics work), you can look for information that may have been "deleted" but not removed from the file. As you can see in Figure 12-3, a simple search of the document reveals information that appears as though it were still included in the document.

To confirm, we open Word and perform an undo to see what comes back. As you can see in Figure 12-4, the data in Figure 12-3 was deleted from the document, and you have recovered it.

This technique will work through multiple changes to the document and can actually go pretty far back in the revision history. You can typically find the data you are looking for using a keyword text search on the document using a tool such as EnCase or a binary editor, and then go back into Word to reconstruct the document.

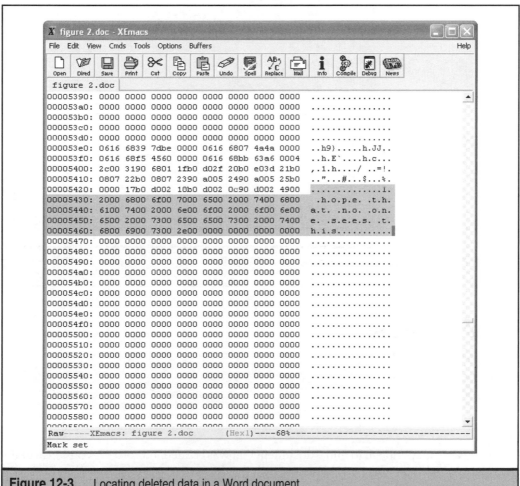

Figure 12-3. Locating deleted data in a Word document

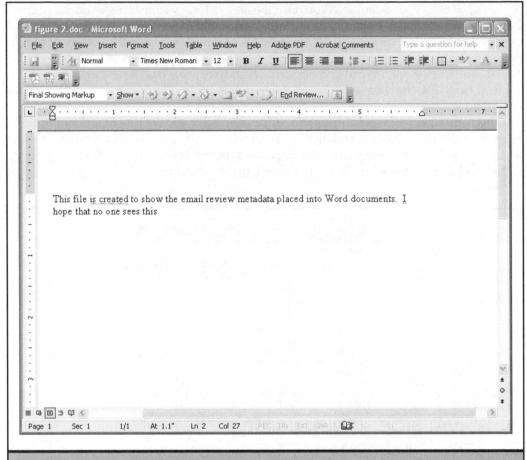

Figure 12-4.   The data after a single undo

Word 97 MAC Address

Popularity:	8
Simplicity:	6
Impact:	7
Risk Rating:	7

If you are lucky enough to find a document that was created in Word 97, you can actually get the MAC address of the machine on which the document was created. A Media Access

Control (MAC) address is like the fingerprint of a network card. A MAC address is typically a number formatted like so: 00-09-5B-E6-24-5D. In the Word document, however, it's formatted a bit differently. Take a look at Figure 12-5, which shows the MAC address in the document itself.

To find the MAC address in a document, open the file in a binary editor and do a search for *PID*. This will bring up the entry. Let's look at the PID-GUID for the Melissa virus document:

```
PID_GUID {572858EA-36DD-11D2-885F-004033E0078E}
```

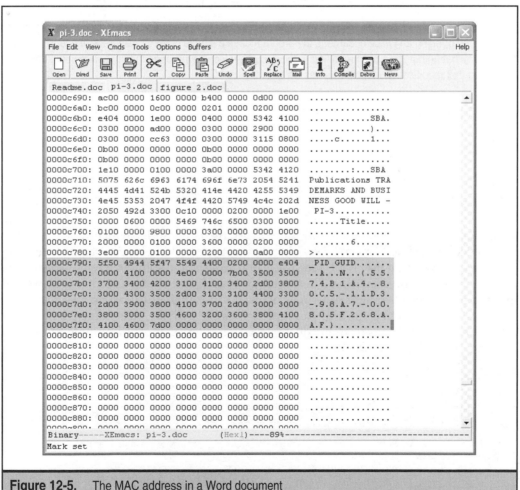

Figure 12-5.   The MAC address in a Word document

If you look at the last chunk of data, *004033E0078E*, and break it down, you get *00-40-33-E0-07-8E*; this is clearly the MAC address of the machine on which the document was created. It must be stated, however, that this number can be modified and is nonauthoritative.

> **TIP** You can do a basic check for a MAC address by looking at the first three pairs of numbers in the MAC address; this is the vendor ID. You can use any number of Internet database lookup sites to find out who owns that MAC address and who created the card. If you are certain that you know on what machine a document was created, you can use this information for cross validation purposes. If the vendor ID and the actual maker of the card do not match, that is a red flag that tampering has occurred.

> **NOTE** When opening an Office document, the program does a couple of very basic file size checks to make sure that nothing has been modified. If the document won't even open in Office, that should be a red flag that modification of metadata has occurred.

Past Filenames

Popularity:	8
Simplicity:	6
Impact:	7
Risk Rating:	7

Older Office documents actually store every filename under which they have ever been saved in the file. This can be very handy if you are looking for directories to go after or network drives that may have been used, or if you need to subpoena removable media to conduct further investigation. The key to this technique is that the filenames are stored in Unicode instead of straight ASCII, so you need to use an application such as strings.exe from Systernals to extract the files. Running strings.exe with the –u argument will output only Unicode text strings from the document. Here's an example of running the strings program on a Word document:

```
Strings -u tester.doc
Strings v2.1
Copyright (C) 1999-2003 Mark Russinovich
Systems Internals - www.sysinternals.com
...
D:\mystuff\test.doc
...
Times New Roman
Root Entry
C:\draft.doc
```

As you can see, multiple filenames and paths are stored in the doument. You can then use your image to trace back these files, and if they point to network shares you can use this data as a reason to conduct further discovery during litigation.

Working with Office Documents

When working with Office documents, remember to be creative and always look beyond what you see when you open the document. You can pull a wealth of information from these documents if you know where to look for it. In fact, ENCASE has built support for reading and searching the unicode into the latest version so as to make this type of investigation easier. One caveat, however, is that the data is nonauthoritative by itself. If you base your court case solely upon this data, you are going to have a bad time. Use this information to corroborate evidence you've obtained from other sources or to develop new leads that you can follow. That said, a little bit of time with an Office document and a low-level editor can point you in the direction you need to go to investigate your case effectively.

TRACKING WEB USAGE

As an investigator, you will frequently find yourself reconstructing a user's web activity. Lucky for you, it seems as though everyone who decides to write a forensic tool writes it in a way that reads a browser's cookies and history. The process of going through the working files and reconstructing activity is actually pretty straightforward, and when properly validated it can be reasonably authoritative. To understand what we are going to be looking at, let's discuss what kind of records a web browser would keep that denotes user activity. First, you have to look at what sites a user visited while using the browser. This information can be obtained from the history file, which stores information on every URL a user has loaded, going back for months. Even if a user has tried to cover her tracks by deleting the history, it may still be recoverable and useful in an investigation. Once you have the URLs that she has visited, you need a way to find out what she did while she was there. Conventionally, this is done using two methods: by looking at the cookies for the site to determine user behavior or reconstructing the web pages from the temporary Internet files. Let's look at how to conduct an investigation for the two most popular browsers: Internet Explorer and Mozilla/Netscape.

Internet Explorer Forensics

Internet Explorer (IE) has been the default web browser for the Microsoft Windows platform since Windows 95. In fact, later versions of Windows have built IE to interact very closely with the operating system, opening some interesting paths for forensic investigation of activity. Covering your tracks in IE is a nontrivial task. Even if you delete the history using the IE facilities, it can still be recovered because of the close interaction with the OS.

Viewing the History

Popularity:	8
Simplicity:	6
Impact:	10
Risk Rating:	9

The history utility in IE, shown in Figure 12-6, creates a convenient audit trail for what a user likes to do on the Internet. It can be used to show whether the user frequents certain types of sites, if she lands on a site inadvertently, and what she is doing when. This information is useful in everything from policy violation cases all the way up to criminal activities.

NOTE ENCASE comes with an enscript that will automatically search the image for IE history and present it in a report format. If you have ENCASE this can greatly speed your investigation, although make sure you understand what the script does and how it does it.

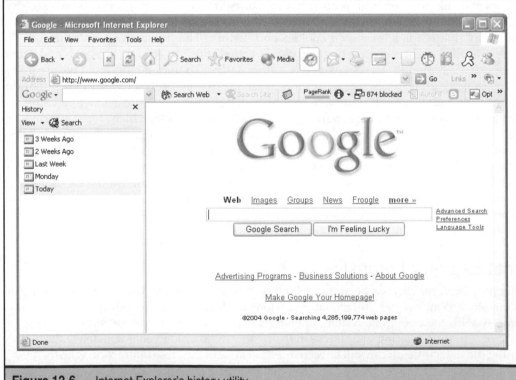

Figure 12-6. Internet Explorer's history utility

Filename	Description
C:\Documents and Settings\ *<username>*\Cookies\index.dat	The audit trail for the cookies that are installed on the system. Useful in locating cookies that are intentionally misnamed and obfuscated.
C:\Documents and Settings\ *<username>*\Local Settings\ History\History.IE5\index.dat	The history for the last calendar day that the browser was in use. Files older than one day roll into a separate folder.
C:\Documents and Settings\ *<username>*\Local Settings\ History\History.IE5\ MSHistXXXXXXXXXXX\ index.dat	Where the history data rolls to after it expires from the above index.dat. Each installation will have several of these directories, indicating yesterday, last week, two weeks ago, last month, and so on.
C:\Documents and Settings\ *<username>*\Local Settings\ Temporary Internet Files\ Content.IE5\index.dat	The audit trail for supporting files such as pictures and includes on the Web site. Look here to help reconstruct documents.
C:\Documents and Settings\ *<username>*\UserData\index.dat	This index.dat holds information about automatic Windows accesses to the Internet, such as Windows update and other utilities.

Table 12-1. Breakdown of File Entries in Windows XP

Luckily, as long as you know where to look, you can use tons of tools to make this job very easy for you. For the sake of demonstration, we will use a freeware command-line utility from Foundstone called Pasco. While completely devoid of any kind of flash or bells and whistles that other commerical products have, it gets the job done. It takes an index.dat file and converts the data into a tab-delimited format. Once you have that, you can import it into Excel and slice and dice it as you see fit. Then the fun begins. If you do a search for index.dat, you will find about five to ten entries. As you can quickly see from looking at any one of them, several different types of entries are included. Table 12-1 shows a breakdown of those that exist in Windows XP, their location, and what each one does.

If you are investigating an older version of Internet Explorer, here are some directories and file locations to look for that will hold the same information:

▼ C:\Windows\Cookies\index.dat

■ C:\Windows\History\index.dat

■ C:\Windows\History\MSHistXXXXXXXXXXXXXXXXXXX\index.dat

- ■ C:\Windows\History\History.IE5\index.dat
- ■ C:\Windows\History\History.IE5\MSHistXXXXXXXXXXXXXXXXXXX\index.dat
- ■ C:\Windows\Temporary Internet Files\index.dat (only in Internet Explorer 4.*x*)
- ■ C:\Windows\Temporary Internet Files\Content.IE5\index.dat
- ■ C:\Windows\UserData\index.dat
- ■ C:\Windows\Profiles*<username>*\Cookies\index.dat
- ■ C:\Windows\Profiles*<username>*\History\index.dat
- ■ C:\Windows\Profiles*<username>*\History\MSHistXXXXXXXXXXXXXXXXXXX\index.dat
- ■ C:\Windows\Profiles*<username>*\History\History.IE5\index.dat
- ■ C:\Windows\Profiles*<username>*\History\History.IE5\MSHistXXXXXXXXXXXXXXXXXXX\index.dat
- ■ C:\Windows\Profiles*<username>*\Temporary Internet Files\index.dat
- ■ C:\Windows\Profiles*<username>*\Temporary Internet Files\Content.IE5\index.dat
- ▲ C:\Windows\Profiles*<username>*\UserData\index.dat

Now that you know where to look, let's examine how these interconnect and how you can use them to trace user activity. The first place you want to go is to the main history to locate what web sites the user has visited. Here's a listing of the History.IE5 directory:

```
06/29/2004   01:22 PM                 163,840 index.dat
06/14/2004   09:48 AM    <DIR>                MSHist012004060720040614
06/21/2004   09:05 AM    <DIR>                MSHist012004061420040621
06/28/2004   11:12 AM    <DIR>                MSHist012004062120040628
06/28/2004   11:12 AM    <DIR>                MSHist012004062820040629
06/29/2004   10:14 AM    <DIR>                MSHist012004062920040630
```

As you can see, five different directories start with *MSHist01* followed by a string of numbers. Let's decipher the sequence that MS uses for this structure.

The number *2004062820040629* looks pretty meaningless at first glance. If you break it up a bit, though, a pattern emerges: *2004-06-28* and *2004-06-29*. If you look at the created time, this suspicion is verified. This is how you tell what dates the directory holds. For our purposes, let's try to find an event that occurred on 2004-06-28, so we would use the index.dat in MSHist012004062120040628. You would go into the directory and actually extract the data from the file.

```
C:\Documents and Settings\<user>\Local Settings\History\History.IE5\MSHis
t012004062120040628>"C:\Documents and Settings\<user>\Desktop\Pasco\pasco
```

```
.exe" index.dat | more
History File: index.dat

TYPE,URL,MODIFIED TIME,ACCESS TIME,FILENAME,DIRECTORY,HTTP HEADERS
,URL,:2004062120040628: <user>@http://www.gnu.org/copyleft/gpl.html,Wed Jun 23
11:37:15 2004 ,Mon Jun 28 16:12:12 2004 ,URL  ,,URL
```

This is one line from the raw output of pasco. As you can see, several fields are stored in the record. You need to determine what each one represents, as shown in Table 12-2.

For those who are unfamiliar with the command line, you can use the following command to dump the history into a text file that you can import into Excel:

```
Pasco <location of index.dat> > <output file>
```

Once you have created the text file and imported it into Excel, you should see something similar to the data shown in Figure 12-7.

From here, you can filter and sort the data to find the information relevant to the case. Most of the all-in-one forensics investigation tools have facilities for searching the history. That being the case, there is still something to be said for this method, because you can leverage the powerful searching and sorting features of a tool like grep or Excel to help speed the investigation along, while still having a step-by-step process to show the court.

Field Name	Explanation
TYPE	The type of request that was made. This will usually be a URL for a GET request.
URL	The actual URL requested along with the name of the user who requested it.
MODIFIED TIME	The time that the page was loaded into the history.
ACCESS TIME	The time that the history entry was last accessed. Through the course of normal operation, this will be the date of loading until the history file rolls back into an older directory; then it will be the date that the entry was added to the aged index.dat.
FILENAME	Used if redirection needs to occur; when a URL is requested this will be URL.
DIRECTORY	The same thing as FILENAME but for the directory. Blank on a URL request.
HTTP HEADERS	Holds any headers that may have form data or whatnot for POST requests. Blank for URL requests.

Table 12-2. What Each Field Represents

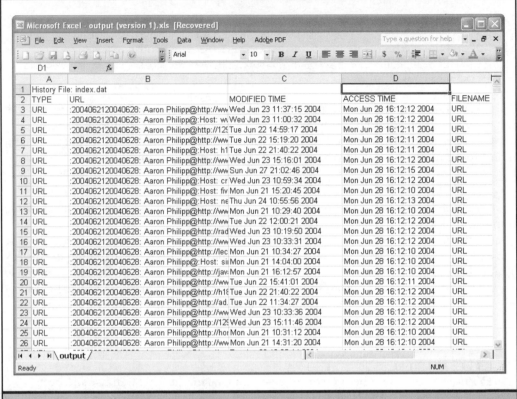

Figure 12-7. History data imported into Excel

Finding Information in Cookies

Popularity:	8
Simplicity:	6
Impact:	10
Risk Rating:	9

Cookies have become the predominant way for web sites to store tracking information about their users. Every time you automatically log into a site, it remembers you and a cookie is involved. A cookie is a small text file earmarked with special data that is pertinent to a specific web site. The information held in these cookies can be invaluable to forensics. Often, the cookie holds information about the username, the user's preferences, and the frequency with which he or she visits the site. Like the history process, pulling information out of cookies is a straightforward process, but the devil is in the details. The first thing you want to do is investigate the history file in the C:\Documents and Settings*<username>*\ Cookies\ directory. This file is identical in structure to the main index.dat files, but instead of URLs, this stores the history of cookies. Here's a line of sample output:

```
TYPE,URL,MODIFIED TIME,ACCESS TIME,FILENAME,DIRECTORY,HTTP HEADERS
URL,Cookie:<user>@imrworldwide.com/cgi-bin,Sun Mar 21 05:25:33 2004 ,Thu
Jun 24 15:08:31 2004 ,<user>@cgi-bin[1].txt,,URL
```

The most notable aspect is the fact that the FILENAME field is populated with the name of the cookie as it's stored on the local hard disk. Notice as well that the filename of the cookie has nothing to do with the web site from which it came. Some of the "shadier" web sites will often name cookies to make it more difficult for you to discover that they are tracking you. This is why it's important to use the history file, because it will show you from where the cookie originated and what server-side code produced it. Since the cookie history is identical in structure to the other histories, you can use the same techniques to search and find specific filenames of cookies.

Oftentimes, the mere existence of a cookie is enough to show that a user was visiting a site. But sometimes you'll need to delve deeper into the user activity and look inside the cookie itself. To do this, you can use a Foundstone tool called galleta. It operates identically to the history tool that we used in the preceding section. A cookie is nothing more than a data structure with a series of variable names and values. However, several fields of metadata are of interest and need explanation, as shown in the following table.

Field Name	Description
SITE	The name and URL of the site from where the cookie came
VARIABLE	The name of the variable stored in the cookie
VALUE	The value stored inside the variable
CREATION TIME	The time the cookie was created, when the web site was accessed
EXPIRE TIME	When the data inside the cookie expires; if a web site pulls a cookie with expired data, it will expunge it and create a new one
FLAGS	Enumerates the flags set for each variable in the cookie; for a complete list of the flags refer to the RFC on cookies

Here is a line created from the galleta program run on a popular web site, www.google.com:

```
C:\Documents and Settings\Admin\Cookies>"C:\Documents and Settings\
Admin\Desktop\galleta\galleta.exe" "admin@google[1].txt"
Cookie File: admin@google[1].txt

SITE      VARIABLE      VALUE    CREATION TIME    EXPIRE TIME     FLAGS
google.com/     PREF     ID=7757897559c7c13d:FF=4:TB=2:LD=en:NR=10:TM=1063258910:
LM=1076737164:S=VyefrLtaPC0FoJTZ         Sat Feb 14 05:39:23 2004      Sun Jan
17 19:14:07 2038       1536
```

Here you can see the variable PREF (presumably for user preferences) with a string value that Google accesses every time this browser goes to the home page. You can often look to cookies to validate that a user spent time and actually logged into a web site and didn't just land on it by accident.

Reconstructing Activity from the Cache

Popularity:	8
Simplicity:	3
Impact:	10
Risk Rating:	9

To speed up the browsing of the Internet, IE caches most of the pages you visit on your hard drive in case you want to go back. Good for forensics examiners, bad for suspects with something to hide. If you can navigate the maze that is the caching structure, you can re-create pages that the user saw and interacted with, including their forms data. There is a problem with caching Internet files, however. Think about what would happen if you cached everything under its original filename. The number of collisions in the cache would render the cache nearly useless (consider the number of pages named index.html, for example). As such, Microsoft has created a naming system that prevents that from occurring. In the cache directory, an index.dat file maps the pages on web sites to files and directories in the cache.

The process for finding things in the cache is identical to the process for finding things in the history. Convert the index.dat to a readable format, slice and dice it to find the files that are important to the investigation, and then use the FILE and DIRECTORY fields to locate the files themselves. This time, the directory that we care about is C:\Documents and Settings\<*Username*>\Local Settings\Temporary Internet Files\Content.IE5\.

Let's look at sample output from the index.dat file:

```
TYPE    URL     MODIFIED TIME    ACCESS TIME      FILENAME        DIRECTORY
HTTP HEADERS
URL     http://hp.msn.com/17/7M{T57_]6423LU+]0D]QKP.jpg Sat Jun 26 00:52:59 2004
        Mon Jun 28 22:01:05 2004        7M{T57_]6423LU+]0D]QKP[1].jpg    0PQLIJYD
        HTTP/1.1 200 OK  Content-Length: 2547  Content-Type: image/jpeg  ETag: "
6ee55ded175bc41:8b1"  P3P: CP="BUS CUR CONo FIN IVDo ONL OUR PHY SAMo TELo"
```

Let's try to make sense of this mess. First, notice that the original URL ties back to an MSN site. You can see a date when it was added to the cache and a date when it was last accessed. The areas where this differs from the history are the FILE, DIRECTORY, and HTTP HEADERS fields. The header field can hold valuable information about the context in which the file was retrieved. The two fields we care most about, however, are the FILE and DIRECTORY fields. These will locate the file in the cache for us. Take a look at the directory structure of the Content.IE5 directory:

```
06/29/2004  11:12 AM   <DIR>          .
06/29/2004  11:12 AM   <DIR>          ..
06/29/2004  10:17 PM   <DIR>          0PQLIJYD
06/30/2004  01:28 PM   <DIR>          S3LJ2IJT
06/30/2004  01:28 PM   <DIR>          UX7W5OVQ
02/12/2004  04:47 PM   <DIR>          W1OJKR87
02/12/2004  04:47 PM   <DIR>          WDQZGTMN
06/29/2004  10:17 PM   <DIR>          WLUFOTEF
06/30/2004  01:28 PM   <DIR>          YNMJAHUB
```

As you can see, several directories have very obscure names. However, if you look at the DIRECTORY field in the index.dat entry, it says *0PQLIJYD*, one of the directories in the hierarchy. Thus, if you go into that directory, you will find a file named 7M{T57_]6423LU+]0D]QKP[1].jpg, or the same value as the FILENAME field. You can repeat this step until all the files for a page including graphics and includes are located, allowing you to reconstruct the page completely that the user loaded and interacted with. The reconstruction process allows you to show pages as the user saw them and interacted with them by evaluating the base HTML documents and then resolving all the links.

Tips for Working with Internet Explorer

Working with IE can quickly get messy. The key to performing investigations on IE-related activities is to understand the overall scheme of how IE stores data. IE always uses an index.dat to serve as a lookup table to find the history, cache, and cookies for the username it's logged in as. As long as you completely understand both the structure of the index.dat and the structure of the data to which it refers, you will be OK. If you try to perform investigations without fully understanding this scheme, you will get lost. Many tools automate this process to one level or another. But realize that even if you use an automated tool, if you are called to testify about the results you must understand what the tool is doing. Don't fall into the temptation of using a graphical tool as a crutch.

Mozilla/Firefox Forensics

Mozilla/Firefox (Mozilla from here out) is the primary browser used in open source circles. It was born out of the "crash-and-burn" that Netscape went through back in 1998. It has been ported to every major operating system and is commonly the Linux browser of choice. Its design focuses on cross-platform compatibility, so the information and metadata that you will be looking for is commonly kept in a file with an industry standard format as opposed to the IE way of doing things. This being said, you will have to deal with some interesting artifacts of the way it was developed (such as the history format) during your investigation.

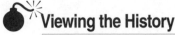

Viewing the History

Popularity:	8
Simplicity:	6
Impact:	10
Risk Rating:	9

The Mozilla history format (MORK) is an example of what happens when open source goes bad. MORK replaced the standard Berkeley database format (DBM), and no one really knows why. In fact, the format is listed as a bug on the Mozilla development tracker. Only one free option is available for viewing the history, a Perl script called Mork.pl. This will extract the history data and put it into plaintext or HTML. If you are working an investigation and must look forensically at the history file, you might want to check out a tool called NetAnalysis, which we will use in the case study, to perform the searching. To become familiar with the format, however, let's look at what the Perl script gives us. The location of the history file will vary based upon operating system. In Windows, the file will be located at C:\Documents and Settings\<*user*>\Application Data\Mozilla\Profiles\<*profile name*>\history.dat, and for Unix/Linux it will be in the ~/ .Mozilla/Profiles/<*profile name*>/history.dat. Now that we know where to look, let's see what we get:

```
1088622307      2          http://www.otc.utexas.edu/"
1088622301      3          http://www.mozilla.org/start/
1088622301      3          http://www.mozilla.org/start/1.7/
```

As you can see, three columns of data are presented. The first column is the last access time in microseconds. The next column represents the number of times that the URL has been accessed. This can be useful in showing that a user didn't just inadvertently end up on a Web site and was actually a repeat visitor. The third column is the URL that was accessed by the request. This is good for a cursory check of what a user was doing on a machine. A ton more information is included in the file that can help with an investigation. Unfortunately, because of the file format, you are going to have to learn to decipher it yourself or buy a tool that does it for you. Unless you have a degree in computer science or at least a strong background in linguistic computing, I recommend the latter.

Finding Information in Cookies

Popularity:	8
Simplicity:	6
Impact:	10
Risk Rating:	9

What Mozilla lacks in a history file format it makes up for with cookies. All of the cookies that the client has are stored in a central file, cookies.txt, which is in the profile directory. If you open it, you will notice that this file is human-readable and no special tools are required to view it. Let's look at a few lines of the file:

```
.amazon.com   TRUE /     FALSE  1089187200  session-id-time   1089187200
.amazon.com   TRUE /     FALSE  2082787201  ubid-main         430-1652529-3243032
.amazon.com   TRUE /     FALSE  1089187200  session-id        104-0716758-6083948
```

This is the cookie and variables for amazon.com, as you can see in the first column. The second value is the flag that says whether or not the cookie allows the POST command. The third column, a directory entry, tells the site for which URLs and sub-URLs the cookie is valid. The fourth value is the flag indicating whether the cookie is used on a secure (SSL/TLS) site. The end of the metadata information contains the expiration time of the cookie in milliseconds. Finally, the last two columns are the variable name and value. As you can see from the entry, this information can be useful because you can see that a session was created with Amazon, denoting a login.

Reconstructing Activity from the Cache

Popularity:	8
Simplicity:	7
Impact:	10
Risk Rating:	9

Cache browsing in Mozilla is actually an easy process. If you can get hold of the cache directory in the profile, you can use Mozilla to navigate it. Make sure that you make the cache read-only and that you properly hash everything before and after doing this, since you will be accessing the data with a non-forensics tool. That being said, fire up Mozilla with the profile of the suspect. Then, in the browser bar, enter the URL **about:cache**, as shown in Figure 12-8.

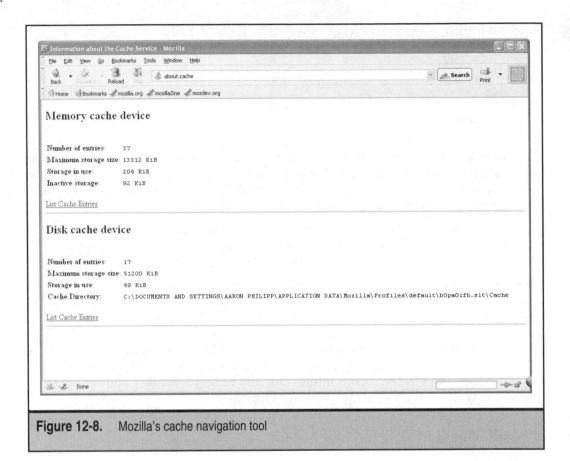

Figure 12-8. Mozilla's cache navigation tool

You are concerned with the cache on the disk, so first ensure that the Cache Directory is set correctly and then click List Cache Entries. After you do this, you will see a listing of every file in the cache along with metadata, as shown in Figure 12-9.

If you need to drill down even further on a specific URL, you can click it to get more information, as shown in Figure 12-10.

As you can see in Figure 12-10, you are presented with everything you would want to know, and more, about the file. The most important part is the local filename, which tells you where to look on the file system to find the cached data. You can use this information to reconstruct entire pages with images and all includes.

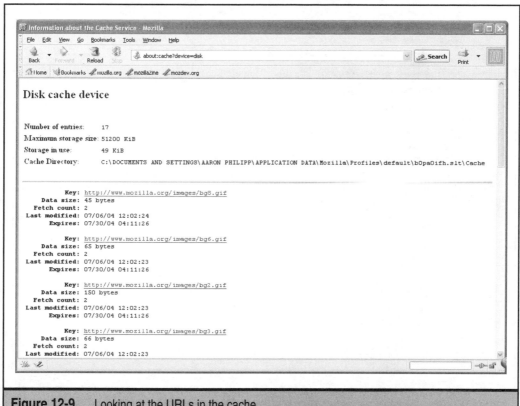

Figure 12-9. Looking at the URLs in the cache

Tips for Working with Mozilla

History file aside, Mozilla is much easier to work with during an investigation than Internet Explorer. Everything you need to look at is consolidated into one central location and the formatting is well documented. In addition, unlike IE, the location of the files stays relatively the same from operating system to operating system. The downfall of Mozilla during an investigation, however, is the history file. If you are doing an investigation that you think may end up in court at some point, save yourself the worry and effort and purchase a tool that can decode the history file for you and present the data in a meaningful manner. As mentioned regarding IE forensics, however, do try and understand what you know and don't know about the format. Several good resources on the MORK format are available; read through these before you use a graphical tool.

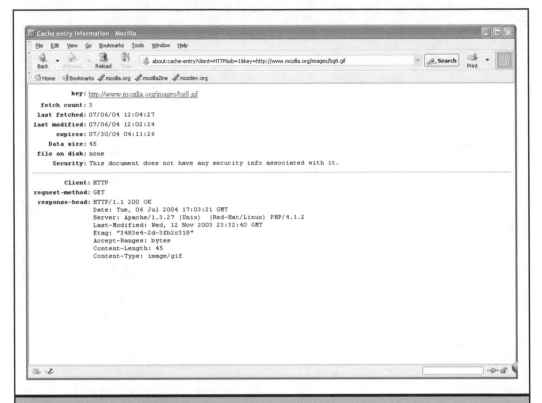

Figure 12-10.   Getting information about a specific URL

Case Study: Using NetAnalysis to Perform an Investigation

NetAnalysis is a graphical tool that makes investigation of web activity easy by pulling everything into one place. Let's look at how you can use this tool to do a complete web investigation.

This case involves an employee who is suspected of working with competitors to leak corporate secrets via the competitor's web site. The suspect was allegedly hacking into servers that contained secret information. We want to find out whether the user's web activity tells us anything about the hack. The user has Windows XP with Mozilla/Firefox as the browser.

Our first step is to check the history and determine whether he has accessed the competitor's site. After we have created a forensic copy of the user's web browser profile and are properly documented, we open the history in NetAnalysis, as shown next. We do this by choosing File | Open History.

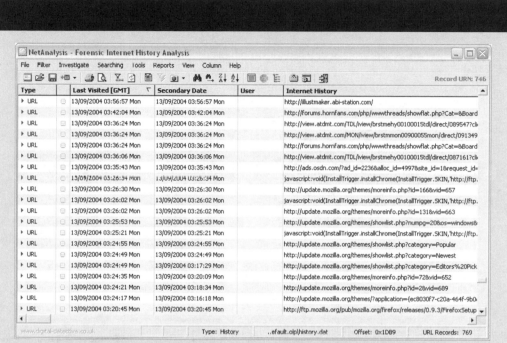

Once open, we can see exactly what our suspect has done. Let's see what he was searching for with Google. The best way to do this is by using a filter. Let's add one for searches we're looking for by choosing Investigate | Google Search Criteria. This will limit the history only to the queries made in Google.

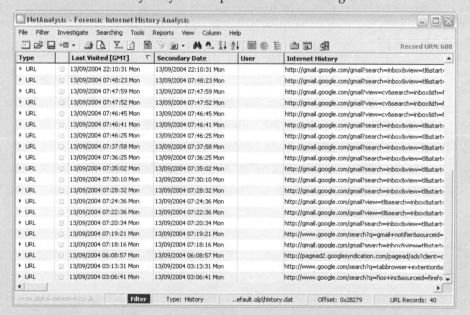

As you can see, the suspect used Google heavily (in fact, he even had a gmail account), as pretty much anyone who uses the Internet does. Let's search the queries that he made and see if he was trolling around for corporate secrets or passwords.

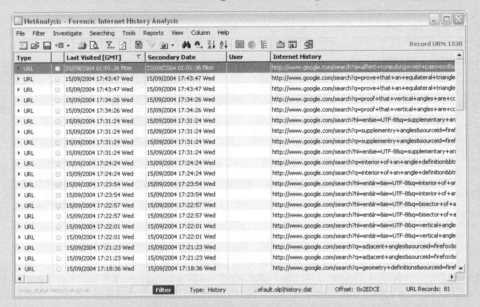

As you can see, he was definitely looking for things he shouldn't have been looking for with Google. This is a common pre-hack tactic to find out information about the company as well as passwords. Next, we follow proper forensic procedures to tag and bag the evidence and create our report for the higher ups.

CHAPTER 13

CELL PHONE AND PDA ANALYSIS

A friend of mine once called personal digital assistants (PDAs) the "pigeons of the technology world." They are small, mobile, absolutely everywhere, and can really make things messy for you unless you're paying attention. All kidding aside, it is true that these devices have permeated our lives, and people are tied to them in ways they never thought possible. On a daily basis, I interact with no less than three PDAs. My wife has a Palm-based device, my cell phone is a combo Mobile Windows/phone, and work has issued me a BlackBerry.

We've come a long way from simple PDAs that just maintain contacts, keep your schedule straight, and allow you to take notes. Today, PDAs have wireless access to corporate e-mail servers and can surf the Web at broadband speeds—in color, mind you. They can also run database applications, create documents with embedded graphics, create spreadsheets, act as clients to terminal services, be cell phones, and—oh, yeah—keep your contacts and schedule straight. Today's PDA is really a computer in every sense of the word; in fact, part of this chapter was authored on my PDA while I was flying home from a business trip. Because PDAs are capable of so many things, it stands to reason that they would be more prevalent during investigations, and, indeed, they have become so.

In the "old" days—prior to 2001—analysis of PDAs was difficult and usually meant using a combination of tools to get the job done. A typical Palm analysis involved backing up the device and using a Palm emulator to see the system as the user did. Today, the forensic examiner has a much wider range of options, from tools that are specifically designed to do nothing but acquire and analyze PDAs, to tools that include this feature as part of a suite of functions.

In this chapter, we cover several types of PDA collections, including Palm OS and Mobile Windows. We also look at various tools and discuss their analytical and reporting capabilities.

GATHERING PDA EVIDENCE—THE COLLECTION

As with everything else in life, there is always a beginning, and in the world of forensics, the work begins with the collection phase, usually my least favorite because it oftentimes takes place in a hostile or semi-hostile environment. People generally aren't thrilled to have a bunch of investigators walking around, picking things up, and bagging evidence.

Mobile Device Power and Peripherals

Popularity:	8
Simplicity:	9
Impact:	10
Risk Rating:	**9**

Before you can collect anything, you must take physical custody of it, a topic that has already been covered in this book. PDAs are just like any other piece of electronic evidence and require the same chain of custody, documentation, and proper handling procedures. However, additional requirements must be met for PDAs that are not needed for desktops, laptops, or servers. Two key requirements are power and peripherals. If you fail to understand these requirements, you may lose your evidence.

Keep Devices Powered and Collect Peripherals

Remember that unlike other types of systems discussed in this book, many PDAs don't have hard drives. These devices store the operating system, basic applications, and anything else the manufacturer doesn't want you to lose on a ROM chip. RAM is the place where your data and any other applications that are added after you purchase the device are stored. The data on the ROM chip will survive if power is lost to the PDA, but data in RAM (that is, your evidence) will not survive.

Therefore, you must ensure a constant supply of power to the PDA for as long as it's in your custody. A great many people have gone through the collection process, gotten these devices into their evidence lockers, and then left them there with no power for weeks—to find out that the batteries are dead when they finally get around to the acquisition stage. "Boss, I've got some bad news," and the conversation can only go downhill from there.

Next are the peripherals. It's very important that you include entries in your collection checklists for the additional items needed when dealing with PDAs; these include the following:

- ▼ Cradle
- ■ Power supply
- ■ Secure digital cards
- ▲ Compact flash cards

Just as you must think about collecting CDs from a desk where you seize a PC, you must think about collecting the storage media that PDAs use.

If collecting the cradle and power supply at the scene is not possible, for whatever reason, you must remember that you don't know exactly how long the device has been off the charger, and time literally is running out on the battery. Therefore, you may want to include some PDA peripherals as part of your standard deployment kit. If, however, you don't have the budget to build an inventory of PDA cradles and power supplies, vendors such as Paraben distribute PDA collection kits that have all the cables and other items you'll likely need.

Imaging Palm PDAs

Popularity:	7
Simplicity:	8
Impact:	9
Risk Rating:	8

Prior to 2001, when a PDA forensics breakthrough allowed easier access to the devices, a typical Palm analysis involved backing up the device and using a Palm emulator to see the system as the user did. The drop in price of PDA devices and the increasing number of form factors using Palm make it the most widely adopted operating system for PDAs and smart phones. People are also quite comfortable with their Palm devices because they are typically close at hand and easy to use. Because of this, the likelihood of relevant data lying around is good.

Collecting Evidence: Palm OS Device Using PDA Seizure

Paraben's PDA Seizure was announced on September 10, 2001, during the High Technology Crime Investigation Association (HTCIA) International conference in Long Beach, California. Hundreds of us sat in a full auditorium waiting for our breakout session on PDA forensics to begin, and when it was over we all knew that PDA forensics had just gotten a whole lot easier. It was the first tool specifically designed to acquire Palm-based and Windows CE devices as its sole purpose; lots of us in that room signed up to be beta testers. The tool has evolved since then, and it now supports Mobile Windows and Research in Motion's (RIM's) BlackBerry.

As with other forensic tools, PDA Seizure creates forensic image files, provides for authentication and verification of data integrity via MD5, and has search and reporting functions. The software also allows the analyst to recover deleted files, launch associated applications, bookmark items of interest, and, in the case of Palm OS systems, launch an emulator allowing for interaction as if working with the device.

Acquisition with PDA Seizure

Make sure the Palm device is powered, in the appropriate cradle, and correctly connected to your acquisition system via either USB or serial port. Disable your Palm Desktop HotSync if you have it running on the acquisition system. HotSync can cause errors during the acquisition. PDA Seizure loads all the appropriate drivers needed to communicate with the Palm device without having to install the Palm Desktop.

1. Start acquisition of a system in PDA Seizure by selecting Tools | Acquire Image or by clicking the Acquire button in the toolbar. This launches the Acquisition Wizard, as shown next:

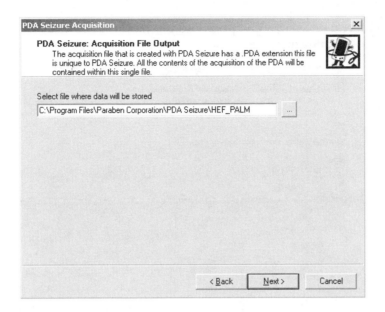

2. After selecting the location of the output .PDA file, choose the type of system to be acquired.

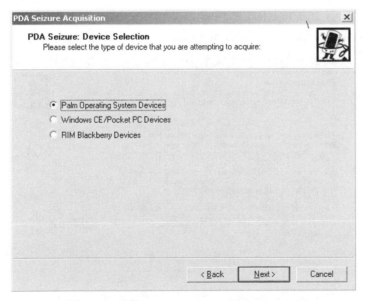

3. Specify the connection settings by selecting the port and speed to be used as well as the option to acquire physical memory and/or logical files. I highly

recommend selecting both options, so you have complete copies as well as flexibility during analysis.

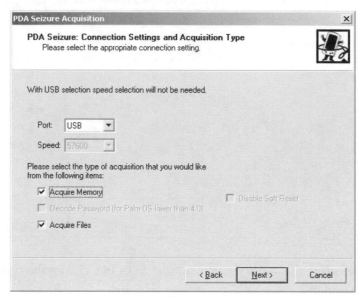

4. If you've chosen the Acquire Memory option, you'll need to place the device in Console Mode—that is, debug mode.

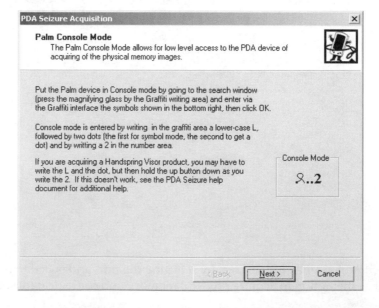

How you get the Palm device into Console Mode depends on the generation of device you're working with. For older models, it involves entering a specific set of characters consisting of a lowercase cursive *L* followed by two single dots in the left-hand graffiti area, and a number 2 in the right-hand graffiti area, as illustrated.

In some of the newer models, the process involves holding the Down scroll button and performing a soft reset, while continuing to hold the Down scroll button for another 10 seconds. If you happen to be working on a model that slides open to reveal the reset button on the back, you've got some extra fun in store. While juggling the cradle, you'll have to coordinate your finger on the Down scroll button and stick a really small object in the reset hole.

Determining when the device is in debug mode is fairly easy based on the model. For older systems, a slightly longer tone followed by a shorter tone tells you the device is in debug mode. Newer systems will show a blinking square in the upper-left corner of the screen.

Additional options during acquisition are as follows:

▼ **Decode Password**   Decoding the password on a Palm-based PDA is determined by the operating system version. Prior to version 4.1, the password can be decoded directly through Console Mode on the device with the aid of third-party software. Post version 4.1, no known recovery techniques are available for password recovery on the device.

▲ **Disable Soft Reset**   This option is used if you want to leave the device in Console Mode after the acquisition is finished. The only significant issue to contend with in this scenario is that the device will drain power faster in Console Mode.

After the memory acquisition finishes, or if you've chosen to perform a logical acquisition, the wizard continues and you must initiate a HotSync.

NOTE   Even though the logical data is also in the physical data, the methods PDA Seizure uses to obtain them can differ. The HotSync protocol is used to obtain the logical data, and the debug protocol is used to obtain the physical data. As with any other kind of media, the time required to obtain the data will vary on how much data there is, connection speeds, and other factors.

After the logical acquisition is complete, you can begin the analysis portion.

Analysis with PDA Seizure

The PDA Seizure interface is divided into four tabs: Files, Search, Graphics, and Bookmark. The Files tab lists all the logical files in the image and their relevant metadata information, identifies whether the files reside in RAM or ROM, and indicates their MD5 hash value. Double-clicking a file will open the PDA Seizure file viewer, allowing you to see the contents of the file in text, hex, or a picture if it's an image.

Similar to other forensic tools, the Search tab is where all the real work gets done in most cases. You can perform text string searches across all the acquired data here. Any matches to the search are displayed in the lower pane, with a view of the text directly in front of and behind the search term. Each row in the lower display represents a different instance of the matched keyword, even though multiple instances of the same word may occur in the same file. Selecting any of the rows in the lower pane will display the complete text in the upper pane. The example shown in Figure 13-1 involves a fictional employee who wishes to take confidential patent info. A search for the word *after* was conducted, and the illustration shows the results.

Figure 13-1, PDA Seizure's search interface, shows a match for our highlighted keyword. Directly above the text associated with the highlighted item is a default warranty memo from Palm.

Other useful functions of PDA Seizure include the ability to bookmark findings, view all graphic files, export files, and report and launch associated applications—all of these options will be discussed in further detail later in the chapter when we get into Windows CE and Mobile Windows analysis.

Focusing on Palm-specific functions for now, we get to the Palm Operating System Emulator (POSE), which allows the analyst to interact with and see the data as the original user did. The POSE interface displays a virtual device that lets you select menus, open memos, access the calendar, and perform other functions, as if you were working on a physical Palm device.

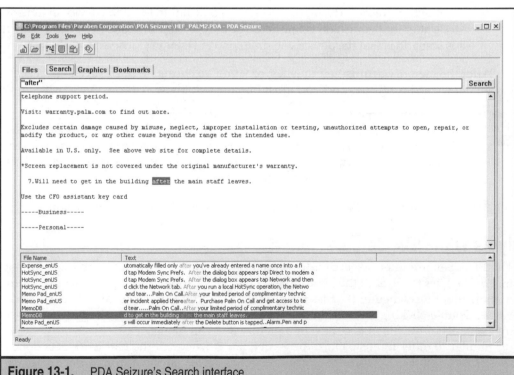

Figure 13-1.   PDA Seizure's Search interface

The current version of PDA Seizure supports emulator functions for the following types of devices:

▼   Palm, Palm Pilot, Palm III, Palm IIIc, Palm IIIe, Palm IIIx, Palm V, Palm Vx, Palm VII, Palm VII(EZ), Palm VIIx, Palm m100, Palm m125, Palm m130, Palm m500, Palm m505, Palm m515, and Palm i750

■   ARM Ref

■   Symbol 1500, Symbol 1700, Symbol 1740

■   TRGpro

■   HandEra 330

▲   Visor, Visor Platinum, Visor Prism, and Visor Edge

The process of starting a POSE session is fairly straightforward and begins by exporting all of the files from the PDA Seizure image file.

1.   Select Tools | Export All Files from the PDA Seizure menu. This will open a dialog box that will allow you to save the files to the location of your choice.

2.   Start POSE by selecting Tools | Run Palm Emulator, or by clicking the Palm Emulator button in the toolbar. Select New, as shown in the next illustration:

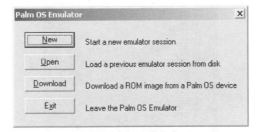

3.   Load the ROM image that was exported from PDA Seizure, as shown next:

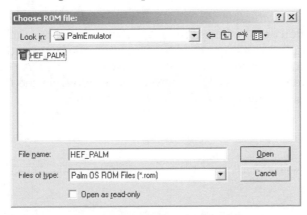

The New Session dialog box will open:

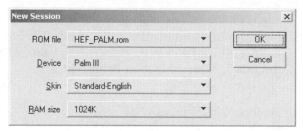

4. The POSE session will begin. To view specific files in the active POSE session, drag and drop the icon from the RAM export folder onto the main POSE screen, as shown next:

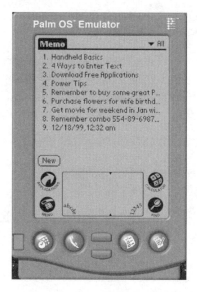

Viewing specific information about each memory card installed in the Palm device at the time of acquisition can also be useful during the course of the analysis. This information includes free and allocated space, user information, the last time the Palm device was synced, and other information, all of which is also part of the PDA Seizure report.

To access this information, choose View | Image Info from the PDA Seizure menu. This will open the PDA Information dialog, as shown next:

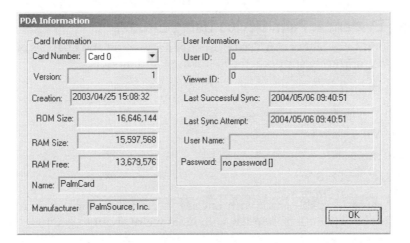

Palm OS Naming Conventions

The naming conventions of Palm OS databases are straightforward and make it easy when you're doing analysis for the first time. For example, NetworkDB is where network connection information such as ISP, type of connection, and username are stored. Also, it's not difficult to figure out what you're likely to find in ToDoDB, MemoDB, and AddressDB. As shown next, PDA Seizure displays the data quite nicely.

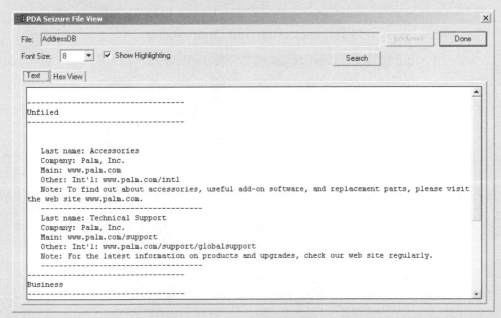

Collecting Evidence: Palm Device Using EnCase

EnCase versions 3 and higher can also be used for acquisition and analysis of Palm-based devices. EnCase currently supports the following Palm models:

▼ Palm IIIx, IIIxe

■ Palm V series

■ Palm VII series

■ Palm m series

▲ Up to Palm OS 3.5

If you've done forensics work with EnCase in the past, or if you've read previous chapters in this book, you'll be familiar with what we're about to get into.

Acquisition with EnCase

As with the previous acquisition example, make sure the Palm device is powered, in the appropriate cradle, and correctly connected to your acquisition system via either USB or serial connection. If you have the Palm Desktop HotSync installed on the acquisition system, it should be disabled.

1. Launch EnCase and put the device into Console (debug) Mode by entering the appropriate characters in the graffiti area.

2. After the device is in Console Mode, click the Add Device button.

3. Choose Local and Palm Pilot in the Add Device dialog.

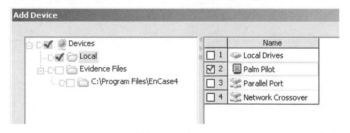

4. You will now be able to preview the contents of the device in the Cases tab and can navigate throughout the different files and/or apply search terms. If you then need to obtain a forensic image of the device, the process is the same as with a hard disk. Find the icon of the Palm device in the Cases tab, right-click it, and choose Acquire from the menu.

   At this point, the wizard allows you to select a password, compression, and evidence file output path, just as you would with any other media. Obviously, the time required to obtain the image will depend on the speed of your connection to the device, the amount of data, and your acquisition system's resources.

Analysis and reporting of a Palm-based device in EnCase is the same as with any other media, as discussed in Chapter 6.

Imaging Mobile Windows and Windows CE Devices

Popularity:	8
Simplicity:	8
Impact:	9
Risk Rating:	**9**

Like the Palm OS, Microsoft's PDA operating systems have been evolving over the years. Unlike Palm, however, Microsoft has chosen to make the Mobile Windows architecture much less dependent on databases, and it incorporates an architecture similar to other Windows systems. Mobile Windows devices pack some serious functionality, including mobile versions of some of the best-selling Office applications as well as virtual private network (VPN) capability out of the box.

Collecting Evidence: Mobile Windows/Windows CE Device Using PDA Seizure

Unlike Palm-based systems, PDA Seizure does not load drivers to communicate with a Windows CE/Mobile Windows device. Therefore, you will need to load Microsoft ActiveSync on the system being used to acquire the device. Before acquisition can begin, make sure the device is powered, in the appropriate cradle, and correctly connected to your acquisition system using the Guest partnership.

 If you don't use the Guest partnership, you will start synchronizing the PDA with your own data, which will really win you points with the boss (not).

Another difference from a Palm OS acquisition is the PDA Seizure Client file, CESeizure.dll, which is a 4K file that is placed on the device in the first available block of memory and removed at the end of the acquisition. Although the insertion of this file seems to violate one of the cornerstone rules of forensics, which is don't alter the original media, the architecture of a Windows CE/Mobile Windows device requires the introduction of this approach to obtain a copy of the physical memory. When this aspect of the acquisition was discussed during the product introduction at the 2001 HTCIA International Conference, the room was filled with law-enforcement folks and district attorneys who all saw it as a purely technical issue dictated by the architecture of the device. The question to ask is, "Do you want some of the data or do you want all of the data?" If you want it all, the introduction of the file has to be done. Continued development of the product is focused on finding a way to acquire the memory without using the DLL.

To counter a possible argument that key files you may find during your analysis could have been altered as a result of the CESeizure.dll installation, it may be a good idea to do a logical file acquisition first. Since CESeizure.dll is required only to obtain the physical memory and is only a single block size, if you have a copy of the logical files with their corresponding MD5 hash values in a completely separate PDA Seizure image taken prior to the physical acquisition, you can compare those hash values with the files that are taken with the use of the CESeizure.dll. Armed with the MD5s prior to the installation of CESeizure.dll, you'll be able to prove to a mathematical certainty that files found during the analysis were not altered. Additionally, PDA Seizure includes a function to compare .PDA acquisition files, so both can be easily viewed side-by-side.

Windows CE/Mobile Windows Acquisition with PDA Seizure

The Windows CE/Mobile Windows acquisition dialog has four options from which to choose.

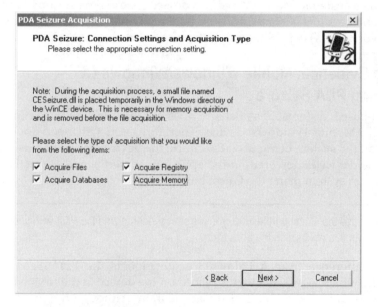

▼ **Acquire Files and Acquire Databases**   Produces the same results as a logical acquisition of a Palm-based system, as described earlier.

■ **Acquire Memory**   The physical acquisition.

▲ **Acquire Registry**   Be prepared for the acquisition to take some time; however, any good analyst knows the importance of being able to look at registry entries in any Windows-based system.

Other unique facets of Window CE/Mobile Windows analysis include the architecture itself. While Palm keeps everything in databases, Microsoft uses databases and files, including DLLs and executables, much like other versions of Windows.

If you acquire the memory, it can be searched like unallocated space in a Windows-based PC; however, complete files associated with any search results cannot be reconstructed at this time.

 Anyone who has done analysis of a Windows-based PC will be very comfortable with a Windows CE/Mobile Windows analysis as compared to Palm-based devices.

Windows CE/Mobile Windows Analysis with PDA Seizure

At this point, the image has been created and brought into PDA Seizure. You will quickly notice the difference in OS architectures and file types between Palm and Windows.

The latest versions of Mobile Windows include a Terminal Services client, MSN Messenger, Pocket Internet Explorer, and Pocket versions of Microsoft Office applications, including Word, Excel, and Outlook, which all come installed standard. However, even if you're comfortable doing analysis of Windows-based systems, you should not think that working with a Mobile Windows/Windows CE environment is a walk in the park. Yes, you're going to find a list of web sites visited in Index.dat, you're going to find an Internet cache in the Temporary Internet Files folder, you're going find a Cookies folder, and you'll be able to analyze some of the data in the same ways as you do in other Windows environments. However, you're not going to find e-mail in a .PST file; instead, you'll find e-mail divided among different databases. You're not going to find contacts in any .PST or .WAB file; instead, you're going to find that information in the Contacts database.

One of the other things to contend with includes the fact that Word and Excel documents are converted to and from Pocket Word and Pocket Excel formats when the PDA is synced. Most Pocket Word documents can be opened by its "un-pocket" counterpart without issue, but that's not the case for Pocket Excel documents. In such cases, you'll need to take the exported .PXL document and convert it back to the Excel format before you can view them outside of the PDA environment.

Earlier in the chapter, you read about analyzing bookmarks, viewing graphics, launching associated applications, exporting files, and reporting functions of PDA Seizure. To help illustrate these, let's examine our fictional case—an employee wants to take patent information associated with internal project number 156987 from his employer, COMPANY XFZ, and sell it to a competitor.

Bookmarking Data

Searching the image based on the fictional project number 156987 has yielded five matches, as shown in Figure 13-2. One match is in an e-mail, one is a Pocket Excel document, and three are Pocket Word documents.

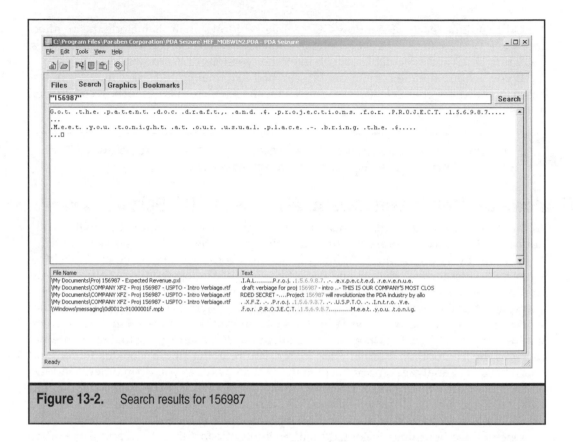

Figure 13-2. Search results for 156987

Looking at the text of the file in the upper pane of the Search tab, you can easily see that it matches the preview of the file identified as 0d0012c91000001f.mpd, located in the Windows\Messaging folder. So you know that this is the body of an e-mail from the employee to the potential buyer. This is a significant find in the investigation, so you'll want to bookmark the text for inclusion in your final report. To do so, select the relevant text in the upper pane, right-click, and select the Bookmark option, as shown in Figure 13-3.

Navigate to the Bookmarks tab, shown in Figure 13-4, and you'll see a list of all the currently bookmarked files, including the filename, a short preview of the bookmarked text, and the descriptions entered. From the Bookmarks tab, you can review, edit, or delete any bookmark.

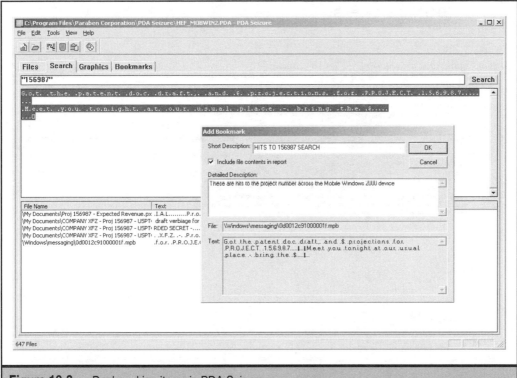

Figure 13-3. Bookmarking items in PDA Seizure

Viewing Graphics

We've all heard that a picture is worth a thousand words, but it's important for you to remember that sometimes a picture is what the whole case may be about. As with many other forensic tools, PDA Seizure has a convenient way to display all the graphics found on the PDA at once. Just click over to the Graphics tab, and there you have it. Since Mobile Windows has an Internet cache, you'll see the images associated with visited web sites, images that were transferred to the device via infrared or sync, as well as those that come with the device.

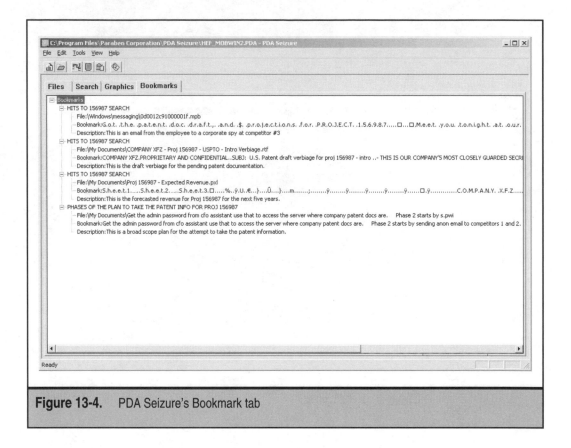

Figure 13-4. PDA Seizure's Bookmark tab

If you want to get a better look at any graphics file you may find of interest, double-click to open the PDA Seizure File View dialog box, as shown in Figure 13-5.

Running Associated Applications

Again, as with most other forensic tools, PDA Seizure allows you to view relevant files in their associated applications. It's just always a plus to view files as they were meant to be instead of as plaintext. Obviously, you can't view files of interest in their associated programs if those programs aren't loaded on your system, so the built-in viewer in PDA Seizure can at least get you most of the way.

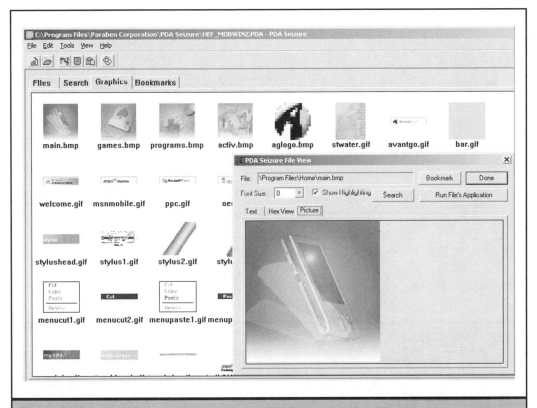

Figure 13-5.   PDA Seizure's Graphics tab and PDA Seizure File View dialog box

One of the useful tools in any PDA is the ability to create an impromptu drawing, or just write down your thoughts in freehand. In our example, the suspect took advantage of this and created a freehand drawing that was later found during the course of the investigation. In a Mobile Windows/Windows CE environment, these .PWI files can be opened by Microsoft Word, as shown in Figures 13-6, 13-7, and 13-8.

Exporting Files

After reviewing some files, you may need to export copies of them from the image. To do so, select the file from the Files tab, right-click, and select Export. The file will automatically be saved to the PDA Seizure folder.

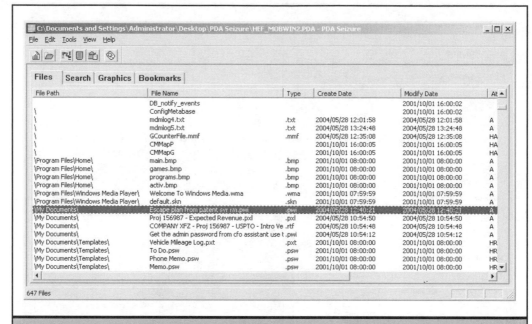

Figure 13-6. Viewing the document in PDA Seizure

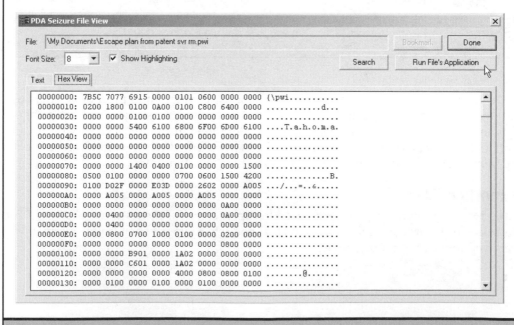

Figure 13-7. The PDA Seizure file viewer and selecting to launch the associated application

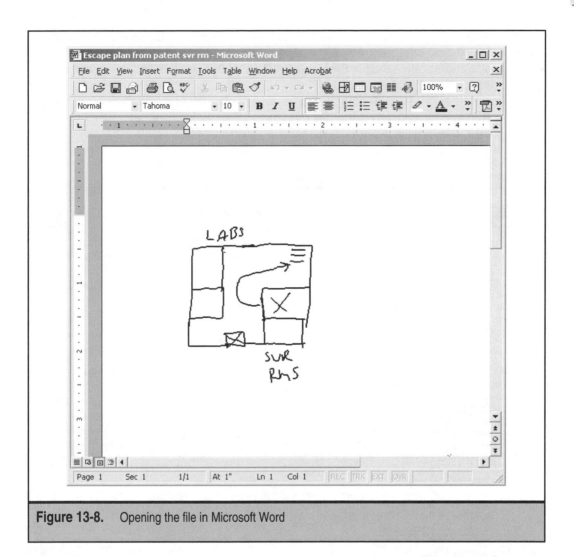

Figure 13-8. Opening the file in Microsoft Word

Reporting

Since it's never over until the paperwork is done, let's look at the PDA Seizure reporting capabilities. Reports are generated by clicking the Report icon on the toolbar or by choosing File | Generate Report. At this point, the PDA Seizure Report Wizard begins and information about the case and the analyst can be entered. At the bottom of the dialog is an option to include a list of all files, which means "every file," not just files that are bookmarked. All bookmarked items, including graphics, are included in the report by default—*all files* in terms of this option means start at the top and list every file on the PDA.

PDA Seizure reports are generated in HTML, so they can be modified with any HTML editor to add a logo or verbiage, such as confidentiality and handing instructions. Reports are automatically saved in the same directory as the case file, and the report usually opens in a browser after it is generated.

Figures 13-9 and 13-10 illustrate the cover and bookmarks for a PDA Seizure report.

Now that we have covered the basic features of PDA Seizure, let's briefly discuss some specific differences when dealing with a Windows CE/Mobile Windows device versus other Windows systems.

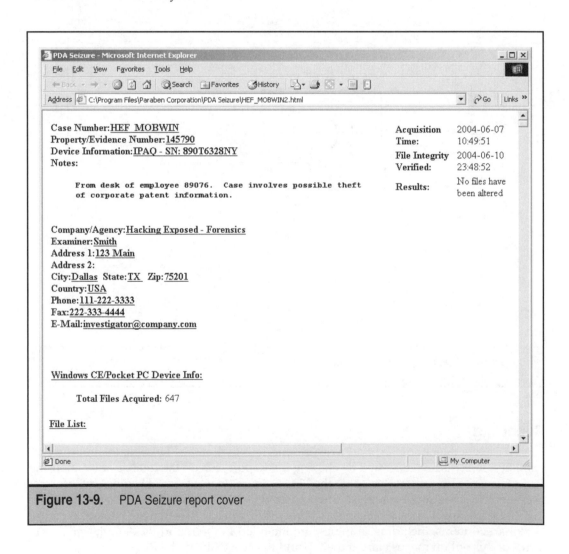

Figure 13-9. PDA Seizure report cover

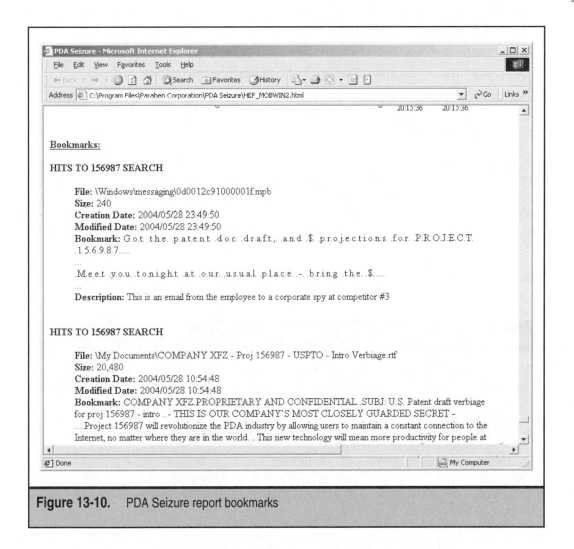

Figure 13-10.   PDA Seizure report bookmarks

E-mail Analysis with Pocket Outlook

Pocket Outlook is not "your daddy's" Outlook. Going back to our sample case, we already found the body of an e-mail sent from the employee to the spy at the competitor, as illustrated in Figure 13-2. As mentioned earlier, with Mobile Windows devices, no container file like a .PST or .DBX, where all e-mail is kept, exists. Rather, Pocket Outlook uses a combination of databases to store files:

▼   E-mails are stored as .MPB files, which are uniquely numbered and reside
   in the Windows\Messaging folder. Filenames will look something like this:
   0a0013438103102.mpb. Opening such files in PDA Seizure will cause the

internal file viewer to open, and you will be able to see associated header information and text of the message.

▲   Attachment information is kept in the pmailAttachs database.

Finally, a discussion of e-mail analysis today must include web-based e-mail. More and more people understand that company e-mail systems are monitored but still think their private web-based e-mail accounts leave no trace. Of course, that's not true.

Because you will find a Temporary Internet Files folder in a Mobile Windows device, as in other versions of the Windows OS, you can search across those files for copies of the HTML associated with web mail sessions. If any are found, it's as easy as launching the associated web browser on your system directly from PDA Seizure, or you can copy and paste the HTML to a text editor if you prefer. You can also examine the Index.dat file or any cookies or other references to web-based e-mail sites. Figures 13-11 and 13-12 illustrate use of the PDA Seizure file viewer to examine an Index.dat file and cookies.

In addition to e-mail, Outlook keeps track of appointments and tasks, which is not a feature of Pocket Outlook. Instead, Mobile Windows keeps track of that information in a set of databases not associated with the Pocket Outlook interface.

Pocket Outlook Tips

Pocket Outlook truncates long e-mails and doesn't download attachments unless the user goes back and marks the message for download. The remainder of the truncated body and any associated attachments will then be downloaded. Pocket Outlook also stores Inbox, Outbox, Deleted Items, and so on, in separate files, which are identified in the pmailFolders file. Here's an example of the data contained in this file:

```
D.e.l.e.t.e.d. .I.t.e.m.s...f.l.d.r.1.0.0.1.9.7.c
D.e.l.e.t.e.d. .I.t.e.m.s...f.l.d.r.1.0.0.1.3.d.5
D.r.a.f.t.s...f.l.d.r.1.0.0.1.9.7.d
D.r.a.f.t.s...f.l.d.r.1.0.0.1.3.d.6
I.n.b.o.x...f.l.d.r.1.0.0.1.9.7.9
I.n.b.o.x...f.l.d.r.1.0.0.1.3.d.2
O.u.t.b.o.x...f.l.d.r.1.0.0.1.3.d.3
O.u.t.b.o.x...f.l.d.r.1.0.0.1.9.7
S.e.n.t. .I.t.e.m.s...f.l.d.r.1.0.0.1.9.7.b
S.e.n.t. .I.t.e.m.s...f.l.d.r.1.0.0.1.3.d
```

All you have to do is find those files and examine their contents to see information about the messages.

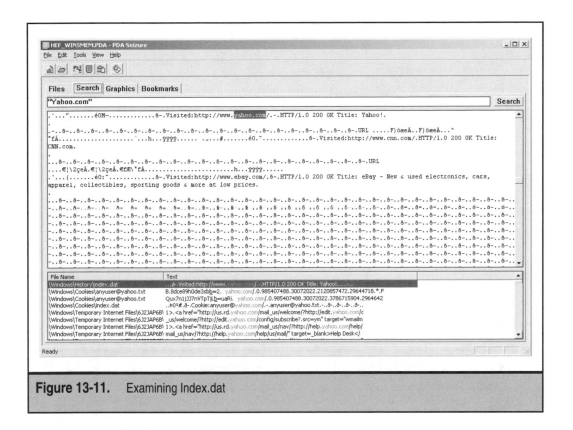

Figure 13-11.   Examining Index.dat

The database DB_notify_queue is where information for all timed activities that have not occurred—such as reminders, appointments, and the like—are stored as well as the application associated with the event. For example, my weekly Monday morning alarm is shown here:

```
W.i.n.d.o.w.s.\.c.l.o.c.k...e.x.e...6.:.0.0. .A.M. . .6./.2.8./.0.4.. W.a.k.e..
.D.a.i.l.y..A.l.a.r.m...A.l.a.r.m.1..C.A.L.N.O.T...E.X.E...A.p.p.R.u.n.A.t.T.i.m.e
...A.p.p.R.u.n.A.t..T.i.m.e...x.e...6.:.0.0. .A.M.  .6./.2.8./.0.4..
W.i.n.d.o.w.s.\.c.l.o.c.k...e.x.e...6.:.0.0. .A.M. . .6./.2.8./.0.4..
W.a.k.e..D.a.i.l.y..A.l.a.r.m...A.l.a.r.m.1..C.A.L.N.O.T...E.X.E
...A.p.p.R.u.n.A.t.T.i.m.e...A.p.p.R.u.n.A.t..T.i.m.e...x.e...
6.:.0.0. .A.M.  .6./.2.8./.0.4..
```

The following was entered by my friend Richard when I let him borrow my PDA in order to "check his e-mail" as we passed the time waiting in the theater line for *Spiderman 2*

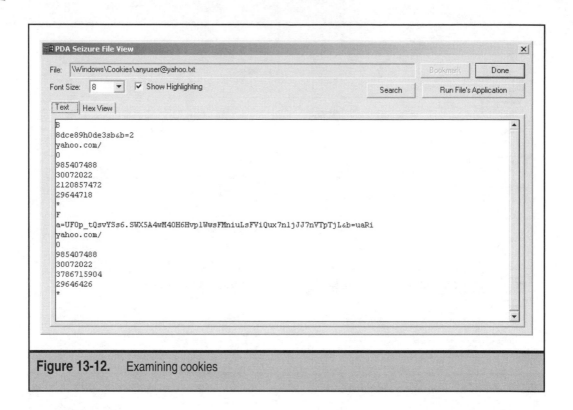

Figure 13-12. Examining cookies

to start at midnight when it opened. (Hey, I got a kitchen pass from my wife; how could I pass it up?)

```
"C.A.L.E.N.D.A.R...E.X.E...R.i.c.h.a.r.d.s. .b.d.a.y..8.:.0.0. .A.M.-.1.1.:.3.0.
.P.M. .8./.3.0./.0.4. .(.B.u.y.
h.i.m..S.t.a.r.w.a.r.s..T.r.i.l.o.g.y..O.n..D.V.D.)...C.a.l.e.n.d.a.r.
.R.e.m.i.n.d.e.r...A.l.a.r.m.1...w.a.v."
"C.A.L.E.N.D.A.R...E.X.E...R.i.c.h.a.r.d.s. .b.d.a.y.
.8.:.0.0. .A.M.-.1.1.:.3.0. .P.M. .8./.3.0./.0.4. .(.B.u.y.
h.i.m..S.t.a.r.w.a.r.s..T.r.i.l.o.g.y..O.n..D.V.D.)
..C.a.l.e.n.d.a.r. .R.e.m.i.n.d.e.r...A.l.a.r.m.1...w.a.v."
```

Another function of Outlook that is not found in Pocket Outlook is the maintaining of contact information. Mobile Windows keeps this information in the Contacts Database file. PDA Seizure does a great job of displaying this information, as shown in Figure 13-13.

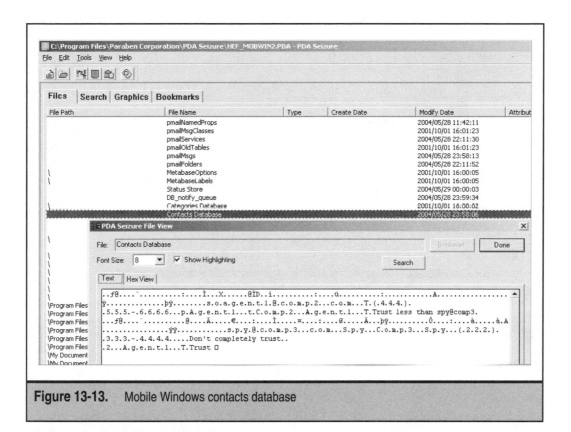

Figure 13-13.   Mobile Windows contacts database

INVESTIGATING TERMINAL SERVICES IN MOBILE WINDOWS

Investigating possible use of the built-in Terminal Services client in Mobile Windows is fairly limited to obtaining the IP address and host name of any servers to which the software has attempted to connect. This information can be found in the registry, as illustrated in Figure 13-14. Because Terminal Server sessions are encrypted by default and the Terminal Services client does not keep records of the session activities, there is no way for you to determine what specific actions were taken by the user during the Terminal session. However, determining whether a Terminal Server connection was made could be significant in any case.

You can search the registry for calls to rdpdr.dll, which should identify the hostname of the Terminal Server and its associated license information. Even though some people

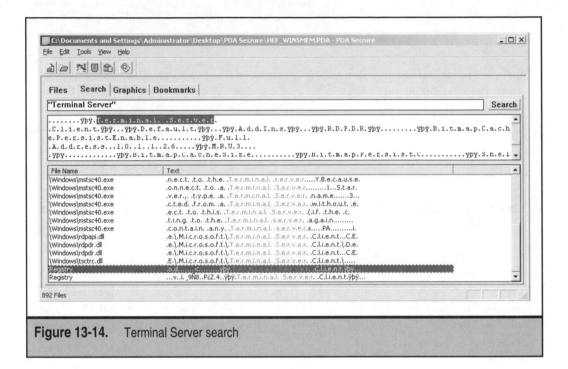

Figure 13-14.   Terminal Server search

tend to under-emphasize the importance of Terminal Services, it is one of the most powerful features around, because it's a fully interactive session with the host system. Aside from examining the registry, if you find an entry in the Index.dat to \TSWeb, this is the default site created by the Windows 2000 Terminal Services web interface. This allows the user to interact with a Terminal Server and conduct a session through Internet Explorer, and it does not require that any client software be installed. Although Pocket Internet Explorer cannot load the ActiveX control required to run the application, any clue as to what servers someone is trying to connect to during any investigation is valuable.

INVESTIGATING MSN MESSENGER

Investigating the possible use of the built-in MSN Messenger Client in Mobile Windows is also best done by searching the registry. The local client does not keep a session log; however, the registry does typically store text of the last session. A typical Messenger session found in the registry will look something like this:

```
..M.S.N.M.e.s.s.e.n.g.e.r.S.e.r.v.i.c.e....I.d.e.n.t.i.t.y.N.a.m.e...S.P.Y.@.C.o.m
.p.3...c.o.m...S.P.Y.@.C.o.m.p.3...c.o.m. .(.E.-.m.a.i.l. .A.d.d.r.e.s.s. .N.o.t.
.V.e.r.i.f.i.e.d.)...M.S.N. .M.e.s.s.e.n.g.e.r.
S.e.r.v.i.c.e...P.r.e.s.e.t.M.s.g.s....*.I. .l.o.v.e. .m.y. .P.o.c.k.e.t.
.P.C.!..&.C.a.l.l. .m.e. .l.a.t.e.r...
```

```
..D.e.f.a.u.l.t..E.x.c.h.a.n...........M.S.N.S....P.a.s.s..U.s.e..P.U...<.C.o.m.p.E
.m.p.l.l.@.C.o.m.p.a.n.y...c.o.m..........M.S.G.S.....,.m.e.s.s.e.n.g.e.r...h.o.t
.m.a.i.l...c.o.m..
```

This brief bit of data encompasses a complete session between our two fictional characters, Spy and CompEmpl1, which breaks down like this:

> Spy uses the PresetMsgs, which Microsoft refers to as "My Text Messages" in the user interface. The conversation consists of "I love my Pocket PC! & Call me later." The server that handled the session was messenger.hotmail.com.

PASSWORDS AND OTHER SECURITY FEATURES YOU MAY ENCOUNTER

One of the issues investigators have to contend with periodically is the suspect protecting his or her data—or at least trying to. Like most everything else in the forensics world, this subject is filled with good news and bad news. Typically, if an investigator encounters an encrypted Microsoft Word or Excel document during a PC forensic case, the options are to have the suspect give you the passwords or decrypt them yourself. If the first option is unsuccessful or impossible, many good tools can be used to do this sort of thing. Luckily for us (at least for now), we don't have to contend with these kinds of issues with PDAs because Pocket Word and Pocket Excel do not support passwords, and if you attempt to upload a password-protected Word or Excel file to a PDA, you'll get an error message.

That's the good news; now for the bad. Just as third-party security applications exist for PCs, they also exist for PDAs. Obviously, they serve very legitimate needs, but that doesn't make them any easier to love when you're trying to find the data you're looking for in a case. At the top of any list in this category has to be PGP Mobile. The name says it all—PGP is synonymous with security, and PGP Mobile has complete OpenPGP RFC 2440 compatibility along with a feature set almost identical to PGP for the desktop, in both Palm OS and Mobile Windows flavors. Slight differences exist in the functionality based upon the supported OS, as well as shared functionality across both.

Both Palm and Mobile Windows PGP Mobile versions feature the following:

▼   E-mail encryption

■   File encryption

■   Clipboard decryption and verification

■   Digital signatures

▲   Complete interoperability with all current PGP products

Palm-specific features include:

▼   PGP Vault, which can be likened to PGP Disk for secure storage of data

■   Free space wiping

▲   The application databases can be encrypted when not in use

Windows-specific features for PGP Mobile include file wiping capabilities.

As with other PGP products, the supported list of symmetric algorithms includes the Advanced Encryption Standard (AES) up to 256-bit, International Data Encryption Algorithm (IDEA), TripleDES (a minor variation of Data Encryption Standard), and CAST (named for its inventors, Carlisle Adams and Stafford Tavares). Supported asymmetric algorithms include RSA (named for its inventors, Ron Rivest, Adi Shamir, and Leonard Adleman) up to 4096-bit, Diffie-Hellman, and Digital Signature Standard (DSS). It also supports both MD5 and Secure Hash Algorithm 1 (SHA1).

As with its desktop cousins, if you encounter files on a PDA that have been secured with PGP Mobile, you should just make note of them and keep on working, because there is nothing you can do in the immediate future.

Password-Protected Windows Devices

Because ActiveSync is required to examine a Mobile Windows device forensically, it is currently not possible to bypass the Mobile Windows password scheme using PDA Seizure. When you attempt to connect to a password-protected Mobile Windows device, ActiveSync will prompt you for the device password.

COLLECTING CELL PHONE EVIDENCE: USING CELL SEIZURE

Although not conventionally thought of as a PDA by many people, the functionality of cell phones has increased so much over the years that it blurs the clear lines of definition. Yes, some integrated phone/PDAs are running on both the Palm and Mobile Windows platforms. However, most non-combination cell phones today come with many of the standard features that PDAs offer:

▼   Web browser

■   E-mail and text messaging

■   Notes

■   Appointment calendar

■   Camera

▲   Contact list

Check out your phone against this list and see how many features you've got.

If PDAs are the pigeons of the technology world, cell phones surely are the insects—there are simply a lot more bugs than birds in the world. With the proliferation of cell phones, it makes sense that almost any case is apt to involve some of these devices. Until recently, if you had to contend with a phone, the first step in most investigations was to send an e-mail to whatever listserve you belonged to and ask whether anyone had ever done one of these before. You could also go to the local cell phone retailer and see whether it offered some way of enabling you to dump the contents—onto paper.

With the 2004 introduction of Cell Seizure from Paraben Corporation, the ability to do a forensic examination of cell phone data has become much less painful. The software supports most models of Nokia, Motorola, Sony Ericsson, and Siemens with the next rollout expected to support Samsung and LG.

Current product features include:

▼   Support for GSM (Global System for Mobile Communications) phones

■   Support for Time Division Multiple Access/Code Division Multiple Access (TDMA/CDMA) phones

■   Acquisition of GSM SIM cards

■   Acquisition of text messages

■   Acquisition of call logs

■   Acquisition of the address book

■   Recovery of deleted data

▲   Verification of file integrity

Although a lot of similarities exist between modern cell phones and PDAs, there are obvious differences in their underlying technology, and as such you cannot think of a phone analysis in traditional forensic terms. One of the first major differences is that phone data storage is proprietary and based on the manufacturer, model, and system. There is no such thing as a "phone forensic image" at this point in time, although that possibility is not too far off. With that in mind, Cell Seizure was designed to allow forensic acquisition of user-entered data and portions of unallocated storage on some devices, but not all.

Current limitations and capabilities identified by Paraben include the following:

▼   Acquires only the phone book on TDMA cell phones because the remaining data is similar to an encrypted file format.

▲   Acquires unallocated space as well as allocated space on portions of SIM cards.

Even with those limitations, the tool is rich in functionality and gives the analyst a comprehensive look into call information, text messages, address books, and more. Now let's jump into the software.

Acquisition with Cell Seizure

The first step in the acquisition is to make sure the phone is correctly connected to the system you will be using. As with PDAs, this means having the appropriate cable to attach the phone to your computer. You can obtain a complete set of cables for the models Cell Seizure supports from Paraben, or you can get them from a phone retailer as needed.

1. After the phone is connected to your system, start the acquisition by choosing Tools | Wizard from the menu or by clicking the Acquire Wizard button on the button bar. Click Next.

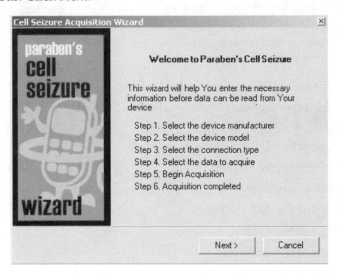

2. Select the location where you will save the resulting Cell Seizure workspace file. The wizard then prompts you to select the phone manufacturer. Depending on your selections here, the options for what data can be acquired will change later in the wizard.

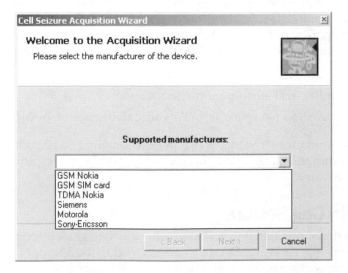

3. The wizard displays the appropriate models supported by the software. If you don't know the exact model or it's obscured on the phone itself, you can have the software autodetect it for you. (Note that if you chose GSM SIM card as the manufacturer, only one option will appear in this dialog.)

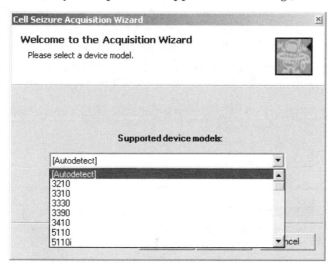

4. Select the appropriate connection type in the next dialog, which is populated based upon the manufacturer and model information you entered previously. You should not expect to see USB, COM1, COM2, and so on, every time.

5. In the next dialog in the wizard, select the data you want to acquire. As mentioned, the items in this dialog are predicated by the specific manufacturer and model you selected previously. Figures 13-15, 13-16, and 13-17 show dialogs for three different examples, based upon a GSM SIM card, a GSM Nokia, and a Motorola.

6. When the wizard completes, click the Acquire button to begin the process and wait for the acquisition to complete. You'll spend a lot of time waiting in computer forensics work; don't let anyone tell you otherwise.

7. When the process is finished, you have the option of ending the wizard or viewing acquisition details by clicking the View Acquisition Report link.

The end result will be a Cell Seizure workspace file (.CSZ) and a hash (.MD5) file with the same name as the workspace file.

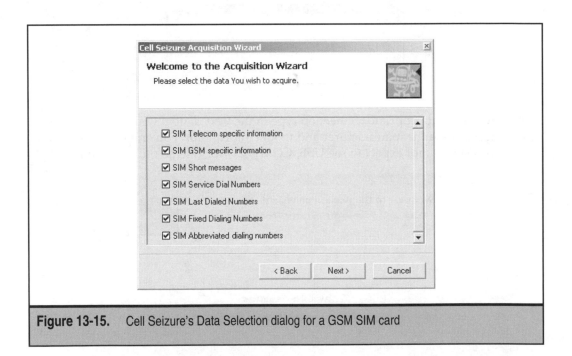

Figure 13-15. Cell Seizure's Data Selection dialog for a GSM SIM card

Cell Seizure Acquisition Wizard

Welcome to the Acquisition Wizard
Please select the data You wish to acquire.

☑ Java Gallery
☑ Sound Gallery
☑ Image Gallery
☑ Sms History
☑ Calendar
☑ Phone Calls
☑ Phonebook

< Back   Next >   Cancel

Figure 13-16.   Cell Seizure's Data Selection dialog for a GSM Nokia

Cell Seizure Acquisition Wizard

Welcome to the Acquisition Wizard
Please select the data You wish to acquire.

☑ SMS and Quick notes memory dump
☑ Datebook
☑ Phone Calls
☑ Sms History
☑ Phonebook

< Back   Next >   Cancel

Figure 13-17.   Cell Seizure's Data Selection dialog for a Motorola

Analysis with Cell Seizure

The first step in analysis is to open the Cell Seizure workspace for the appropriate device.

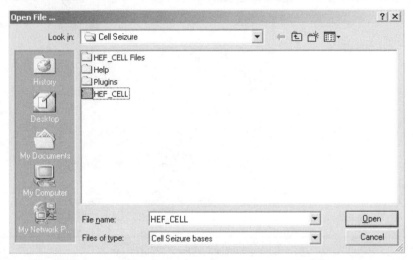

Once opened, you will be able to see the data associated with the device, as illustrated next. At this point, you can run keyword searches and bookmark findings for later inclusion in the final report.

As Figures 13-18 and 13-19 illustrate, the Cell Seizure interface makes it easy to view the phone book, calling history, text messaging activity, and other artifacts relevant to your investigation.

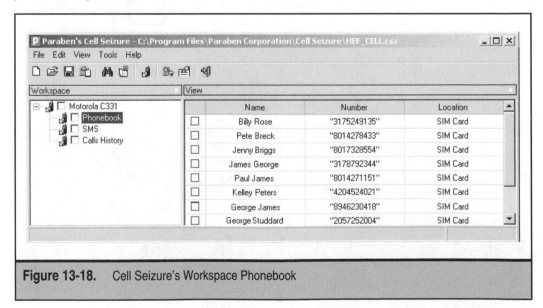

Figure 13-18. Cell Seizure's Workspace Phonebook

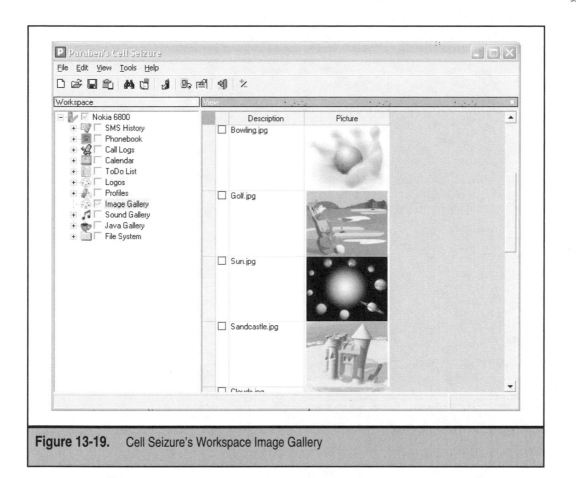

Figure 13-19. Cell Seizure's Workspace Image Gallery

To document your findings, the reporting functions are accessible by choosing File | Report or by clicking the Report button on the button bar. The software will then prompt you to select the location where you would like the resulting .HTML file to be saved. After saving, the file can be opened with an editor to add a logo, handling and classification information, and other data.

PART IV

PRESENTING YOUR FINDINGS

CASE STUDY: WRAPPING UP THE CASE

During and at the conclusion of the ACME Services case, we drafted several reports to council that were used to make decisions. With council's advisement, we produced reports and summaries of the evidence found for the US Attorney's Office and the US Secret Service. We did this so they could understand and re-create what we had found.

He Said, She Said...

Civil investigators need to understand what happens when the line is crossed and the findings become part of a criminal case. No one can testify to facts that were told to them by another party—this is considered hearsay—so the findings must be repeatable and verifiable by other investigators. We carefully document our procedures so other investigators can rediscover what we find. When another party re-creates our findings, they have first-party knowledge, which makes the evidence they recover admissible in court.

We carefully documented our methodologies and search terms to aide the US Secret Service so they could re-create our findings. The Secret Service was now involved in a criminal case and had to have first-party knowledge of the investigation's findings to testify on the matter.

The US Attorney's Office then brought the suspect into court with the Secret Service acting as their expert witnesses. With a solid case in front of him, the judge revoked Charlie Blink's bail and placed him in custody pending trial. The trial was successful for the prosecution, and Blink was found guilty. Charlie Blink remains in prison today.

CHAPTER 14

DOCUMENTING THE INVESTIGATION

After you complete an investigation, you must deal with the most nontechnical part of the process, commonly viewed as the least entertaining part of the job: reporting. However, reporting is one of the most crucial parts of an investigation, because if you cannot clearly relate the facts of the matter to your audience, all of your hard work will be for naught.

READ ME

Your report is the one common tool that you and nontechnical people will use to discuss and understand your findings. Being able to write a clear, concise, and factual report is one of the more difficult aspects of the job for a technically oriented person, because your audience is usually not technical, so they will not understand all the terms and technology that you have employed in your investigation and may not be able to understand the impact of the "smoking gun" you found.

Such communication can be difficult. You must use care in your explanations to be sure that what you report can be understood and supported with evidence. If, for example, you tell someone what you know to be true based on the evidence you reviewed, you must make sure that your evidence proves what you say. Assumptions can lead to lawsuits or criminal complaints if your opinion is not based on hard, reliable evidence.

Events that can be reconstructed, re-created, or at least given credibility through some outside source are the only events you should represent as facts in a report. No matter how convinced you are of someone's intentions, motive, or guilt, it is your place as the forensic examiner to report only what the evidence tells you. You can offer your opinions during a conversation about the case, but you must not document these opinions in your report. Documenting opinions that are not based on factual evidence can be used against you at a later time, as being biased in your judgment.

Different kinds of reports are used for different situations. The type of report you are being asked to generate should indicate the magnitude of the work you are about to undertake. While an internal report to your manager may be informal and represent basic facts, an expert report to the court must be prepared with care and submitted only when you are confident with each fact and opinion you have put to page.

The reports discussed in this chapter are shown in Table 14-1.

In every kind of report, some specific items should be considered or included. Screenshots and any other illustration or visualization that you can provide are extremely helpful. Not all managers, attorneys, or judges are technically savvy and many have not had to handle digital evidence before. The more straightforward your evidence and the more support you give for evidence through visual representations and reconstruction, the more compelling your argument becomes.

Type of Report	Description
Internal reports	Reports whose intended audience is local counsel or your manager.
Affidavits	Reports whose intended audience is the court; such documents are signed in front of a notary and the statements within them are taken as though they were sworn under oath.
Declarations	Reports whose intended audience is the court; these documents are not signed in front of a notary but are assumed to be factual.
Expert reports	Reports whose intended audience is the court; these documents are filed as a report of your findings to a judge upon being appointed an expert witness.

Table 14-1.   Types of Reports

INTERNAL REPORT

The internal report is by far the most common report you will create. While the internal report is not a formal representation to the courts, it is a serious document. When you finish an internal report, it normally is first reviewed by your manager and then, if action is warranted, is passed on to your general counsel. The general counsel (your company's head internal attorney) may decide to take legal action against some person(s) depending on what you documented in your report.

Always explain every detail clearly to your attorney, whether he or she be internal to the company or from an outside firm, as the need to understand any legal assumptions or risks as the result of taking action based upon the evidence in your report is paramount. All communication with the attorney and documents that you create at the direction of your attorney are held as attorney-client privilege. This means that whatever you tell your attorney is going to remain private and will not be given to the opposing counsel as evidence. However, if legal action is undertaken, you may be asked to create a declaration or affidavit that restates your findings for the court. Anything you produce in these documents will be heavily scrutinized by the opposing counsel.

In some cases, you may be acting in a consultative role for the company. Many companies choose to hire outside consultants either to verify an internal investigation or handle the investigation completely. The most common reason for hiring outside the company is that employees who do the internal investigations can become fact witnesses. This means that the employees can be subpoenaed by the opposing counsel or by their own attorney to testify their first-person knowledge of events in front of a judge. This can be a risky endeavor, as an employee will always know more personal and nonrelevant information about a coworker, and this can be used by opposing counsel to claim a bias against the suspect.

When acting as a consultant, you should always follow the general principles of internal reporting: create clear, concise, and informal reports that explain in detail the matter at hand. Obviously, as a hired consultant, a higher expectation of quality and professionalism is expected, as this is hopefully the product of a well-paid consultant. As a consultant working at the direction of the attorneys, you also are covered by attorney-client privilege—any communication and work product created for the attorneys cannot be subpoenaed by the opposing counsel.

However, as a legal case enters the system, you may become what is known as an "expert consultant" or "expert witness." Be aware of an important and distinct difference between these rules. An expert consultant acts in an advisory role to the attorneys and is covered by attorney-client privilege. An expert witness does not have this privilege; all communication that is relevant to the case at hand, whether created during or before your appointment as an expert witness, is discoverable. This includes conversations you are part of or have overheard; e-mails you have sent, received, or have been copied on; and any reports you may have created. Make sure that you communicate to your attorney early and often about your role in any litigation to make sure that you and your attorney understand the impact of your report. While an early doubt expressed in a report may be clarified and reinforced at a later date, the existence of the doubt can be used against you by the opposing counsel.

Construction of an Internal Report

Some forensic tools such as ASR Data's SMART, Guidance Software's EnCase, Paraben's P2 suite, and AccessData's Forensic Tool Kit allow you to create reports. The reports generated by these tools are normally a collection of bookmarked evidence that you have noted during your investigation, along with the structure of the disk in question, some information about the image itself (such as the MD5 hash), and any notes you might have created during your investigation. While this is valuable information and contains key evidence that will support your report, it should not be your end product.

Most internal reports begin with a statement describing the specific situation. Oftentimes, this is encompassed in an *executive summary*. An executive summary is a summary of the facts written at a high level that an executive from your company or your client should be able to read to ascertain what you have done. An executive summary might look something like this:

> *I, Ima Investigator, was asked to investigate Mr. Suspect by Ms. Supervisor in regards to Mr. Suspect's e-mail communications with competing companies. I was requested by Ms. Supervisor to create an image of Mr. Suspect's computer system on this date. The following report serves as a summary of my findings.*

The next section should provide a summary of your conclusions, called the *results section*. This should state what you were directed to do, what evidence you have found, and what subsequent requests were made. Remember that this will be the last part of your report that many people see and understand before you get into the "technical voodoo," so be sure that you make every point in this section that you plan to reinforce with evidence within the report itself. An example of the results section is shown here:

After imaging the system of Mr. Suspect, I was instructed by Ms. Supervisor to identify and analyze all e-mails sent between Mr. Suspect and Mr. Ex-employee. Upon reviewing the recovered e-mails, it is my opinion that Mr. Suspect has been supplying confidential information to Mr. Ex-employee and evidence of this can be found in section X of this report. Upon notification of this, Ms. Supervisor asked that further analysis be done to determine what other Internet-based activities Mr. Suspect had been involved in and what files were recently deleted. It is my opinion that Mr. Suspect is using company resources to distribute materials and send spam e-mails.

Following that section is the evidence you have recovered from the suspect's system. You should annotate each piece of evidence, explaining what it is and why you believe it to be of relevance. It is also recommended that you convert your report to a format such as Portable Document Format (PDF) or something similar so that you can have some confidence that your report will not be inadvertently modified as people review it and pass it to others.

Figures 14-1 and 14-2 show examples of the information that may be contained in an internal report. The information shown here is from a consultative perspective, but the exact same model can be applied to any internal report.

Final Report of Findings for
Acme Funds Inc.

**Prepared by
David Cowen**

Description: Investigation of Mr. Suspect

Figure 14-1.   The cover page of a report

1.1 Executive Summary

I was called into an investigation of the activities of Mr. Suspect on December 25, 2020. Investigators were briefed by Acme's head of investigations, Mr. Supervisor, on the suspected activities and asked to create an image of the suspect's computer system for analysis. This report serves as a final report of our findings in the matter.

1.2 Results

The initial request to investigators was to search for any access to prohibited web sites by Mr. Suspect and to determine if Mr. Suspect had misappropriated any of Acme's confidential materials.

With this search, investigators were successful in finding a series of e-mails that Mr. Suspect had sent to his personal Internet e-mail account that contained files marked as confidential. Evidence was also found that these e-mails were then forwarded to Mr. Ex Exployee at Emca.

During the search for Mr. Suspect's Internet history, investigators also discovered that Mr. Suspect spends most of his working hours running a marketing company and misuses company resources in distributing materials and sending spam e-mails from an internal company web server.

2.1 E-mails containing files received by Mr. Suspect

The e-mails included below are shown in chronological order.

2.1.1 Earliest e-mail 12/23/2020 11:57PM
Here Mr. Suspect is sending a file from his Acme account to a Mr. Ex Employee. The file in question is OurSpamPlan.doc.

Figure 14-2. An example internal report

DECLARATION

After you have written your initial report of an investigation and the attorneys decide to proceed with legal action, you will normally be asked to draft a declaration. Declarations are used by attorneys to support motions they present to the court. A motion can be just about any type of action that someone is requesting the court to take, such as motions to compel, temporary restraining orders, motions to dismiss, motions for summary judgment, motions for expedited discovery, and others. Your declaration would provide the technical merit for your attorney's argument.

A declaration differs from an internal report in that it is meant to be viewed and understood by a judge and opposing counsel. More so than in an internal report, you must ensure that all of your statements make sense to someone who does not have technical knowledge and that your conclusions are not lost in a maze of technical details. You should also be aware that the opposing counsel will base their arguments partly on the report you create; this means that any evidence you state and support will be examined and possibly attacked. Be prepared to defend any statement you have made, and realize that any evidence you reference could be requested or subpoenaed by the opposing counsel.

When the opposing counsel subpoenas some evidence, it means that they have gone to the judge and gotten a written order stating that whatever evidence they have referenced must now be produced in whatever manner the judge has granted them. Sometimes this means that an image will be handed over; other times it means that the original system will be produced to the opposing counsel and their expert will re-image the system and try to re-create your findings. If any of your conclusions were based on assumptions or any accidental access to the original evidence—and this can and will happen—and you did not state such in your declaration, the opposing counsel will challenge the evidence itself.

The same scenario plays both ways; if you are working for the defense and the plaintiff's expert has produced some evidence that shows signs of accidental or intentional tampering, you would most likely be asked to create a declaration stating this case. You must be careful, though, when moving toward these kinds of motions, as you never know all of what happened during the lifetime of the evidence. Make such suggestion to the attorneys only when you believe you have ample evidence to support your claims.

A declaration is also meant to be a factual statement. While you are not getting a notary to witness your signing of the document, as you do with an affidavit, you are still swearing to the fact that the statements you have written are true. This is important, as making knowingly false statements can bring serious repercussions. Though I doubt that making false statements in a declaration is something you aspire to do, many attorneys who do understand the details of the technology you are dealing with may ask you to reinterpret or more forcefully support a conclusion than you are comfortable with. This is understandable, as the attorneys believe that your new conclusions may just be a point of view and not the actual factual representation that you and the opposing expert would understand. Remember that no matter who is paying you, your name is being signed on these documents, and you are liable for any false statements that are made.

Construction of a Declaration

Declarations have a very standard form as to how they begin and end. It is what goes in the middle that lets you create a unique document. You should make sure to express your opinions in the matter, but remember to be as professional as possible. All declarations should begin with a statement similar to the following; the sections that you should fill in are underlined:

I, your name here, declare as follows:
I am a your title with your company, a description of what your company does. Your company

has been retained by counsel for the plaintiffs/defense (name of the plaintiff/ defendant) in abc v. def, Civil Action No. some number (D. some state) to render an opinion regarding the possibility of what you where asked to do. The following contains my the opinion that you are planning to defend based upon my experience in the field and my knowledge of the current case.

The next section of a declaration is a primer on your background, stating what makes you qualified as an expert to make the opinions and conclusions you are about to state to the court. It should look something like the following, but it will be unique to you based on how you choose to represent yourself and your experience. The parts you should change or fill in are underlined.

My educational background is mainly technological/academic in nature, featuring more than some years of direct experience in the areas of what you have done and your job duties relating to this case or your investigation. I currently hold any certificates you might have. I am also an active member of any associations you may be a part of that have some bearing on your ability to be an expert. I have been trained in whatever and whoever has trained you in the areas relevant to the opinion you are making. If you are a consultant, you should name the company you work for and indicate your billing rate here.

After this, you should begin stating on what you have been asked to base your opinion and what you have reviewed in doing so. You should explain in layman's terms the technical aspects of whatever processes you have undertaken and discuss the evidence you have reviewed. This is important, as you can make opinions and conclusions based only on firsthand knowledge. Making a statement like "I was told by Ms. Jones that he arrived at work at 10 a.m." would be considered hearsay. Be sure to ask for and review any documents or records that you will discuss in your declaration.

A declaration has no particular minimum or maximum page length requirements. If you can make all of your points and conclusions in one page, and it is understandable to a layman, that's fine. When you are done stating your opinions, you should end your declaration with a conclusion that covers all of your opinions and conclusions about the matter and reaffirms your overall statement and support for the motion. An example of a conclusion is shown here:

After reviewing and analyzing all of the whatever evidence you reviewed in making your opinions, I am left with the opinion that whatever conclusion you have come to. Discuss the ramifications of what this opinion means to the motion at hand. In my opinion, state your overall conclusion and support for the motion.

An example of a declaration is shown in Figures 14-3 and 14-4. This declaration is taken more from a consultative perspective, but the exact same model can be applied to any declaration.

You do not have the same document modification concerns for a declaration after you have submitted it, since your signature must be in place on a printed document.

UNITED STATES DISTRICT COURT
SOUTHERN DISTRICT OF TEXAS,
HOUSTON DIVISION

ABC

           Plaintiff

    v.   Civil Action No._____

DEF

           Defendants

**DECLARATION OF DAVID COWEN IN SUPPORT OF PLAINTIFF ABC
MOTION FOR SANCTIONS AGAINST DEFENDANT DEF**

I, DAVID COWEN, declare as follows:

1.   I am a Senior Consultant with Fios, a computer consulting company that focuses on digital litigation support and forensic analysis. S3 Partners has been retained by counsel for the plaintiffs ("ABC") to render an opinion regarding the time and possibility of recovering relevant digital data from the Defendants' ("DEF") systems. I submit this declaration in support of Plaintiff ABC Motion for Sanctions Against Defendant DEF.

My educational background is technological in nature, featuring more than seven years of experience in the areas of integration, architecture, assessment, programming, forensic analysis and investigation. I currently hold the Certified Information Systems Security Professional certification from (ISC).˙ I have been trained in proper forensics practices by the High Tech Crime Investigators Association, Guidance Software, amongst others. I am an active member of the computer security community, including the High Technology Crime Investigators Association, where I frequently present and train on various forensic topics. I have managed, created, and worked with multiple forensics teams and associated forensic procedures. My experience spans a variety of environments ranging from high security military installations to large/small private sector companies. My billing rate as a senior consultant with FIOS is $sorry guys per hour.

**DECLARATION OF DAVID COWEN IN SUPPORT OF PLAINTIFF ABC MOTION
FOR SANCTIONS AGAINST DEFENDANT DEF PAGE 1**

Figure 14-3.   Front page of a sample declaration

9. After reviewing and analyzing all of the seized evidence with the data first provided and then later discovered in subsequent searches, I am left with the opinion that evidence must exist in some form (i.e., on another system or storage media) that DEF has refused to produce to date. Without access to this additional evidence, we cannot determine the extent that DEF has infringed on ABC's intellectual property rights. In my opinion, DEF's expert has made significant misstatements and omissions to the court and has refused to deliver to the court those relevant documents ordered for production.

I declare under penalty of perjury that the foregoing is true and correct.

Dated: June 30, 2020
Dallas, Texas

_____

David Cowen

90037852.2doc

Figure 14-4.   Last page of a sample declaration

However, you should carefully review any document that is put in front of you to sign, to make sure that no last-minute revisions were made that are inaccurate or that you cannot stand behind.

At the end of your declaration, you may want to add a glossary with a section name, such as "Definitions." Within this section, you should define any technical terms you have not explained in the declaration as well as any specific methodologies you followed. The glossary becomes a powerful tool for you in restricting the interpretability of your statements in that you can limit the scope and impact of particular technical terminology. This is very useful as you deal with opposing attorneys and experts who may be aggressive in trying to rebuke your otherwise factual declaration.

AFFIDAVIT

Affidavits are much like declarations, except that they require a notarized signature on the document. Affidavits are viewed as "stronger" documents than declarations because of this, but the request for an affidavit or a declaration will be based on the court's needs, whether state or federal, and type of motion you are supporting. Otherwise, an affidavit can be structured much like a declaration with the same rules applied, as discussed earlier.

EXPERT REPORT

Expert reports are the pinnacle of formal reports to a court. The expert report is your dissertation to the court on the matter at hand and your opinions regarding them. If you are being asked to create an expert report, it is because you have been deemed an expert witness by your attorney and you must readily adhere to the warning mentioned earlier in the chapter regarding such documentation.

While a declaration and an affidavit are made in support of a motion, an expert report stands alone as a document submitted to the courts. The expert report shows your abilities as an expert to state facts, explain details, and clearly support conclusions and opinions. Remember that as an expert, you have the ability and right to make opinions that are aggregated from the evidence you have reviewed, but you should do so carefully. Opposing counsel will have their own experts, possibly even one of the authors of this book, who will be scrutinizing every word of your report. If you have offered any opinions that are based mainly on speculation, they will be quickly opposed and refuted. Any opinion you can make based on reconstructed evidence and outside support will stand much better against the opposing onslaught.

It also works the other way, though. As the expert witness, you will review the opposing expert's opinion and will have the opportunity to respond by providing supplemental reports that address other documents that have been submitted to the court. This includes expert reports, declarations, affidavits, deposition testimony, and any other evidence that has been submitted to the court. Your expert report will also be used against you and the opposing expert when and if you are asked to testify in front of the courts.

When testifying, make sure that you make reference to your report and quote it when you can. Going back to your expert report allows you to reiterate your opinions to the judge and allows you to stand firm behind previous statements. Many attorneys will simply try to get you to restate your opinion in contrast to your report as a tactic to discredit you. Referring back to your report allows you to defend yourself and your opinions from attack.

When making any type of conclusion in your report, it is always a good idea to make use of an outside party's formal papers and reports. This is not considered hearsay, as you have personal knowledge of some published research paper or standard that is available for public use. This is especially true any time you are dealing with some kind of standard, whether it is a network protocol or a function of communication of a standardized service, such as HTTP. Making direct quotations and citing these public works enhances the credibility of your documentation.

You should also carefully research any public articles or presentations you have made in the past. Any public documents you have created in the past can be used against you if they pertain to the matter at hand. For instance, if at some point in the past you wrote an article about intrusion-detection systems and their inability to provide accurate reporting, you should be wary of making a statement in an expert report later stating that you believe the reports generated from the intrusion-detection system are always valid and factual.

Construction of an Expert Report

Expert reports can vary in their construction from expert to expert, but the form put forward here is fairly standard. You should begin the report with a cover page that states that this is your expert report in the following case. Next, the actual report begins. Expert reports are usually separated by sections that are numbered with Roman numerals. The first numbered section in this example is "I. Overview." The overview should state who you have been retained by, the matter name (the names of the entities suing each other), and what you where retained to do. An example overview follows:

I. OVERVIEW
I have been retained by <u>ABC</u> in the matter styled <u>ABC v. DEF</u> to analyze the items seized from <u>DEF</u> during the court-ordered seizure of systems from <u>DEF</u>. This report sets forth my analysis and my expert opinions.

The next section, entitled "II. Qualifications," is much like the qualifications section that you would write for a declaration. The following section, though, is unique to expert reports.

The next section is entitled "III. Prior Expert Witness Experience." In this section, you must list every case with which you have been involved and for which you have been declared the expert. This is a very specific list, as it applies only when as an expert, you took some action in the suit. So if you were declared the expert in a lawsuit that then settled, you should not include that suit here, since you provided no actual services to the client. Unlike in the security world, where most client engagements are confidential and you cannot reveal the names of your clients, the legal world expects to see each case as soon as it is filed, as the lawsuit becomes public knowledge. While motions may be filed under seal, the overlying case will always be public record. This means that you cannot attempt to show some kind of expert experience without listing a public case that the court and opposing counsel can research and verify. Attempting to mislead or take out of context your role in a case would quickly lead to your removal as an expert in a case. The qualifications section should resemble something like the following:

III. PRIOR EXPERT WITNESS EXPERIENCE
I have previously been designated as testify expert witness in the following lawsuits: <u>XYZ v. 123 (Anytown District Court)</u>, <u>Bob v Jane (D. Anystate)</u>.

The next sections are relatively straightforward; you must include a section stating your compensation for the work, if any, and what exactly you have reviewed in preparation for this report. The "Items Reviewed" section is important, because you are basically limiting yourself to these sources as potential evidence that you can quote from and show as support in your report. Make sure that you do not omit any evidence that you reviewed, as that will possibly create an argument without basis, which is an easy argument to refute.

Your next section would be "Analysis." The analysis portion of your expert report is the bulk of the document, where you refer to your expert knowledge and the evidence you referred to in the previous section to make your opinions and conclusions.

 NOTE It is important always to be a professional and as concise as possible. Remember that a judge will be reading your statements and needs to be able to understand all of the technical points to understand and uphold your point of view.

The last section is the "Conclusion" section. Much like declarations and affidavits, the conclusion section is where you restate your conclusions and opinions and state their impacts on the matter at hand. In this section, you should quickly and concisely state your overall opinion and what harm you believe has occurred. Examples of an expert report are shown in Figures 14-5, 14-6, and 14-7.

**Expert Report of
David L. Cowen**

ABC v. DEF

Figure 14-5. The cover of an expert report

I.   **OVERVIEW**

I have been retained by ABC in the matter styled ABC v. DEF. I have been retained to analyze the items seized from DEF and from the homes of the president and chief operating officer of DEF. This report sets forth my analysis and my expert opinions.

II.   **QUALIFICATIONS**

My educational background is technological in nature. I have more than seven years of experience in the areas of integration, architecture, assessment, programming, forensic analysis and investigation. I currently hold the Certified Information Systems Security Professional certification from (ISC). I have been trained in proper forensics practices by the High Tech Crime Investigators Association, Guidance Software, amongst others.

I am also an active member of the computer security community, including the High Technology Crime Investigators Association. As a member of that community, I frequently present and train on various forensic topics. I have managed, created, and worked with multiple forensics teams and associated forensic procedures. My experience spans a variety of environments ranging from high security military installations to large/small private sector companies.

III.   **PRIOR EXPERT WITNESS EXPERIENCE**

I have previously been designated as testifying expert witness in the following lawsuits: TXU v. Mosby (Dallas District Court), Trocciola v. Quris (D. Colo.), Measurement Computing v. National Instruments (D. Massachusetts), BMC v. Crabbyhacker (D. Texas). I also testified during this case at Temporary Restraining Order, Preliminary Injunction, and Sanctions Motion hearings.

IV.   **COMPENSATION**

Sorry guys

V.   **ITEMS REVIEWED**

I reviewed the following items to complete my analysis in this lawsuit:

a.   Items seized from DEF

VI.   **ANALYSIS**

For purposes of this expert report, I have reviewed the evidence seized in this lawsuit to determine whether DEF is withholding evidence related to their development, sales, and distribution of the 123 program. As shown below, it is my expert opinion that

Figure 14-6.   The first page of an expert report

DEF has withheld evidence in this lawsuit, such as the source code and executable for the latest version of 123 and evidence related to the development, sales and distribution of 123. As a result, DEF is currently free to continue to cause substantial and irreparable injury to ABC.

VII. CONCLUSION

After reviewing and analyzing all of the seized evidence with the data first provided and then later discovered in subsequent searches, it is my opinion that evidence must exist in some form (i.e., on another system or storage media) that DEF has withheld.

_____

David L. Cowen

September 19, 2020

Figure 14-7. The last page of an expert report

CHAPTER 15

THE JUSTICE SYSTEM

So far in this book, we've talked about how to collect and analyze evidence and even how to create reports based on that evidence. What remains is how the ultimate arbiter—the courts—will judge your efforts. This chapter focuses on how the United States court system views the presentation of electronic evidence.

Essentially three types of forensic investigators are working in the field today—law enforcement–trained investigators, military-trained investigators, and the fastest growing group of all, industry-trained investigators. Law enforcement–trained investigators are educated in proper practices by government agencies, including police departments and state police. Military-trained investigators are educated in proper practices that relate to the investigation of military personnel or recovered systems from opposing forces. As a result, these two types of investigators are trained extensively in the best practices of evidence for the purposes of presenting to the court. Industry-trained investigators, however, do not have the formal background of military or law enforcement investigators and as a result do not have much in the way of experience in best practices of gathering and producing evidence for court.

In the last few years, computer forensics has emerged as an industry with easier to use tools being developed for the commercial market to assist in investigations and more opportunities for private sector consultants. These investigators typically are highly technical and formally trained by private firms but lack the knowledge of best practices of evidence and the courts. If this fits your description as an investigator, this chapter is written primarily with you in mind and is intended to help you understand the system and allay any fears that you might harbor regarding rumors and myths surrounding the complicated justice system. In this chapter, we discuss the two different court systems, criminal court and civil court, and show how forensic consultants as designated experts relate to these courts during trial.

Both criminal and civil court systems make significant use of forensic experts. Each system has distinctly different rules of procedure and rules of evidence. We provide a brief overview of both systems and how expert consultants are affected by the different rules.

THE CRIMINAL COURT SYSTEM

The criminal system allows the complainant to lodge a complaint only with a local prosecutor. It is up to the prosecutor to decide whether or not to pursue the complaint. The attorney who brings criminal charges is representing the government at some level—be it the district attorney's office, the state attorney general's office, the U.S. Attorney General's Office, or the Securities Exchange Commission, for example. This means a private citizen or company can approach law enforcement or government attorneys and ask them to open an investigation into some criminal activity. It is up to the government attorneys to decide whether they are willing to take the case and what charges to press. This also means that once the complaint is lodged, control over the prosecution of the case is in the hands of the government. As the complainant, you risk losing control over your own data in a criminal suit.

The other important aspect to understand about the criminal system is that in order to produce, validate, and testify to evidence, law enforcement must seize the original media. Chain of custody concerns often dictate that the government take control of the original media rather than accept an image created by a private citizen. This is specifically because, without original media, the government cannot testify with first-party knowledge as to how the image was created or if any findings that result from its use are valid.

Before you call law enforcement into an investigation, you must understand that you could lose control over the scene of the crime—which could include your databases. While law enforcement today makes great attempts to work with the private sector, government officers and investigators still have to maintain the chain of custody of evidence that they are going to be using in their investigation. Be aware of this, and understand when to bring law enforcement into an investigation and when to authorize private investigations. At a minimum, you would be well served to create a forensically sound image of the system in question so that you can restore it into operation before calling law enforcement and losing access to a critical system.

Nearly as important an issue is that once the government has brought charges against a party, the complainant is not in a position to stop the proceedings. That is, even if an amicable settlement is reached between the parties, the government is under no obligation to drop the criminal charges. Once the government has filed charges, the case belongs to the government, which typically will not let a guilty suspect walk free. Criminal charges can come with some amount of monetary restitution ordered, but criminal charges primarily entail jail time for the suspect.

CIVIL COURT

For most corporate parties involved in litigation, civil court offers the more favorable elements to address wrongs. Civil courts allow parties to litigate their grievances without the intrusion of governmental entities and with the freedom to cease litigation in the event of settlement. Parties to a civil suit can agree beforehand on the manner of discovery, such as what data will be subject to production and how the data will be produced. In addition, the time and manner of collection can be controlled by the parties so as to keep business interruption to a minimum. Simply put, civil court allows the parties to control the scope and flow of discovery. Civil suits consist of several phases.

Phase One: Investigation

During the investigatory phase of a lawsuit, legal papers are not filed, motions are not made, and depositions are not taken, yet this is perhaps the most important phase in pursuing a civil lawsuit. It is at this phase that the core facts of a case are gathered and a determination is made whether to pursue the claim. It is also at this phase that vital data can be identified and preserved before destruction policies take place. As an expert, you can provide your opinions on where relevant data could be located, how the data is stored, forensically search in the unallocated space of hard drives of suspect custodians, and offer advice on the best ways to gather data from the opposing party.

Phase Two: Filing of the Lawsuit

Once the investigation is complete and the relevant facts and data are in order, attorneys file documents with the court. Several types of filings can occur at this stage: a formal intent to sue, a temporary restraining order, or a formal lawsuit against the opposing party. No matter what the purpose of the filing, it will become public knowledge unless it is filed "under seal." Filing under seal means that the documents and your supporting documents are put into a sealed envelope at the court and will be opened only by the judge until they are served upon the opposing counsel. Filings under seal will be permitted by the court only when sensitive, confidential information is involved and one of the parties has shown cause as to why it would be harmful if this information were made public. Most cases involving sealed filings relate to patent and trade-secret infringement matters. In any event, the filing of the lawsuit starts the clock on the discovery phase and officially engages the role of the court as the mediator of all discovery disputes.

Phase Three: Discovery

During the discovery phase, both parties make requests of each other to provide relevant information. This information can be produced in many forms that are governed by the type of discovery request being made. Three primary elements make up the discovery phase: requests for production, interrogatories, and depositions. Interrogatories are a series of questions that are being asked of the opposing party that must be answered or refuted on some ground. Request for production are formal requests for the production of documents, whether paper or electronic. At this point, both parties also establish persons who have knowledge of the facts. The primary focus of the discovery phase is to seek and review relevant evidence from the opposing party and use that information during the deposition of the witnesses to build a case.

The discovery phase commences at the filing of the lawsuit and typically ends 30 to 60 days before the scheduled trial date. The timing and scope of discovery can be altered from the local rules by agreement of the parties involved in the lawsuit with the court's approval.

Request for Production

A request for production asks the responding party to produce tangible items to the requesting party within 30 days of receipt of the request. Tangible items can be anything from a one-page document to all of the corporate e-mails related to the particular event in question. The production request must be in relation to the case and its scope will reflect that. However, in some cases, that scope can be extremely broad, as in anti-trust cases where almost any document might be considered relevant. In such cases, data produced could range in the terabytes. The lion's share of a forensics consultant's work will occur in relation to a request for production. Attorneys are quickly learning the value of electronic data and the secrets it holds. However, two types of documents do not have to be produced—privileged and nonrelevant documents.

Privileged Documents   *Privilege* means that a legal basis exists for the withholding of a document due to the nature of either its creation or to whom it was sent. For example, any document sent to an attorney or from an attorney or containing the attorney's thoughts on the matter at hand can be considered to be attorney work product and privileged. Likewise, correspondence between a client and his or her attorney can be considered privileged by virtue of the attorney-client privilege. Finally, and most importantly for the purposes of this chapter, correspondence between you, the expert, and the attorney can be withheld as privileged under the attorney work product privilege. This privilege extends to agents of the attorney, such as non-testifying expert consultants who are involved in the preparation of the case. However, all privileged documents must be tracked in a privilege log, and their status as privileged may be challenged by the opposing party. It is up to the requesting party to challenge the designation of privileged. At that point, the responding party will provide a privilege log to the court, which will then review the documents privately, or in camera, and make a determination as to whether the privilege applies to the documents.

Nonrelevant Documents   Documents can be deemed nonrelevant by an attorney or the court. It is not a designation to be made by an expert. As an expert, you can render an opinion, but the actual act of declaring something nonrelevant is not your place. The responsibility of a production falls directly on an attorney and his or her client, so the ultimate decision must stay with them. A document is declared nonrelevant if the information contained within the document does not relate to the matter at hand.

Interrogatory

An interrogatory is similar to a request for production in that it is a tool used to learn new information. However, in an interrogatory, the requesting party is seeking answers and not tangible things. Using this discovery tool, counsel discovers the basis of the cause of the action, the names of the relevant witnesses, the names of the designated testifying experts, as well as any background information deemed to be relevant. For the purposes of computer forensics, this discovery tool has very little to do with your job.

Deposition

Depositions take place during the discovery phase of a trial. During this phase, both parties are seeking evidence that can bolster their cases. A deposition is a formal question-and-answer session in which the lawyers who retained your services and opposing counsel take turns asking you questions. The questions and their answers will be part of the official court record and will be on file in the court. All statements are recorded and transcribed by a court reporter, who has obtained a court reporter certificate and transcribes all statements made during the deposition. In addition to a court reporter, the lawyers can ask that a videographer attend a deposition. Video is a powerful tool in that it allows the judge and jury to see, in a deponent's reluctance or slowness in responding, what a written transcription might miss.

For a period of time after deposition testimony, the *deponent* (the person whose deposition was taken) can correct the transcript before it is entered into the court record. Deponents can use this opportunity either to correct possible errors made by the court reporter, fill in answers that were not known at the time of the deposition, or add information to answers that were originally left incomplete. A deposition can take place at an attorney's office, your office, opposing counsel's office, or, in the very rare occasion, a courtroom. The location does not change the fact that you are making sworn testimony to the court. Transcription will begin when you "go on the record" and will stop any time counsel from either side requests that you "go off the record." When off the record, any statements made will not be transcribed, but they are still admissible in court.

Depositions begin with the swearing in of the witness to ensure that what is said during the deposition is considered testimony to the court and as such carries the burden of perjury. To commit *perjury* is to make false statements knowingly under oath, considered a felony that carries with it the penalty of imprisonment. During the deposition, counsel will take turns asking questions. The attorney requesting the deposition will begin and continue questioning until complete. The responding party may then ask questions of his or her own witness. Both parties will then have another chance to ask questions or end the deposition after the first round. The attorney representing you will have the opportunity to object to questions asked by opposing counsel. Be careful not to talk over the attorney's objections, and make certain that you do not answer the question before asking counsel for permission to answer. Opposing counsel will frequently look for ways to get confidential information from the witness. It is your attorney's job to keep that information from being shared, because of the privileged nature of the information. Always be careful of your statements, as they may contain privileged information. We will discuss more on privilege later in the chapter in the section "Expert Status."

Frequently, local or state rules mandate time limits on an individual's deposition. However, a deposition can last as little as 10 minutes or as long as five days—it simply depends on whether an agreement was reached between the parties regarding the length of depositions. In fact, for example, a deposition could last five days and then be put on hold. This means that the attorney can reopen the deposition at a later date because, as of today, they do not feel that they have adequate information to ask you all of the relevant questions.

Phase Four: The Trial

The trial phase is the final phase, wherein the fruits of the discovery are brought into the courtroom. At this point, testimony from the particular experts has already been elicited during depositions. The trial phase can take anywhere from one day to several months, and parties can agree to a trial by jury or judge. A typical trial consists of four phases: opening arguments, plaintiff's case, defendant's case, and then closing arguments. Expert testimony takes place during the presentation of the plaintiff's and defendant's cases.

Trial testimony takes place under oath in the courtroom in front of a judge and possibly a jury. Unlike deposition testimony, however, trial testimony allows for questions from a third party—the judge is allowed at any time to ask a question of the witness. Oftentimes, a judge will do this to get clarification on a topic or to determine your bias toward an opinion. There are no time limits. Testimony can last for 10 minutes to five days. Like depositions, both parties will have an opportunity to ask questions.

EXPERT STATUS

In the preceding chapter, we talked about experts in the creation of reports. Specifically, we discussed what kind of reports should be created when you are deemed an expert for a certain capacity. You cannot simply deem yourself the expert; an expert must be retained by whatever attorney is litigating the case, and in some special cases by the court itself.

Expert Credentials

An *expert witness*, by definition, is a person who has more knowledge of some field than an ordinary person. What qualifies an expert is his or her ability to demonstrate his or her proficiency in his or her specialized area through statements and prior work history and training. No special class or certificate is necessary to become an expert. However, if challenged by the opposing party, the party presenting the witness must show to the court that the witness is a qualified expert in the field he or she is being asked to testify about. This is typically demonstrated through a series of questions regarding the expert's educational and occupational history and previous cases for which the expert may have testified. The ultimate arbiter as to whether a witness qualifies as an expert is the presiding judge.

Nontestifying Expert Consultant

A *nontestifying expert consultant* is an expert who works for the attorney and whose work under advisement of the attorney is considered privileged. As an expert consultant, you will be asked to investigate and review confidential documents in the suit so that you can render an opinion to the attorney. You, at times, may also be asked to communicate with the chosen testifying expert witness to give specific information or evidence for his or her review. You may also be asked to write declarations and affidavits in support of some work you have done. Typically, nontestifying expert consultants are exempt from being deposed or called to testify, as they have not been designated as testifying experts. Their existence is usually shielded by counsel and nothing requires that a nontestifying witness be identified as a person with knowledge of relevant facts. As such, the nontestifying expert can conduct his or her work in complete anonymity. However, a nontestifying expert may be asked to testify if the party requesting the testimony can show the court that the witness has firsthand knowledge of the facts at issue. Since most consulting experts learn the facts of a case through the eyes of others, they are rarely required to testify.

Testifying Expert Witness

A *testifying expert witness* is an expert who is employed by the attorney to review evidence and render an independent opinion based on his or her expertise in the area. As stated in Chapter 14, no privilege is implied for any work or communication that an expert witness carries out in relation to a lawsuit. As a testifying expert witness, any document you are shown and conversation you overhear or are a part of is open for questioning. Also, any document you create, from an electronic document to an e-mail to a doodle on a napkin, is considered work product. Any work product you create can be requested for production by opposing counsel, so be aware of this when you are creating your notes. Attorneys will generally ask their testifying experts to refrain from drafting any notes that include legal conclusions or the work product of the attorney. Reports are not to be prepared until a specific request is issued from either counsel. At times, your opinion as an expert will harm the client's case. For that reason, your client may not want an expert report until it is specifically requested by opposing counsel. If it is not requested, counsel will likely try to de-designate you as an expert, not call you to testify at deposition or trial.

Expert for the Court

Sometimes a judge will appoint an expert to act as an independent expert for both parties. This happens often in criminal cases and smaller civil cases, where neither party has the knowledge or finances to find an expert on the subject. In addition, when a discovery dispute exists between the parties, a court will often designate an independent expert to look into the conflict and determine whether an alternative solution exists. As an expert for the court, all of the rules applied to an expert witness apply, but in addition you are required to be subjective as you are employed and paid by the court, not either attorney.

Expert Interaction with the Court

As an expert representing a party, you cannot directly address the court or file motions stating your opinion. Instead, your ability to make written statements to the court is limited to affidavits and declarations in support of motions and expert reports like those covered in Chapter 14. Other opportunities for you to make statements to the court do exist. Through testimony elicited by counsel for either party, you can state your opinion on the record at trial or at deposition. In addition, as previously discussed, if an expert report is prepared, it will likely be entered into the court record.

PART V

APPENDIXES

APPENDIX A

FORENSIC FORMS AND CHECKLISTS

Forms, checklists, and procedures are critical to reliable and trusted outcomes during investigations. They ensure that you complete all the steps, document the findings, and bring control to a serious process. In the corporate environment, many times someone's job is at stake, so such considerations are important.

Where is the evidence? How do you know it wasn't tampered with prior to the examiner investigating the electronic media? How do you know the examination was complete? How do you communicate to the business manager the status of his business assets?

In the following pages, sample forms and checklists are provided to help you in your examinations. These are also located on http://hackingexposedforensics.com for you to customize for your needs and print as necessary. Additional material online includes examples of lab inventory and history forms.

Evidence Receipt

Case Number:	Receipt Number:
Items Relinquished By / Title:	Date / Time:
Organization / Company:	Location / Address:

Computer(s):

Desktop	Laptop	Server	Hard Drive	Serial Number
☐	☐	☐	☐	
☐	☐	☐	☐	
☐	☐	☐	☐	

Storage Media:

CD-ROM	USB Media	Floppy / Zip	Tape	Subject/SN
☐	☐	☐	☐	
☐	☐	☐	☐	
☐	☐	☐	☐	

Other Materials:

Items Received By / Title:	Signature:
Organization / Company:	Location / Address:

Evidence Receipt Checklist

☐	Took evidence with authorization
☐	Created unique case and evidence number
☐	Documented some asset tag or serial number that uniquely identifies the evidence
☐	Received signature from owner or manager
☐	Noted date and time of seizure
☐	Completed receipt for all evidence taken
☐	Provided copies to owner or manager

Chain of Custody Form

Case Number:		Evidence Number:	
Client:		Date / Time Received:	
Bios Time:		Location Found:	

Evidence Description:			Size:
Manufacturer:		Model:	SN:

History / Chain of Custody:

Date / Time:	By:	Action:

Notes:

Chain of Custody Checklist

☐	Created unique case and evidence number
☐	Documented some asset tag or serial number that uniquely identifies the evidence
☐	Documented make and model of system the data was taken from
☐	Documented BIOS time
☐	Documented location the evidence was found in (inside case, inside drawer of desk, inside briefcase)
☐	Documented physical description of evidence
☐	Annotated notes for any accesses to the evidence before you arrived
☐	Annotated notes for any step that occurs outside of your normal process
☐	Filled in history annotating when you received the drive and from whom
☐	Updated chain of custody for each action taken with the original evidence

Imaging Checklist

☐   Computer is powered off
☐   Drive is removed and serial number recorded
☐   System is booted with drive removed and BIOS time recorded
☐   Chain of custody form filled out
☐   Drive is imaged with forensically sound method
☐   Chain of custody updated
☐   Drive either given back or taken with evidence receipt given

Linux Examination Checklist

☐	Linux distribution and version documented
☐	Last boot time documented
☐	Last shutdown time documented
☐	"Local" vs. "real" date/time delta identified and resolved
☐	Drive searched for remnants of file system partitions
☐	Swap space examined
☐	Log files recovered and examined
☐	User shell history files checked
☐	Drive searched for mail spools and Internet mail
☐	Internet history recovered
☐	Documents recovered from unallocated (Microsoft Office, PDF, etc.)
☐	Drive checked for wiping
☐	Deleted files recovered
☐	Printer spools recovered
☐	Archives decompressed and examined
☐	Keyword searches conducted as appropriate
☐	Summary of findings/report/conclusions/opinion written

Macintosh Examination Checklist

- ☐ OS version documented
- ☐ Last boot time documented
- ☐ Last shutdown time documented
- ☐ "Local" vs. "real" date/time delta identified and resolved
- ☐ Partition waste space searched for file system artifacts
- ☐ Large files and image files examined
- ☐ Log files recovered and examined
- ☐ User shell history files checked
- ☐ Drive searched for mail spools
- ☐ Internet history recovered
- ☐ Documents carved from unallocated (Microsoft Office, PDF, etc.)
- ☐ Drive checked for wiping
- ☐ Deleted files recovered
- ☐ Cache files and mbox files preprocessed
- ☐ Archives decompressed and examined
- ☐ Keyword searches conducted as appropriate
- ☐ Summary of findings/report/conclusions/opinion written

Windows Examination Checklist

☐	Windows version documented
☐	Last boot time documented
☐	Last shutdown time documented
☐	"Local" vs. "real" date/time delta identified and resolved
☐	Drive searched for remnants of file system partitions
☐	Large files and image files examined
☐	Log files recovered and examined
☐	Drive searched for mail spools and Internet mail
☐	INFO2 records recovered
☐	Internet history recovered
☐	Documents carved from unallocated (Microsoft Office, PDF, etc.)
☐	Drive checked for wiping
☐	Deleted files recovered
☐	Printer spools recovered
☐	XP–User Assist records recovered
☐	Archives decompressed and examined
☐	Keyword searches conducted as appropriate
☐	Summary of findings/report/conclusions/opinion written

Computer Forensic Lab Checklist

☐	Ensure your lab door locks and you have controlled access to the keys and/or combination
☐	Ensure your cleaning staff and others do not have access to the facility unless they are properly escorted
☐	Ensure the walls and ceiling are constructed in such way that easy access is prevented (e.g., no one can climb over the wall and drop through the ceiling)
☐	Ensure protective mechanisms are in place for disastrous events such as fire, flooding, lightning, and other events common to the environment
☐	Ensure there is a physically secure evidence room or locker within the lab with a separate key or combination lock than what's used to get into the lab
☐	Ensure there are written policies and procedures for lab controls, evidence controls, forensic examinations, and validation of tools and equipment
☐	Ensure a formal case-management system is in place
☐	Ensure there is a separate network connection for Internet access that is separate from the forensic examination computer
☐	Ensure the forensic examination computer is isolated from the network
☐	Ensure there is a central place to store documents (could be in the evidence room or locker if it's large enough and fits your storage needs)
☐	Ensure there is a designated document librarian for centralized and consistent control of case data
☐	Ensure there is a standard validated field kit including the hardware and software tools you use the most in your investigations
☐	Ensure you have extra copies of forms, like Chain of Custody forms and Evidence Receipts
☐	Ensure your hardware and storage are consistent with the environment you commonly investigate, including access to special equipment, extra drives, and other needed media
☐	Ensure your hardware and storage are consistent with the environment you commonly investigate, including access to special equipment, extra drives, and other needed media

Computer Forensic Lab Checklist *(continued)*

☐ Ensure you have hardware and/or software tools for
- Write protection
- Acquisition
- Data recovery/discovery
- Internet history, images, e-mail
- Password cracking
- Mobile devices (PDA/cell phone)
- Malware/virus detection
- Binary analysis
- Large storage analysis
- Multifunction use (e.g., EnCase, Paraben Tools, FTK, SMART)
- And other specialized tools helpful for the environments you investigate

Computer Forensic Fly-Away Kit

☐ Assorted hand tools including screwdrivers, nut drivers, pliers, snips, flashlight, magnifying glass, and other tools common for your environment

☐ Digital camera with date/time stamp ensures you know how the scene was laid out before you began your work (e.g., covert civil operations)

☐ Digital and hard copy of prepared forms such as Evidence Receipts, Chain of Custody, evidence labels, procedure checklists, and others commonly used

☐ Digital or hard copy of policies and procedures

☐ Evidence bag for storing and locking evidence during travel

☐ Manuals, digital or otherwise, for the tools you use

☐ Large storage media (e.g., IDE drives) for capturing data

☐ Hardware and/or software tools for
  - Write protection
  - Acquisition
  - Data recovery/discovery
  - Internet history, images, e-mail
  - Password cracking
  - Mobile devices (PDA/cell phone)
  - Malware/virus detection
  - Binary analysis
  - Large storage analysis
  - Multifunction use (e.g., EnCase, Paraben Tools, FTK, SMART)
  - And other specialized tools helpful for the environments you investigate

APPENDIX B

UNDERSTANDING LEGAL CONCERNS

This appendix discusses recent cases that have greatly influenced the computer forensics and electronic discovery community. First, the case is summarized, and then the ruling the judge issued on the case is presented. Reading the judge's opinion and decision on a case helps you understand how the court handles and accepts digital evidence.

ZUBULAKE V. UBS WARBURG

Laura Zubulake's case was a gender-discrimination case that involved electronic evidence. A question that quickly arose in the case was "Who pays for the costs of electronic discovery?" The electronic evidence in this case was e-mail that existed on backup tapes. Judge Scheindlin set forth in this ruling the procedure to follow when deciding how to split the costs of electronic discovery. These seven rules, as originally outlined by Judge Scheindlin, determine whether cost-shifting is appropriate for the discovery of inaccessible data.

The following factors should be considered, weighted more-or-less in the following order:

▼ The extent to which the request is specifically tailored to discover relevant information

■ The availability of such information from other sources

■ The total cost of production, compared to the amount in controversy

■ The total cost of production, compared to the resources available to each party

■ The relative ability of each party to control costs and its incentive to do so

■ The importance of the issues at stake in the litigation

▲ The relative benefits to the parties of obtaining the information

The transcription of the case details the circumstances and reasons for the ruling. The resulting important case law set the precedent for future cases involving electronic discovery.

Case Transcription

Following is the transcription of the case, as provided by the U.S. District Court of the Southern District of New York. The transcription can also be found at http://www.nysd .uscourts.gov/rulings/02cv01243_072403.pdf.

UNITED STATES DISTRICT COURT

SOUTHERN DISTRICT OF NEW YORK

Plaintiff: LAURA ZUBULAKE

Defendants: UBS WARBURG LLC, UBS WARBURG, and UBS AG

SHIRA A. SCHEINDLIN, U.S.D.J.:

On May 13, 2003, I ordered defendants UBS Warburg LLC, UBS Warburg, and UBS AG (collectively "UBS") to restore and produce certain e-mails from a small group of backup tapes. Having reviewed the results of this sample restoration, Laura Zubulake now moves for an order compelling UBS to produce all remaining backup e-mails at its expense. UBS argues that based on the sampling, the costs should be shifted to Zubulake.

For the reasons fully explained below, Zubulake must share in the costs of restoration, although UBS must bear the bulk of that expense. In addition, UBS must pay for any costs incurred in reviewing the restored documents for privilege.

I. BACKGROUND

The background of this lawsuit and the instant discovery dispute are recounted in two prior opinions, familiarity with which is presumed. In brief, Zubulake, an equities trader who earned approximately $650,000 a year with UBS, is now suing UBS for gender discrimination, failure to promote, and retaliation under federal, state, and city law. To support her claim, Zubulake seeks evidence stored on UBS's backup tapes that is only accessible through costly and time-consuming data retrieval. In particular, Zubulake seeks e-mails relating to her that were sent to or from five UBS employees: Matthew Chapin (Zubulake's immediate supervisor and the alleged primary discriminator), Jeremy Hardisty (Chapin's supervisor and the individual to whom Zubulake originally complained about Chapin), Rose Tong (a human relations representative who was assigned to handle issues concerning Zubulake), Vinay Datta (a coworker), and Andrew Clarke (another coworker). The question presented in this dispute is which party should pay for the costs incurred in restoring and producing these backup tapes.

In order to obtain a factual basis to support the cost-shifting analysis, I ordered UBS to restore and produce e-mails from five of the ninety-four backup tapes that UBS had then identified as containing responsive documents; Zubulake was permitted to select the five tapes to be restored. UBS now reports, however, that there are only seventy-seven backup tapes that contain responsive data, including the five already restored. I further ordered UBS to "prepare an affidavit detailing the results of its search, as well as the time and money spent." UBS has complied by submitting counsel's declaration.

According to the declaration, Zubulake selected the backup tapes corresponding to Matthew Chapin's e-mails from May, June, July, August, and September 2001. That period includes the time from Zubulake's initial EEOC charge of discrimination (August 2001) until just before her termination (in the first week of October 2001). UBS hired an outside vendor, Pinkerton Consulting & Investigations, to perform the restoration.

Pinkerton was able to restore each of the backup tapes, yielding a total of 8,344 e-mails. That number is somewhat inflated, however, because it does not account for duplicates. Because each month's backup tape was a snapshot of Chapin's server for that month—and not an incremental backup reflecting only new material—an e-mail that was on the server for more than one month would appear on more than one backup tape. For example, an e-mail received in January 2001 and deleted in November 2001 would have been restored from all five backup tapes. With duplicates eliminated, the total number of unique e-mails restored was 6,203.

Pinkerton then performed a search for e-mails containing (in either the e-mail's text or its header information, such as the "subject" line) the terms "Laura", "Zubulake", or "LZ". The searches yielded 1,541 e-mails, or 1,075 if duplicates are eliminated. Of these 1,541 e-mails, UBS deemed approximately 600 to be responsive to Zubulake's document request and they were produced. UBS also produced, under the terms of the May 13 Order, fewer than twenty e-mails extracted from UBS's optical disk storage system.

Pinkerton billed UBS 31.5 hours for its restoration services at an hourly rate of $245, six hours for the development, refinement and execution of a search script at $245 an hour, and 101.5 hours of "CPU Bench Utilization" time for use of Pinkerton's computer systems at a rate of $18.50 per hour. Pinkerton also included a five percent "administrative overhead fee" of $459.38. Thus, the total cost of restoration and search was $11,524.63. In addition, UBS incurred the following costs: $4,633 in attorney time for the document review (11.3 hours at $410 per hour) and $2,845.80 in paralegal time for tasks related to document production (16.74 hours at $170 per hour). UBS also paid $432.60 in photocopying costs, which, of course, will be paid by Zubulake and is not part of this cost-shifting analysis. The total cost of restoration and production from the five backup tapes was $19,003.43.

UBS now asks that the cost of any further production—estimated to be $273,649.39, based on the cost incurred in restoring five tapes and producing responsive documents from those tapes—be shifted to Zubulake. The total figure includes $165,954.67 to restore and search the tapes and $107,694.72 in attorney and paralegal review costs. These costs will be addressed separately below.

II. LEGAL STANDARD

The Federal Rules of Civil Procedure specify that "any matter, not privileged, that is relevant to the claim or defense of any party" is discoverable, except where:

> (i) the discovery sought is unreasonably cumulative or duplicative, or is obtainable from some other source that is more convenient, less burdensome, or less expensive;

> (ii) the party seeking discovery has had ample opportunity by discovery in the action to obtain the information sought; or

> (iii) the burden or expense of the proposed discovery outweighs its likely benefit, taking into account the needs of the case, the amount in controversy, the parties' resources, the importance of the issues at stake in the litigation, and the importance of the proposed discovery in resolving the issues.

Although "the presumption is that the responding party must bear the expense of complying with discovery requests," requests that run afoul of the Rule 26(b)(2) proportionality test may subject the requesting party to protective orders under Rule 26(c), "including orders conditioning discovery on the requesting party's payment of the costs of discovery." A court will order such a cost-shifting protective order only upon motion of the responding party to a discovery request, and "for good cause shown." Thus, the responding party has the burden of proof on a motion for cost-shifting.

III. DISCUSSION

A. Cost-Shifting Generally

In Zubulake I, I considered plaintiff's request for information contained only on backup tapes and determined that cost-shifting might be appropriate. It is worth emphasizing again that cost-shifting is potentially appropriate only when inaccessible data is sought. When a discovery request seeks accessible data—for example, active on-line or near-line data—it is typically inappropriate to consider cost-shifting.

In order to determine whether cost-shifting is appropriate for the discovery of inaccessible data, "the following factors should be considered, weighted more-or-less in the following order":

1. The extent to which the request is specifically tailored to discover relevant information;

2. The availability of such information from other sources;

3. The total cost of production, compared to the amount in controversy;

4. The total cost of production, compared to the resources available to each party;

5. The relative ability of each party to control costs and its incentive to do so;

6. The importance of the issues at stake in the litigation; and

7. The relative benefits to the parties of obtaining the information.

In establishing this test, I modified the list of factors articulated in Rowe Entertainment, Inc. v. William Morris Agency, Inc., to meet the legitimate concern of those commentators who have argued that "the factors articulated in Rowe tend to favor the responding party, and frequently result in shifting the costs of electronic discovery to the requesting party." Thus, the seven-factor test articulated in Zubulake I was designed to simplify application of the Rule 26(b)(2) proportionality test in the context of electronic data and to reinforce the traditional presumptive allocation of costs.

B. Application of the Seven Factor Test

1. Factors One and Two

As I explained in Zubulake I, the first two factors together comprise the "marginal utility test" announced in McPeek v. Ashcroft:

The more likely it is that the backup tape contains information that is relevant to a claim or defense, the fairer it is that the [responding party] search at its own expense. The less likely it is, the more unjust it would be to make the [responding party] search at its own expense. The difference is "at the margin."

These two factors should be weighted the most heavily in the cost-shifting analysis.

a. The Extent to Which the Request Is Specifically Tailored to Discover Relevant Information

The document request at issue asks for "[a]ll documents concerning any communication by or between UBS employees concerning Plaintiff," and was subsequently narrowed to pertain to only five employees (Chapin, Hardisty, Tong, Datta, and Clarke) and to the period from August 1999 to December 2001. This is a relatively limited and targeted request, a fact borne out by the e-mails UBS actually produced, both initially and as a result of the sample restoration.

At oral argument, Zubulake presented the court with sixty-eight e-mails (of the 600 she received) that she claims are "highly relevant to the issues in this case" and thus require, in her view, that UBS bear the cost of production. And indeed, a review of these e-mails reveals that they are relevant. Taken together, they tell a compelling story of the dysfunctional atmosphere surrounding UBS's U.S. Asian Equities Sales Desk (the "Desk"). Presumably, these sixty-eight e-mails are reasonably representative of the seventy-seven backup tapes.

A number of the e-mails complain of Zubulake's behavior. Zubulake was described by Clarke as engaging in "bitch sessions about the horrible men on the [Desk]," and as a "conduit for a steady stream of distortions, accusations and good ole fashioned back stabbing," and Hardisty noted that Zubulake was disrespectful to Chapin and other members of the Desk. And Chapin takes frequent snipes at Zubulake. There are also complaints about Chapin's behavior. In addition, Zubulake argues that several of the e-mails contradict testimony given by UBS employees in sworn depositions.

In particular, six e-mails singled out by Zubulake as particularly "striking" include:

▼ An e-mail from Hardisty, Chapin's supervisor, chastising Chapin for saying one thing and doing another with respect to Zubulake. Hardisty said, "As I see it, you do not appear to be upholding your end of the bargain to work with her." This e-mail stands in contrast to UBS's response to Zubulake's EEOC charges, which says that "Mr. Chapin was receptive to Mr. Hardisty's suggestions [for improving his relationship with Zubulake]."

■ An e-mail from Chapin to one of his employees on the Desk, Joy Kim, suggesting to her how to phrase a complaint against Zubulake. A few hours later, Joy Kim did in fact send an e-mail to Chapin complaining about Zubulake, using precisely the same words that Chapin had suggested. But at his deposition (taken before these e-mails were restored), Chapin claimed that he did not solicit the complaint.

■ An e-mail from Chapin to the human resources employee handling Zubulake's case listing the employees on the Desk and categorizing them as senior, mid-level, or junior salespeople. In its EEOC filing, however, UBS claimed in response to Zubulake's argument that she was the only senior salesperson on the desk, that it "does not categorize salespeople as 'junior' or 'senior.'" In addition, UBS claimed in its EEOC papers that there were four female salespeople on the Desk, but this e-mail shows only two.

- An e-mail from Chapin to Hardisty acknowledging that Zubulake's "ability to do a good job…is clear," and that she is "quite capable."

- An e-mail from Derek Hillan, presumably a UBS employee, to Chapin and Zubulake using vulgar language, although UBS claims that it does not tolerate such language.

▲ An e-mail from Michael Oertli, presumably a UBS employee, to Chapin explaining that UBS's poor performance in Singapore was attributable to the fact that it only "covered" eight or nine of twenty-two accounts, and not to Zubulake's poor performance, as UBS has argued.

Not surprisingly, UBS argued that these e-mails have very little, if any, relevance to the issues in the case. While all of these e-mails are likely to have some "tendency to make the existence of any fact that is of consequence to the determination of the action more probable or less probable than it would be without the evidence," none of them provide any direct evidence of discrimination. To be sure, the e-mails reveal a hostile relationship between Chapin and Zubulake—UBS does not contest this. But nowhere (in the sixty-eight e-mails produced to the Court) is there evidence that Chapin's dislike of Zubulake related to her gender.

b. The Availability of Such Information from Other Sources

The other half of the marginal utility test is the availability of the relevant data from other sources. Neither party seemed to know how many of the 600 e-mails produced in response to the May 13 Order had been previously produced. UBS argues that "nearly all of the restored e-mails that relate to plaintiff's allegations in this matter or to the merits of her case were already produced." This statement is perhaps too careful, because UBS goes on to observe that "the vast majority of the restored e-mails that were produced do not relate at all to plaintiff's allegations in this matter or to the merits of her case." But this determination is not for UBS to make; as the saying goes, "one man's trash is another man's treasure."

It is axiomatic that a requesting party may obtain "any matter, not privileged, that is relevant to the claim or defense of any party." The simple fact is that UBS previously produced only 100 pages of e-mails, but has now produced 853 pages (comprising the 600 responsive e-mails) from the five selected backup tapes alone. UBS itself decided that it was obliged to provide these 853 pages of e-mail pursuant to the requirements of Rule 26. Having done so, these numbers lead to the unavoidable conclusion that there are a significant number of responsive e-mails that now exist only on backup tapes.

If this were not enough, there is some evidence that Chapin was concealing and deleting especially relevant e-mails. When Zubulake first filed her EEOC charge in August 2001, all UBS employees were instructed to save documents relevant to her case. In furtherance of this policy, Chapin maintained separate files on Zubulake. However, certain e-mails sent after the initial EEOC charge—and particularly relevant to Zubulake's retaliation claim—were apparently not saved at all. For example, the e-mail from Chapin to Joy Kim instructing her on how to file a complaint against Zubulake was not saved, and it bears the subject line "UBS client attorney priviledge [sic] only," although no attorney is copied on the e-mail. This potentially useful e-mail was deleted and resided only on UBS's backup tapes.

In sum, hundreds of the e-mails produced from the five backup tapes were not previously produced, and so were only available from the tapes. The contents of these e-mails are also new. Although some of the substance is available from other sources (e.g., evidence of the sour relationship between Chapin and Zubulake), a good deal of it is only found on the backup tapes (e.g., inconsistencies with UBS's EEOC filing and Chapin's deposition testimony). Moreover, an e-mail contains the precise words used by the author. Because of that, it is a particularly powerful form of proof at trial when offered as an admission of a party opponent.

c. Weighing Factors One and Two

The sample restoration, which resulted in the production of relevant e-mail, has demonstrated that Zubulake's discovery request was narrowly tailored to discover relevant information. And while the subject matter of some of those e-mails was addressed in other documents, these particular e-mails are only available from the backup tapes. Thus, direct evidence of discrimination may only be available through restoration. As a result, the marginal utility of this additional discovery may be quite high.

While restoration may be the only means for obtaining direct evidence of discrimination, the existence of that evidence is still speculative. The best that can be said is that Zubulake has demonstrated that the marginal utility is potentially high. All-in-all, because UBS bears the burden of proving that cost-shifting is warranted, the marginal utility test tips slightly against cost-shifting.

2. Factors Three, Four and Five

"The second group of factors addresses cost issues: 'How expensive will this production be?' and, 'Who can handle that expense?'"

a. The Total Cost of Production Compared to the Amount in Controversy

UBS spent $11,524.63, or $2,304.93 per tape, to restore the five backup tapes. Thus, the total cost of restoring the remaining seventy-two tapes extrapolates to $165,954.67.

In order to assess the amount in controversy, I posed the following question to the parties: Assuming that a jury returns a verdict in favor of plaintiff, what economic damages can the plaintiff reasonably expect to recover? Plaintiff answered that reasonable damages are between $15,271,361 and $19,227,361, depending upon how front pay is calculated. UBS answered that damages could be as high as $1,265,000.

Obviously, this is a significant disparity. At this early stage, I cannot assess the accuracy of either estimate. Plaintiff had every incentive to high-ball the figure and UBS had every incentive to low-ball it. It is clear, however, that this case has the potential for a multi-million dollar recovery. Whatever else might be said, this is not a nuisance value case, a small case or a frivolous case. Most people do not earn $650,000 a year. If Zubulake prevails, her damages award undoubtedly will be higher than that of the vast majority of Title VII plaintiffs.

In an ordinary case, a responding party should not be required to pay for the restoration of inaccessible data if the cost of that restoration is significantly disproportionate to the value of the case. Assuming this to be a multi-million dollar case, the cost of restoration is surely not "significantly disproportionate" to the projected value of this case. This factor weighs against cost-shifting.

b. The Total Cost of Production Compared to the Resources Available to Each Party

There is no question that UBS has exponentially more resources available to it than Zubulake. While Zubulake is an accomplished equities trader, she has now been unemployed for close to two years. Given the difficulties in the equities market and the fact that she is suing her former employer, she may not be particularly marketable. On the other hand, she asserts that she has a $19 million claim against UBS. So while UBS's resources clearly dwarf Zubulake's, she may have the financial wherewithal to cover at least some of the cost of restoration. In addition, it is not unheard of for plaintiff's firms to front huge expenses when multi-million dollar recoveries are in sight. Thus, while this factor weighs against cost-shifting, it does not rule it out.

c. The Relative Ability of Each Party to Control Costs and Its Incentive to Do So

Restoration of backup tapes must generally be done by an outside vendor. Here, UBS had complete control over the selection of the vendor. It is entirely possible that a less-expensive vendor could have been found. However, once that vendor is selected, costs are not within the control of either party. In addition, because these backup tapes are relatively well-organized—meaning that UBS knows what e-mails can be found on each tape—there is nothing more that Zubulake can do to focus her discovery request or reduce its cost. Zubulake has already made a targeted discovery request and the restoration of the sample tapes has not enabled her to cut back on that request. Thus, this factor is neutral.

3. Factor Six: The Importance of the Issues at Stake in the Litigation

As noted in Zubulake I, this factor "will only rarely come into play." Although this case revolves around a weighty issue—discrimination in the workplace—it is hardly unique. Claims of discrimination are common, and while discrimination is an important problem, this litigation does not present a particularly novel issue. If I were to consider the issues in this discrimination case sufficiently important to weigh in the cost-shifting analysis, then this factor would be virtually meaningless. Accordingly, this factor is neutral.

4. Factor Seven: The Relative Benefits to the Parties of Obtaining the Information

Although Zubulake argues that there are potential benefits to UBS in undertaking the restoration of these backup tapes—in particular, the opportunity to obtain evidence that may be useful at summary judgment or trial—there can be no question that Zubulake stands to gain far more than does UBS, as will typically be the case. Certainly, absent an order, UBS would not restore any of this data of its own volition. Accordingly, this factor weighs in favor of cost-shifting.

5. Summary and Conclusion

Factors one through four tip against cost-shifting (although factor two only slightly so). Factors five and six are neutral, and factor seven favors cost-shifting. As noted in my earlier opinion in this case, however, a list of factors is not merely a matter of counting and adding; it is only a guide. Because some of the factors cut against cost-shifting, but only slightly so—in particular, the possibility that the continued production will produce valuable new information—some cost-shifting is appropriate in this case, although UBS should pay the majority of the costs. There is plainly relevant evidence that is only available on UBS's backup tapes. At the same time, Zubulake has not been able to show that there is indispensable evidence on those backup tapes (although the fact that Chapin apparently deleted certain e-mails indicates that such evidence may exist).

The next question is how much of the cost should be shifted. It is beyond cavil that the precise allocation is a matter of judgment and fairness rather than a mathematical consequence of the seven factors discussed above. Nonetheless, the analysis of those factors does inform the exercise of discretion. Because the seven factor test requires that UBS pay the lion's share, the percentage assigned to Zubulake must be less than fifty percent. A share that is too costly may chill the rights of litigants to pursue meritorious claims. However, because the success of this search is somewhat speculative, any cost that fairly can be assigned to Zubulake is appropriate and ensures that UBS's expenses will not be unduly burdensome. A twenty-five percent assignment to Zubulake meets these goals.

C. Other Costs

The final question is whether this result should apply to the entire cost of the production, or only to the cost of restoring the backup tapes. The difference is not academic—the estimated cost of restoring and searching the remaining backup tapes is $165,954.67, while the estimated cost of producing them (restoration and searching costs plus attorney and paralegal costs) is $273,649.39 ($19,003.43 for the five sample tapes, or $3,800.69 per tape, times seventy-two unrestored tapes), a difference of $107,694.72.

As a general rule, where cost-shifting is appropriate, only the costs of restoration and searching should be shifted. Restoration, of course, is the act of making inaccessible material accessible. That "special purpose" or "extraordinary step" should be the subject of cost-shifting. Search costs should also be shifted because they are so intertwined with the restoration process; a vendor like Pinkerton will not only develop and refine the search script, but also necessarily execute the search as it conducts the restoration. However, the responding party should always bear the cost of reviewing and producing electronic data once it has been converted to an accessible form. This is so for two reasons.

First, the producing party has the exclusive ability to control the cost of reviewing the documents. In this case, UBS decided—as is its right—to have a senior associate at a top New York City law firm conduct the privilege review at a cost of $410 per hour. But the job could just as easily have been done (while perhaps not as well) by a first-year associate or contract attorney at a far lower rate. UBS could similarly have obtained paralegal assistance for far less than $170 per hour.

Moreover, the producing party unilaterally decides on the review protocol. When reviewing electronic data, that review may range from reading every word of every document to conducting a series of targeted key word searches. Indeed, many parties to document-intensive litigation enter into so-called "claw-back" agreements that allow the parties to forego privilege review altogether in favor of an agreement to return inadvertently produced privileged documents. The parties here can still reach such an agreement with respect to the remaining seventy-two tapes and thereby avoid any cost of reviewing these tapes for privilege.

Second, the argument that all costs related to the production of restored data should be shifted misapprehends the nature of the cost-shifting inquiry. Recalling that cost-shifting is only appropriate for inaccessible—but otherwise discoverable—data, it necessarily follows that once the data has been restored to an accessible format and responsive documents located, cost-shifting is no longer appropriate. Had it always been accessible, there is no question that UBS would have had to produce the data at its own cost. Indeed, this is precisely what I ordered in Zubulake I with respect to certain e-mails kept on UBS's optical disk system.

Documents stored on backup tapes can be likened to paper records locked inside a sophisticated safe to which no one has the key or combination. The cost of accessing those documents may be onerous, and in some cases the parties should split the cost of breaking into the safe. But once the safe is opened, the production of the documents found inside is the sole responsibility of the responding party. The point is simple: technology may increasingly permit litigants to reconstruct lost or inaccessible information, but once restored to an accessible form, the usual rules of discovery apply.

IV. CONCLUSION

For the reasons set forth above, the costs of restoring any backup tapes are allocated between UBS and Zubulake seventy-five percent and twenty-five percent, respectively. All other costs are to be borne exclusively by UBS. Notwithstanding this ruling, UBS can potentially impose a shift of all of its costs, attorney's fees included, by making an offer to the plaintiff under Rule 68.

SO ORDERED:

Shira A. Scheindlin

U.S.D.J.

Dated: New York, New York

July 24, 2003

CASE SUMMARIES

The following web sites keep up with case law and contain summaries of cases relevant to the chapters in the book. You should be aware of these cases, as many courts use these as case law on which to base their rulings.

Web Site	URL	Description
Fios	http://www.discoveryresources.org/	Fios provides a public blog where its internal lawyers give updates on the state of electronic discovery.
Kroll Ontrack	http://www.krollontrack.com/legalresources/	Kroll Ontrack has an excellent and continuously updated list of cases and case law as it occurs.
Guidance Software	http://www.guidancesoftware.com/corporate/legal/index.shtm	Guidance software keeps up with cases that directly relate to the use of their software and case law in general.

APPENDIX C

THE DIGITAL EVIDENCE LEGAL PROCESS

We discuss and highlight the Federal Rules of Evidence and the Federal Rules of Civil Procedure in this appendix. The Federal Rules of Evidence discuss how to handle and admit evidence into court. The Federal Rules of Civil Procedure define the processes the court will go through to bring judgment in a civil suit. As an expert witness, you need to understand these processes.

FEDERAL RULES OF EVIDENCE: OVERVIEW

The Federal Rules of Evidence are the most relevant rules of law for the forensic investigator. They explain what can and cannot be admitted as evidence. This ultimately determines what can be admitted as evidence into a federal court. The Federal Rules of Evidence is the supporting document used for all electronic evidence admissibility, especially forensic images.

 We removed sections we believed were less relevant to the role of the forensic investigator. The Legal Information Institute, maintained by Cornell Law School, maintains a copy you can read here: http://www.law.cornell.edu/rules/fre/overview.html.

FEDERAL RULES OF EVIDENCE (FRE)

ARTICLE I. GENERAL PROVISIONS

Rule 101. Scope
These rules govern proceedings in the courts of the United States and before United States bankruptcy judges and United States magistrate judges, to the extent and with the exceptions stated in rule 1101.

Rule 102. Purpose and Construction
These rules shall be construed to secure fairness in administration, elimination of unjustifiable expense and delay, and promotion of growth and development of the law of evidence to the end that the truth may be ascertained and proceedings justly determined.

Rule 103. Rulings on Evidence
(a) Effect of erroneous ruling.
Error may not be predicated upon a ruling which admits or excludes evidence unless a substantial right of the party is affected, and

(1) Objection. - In case the ruling is one admitting evidence, a timely objection or motion to strike appears of record, stating the specific ground of objection, if the specific ground was not apparent from the context; or

(2) Offer of proof. - In case the ruling is one excluding evidence, the substance of the evidence was made known to the court by offer or was apparent from the context within which questions were asked.

Once the court makes a definitive ruling on the record admitting or excluding evidence, either at or before trial, a party need not renew an objection or offer of proof to preserve a claim of error for appeal.

(b) Record of offer and ruling.
The court may add any other or further statement which shows the character of the evidence, the form in which it was offered, the objection made, and the ruling thereon. It may direct the making of an offer in question and answer form.

(c) Hearing of jury.
In jury cases, proceedings shall be conducted, to the extent practicable, so as to prevent inadmissible evidence from being suggested to the jury by any means, such as making statements or offers of proof or asking questions in the hearing of the jury.

(d) Plain error.
Nothing in this rule precludes taking notice of plain errors affecting substantial rights although they were not brought to the attention of the court.

Rule 104. Preliminary Questions

(a) Questions of admissibility generally.
Preliminary questions concerning the qualification of a person to be a witness, the existence of a privilege, or the admissibility of evidence shall be determined by the court, subject to the provisions of subdivision (b). In making its determination it is not bound by the rules of evidence except those with respect to privileges.

(b) Relevancy conditioned on fact.
When the relevancy of evidence depends upon the fulfillment of a condition of fact, the court shall admit it upon, or subject to, the introduction of evidence sufficient to support a finding of the fulfillment of the condition.

(c) Hearing of jury.
Hearings on the admissibility of confessions shall in all cases be conducted out of the hearing of the jury. Hearings on other preliminary matters shall be so conducted when the interests of justice require, or when an accused is a witness and so requests.

(d) Testimony by accused.
The accused does not, by testifying upon a preliminary matter, become subject to cross-examination as to other issues in the case.

(e) Weight and credibility.
This rule does not limit the right of a party to introduce before the jury evidence relevant to weight or credibility.

Rule 105. Limited Admissibility

When evidence which is admissible as to one party or for one purpose but not admissible as to another party or for another purpose is admitted, the court, upon request, shall restrict the evidence to its proper scope and instruct the jury accordingly.

Rule 106. Remainder of or Related Writings or Recorded Statements

When a writing or recorded statement or part thereof is introduced by a party, an adverse party may require the introduction at that time of any other part or any other writing or recorded statement which ought in fairness to be considered contemporaneously with it.

ARTICLE II. JUDICIAL NOTICE

Rule 201. Judicial Notice of Adjudicative Facts

(a) Scope of rule.

This rule governs only judicial notice of adjudicative facts.

(b) Kinds of facts.

A judicially noticed fact must be one not subject to reasonable dispute in that it is either (1) generally known within the territorial jurisdiction of the trial court or (2) capable of accurate and ready determination by resort to sources whose accuracy cannot reasonably be questioned.

(c) When discretionary.

A court may take judicial notice, whether requested or not.

(d) When mandatory.

A court shall take judicial notice if requested by a party and supplied with the necessary information.

(e) Opportunity to be heard.

A party is entitled upon timely request to an opportunity to be heard as to the propriety of taking judicial notice and the tenor of the matter noticed. In the absence of prior notification, the request may be made after judicial notice has been taken.

(f) Time of taking notice.

Judicial notice may be taken at any stage of the proceeding.

(g) Instructing jury.

In a civil action or proceeding, the court shall instruct the jury to accept as conclusive any fact judicially noticed. In a criminal case, the court shall instruct the jury that it may, but is not required to, accept as conclusive any fact judicially noticed.

ARTICLE III. PRESUMPTIONS IN CIVIL ACTIONS AND PROCEEDINGS

Rule 301. Presumptions in General Civil Actions and Proceedings

In all civil actions and proceedings not otherwise provided for by Act of Congress or by these rules, a presumption imposes on the party against whom it is directed the burden of going forward with evidence to rebut or meet the presumption, but does not shift to such party the burden of proof in the sense of the risk of nonpersuasion, which remains throughout the trial upon the party on whom it was originally cast.

Rule 302. Applicability of State Law in Civil Actions and Proceedings

In civil actions and proceedings, the effect of a presumption respecting a fact which is an element of a claim or defense as to which State law supplies the rule of decision is determined in accordance with State law.

ARTICLE IV. RELEVANCY AND ITS LIMITS

Rule 401. Definition of "Relevant Evidence"

"Relevant evidence" means evidence having any tendency to make the existence of any fact that is of consequence to the determination of the action more probable or less probable than it would be without the evidence.

Rule 402. Relevant Evidence Generally Admissible; Irrelevant Evidence Inadmissible

All relevant evidence is admissible, except as otherwise provided by the Constitution of the United States, by Act of Congress, by these rules, or by other rules prescribed by the Supreme Court pursuant to statutory authority. Evidence which is not relevant is not admissible.

Rule 403. Exclusion of Relevant Evidence on Grounds of Prejudice, Confusion, or Waste of Time

Although relevant, evidence may be excluded if its probative value is substantially outweighed by the danger of unfair prejudice, confusion of the issues, or misleading the jury, or by considerations of undue delay, waste of time, or needless presentation of cumulative evidence.

Rule 406. Habit; Routine Practice

Evidence of the habit of a person or of the routine practice of an organization, whether corroborated or not and regardless of the presence of eyewitnesses, is relevant to prove that the conduct of the person or organization on a particular occasion was in conformity with the habit or routine practice.

Rule 408. Compromise and Offers to Compromise

Evidence of (1) furnishing or offering or promising to furnish, or (2) accepting or offering or promising to accept, a valuable consideration in compromising or attempting to compromise a claim which was disputed as to either validity or amount, is not admissible to prove liability for or invalidity of the claim or its amount. Evidence of conduct or statements made in compromise negotiations is likewise not admissible. This rule does not require the exclusion of any evidence otherwise discoverable merely because it is presented in the course of compromise negotiations. This rule also does not require exclusion when the evidence is offered for another purpose, such as proving bias or prejudice of a witness, negativing a contention of undue delay, or proving an effort to obstruct a criminal investigation or prosecution.

Rule 409. Payment of Medical and Similar Expenses

ARTICLE V. PRIVILEGES

Rule 501. General Rule

Except as otherwise required by the Constitution of the United States or provided by Act of Congress or in rules prescribed by the Supreme Court pursuant to statutory authority, the privilege of a witness, person, government, State, or political subdivision thereof shall be governed by the principles of the common law as they may be interpreted by the courts of the United States in the light of reason and experience. However, in civil actions and proceedings, with respect to an element of a claim or defense as to which State law supplies the rule of decision, the privilege of a witness, person, government, State, or political subdivision thereof shall be determined in accordance with State law.

ARTICLE VI. WITNESSES

Rule 601. General Rule of Competency

Every person is competent to be a witness except as otherwise provided in these rules. However, in civil actions and proceedings, with respect to an element of a claim or defense as to which State law supplies the rule of decision, the competency of a witness shall be determined in accordance with State law.

Rule 602. Lack of Personal Knowledge

A witness may not testify to a matter unless evidence is introduced sufficient to support a finding that the witness has personal knowledge of the matter. Evidence to prove personal knowledge may, but need not, consist of the witness' own testimony. This rule is subject to the provisions of rule 703, relating to opinion testimony by expert witnesses.

Rule 603. Oath or Affirmation

Before testifying, every witness shall be required to declare that the witness will testify truthfully, by oath or affirmation administered in a form calculated to awaken the witness' conscience and impress the witness' mind with the duty to do so.

Rule 604. Interpreters

An interpreter is subject to the provisions of these rules relating to qualification as an expert and the administration of an oath or affirmation to make a true translation.

Rule 605. Competency of Judge as Witness

The judge presiding at the trial may not testify in that trial as a witness. No objection need be made in order to preserve the point.

Rule 607. Who May Impeach

The credibility of a witness may be attacked by any party, including the party calling the witness.

Rule 608. Evidence of Character and Conduct of Witness

(a) Opinion and reputation evidence of character.

The credibility of a witness may be attacked or supported by evidence in the form of opinion or reputation, but subject to these limitations: (1) the evidence may refer only to character for truthfulness or untruthfulness, and (2) evidence of truthful character is admissible only after the character of the witness for truthfulness has been attacked by opinion or reputation evidence or otherwise.

(b) Specific instances of conduct.

Specific instances of the conduct of a witness, for the purpose of attacking or supporting the witness' character for truthfulness, other than conviction of crime as provided in rule 609, may not be proved by extrinsic evidence. They may, however, in the discretion of the court, if probative of truthfulness or untruthfulness, be inquired into on cross-examination of the witness (1) concerning the witness' character for truthfulness or untruthfulness, or (2) concerning the character for truthfulness or untruthfulness of another witness as to which character the witness being cross-examined has testified.

The giving of testimony, whether by an accused or by any other witness, does not operate as a waiver of the accused's or the witness' privilege against self-incrimination when examined with respect to matters that relate only to character for truthfulness.

Rule 609. Impeachment by Evidence of Conviction of Crime

(a) General rule.

For the purpose of attacking the credibility of a witness,

(1) evidence that a witness other than an accused has been convicted of a crime shall be admitted, subject to Rule 403, if the crime was punishable by death or imprisonment in excess of one year under the law under which the witness was convicted, and evidence that an accused has been convicted of such a crime shall be admitted if the court determines that the probative value of admitting this evidence outweighs its prejudicial effect to the accused; and

(2) evidence that any witness has been convicted of a crime shall be admitted if it involved dishonesty or false statement, regardless of the punishment.

(b) Time limit.

Evidence of a conviction under this rule is not admissible if a period of more than ten years has elapsed since the date of the conviction or of the release of the witness from the confinement imposed for that conviction, whichever is the later date, unless the court determines, in the interests of justice, that the probative value of the conviction supported by specific facts and circumstances substantially outweighs its prejudicial effect. However, evidence of a conviction more than 10 years old as calculated herein, is not admissible unless the proponent gives to the adverse party sufficient advance written notice of intent to use such evidence to provide the adverse party with a fair opportunity to contest the use of such evidence.

(c) Effect of pardon, annulment, or certificate of rehabilitation.

Evidence of a conviction is not admissible under this rule if (1) the conviction has been the subject of a pardon, annulment, certificate of rehabilitation, or other equivalent procedure based on a finding of the rehabilitation of the person convicted, and that person has not been convicted of a subsequent crime which was punishable by death or imprisonment in excess of one year, or (2) the conviction has been the subject of a pardon, annulment, or other equivalent procedure based on a finding of innocence.

(d) Juvenile adjudications.

Evidence of juvenile adjudications is generally not admissible under this rule. The court may, however, in a criminal case allow evidence of a juvenile adjudication of a witness other than the accused if conviction of the offense would be admissible to attack the credibility of an adult and the court is satisfied that admission in evidence is necessary for a fair determination of the issue of guilt or innocence.

(e) Pendency of appeal.

The pendency of an appeal therefrom does not render evidence of a conviction inadmissible. Evidence of the pendency of an appeal is admissible.

Rule 610. Religious Beliefs or Opinions

Evidence of the beliefs or opinions of a witness on matters of religion is not admissible for the purpose of showing that by reason of their nature the witness' credibility is impaired or enhanced.

Rule 611. Mode and Order of Interrogation and Presentation

(a) Control by court.

The court shall exercise reasonable control over the mode and order of interrogating witnesses and presenting evidence so as to (1) make the interrogation and presentation effective for the ascertainment of the truth, (2) avoid needless consumption of time, and (3) protect witnesses from harassment or undue embarrassment.

(b) Scope of cross-examination.

Cross-examination should be limited to the subject matter of the direct examination and matters affecting the credibility of the witness. The court may, in the exercise of discretion, permit inquiry into additional matters as if on direct examination.

(c) Leading questions.

Leading questions should not be used on the direct examination of a witness except as may be necessary to develop the witness' testimony. Ordinarily leading questions should be permitted on cross-examination. When a party calls a hostile witness, an adverse party, or a witness identified with an adverse party, interrogation may be by leading questions.

Rule 612. Writing Used to Refresh Memory

Except as otherwise provided in criminal proceedings by section 3500 of title 18, United States Code, if a witness uses a writing to refresh memory for the purpose of testifying, either—

(1) while testifying, or

(2) before testifying, if the court in its discretion determines it is necessary in the interests of justice,

an adverse party is entitled to have the writing produced at the hearing, to inspect it, to cross-examine the witness thereon, and to introduce in evidence those portions which relate to the testimony of the witness. If it is claimed that the writing contains matters not related to the subject matter of the testimony the court shall examine the writing in camera, excise any portions not so related, and order delivery of the remainder to the party entitled thereto. Any portion withheld over objections shall be preserved and made available to the appellate court in the event of an appeal. If a writing is not produced or delivered pursuant to order under this rule, the court shall make any order justice requires, except that in criminal cases when the prosecution elects not to comply, the order shall be one striking the testimony or, if the court in its discretion determines that the interests of justice so require, declaring a mistrial.

Rule 613. Prior Statements of Witnesses

(a) Examining witness concerning prior statement.

In examining a witness concerning a prior statement made by the witness, whether written or not, the statement need not be shown nor its contents disclosed to the witness at that time, but on request the same shall be shown or disclosed to opposing counsel.

(b) Extrinsic evidence of prior inconsistent statement of witness.

Extrinsic evidence of a prior inconsistent statement by a witness is not admissible unless the witness is afforded an opportunity to explain or deny the same and the opposite party is afforded an opportunity to interrogate the witness thereon, or the interests of justice otherwise require. This provision does not apply to admissions of a party-opponent as defined in rule 801(d)(2).

Rule 614. Calling and Interrogation of Witnesses by Court

(a) Calling by court.

The court may, on its own motion or at the suggestion of a party, call witnesses, and all parties are entitled to cross-examine witnesses thus called.

(b) Interrogation by court.

The court may interrogate witnesses, whether called by itself or by a party.

(c) Objections.

Objections to the calling of witnesses by the court or to interrogation by it may be made at the time or at the next available opportunity when the jury is not present.

Rule 615. Exclusion of Witnesses

At the request of a party the court shall order witnesses excluded so that they cannot hear the testimony of other witnesses, and it may make the order of its own motion. This rule does not authorize exclusion of (1) a party who is a natural person, or (2) an officer or employee of a party which is not a natural person designated as its representative by its attorney, or (3) a person whose presence is shown by a party to be essential to the presentation of the party's cause, or (4) a person authorized by statute to be present.

ARTICLE VII. OPINIONS AND EXPERT TESTIMONY

Rule 701. Opinion Testimony by Lay Witnesses

If the witness is not testifying as an expert, the witness' testimony in the form of opinions or inferences is limited to those opinions or inferences which are (a) rationally based on the perception of the witness, and (b) helpful to a clear understanding of the witness' testimony or the determination of a fact in issue, and (c) not based on scientific, technical, or other specialized knowledge within the scope of Rule 702.

Rule 702. Testimony by Experts

If scientific, technical, or other specialized knowledge will assist the trier of fact to understand the evidence or to determine a fact in issue, a witness qualified as an expert by knowledge, skill, experience, training, or education, may testify thereto in the form of an opinion or otherwise, if (1) the testimony is based upon sufficient facts or data, (2) the testimony is the product of reliable principles and methods, and (3) the witness has applied the principles and methods reliably to the facts of the case.

Rule 703. Bases of Opinion Testimony by Experts

The facts or data in the particular case upon which an expert bases an opinion or inference may be those perceived by or made known to the expert at or before the hearing. If of a type reasonably relied upon by experts in the particular field in forming opinions or inferences upon the subject, the facts or data need not be admissible in evidence in order for the opinion or inference to be admitted. Facts or data that are otherwise inadmissible shall not be disclosed to the jury by the proponent of the opinion or inference unless the court determines that their probative value in assisting the jury to evaluate the expert's opinion substantially outweighs their prejudicial effect.

Rule 704. Opinion on Ultimate Issue

(a) Except as provided in subdivision (b), testimony in the form of an opinion or inference otherwise admissible is not objectionable because it embraces an ultimate issue to be decided by the trier of fact.

(b) No expert witness testifying with respect to the mental state or condition of a defendant in a criminal case may state an opinion or inference as to whether the defendant did or did not have the mental state or condition constituting an element of the crime charged or of a defense thereto. Such ultimate issues are matters for the trier of fact alone.

Rule 705. Disclosure of Facts or Data Underlying Expert Opinion

The expert may testify in terms of opinion or inference and give reasons therefor without first testifying to the underlying facts or data, unless the court requires otherwise. The expert may in any event be required to disclose the underlying facts or data on cross-examination.

Rule 706. Court Appointed Experts

(a) Appointment.

The court may on its own motion or on the motion of any party enter an order to show cause why expert witnesses should not be appointed, and may request the parties to submit nominations. The court may appoint any expert witnesses agreed upon by the parties, and may appoint expert witnesses of its own selection. An expert witness shall not be appointed by the court unless the witness consents to act. A witness so appointed shall be informed of the witness' duties by the court in writing, a copy of which shall be filed with the clerk, or at a conference in which the parties shall have opportunity to participate. A witness so appointed shall advise the parties of the witness' findings, if any; the witness' deposition may be taken by any party; and the witness may be called to testify by the court or any party. The witness shall be subject to cross-examination by each party, including a party calling the witness.

(b) Compensation.

Expert witnesses so appointed are entitled to reasonable compensation in whatever sum the court may allow. The compensation thus fixed is payable from funds which may be provided by law in criminal cases and civil actions and proceedings involving just compensation under the fifth amendment. In other civil actions and proceedings the compensation shall be paid by the parties in such proportion and at such time as the court directs, and thereafter charged in like manner as other costs.

(c) Disclosure of appointment.

In the exercise of its discretion, the court may authorize disclosure to the jury of the fact that the court appointed the expert witness.

(d) Parties' experts of own selection.

Nothing in this rule limits the parties in calling expert witnesses of their own selection.

ARTICLE VIII. HEARSAY

Rule 801. Definitions

The following definitions apply under this article:

(a) Statement.
A "statement" is (1) an oral or written assertion or (2) nonverbal conduct of a person, if it is intended by the person as an assertion.

(b) Declarant.
A "declarant" is a person who makes a statement.

(c) Hearsay.
"Hearsay" is a statement, other than one made by the declarant while testifying at the trial or hearing, offered in evidence to prove the truth of the matter asserted.

(d) Statements which are not hearsay.
A statement is not hearsay if—

(1) *Prior statement by witness.* The declarant testifies at the trial or hearing and is subject to cross-examination concerning the statement, and the statement is (A) inconsistent with the declarant's testimony, and was given under oath subject to the penalty of perjury at a trial, hearing, or other proceeding, or in a deposition, or (B) consistent with the declarant's testimony and is offered to rebut an express or implied charge against the declarant of recent fabrication or improper influence or motive, or (C) one of identification of a person made after perceiving the person; or

(2) *Admission by party-opponent.* The statement is offered against a party and is

(A) the party's own statement, in either an individual or a representative capacity, or

(B) a statement of which the party has manifested an adoption or belief in its truth, or

(C) a statement by a person authorized by the party to make a statement concerning the subject, or

(D) a statement by the party's agent or servant concerning a matter within the scope of the agency or employment, made during the existence of the relationship, or

(E) a statement by a coconspirator of a party during the course and in furtherance of the conspiracy.

The contents of the statement shall be considered but are not alone sufficient to establish the declarant's authority under subdivision (C), the agency or employment relationship and scope thereof under subdivision (D), or the existence of the conspiracy and the participation therein of the declarant and the party against whom the statement is offered under subdivision (E).

Rule 802. Hearsay Rule

Hearsay is not admissible except as provided by these rules or by other rules prescribed by the Supreme Court pursuant to statutory authority or by Act of Congress.

Rule 803. Hearsay Exceptions; Availability of Declarant Immaterial

The following are not excluded by the hearsay rule, even though the declarant is available as a witness:

(1) Present sense impression.

A statement describing or explaining an event or condition made while the declarant was perceiving the event or condition, or immediately thereafter.

(2) Excited utterance.

A statement relating to a startling event or condition made while the declarant was under the stress of excitement caused by the event or condition.

(3) Then existing mental, emotional, or physical condition.

A statement of the declarant's then existing state of mind, emotion, sensation, or physical condition (such as intent, plan, motive, design, mental feeling, pain, and bodily health), but not including a statement of memory or belief to prove the fact remembered or believed unless it relates to the execution, revocation, identification, or terms of declarant's will.

(4) Statements for purposes of medical diagnosis or treatment.

Statements made for purposes of medical diagnosis or treatment and describing medical history, or past or present symptoms, pain, or sensations, or the inception or general character of the cause or external source thereof insofar as reasonably pertinent to diagnosis or treatment.

(5) Recorded recollection.

A memorandum or record concerning a matter about which a witness once had knowledge but now has insufficient recollection to enable the witness to testify fully and accurately, shown to have been made or adopted by the witness when the matter was fresh in the witness' memory and to reflect that knowledge correctly. If admitted, the memorandum or record may be read into evidence but may not itself be received as an exhibit unless offered by an adverse party.

(6) Records of regularly conducted activity.

A memorandum, report, record, or data compilation, in any form, of acts, events, conditions, opinions, or diagnoses, made at or near the time by, or from information transmitted by, a person with knowledge, if kept in the course of a regularly conducted business activity, and if it was the regular practice of that business activity to make the memorandum, report, record or data compilation, all as shown by the testimony of the custodian or other qualified witness, or by certification that complies with Rule 902(11), Rule 902(12), or a statute permitting certification, unless the source of information or the method or circumstances of preparation indicate lack of trustworthiness. The term "business" as used in this paragraph includes business, institution, association, profession, occupation, and calling of every kind, whether or not conducted for profit.

(7) Absence of entry in records kept in accordance with the provisions of paragraph (6).

Evidence that a matter is not included in the memoranda reports, records, or data compilations, in any form, kept in accordance with the provisions of paragraph (6), to prove the nonoccurrence or nonexistence of the matter, if the matter was of a kind of which a memorandum, report, record, or data compilation was regularly made and preserved, unless the sources of information or other circumstances indicate lack of trustworthiness.

(8) Public records and reports.

Records, reports, statements, or data compilations, in any form, of public offices or agencies, setting forth (A) the activities of the office or agency, or (B) matters observed pursuant to duty imposed by law as to which matters there was a duty to report, excluding, however, in criminal cases matters observed by police officers and other law enforcement personnel, or (C) in civil actions and proceedings and against the Government in criminal cases, factual findings resulting from an investigation made pursuant to authority granted by law, unless the sources of information or other circumstances indicate lack of trustworthiness.

(9) Records of vital statistics.

Records or data compilations, in any form, of births, fetal deaths, deaths, or marriages, if the report thereof was made to a public office pursuant to requirements of law.

(10) Absence of public record or entry.

To prove the absence of a record, report, statement, or data compilation, in any form, or the nonoccurrence or nonexistence of a matter of which a record, report, statement, or data compilation, in any form, was regularly made and preserved by a public office or agency, evidence in the form of a certification in accordance with rule 902, or testimony, that diligent search failed to disclose the record, report, statement, or data compilation, or entry.

(11) Records of religious organizations.

Statements of births, marriages, divorces, deaths, legitimacy, ancestry, relationship by blood or marriage, or other similar facts of personal or family history, contained in a regularly kept record of a religious organization.

(12) Marriage, baptismal, and similar certificates.

Statements of fact contained in a certificate that the maker performed a marriage or other ceremony or administered a sacrament, made by a clergyman, public official, or other person authorized by the rules or practices of a religious organization or by law to perform the act certified, and purporting to have been issued at the time of the act or within a reasonable time thereafter.

(13) Family records.

Statements of fact concerning personal or family history contained in family Bibles, genealogies, charts, engravings on rings, inscriptions on family portraits, engravings on urns, crypts, or tombstones, or the like.

(14) Records of documents affecting an interest in property.

The record of a document purporting to establish or affect an interest in property, as proof of the content of the original recorded document and its execution and delivery by each person by whom it purports to have been executed, if the record is a record of a public office and an applicable statute authorizes the recording of documents of that kind in that office.

(15) Statements in documents affecting an interest in property.

A statement contained in a document purporting to establish or affect an interest in property if the matter stated was relevant to the purpose of the document, unless dealings with the property since the document was made have been inconsistent with the truth of the statement or the purport of the document.

(16) Statements in ancient documents.

Statements in a document in existence twenty years or more the authenticity of which is established.

(17) Market reports, commercial publications.

Market quotations, tabulations, lists, directories, or other published compilations, generally used and relied upon by the public or by persons in particular occupations.

(18) Learned treatises.

To the extent called to the attention of an expert witness upon cross-examination or relied upon by the expert witness in direct examination, statements contained in published treatises, periodicals, or pamphlets on a subject of history, medicine, or other science or art, established as a reliable authority by the testimony or admission of the witness or by other expert testimony or by judicial notice. If admitted, the statements may be read into evidence but may not be received as exhibits.

(19) Reputation concerning personal or family history.

Reputation among members of a person's family by blood, adoption, or marriage, or among a person's associates, or in the community, concerning a person's birth, adoption, marriage, divorce, death, legitimacy, relationship by blood, adoption, or marriage, ancestry, or other similar fact of personal or family history.

(20) Reputation concerning boundaries or general history.

Reputation in a community, arising before the controversy, as to boundaries of or customs affecting lands in the community, and reputation as to events of general history important to the community or State or nation in which located.

(21) Reputation as to character.

Reputation of a person's character among associates or in the community.

(22) Judgment of previous conviction.

Evidence of a final judgment, entered after a trial or upon a plea of guilty (but not upon a plea of nolo contendere), adjudging a person guilty of a crime punishable by death or imprisonment in excess of one year, to prove any fact essential to sustain the judgment, but not including, when offered by the Government in a criminal prosecution for purposes other than impeachment, judgments against persons other than the accused. The pendency of an appeal may be shown but does not affect admissibility.

(23) Judgment as to personal, family or general history, or boundaries.
Judgments as proof of matters of personal, family or general history, or boundaries, essential to the judgment, if the same would be provable by evidence of reputation.

(24) [Other exceptions.]
[Transferred to Rule 807]

Rule 804. Hearsay Exceptions; Declarant Unavailable

(a) Definition of unavailability.
"Unavailability as a witness" includes situations in which the declarant—

(1) is exempted by ruling of the court on the ground of privilege from testifying concerning the subject matter of the declarant's statement; or

(2) persists in refusing to testify concerning the subject matter of the declarant's statement despite an order of the court to do so; or

(3) testifies to a lack of memory of the subject matter of the declarant's statement; or

(4) is unable to be present or to testify at the hearing because of death or then existing physical or mental illness or infirmity; or

(5) is absent from the hearing and the proponent of a statement has been unable to procure the declarant's attendance (or in the case of a hearsay exception under subdivision (b)(2), (3), or (4), the declarant's attendance or testimony) by process or other reasonable means.

A declarant is not unavailable as a witness if exemption, refusal, claim of lack of memory, inability, or absence is due to the procurement or wrongdoing of the proponent of a statement for the purpose of preventing the witness from attending or testifying.

(b) Hearsay exceptions.
The following are not excluded by the hearsay rule if the declarant is unavailable as a witness:

(1) **Former testimony.** Testimony given as a witness at another hearing of the same or a different proceeding, or in a deposition taken in compliance with law in the course of the same or another proceeding, if the party against whom the testimony is now offered, or, in a civil action or proceeding, a predecessor in interest, had an opportunity and similar motive to develop the testimony by direct, cross, or redirect examination.

(2) **Statement under belief of impending death.** In a prosecution for homicide or in a civil action or proceeding, a statement made by a declarant while believing that the declarant's death was imminent, concerning the cause or circumstances of what the declarant believed to be impending death.

(3) **Statement against interest.** A statement which was at the time of its making so far contrary to the declarant's pecuniary or proprietary interest, or so far tended to subject the declarant to civil or criminal liability, or to render invalid a claim by the declarant against another, that a reasonable person in the declarant's position would not have made the statement unless believing it to be true. A statement tending to expose the declarant to criminal liability and offered to exculpate the accused is not admissible unless corroborating circumstances clearly indicate the trustworthiness of the statement.

(4) **Statement of personal or family history.** (A) A statement concerning the declarant's own birth, adoption, marriage, divorce, legitimacy, relationship by blood, adoption, or marriage, ancestry, or other similar fact of personal or family history, even though declarant had no means of acquiring personal knowledge of the matter stated; or (B) a statement concerning the foregoing matters, and death also, of another person, if the declarant was related to the other by blood, adoption, or marriage or was so intimately associated with the other's family as to be likely to have accurate information concerning the matter declared.

(5) **[Other exceptions.]**[Transferred to Rule 807]

(6) **Forfeiture by wrongdoing.** A statement offered against a party that has engaged or acquiesced in wrongdoing that was intended to, and did, procure the unavailability of the declarant as a witness.

Rule 805. Hearsay Within Hearsay

Hearsay included within hearsay is not excluded under the hearsay rule if each part of the combined statements conforms with an exception to the hearsay rule provided in these rules.

Rule 806. Attacking and Supporting Credibility of Declarant

When a hearsay statement, or a statement defined in Rule 801(d)(2)(C), (D), or (E), has been admitted in evidence, the credibility of the declarant may be attacked, and if attacked may be supported, by any evidence which would be admissible for those purposes if declarant had testified as a witness. Evidence of a statement or conduct by the declarant at any time, inconsistent with the declarant's hearsay statement, is not subject to any requirement that the declarant may have been afforded an opportunity to deny or explain. If the party against whom a hearsay statement has been admitted calls the declarant as a witness, the party is entitled to examine the declarant on the statement as if under cross-examination.

Rule 807. Residual Exception

A statement not specifically covered by Rule 803 or 804 but having equivalent circumstantial guarantees of trustworthiness, is not excluded by the hearsay rule, if the court determines that (A) the statement is offered as evidence of a material fact; (B) the statement is more probative on the point for which it is offered than any other evidence which the proponent can procure through reasonable efforts; and (C) the general purposes of these rules and the interests of justice will best be served by admission of the statement into evidence. However, a statement may not be admitted under this exception unless the proponent of it makes known to the adverse party sufficiently in advance of the trial or hearing to provide the adverse party with a fair opportunity to prepare to meet it, the proponent's intention to offer the statement and the particulars of it, including the name and address of the declarant.

ARTICLE IX. AUTHENTICATION AND IDENTIFICATION

Rule 901. Requirement of Authentication or Identification

(a) General provision.

The requirement of authentication or identification as a condition precedent to admissibility is satisfied by evidence sufficient to support a finding that the matter in question is what its proponent claims.

(b) Illustrations.

By way of illustration only, and not by way of limitation, the following are examples of authentication or identification conforming with the requirements of this rule:

(1) **Testimony of witness with knowledge.** Testimony that a matter is what it is claimed to be.

(2) **Nonexpert opinion on handwriting.** Nonexpert opinion as to the genuineness of handwriting, based upon familiarity not acquired for purposes of the litigation.

(3) **Comparison by trier or expert witness.** Comparison by the trier of fact or by expert witnesses with specimens which have been authenticated.

(4) **Distinctive characteristics and the like.** Appearance, contents, substance, internal patterns, or other distinctive characteristics, taken in conjunction with circumstances.

(5) **Voice identification.** Identification of a voice, whether heard firsthand or through mechanical or electronic transmission or recording, by opinion based upon hearing the voice at any time under circumstances connecting it with the alleged speaker.

(6) **Telephone conversations.** Telephone conversations, by evidence that a call was made to the number assigned at the time by the telephone company to a particular person or business, if (A) in the case of a person, circumstances, including self-identification, show the person answering to be the one called, or (B) in the case of a business, the call was made to a place of business and the conversation related to business reasonably transacted over the telephone.

(7) **Public records or reports.** Evidence that a writing authorized by law to be recorded or filed and in fact recorded or filed in a public office, or a purported public record, report, statement, or data compilation, in any form, is from the public office where items of this nature are kept.

(8) **Ancient documents or data compilation.** Evidence that a document or data compilation, in any form, (A) is in such condition as to create no suspicion concerning its authenticity, (B) was in a place where it, if authentic, would likely be, and (C) has been in existence 20 years or more at the time it is offered.

(9) **Process or system.** Evidence describing a process or system used to produce a result and showing that the process or system produces an accurate result.

(10) **Methods provided by statute or rule.** Any method of authentication or identification provided by Act of Congress or by other rules prescribed by the Supreme Court pursuant to statutory authority.

Rule 902. Self-authentication

Extrinsic evidence of authenticity as a condition precedent to admissibility is not required with respect to the following:

(1) **Domestic public documents under seal.** A document bearing a seal purporting to be that of the United States, or of any State, district, Commonwealth, territory, or insular possession thereof, or the Panama Canal Zone, or the Trust Territory of the Pacific Islands, or of a political subdivision, department, officer, or agency thereof, and a signature purporting to be an attestation or execution.

(2) **Domestic public documents not under seal.** A document purporting to bear the signature in the official capacity of an officer or employee of any entity included in paragraph (1) hereof, having no seal, if a public officer having a seal and having official duties in the district or political subdivision of the officer or employee certifies under seal that the signer has the official capacity and that the signature is genuine.

(3) **Foreign public documents.** A document purporting to be executed or attested in an official capacity by a person authorized by the laws of a foreign country to make the execution or attestation, and accompanied by a final certification as to the genuineness of the signature and official position (A) of the executing or attesting person, or (B) of any foreign official whose certificate of genuineness of signature and official position relates to the execution or attestation or is in a chain of certificates of genuineness of signature and official position relating to the execution or attestation. A final certification may be made by a secretary of an embassy or legation, consul general, consul, vice consul, or consular agent of the United States, or a diplomatic or consular official of the foreign country assigned or accredited to the United States. If reasonable opportunity has been given to all parties to investigate the authenticity and accuracy of official documents, the court may, for good cause shown, order that they be treated as presumptively authentic without final certification or permit them to be evidenced by an attested summary with or without final certification.

(4) **Certified copies of public records.** A copy of an official record or report or entry therein, or of a document authorized by law to be recorded or filed and actually recorded or filed in a public office, including data compilations in any

form, certified as correct by the custodian or other person authorized to make the certification, by certificate complying with paragraph (1), (2), or (3) of this rule or complying with any Act of Congress or rule prescribed by the Supreme Court pursuant to statutory authority.

(5) **Official publications.** Books, pamphlets, or other publications purporting to be issued by public authority.

(6) **Newspapers and periodicals.** Printed materials purporting to be newspapers or periodicals.

(7) **Trade inscriptions and the like.** Inscriptions, signs, tags, or labels purporting to have been affixed in the course of business and indicating ownership, control, or origin.

(8) **Acknowledged documents.** Documents accompanied by a certificate of acknowledgment executed in the manner provided by law by a notary public or other officer authorized by law to take acknowledgments.

(9) **Commercial paper and related documents.** Commercial paper, signatures thereon, and documents relating thereto to the extent provided by general commercial law.

(10) **Presumptions under Acts of Congress.** Any signature, document, or other matter declared by Act of Congress to be presumptively or prima facie genuine or authentic.

(11) **Certified domestic records of regularly conducted activity.** The original or a duplicate of a domestic record of regularly conducted activity that would be admissible under Rule 803(6) if accompanied by a written declaration of its custodian or other qualified person, in a manner complying with any Act of Congress or rule prescribed by the Supreme Court pursuant to statutory authority, certifying that the record:

(A) was made at or near the time of the occurrence of the matters set forth by, or from information transmitted by, a person with knowledge of those matters;

(B) was kept in the course of the regularly conducted activity; and

(C) was made by the regularly conducted activity as a regular practice.

A party intending to offer a record into evidence under this paragraph must provide written notice of that intention to all adverse parties, and must make the record and declaration available for inspection sufficiently in advance of their offer into evidence to provide an adverse party with a fair opportunity to challenge them.

(12) **Certified foreign records of regularly conducted activity.** In a civil case, the original or a duplicate of a foreign record of regularly conducted activity that would be admissible under Rule 803(6) if accompanied by a written declaration by its custodian or other qualified person certifying that the record:

(A) was made at or near the time of the occurrence of the matters set forth by, or from information transmitted by, a person with knowledge of those matters;

(B) was kept in the course of the regularly conducted activity; and

(C) was made by the regularly conducted activity as a regular practice.

The declaration must be signed in a manner that, if falsely made, would subject the maker to criminal penalty under the laws of the country where the declaration is signed. A party intending to offer a record into evidence under this paragraph must provide written notice of that intention to all adverse parties, and must make the record and declaration available for inspection sufficiently in advance of their offer into evidence to provide an adverse party with a fair opportunity to challenge them.

Rule 903. Subscribing Witness' Testimony Unnecessary

The testimony of a subscribing witness is not necessary to authenticate a writing unless required by the laws of the jurisdiction whose laws govern the validity of the writing.

ARTICLE X. CONTENTS OF WRITINGS, RECORDINGS, AND PHOTOGRAPHS

Rule 1001. Definitions

For purposes of this article, the following definitions are applicable:

(1) **Writings and recordings.** "Writings" and "recordings" consist of letters, words, or numbers, or their equivalent, set down by handwriting, typewriting, printing, photostating, photographing, magnetic impulse, mechanical or electronic recording, or other form of data compilation.

(2) **Photographs.** "Photographs" include still photographs, X-ray films, video tapes, and motion pictures.

(3) **Original.** An "original" of a writing or recording is the writing or recording itself or any counterpart intended to have the same effect by a person executing or issuing it. An "original" of a photograph includes the negative or any print therefrom. If data are stored in a computer or similar device, any printout or other output readable by sight, shown to reflect the data accurately, is an "original".

(4) **Duplicate.** A "duplicate" is a counterpart produced by the same impression as the original, or from the same matrix, or by means of photography, including enlargements and miniatures, or by mechanical or electronic re-recording, or by chemical reproduction, or by other equivalent techniques which accurately reproduces the original.

Rule 1002. Requirement of Original

To prove the content of a writing, recording, or photograph, the original writing, recording, or photograph is required, except as otherwise provided in these rules or by Act of Congress.

Rule 1003. Admissibility of Duplicates

A duplicate is admissible to the same extent as an original unless (1) a genuine question is raised as to the authenticity of the original or (2) in the circumstances it would be unfair to admit the duplicate in lieu of the original.

Rule 1004. Admissibility of Other Evidence of Contents

The original is not required, and other evidence of the contents of a writing, recording, or photograph is admissible if—

(1) **Originals lost or destroyed.** All originals are lost or have been destroyed, unless the proponent lost or destroyed them in bad faith; or

(2) **Original not obtainable.** No original can be obtained by any available judicial process or procedure; or

(3) **Original in possession of opponent.** At a time when an original was under the control of the party against whom offered, that party was put on notice, by the pleadings or otherwise, that the contents would be a subject of proof at the hearing, and that party does not produce the original at the hearing; or

(4) **Collateral matters.** The writing, recording, or photograph is not closely related to a controlling issue.

Rule 1005. Public Records

The contents of an official record, or of a document authorized to be recorded or filed and actually recorded or filed, including data compilations in any form, if otherwise admissible, may be proved by copy, certified as correct in accordance with rule 902, or testified to be correct by a witness who has compared it with the original. If a copy which complies with the foregoing cannot be obtained by the exercise of reasonable diligence, then other evidence of the contents may be given.

Rule 1006. Summaries

The contents of voluminous writings, recordings, or photographs which cannot conveniently be examined in court may be presented in the form of a chart, summary, or calculation. The originals, or duplicates, shall be made available for examination or copying, or both, by other parties at a reasonable time and place. The court may order that they be produced in court.

Rule 1007. Testimony or Written Admission of Party

Contents of writings, recordings, or photographs may be proved by the testimony or deposition of the party against whom offered or by that party's written admission, without accounting for the nonproduction of the original.

Rule 1008. Functions of Court and Jury

When the admissibility of other evidence of contents of writings, recordings, or photographs under these rules depends upon the fulfillment of a condition of fact, the question whether the condition has been fulfilled is ordinarily for the court to determine in accordance with the provisions of rule 104. However, when an issue is raised (a) whether the asserted writing ever existed, or (b) whether another writing, recording, or photograph produced at the trial is the original, or (c) whether other evidence of contents correctly reflects the contents, the issue is for the trier of fact to determine as in the case of other issues of fact.

ARTICLE XI: MISCELLANEOUS RULES

Rule 1101. Applicability of Rules

(a) Courts and judges.
These rules apply to the United States district courts, the District Court of Guam, the District Court of the Virgin Islands, the District Court for the Northern Mariana Islands, the United States courts of appeals, the United States Claims Court, and to the United States bankruptcy judges and United States magistrate judges, in the actions, cases, and proceedings and to the extent hereinafter set forth. The terms "judge" and "court" in these rules include United States bankruptcy judges and United States magistrate judges.

(b) Proceedings generally.
These rules apply generally to civil actions and proceedings, including admiralty and maritime cases, to criminal cases and proceedings, to contempt proceedings except those in which the court may act summarily, and to proceedings and cases under title 11, United States Code.

(c) Rule of privilege.
The rule with respect to privileges applies at all stages of all actions, cases, and proceedings.

(d) Rules inapplicable.
The rules (other than with respect to privileges) do not apply in the following situations:

(1) **Preliminary questions of fact.** The determination of questions of fact preliminary to admissibility of evidence when the issue is to be determined by the court under rule 104.

(2) **Grand jury.** Proceedings before grand juries.

(3) **Miscellaneous proceedings.** Proceedings for extradition or rendition; preliminary examinations in criminal cases; sentencing, or granting or revoking probation; issuance of warrants for arrest, criminal summonses, and search warrants; and proceedings with respect to release on bail or otherwise.

(e) Rules applicable in part.
In the following proceedings, these rules apply to the extent that matters of evidence are not provided for in the statutes which govern procedure therein or in other rules prescribed by the Supreme Court pursuant to statutory authority: the trial of misdemeanors and other petty offenses before a United States magistrate judge; review of agency actions when the facts are subject to trail de novo under section 706(2)(F) of title 5, United States Code;

review of orders of the Secretary of Agriculture under section 2 of the Act entitled "An Act to authorize association of producers of agricultural products", approved February 18, 1922 (7 U.S.C. 292), and under section 6 and 7(c) of the Perishable Agricultural Commodities Act, 1930 (7 U.S.C. 499f, 499g(c)); naturalization and revocation of naturalization under sections 310-318 of the Immigration and Nationality Act (8 U.S.C. 1421-1429); prize proceedings in admiralty under sections 7651-7681 of title 10, United States Code; review of orders of the Secretary of the Interior under section 2 of the Act entitled "An Act authorizing associations of producers of aquatic products", approved June 25, 1934 (15 U.S.C. 522); review of orders of petroleum control boards under section 5 of the Act entitled "An Act to regulate interstate and foreign commerce in petroleum and its products by prohibiting the shipment in such commerce of petroleum and its products produced in violation of State law, and for other purposes", approved February 22, 1935 (15 U.S.C. 715d); actions for fines, penalties, or forfeitures under part V of title IV of the Tariff Act of 1930 (19 U.S.C. 1581-1624), or under the Anti-Smuggling Act (19 U.S.C. 1701-1711); criminal libel for condemnation, exclusion of imports, or other proceedings under the Federal Food, Drug, and Cosmetic Act (21 U.S.C. 301-392); disputes between seamen under sections 4079, 4080, and 4081 of the Revised Statutes (22 U.S.C. 256-258); habeas corpus under sections 2241-2254 of title 28, United States Code; motions to vacate, set aside, or correct sentence under section 2255 of title 28, United States Code; actions for penalties for refusal to transport destitute seamen under section 4578 of the Revised Statutes (46 U.S.C. 679); actions against the United States under the Act entitled "An Act authorizing suits against the United States in admiralty for damage caused by and salvage service rendered to public vessels belonging to the United States, and for other purposes", approved March 3, 1925 (46 U.S.C. 781-790), as implemented by section 7730 of title 10, United States Code.

Rule 1102. Amendments

Amendments to the Federal Rules of Evidence may be made as provided in section 2072 of title 28 of the United States Code.

Rule 1103. Title

These rules may be known and cited as the Federal Rules of Evidence.

FEDERAL RULES OF CIVIL PROCEDURE: OVERVIEW

Civil Procedure is the complex and sometimes confusing body of rules and regulations establishing the format under which civil lawsuits are filed, pursued, and tried. Multiple sources for civil procedure are available, set out in both state (usually Code of Civil Procedure) and federal (Federal Code of Procedure). The Federal Rules of Civil Procedure govern all federal civil courts and form the foundation for the state and local Rules of Civil Procedure.

Civil procedure refers to the rules by which courts conduct civil trials. *Civil trials* concern the judicial resolution of claims by one individual or group against another individual or group, whereas *criminal trials* concern state prosecution of an individual for violating criminal law.

Procedure is different from substantive law in that substantive law describes the boundaries in which we work, play, and enjoy life. They are the laws, as most people understand them, which give people the right to sue or defend a lawsuit. Procedural laws are "the rules that prescribe the steps for having a right or duty judicially enforced, as opposed to the [substantive] law that defines the specific rights or duties themselves" (*Black's Law Dictionary*, 7th ed. 1999). Thus, these rules govern litigation and are the rules that the parties must follow as they bring their case and the rules for the court administration of the case.

What follows is a subset of the Federal Rules of Civil Procedure (FRCP), from which other Codes build. We kept the most important rules for the forensic examiner in the following text, but you should review the entire set if you are going to court.

Lower courts can always add restrictions to the FRCP but rarely loosen them. Because the result may be different from what you expect, you should consult an attorney and your local codes before you go to trial. Check http://www.law.cornell.edu/rules/frcp/overview.htm for an easy-to-read online version of the FRCP.

 We removed sections we believed were less relevant to the role of the forensic investigator. The Legal Information Institute, maintained by Cornell Law School, maintains a complete copy you can read here: http://www.law.cornell.edu/rules/frcp/overview.htm.

FEDERAL RULES OF CIVIL PROCEDURE (FRCP)

I. Scope of Rules—One Form of Action

Rule 1—Scope and Purpose of Rules

These rules govern the procedure in the United States district courts in all suits of a civil nature whether cognizable as cases at law or in equity or in admiralty, with the exceptions stated in Rule 81. They shall be construed and administered to secure the just, speedy, and inexpensive determination of every action.

Rule 2—One Form of Action

There shall be one form of action to be known as "civil action."

II. Commencement of Action; Service of Process, Pleadings, Motions, and Orders

Rule 3—Commencement of Action

A civil action is commenced by filing a complaint with the court.

Rule 7—Pleadings Allowed; Forms of Motions

(a) Pleadings.

There shall be a complaint and an answer; a reply to a counterclaim denominated as such; an answer to a cross-claim, if the answer contains a cross-claim; a third-party complaint, if a person who was not an original party is summoned under the provisions of Rule 14; and a third-party answer, if a third-party complaint is served. No other pleading shall be allowed, except that the court may order a reply to an answer or a third-party answer.

(b) Motions and Other Papers.

(1) An application to the court for an order shall be by motion which, unless made during a hearing or trial, shall be made in writing, shall state with particularity the grounds therefor, and shall set forth the relief or order sought. The requirement of writing is fulfilled if the motion is stated in a written notice of the hearing of the motion.

(2) The rules applicable to captions and other matters of form of pleadings apply to all motions and other papers provided for by these rules.

(3) All motions shall be signed in accordance with Rule 11.

(c) Demurrers, Pleas, Etc.

Abolished. Demurrers, pleas, and exceptions for insufficiency of a pleading shall not be used.

Rule 8—General Rules of Pleading

(a) Claims for Relief.

A pleading which sets forth a claim for relief, whether an original claim, counterclaim, cross-claim, or third-party claim, shall contain

(1) a short and plain statement of the grounds upon which the court's jurisdiction depends, unless the court already has jurisdiction and the claim needs no new grounds of jurisdiction to support it;

(2) a short and plain statement of the claim showing that the pleader is entitled to relief; and

(3) a demand for judgment for the relief the pleader seeks. Relief in the alternative or of several different types may be demanded.

(b) Defenses; Form of Denials.

A party shall state in short and plain terms the party's defenses to each claim asserted and shall admit or deny the averments upon which the adverse party relies. If a party is without knowledge or information sufficient to form a belief as to the truth of an averment, the party shall so state and this has the effect of a denial. Denials shall fairly meet the substance of the averments denied. When a pleader intends in good faith to deny only a part or a qualification of an averment, the pleader shall specify so much of it as is true and material and shall deny only the remainder. Unless the pleader intends in good faith to controvert all the averments of the preceding pleading, the pleader may make denials as specific denials of designated averments or paragraphs or may generally deny all the averments except such designated averments or paragraphs as the pleader expressly admits; but, when the pleader does so intend to controvert all its averments, including averments of the grounds upon which the court's jurisdiction depends, the pleader may do so by general denial subject to the obligations set forth in Rule 11.

(c) Affirmative Defenses.
In pleading to a preceding pleading, a party shall set forth affirmatively accord and satisfaction, arbitration and award, assumption of risk, contributory negligence, discharge in bankruptcy, duress, estoppel, failure of consideration, fraud, illegality, injury by fellow servant, laches, license, payment, release, res judicata, statute of frauds, statute of limitations, waiver, and any other matter constituting an avoidance or affirmative defense. When a party has mistakenly designated a defense as a counterclaim or a counterclaim as a defense, the court on terms, if justice so requires, shall treat the pleading as if there had been a proper designation.

(d) Effect of Failure to Deny.
Averments in a pleading to which a responsive pleading is required, other than those as to the amount of damage, are admitted when not denied in the responsive pleading. Averments in a pleading to which no responsive pleading is required or permitted shall be taken as denied or avoided.

(e) Pleading to be Concise and Direct; Consistency.

(1)Each averment of a pleading shall be simple, concise, and direct. No technical forms of pleading or motions are required.

(2) A party may set forth two or more statements of a claim or defense alternately or hypothetically, either in one count or defense or in separate counts or defenses. When two or more statements are made in the alternative and one of them if made independently would be sufficient, the pleading is not made insufficient by the insufficiency of one or more of the alternative statements. A party may also state as many separate claims or defenses as the party has regardless of consistency and whether based on legal, equitable, or maritime grounds. All statements shall be made subject to the obligations set forth in Rule 11.

(f) Construction of Pleadings.
All pleadings shall be so construed as to do substantial justice.

Rule 10—Form of Pleadings
(a) Caption; Names of Parties.
Every pleading shall contain a caption setting forth the name of the court, the title of the action, the file number, and a designation as in Rule 7(a). In the complaint the title of the action shall include the names of all the parties, but in other pleadings it is sufficient to state the name of the first party on each side with an appropriate indication of other parties.

(b) Paragraphs; Separate Statements.

All averments of claim or defense shall be made in numbered paragraphs, the contents of each of which shall be limited as far as practicable to a statement of a single set of circumstances; and a paragraph may be referred to by number in all succeeding pleadings. Each claim founded upon a separate transaction or occurrence and each defense other than denials shall be stated in a separate count or defense whenever a separation facilitates the clear presentation of the matters set forth.

(c) Adoption by Reference; Exhibits.

Statements in a pleading may be adopted by reference in a different part of the same pleading or in another pleading or in any motion. A copy of any written instrument which is an exhibit to a pleading is a part thereof for all purposes.

V. Depositions and Discovery

Rule 26—General Provisions Governing Discovery; Duty of Disclosure

(a) Required Disclosures; Methods to Discover Additional Matter.

(1) **Initial Disclosures.**

Except in categories of proceedings specified in Rule 26(a)(1)(E), or to the extent otherwise stipulated or directed by order, a party must, without awaiting a discovery request, provide to other parties:

(A) the name and, if known, the address and telephone number of each individual likely to have discoverable information that the disclosing party may use to support its claims or defenses, unless solely for impeachment, identifying the subjects of the information;

(B) a copy of, or a description by category and location of, all documents, data compilations, and tangible things that are in the possession, custody, or control of the party and that the disclosing party may use to support its claims or defenses, unless solely for impeachment;

(C) a computation of any category of damages claimed by the disclosing party, making available for inspection and copying as under Rule 34 the documents or other evidentiary material, not privileged or protected from disclosure, on which such computation is based, including materials bearing on the nature and extent of injuries suffered; and

(D) for inspection and copying as under Rule 34 any insurance agreement under which any person carrying on an insurance business may be liable to satisfy part or all of a judgment which may be entered in the action or to indemnify or reimburse for payments made to satisfy the judgment.

(E) The following categories of proceedings are exempt from initial disclosure under Rule 26(a)(1):

(i) an action for review on an administrative record;

(ii) a petition for habeas corpus or other proceeding to challenge a criminal conviction or sentence;

(iii) an action brought without counsel by a person in custody of the United States, a state, or a state subdivision;

(iv) an action to enforce or quash an administrative summons or subpoena;

(v) an action by the United States to recover benefit payments;

(vi) an action by the United States to collect on a student loan guaranteed by the United States;

(vii) a proceeding ancillary to proceedings in other courts; and

(viii) an action to enforce an arbitration award.

These disclosures must be made at or within 14 days after the Rule 26(f) conference unless a different time is set by stipulation or court order, or unless a party objects during the conference that initial disclosures are not appropriate in the circumstances of the action and states the objection in the Rule 26(f) discovery plan. In ruling on the objection, the court must determine what disclosures—if any—are to be made, and set the time for disclosure. Any party first served or otherwise joined after the Rule 26(f) conference must make these disclosures within 30 days after being served or joined unless a different time is set by stipulation or court order. A party must make its initial disclosures based on the information then reasonably available to it and is not excused from making its disclosures because it has not fully completed its investigation of the case or because it challenges the sufficiency of another party's disclosures or because another party has not made its disclosures.

(2) **Disclosure of Expert Testimony.**

(A) In addition to the disclosures required by paragraph (1), a party shall disclose to other parties the identity of any person who may be used at trial to present evidence under Rules 702, 703, or 705 of the Federal Rules of Evidence.

(B) Except as otherwise stipulated or directed by the court, this disclosure shall, with respect to a witness who is retained or specially employed to provide expert testimony in the case or whose duties as an employee of the party regularly involve giving expert testimony, be accompanied by a written report prepared and signed by the witness. The report shall contain a complete statement of all opinions to be expressed and the basis and reasons therefor; the data or other information considered by the witness in forming the opinions; any exhibits to be used as a summary of or support for the opinions; the qualifications of the witness, including a list of all publications authored by the witness within the preceding ten years; the compensation to be paid for the study and testimony; and a listing of any other cases in which the witness has testified as an expert at trial or by deposition within the preceding four years.

(C) These disclosures shall be made at the times and in the sequence directed by the court. In the absence of other directions from the court or stipulation by the parties, the disclosures shall be made at least 90 days before the trial date or the date the case is to be ready for trial or, if the evidence is intended solely to contradict or rebut evidence on the same subject matter identified by another party under paragraph (2)(b), within 30 days after the disclosure made by the other party. The parties shall supplement these disclosures when required under subdivision (e)(1).

(3) **Pretrial Disclosures.**

In addition to the disclosures required in the preceding paragraphs, a party shall provide to other parties the following information regarding the evidence that it may present at trial other than solely for impeachment purposes:

(A) the name and, if not previously provided, the address and telephone number of each witness, separately identifying those whom the party expects to present and those whom the party may call if the need arises;

(B) the designation of those witnesses whose testimony is expected to be presented by means of a deposition and, if not taken stenographically, a transcript of the pertinent portions of the deposition testimony; and

(C) an appropriate identification of each document or other exhibit, including summaries of other evidence, separately identifying those which the party expects to offer and those which the party may offer if the need arises.

Unless otherwise directed by the court, these disclosures shall be made at least 30 days before trial. Within 14 days thereafter, unless a different time is specified by the court, a party may serve and file a list disclosing

(i) any objections to the use under Rule 32(a) of a deposition designated by another party under subparagraph (B); and

(ii) any objection, together with the grounds therefor, that may be made to the admissibility of materials identified under subparagraph (C).

Objections not so disclosed, other than objections under Rules 402 and 403 of the Federal Rules of Evidence, shall be deemed waived unless excused by the court for good cause shown.

(4) **Forms of Disclosure; Filing.**

Unless otherwise directed by order or local rule, all disclosures under paragraphs (1) through (3) shall be made in writing, signed, served, and promptly filed with the court.

(5) **Methods to Discover Additional Matter.**

Parties may obtain discovery by one or more of the following methods: depositions upon oral examination or written questions; written interrogatories; production of documents or things or permission to enter upon land or other property under Rule 34 or 45(a)(1)(C), for inspection and other purposes; physical and mental examinations; and requests for admission.

(b) Discovery Scope and Limits.

Unless otherwise limited by order of the court in accordance with these rules, the scope of discovery is as follows:

(1) In General.

Parties may obtain discovery regarding any matter, not privileged, which is relevant to the subject matter involved in the pending action, whether it relates to the claim or defense of the party seeking discovery or to the claim or defense of any other party, including the existence, description, nature, custody, condition and location of any books, documents, or other tangible things and the identity and location of persons having knowledge of any discoverable matter. The information sought need not be admissible at the trial if the information sought appears reasonably calculated to lead to the discovery of admissible evidence.

(2) Limitations.

By order or by local rule, the court may alter the limits in these rules on the number of depositions and interrogatories and may also limit the length of depositions under Rule 30 and the number of requests under Rule 36. The frequency or extent of use of the discovery methods otherwise permitted under these rules and by any local rule shall be limited by the court if it determines that:

> (i) the discovery sought is unreasonably cumulative or duplicative, or is obtainable from some other source that is more convenient, less burdensome, or less expensive;
>
> (ii) the party seeking discovery has had ample opportunity by discovery in the action to obtain the information sought; or
>
> (iii) the burden or expense of the proposed discovery outweighs its likely benefit, taking into account the needs of the case, the amount in controversy, the parties' resources, the importance of the issues at stake in the litigation, and the importance of the proposed discovery in resolving the issues. The court may act upon its own initiative after reasonable notice or pursuant to a motion under subdivision (c).

(3) Trial Preparation: Materials.

Subject to the provisions of subdivision (b)(4) of this rule, a party may obtain discovery of documents and tangible things otherwise discoverable under subdivision (b)(1) of this rule and prepared in anticipation of litigation or for the trial by or for another party or by or for that other party's representative (including the other party's attorney, consultant, surety, indemnitor, insurer, or agent) only upon a showing that the party seeking discovery has substantial need of the materials in the preparation of the party's case and that the party is unable without undue hardship to obtain the substantial equivalent of the materials by other means. In ordering discovery of such materials when the required showing has been made, the court shall protect against disclosure of the mental impressions, conclusions, opinions, or legal theories of an attorney or other representative of a party concerning the litigation.

A party may obtain without the required showing a statement concerning the action or its subject matter previously made by that party. Upon request, a person not a party may obtain without the required showing a statement concerning the action or its subject matter previously made by that person. If the request is refused, the person may move for a court order. The provisions of Rule 37(a)(4) apply to the award of expenses incurred in relation to the motion. For purposes of this paragraph, a statement previously made is

(A) a written statement signed or otherwise adopted or approved by the person making it, or

(B) a stenographic, mechanical, electrical, or other recording, or a transcription thereof, which is a substantially verbatim recital of an oral statement by the person making it and contemporaneously recorded.

(4) **Trial Preparation: Experts.**

(A) A party may depose any person who has been identified as an expert whose opinions may be presented at trial. If a report from the expert is required under subdivision (a)(2)(B), the deposition shall not be conducted until after the report is provided.

(B) A party may, through interrogatories or by deposition, discover facts known or opinions held by an expert who has been retained or specially employed by another party in anticipation of litigation or preparation for trial and who is not expected to be called as a witness at trial only as provided in Rule 35(b) or upon a showing of exceptional circumstances under which it is impracticable for the party seeking discovery to obtain facts or opinions on the same subject by other means.

(C) Unless manifest injustice would result,

(i) the court shall require that the party seeking discovery pay the expert a reasonable fee for time spent in responding to discovery under this subdivision; and

(ii) with respect to discovery obtained under subdivision (b)(4)(B) of this rule the court shall require the party seeking discovery to pay the other party a fair portion of the fees and expenses reasonably incurred by the latter party in obtaining facts and opinions from the expert.

(5) **Claims of Privilege or Protection of Trial Preparation Materials.**

When a party withholds information otherwise discoverable under these rules by claiming that it is privileged or subject to protection as trial preparation material, the party shall make the claim expressly and shall describe the nature of the documents, communications, or things not produced or disclosed in a manner that, without revealing information itself privileged or protected, will enable other parties to assess the applicability of the privilege or protection.

(c) Protective Orders.

Upon motion by a party or by the person from whom discovery is sought, accompanied by a certification that the movant has in good faith conferred or attempted to confer with other affected parties in an effort to resolve the dispute without court action, and for good cause shown, the court in which the action is pending or alternatively, on matters relating to a deposition, the court in the district where the deposition is to be taken may make any order which justice requires to protect a party or person from annoyance, embarrassment, oppression, or undue burden or expense, including one or more of the following:

(1) that the disclosure or discovery not be had;

(2) that the disclosure or discovery may be had only on specified terms and conditions, including a designation of the time or place;

(3) that the discovery may be had only by a method of discovery other than that selected by the party seeking discovery;

(4) that certain matters not be inquired into, or that the scope of the disclosure or discovery be limited to certain matters;

(5) that discovery be conducted with no one present except persons designated by the court;

(6) that a deposition, after being sealed, be opened only by order of the court;

(7) that a trade secret or other confidential research, development, or commercial information not be revealed or be revealed only in a designated way; and

(8) that the parties simultaneously file specified documents or information enclosed in sealed envelopes to be opened as directed by the court.

If the motion for a protective order is denied in whole or in part, the court may, on such terms and conditions as are just, order that any party or person provide or permit discovery. The provisions of Rule 37(a)(4) apply to the award of expenses incurred in relation to the motion.

(d) Timing and Sequence of Discovery.

Except when authorized under these rules or by local rule, order, or agreement of the parties, a party may not seek discovery from any source before the parties have met and conferred as required by subdivision (f). Unless the court upon motion, for the convenience of parties and witnesses and in the interests of justice, orders otherwise, methods of discovery may be used in any sequence and the fact that a party is conducting discovery, whether by deposition or otherwise, shall not operate to delay any other party's discovery.

(e) Supplementation of Disclosures and Responses.

A party who has made a disclosure under subdivision (a) or responded to a request for discovery with a disclosure or response is under a duty to supplement or correct the disclosure or response to include information thereafter acquired if ordered by the court or in the following circumstances:

(1) A party is under a duty to supplement at appropriate intervals its disclosures under subdivision (a) if the party learns that in some material respect the information disclosed is incomplete or incorrect and if the additional or corrective information has not otherwise been made known to the other parties during the discovery process or in writing. With respect to testimony of an expert from whom a report is required under subdivision (a)(2)(B), the duty extends both to information contained in the report and to information provided through a deposition of the expert, and any additions or other changes to this information shall be disclosed by the time the party's disclosures under Rule 26(a)(3) are due.

(2) A party is under a duty seasonably to amend a prior response to an interrogatory, request for production, or request for admission if the party learns that the response is in some material respect incomplete or incorrect and if the additional or corrective information has not otherwise been made known to the other parties during the discovery process or in writing.

(f) Meeting of Parties; Planning for Discovery.

Except in categories of proceedings exempted from initial disclosure under Rule 26(a)(1)(E) or when otherwise ordered, the parties must, as soon as practicable and in any event at least 21 days before a scheduling conference is held or a scheduling order is due under Rule 16(b), confer to consider the nature and basis of their claims and defenses and the possibilities for a prompt settlement or resolution of the case, to make or arrange for the disclosures required by Rule 26(a)(1), and to develop a proposed discovery plan that indicates the parties' views and proposals concerning:

(1) what changes should be made in the timing, form, or requirement for disclosures under Rule 26(a), including a statement as to when disclosures under Rule 26(a)(1) were made or will be made;

(2) the subjects on which discovery may be needed, when discovery should be completed, and whether discovery should be conducted in phases or be limited to or focused upon particular issues;

(3) what changes should be made in the limitations on discovery imposed under these rules or by local rule, and what other limitations should be imposed; and

(4) any other orders that should be entered by the court under Rule 26(c) or under Rule 16(b) and (c).

The attorneys of record and all unrepresented parties that have appeared in the case are jointly responsible for arranging the conference, for attempting in good faith to agree on the proposed discovery plan, and for submitting to the court within 14 days after the conference a written report outlining the plan. A court may order that the parties or attorneys attend the conference in person. If necessary to comply with its expedited schedule for Rule 16(b) conferences, a court may by local rule (i) require that the conference between the parties occur fewer than 21 days before the scheduling conference is held or a scheduling order is due under Rule 16(b), and (ii) require that the written report outlining the discovery plan be filed fewer than 14 days after the conference between the parties, or excuse the parties from submitting a written report and permit them to report orally on their discovery plan at the Rule 16(b) conference.

(g) Signing of Disclosures, Discovery Requests, Responses, and Objections.

(1) Every disclosure made pursuant to subdivision (a)(1) or subdivision (a)(3) shall be signed by at least one attorney of record in the attorney's individual name, whose address shall be stated. An unrepresented party shall sign the disclosure and state the party's address. The signature of the attorney or party constitutes a certification that to the best of the signer's knowledge, information, and belief, formed after a reasonable inquiry, the disclosure is complete and correct as of the time it is made.

(2) Every discovery request, response, or objection made by a party represented by an attorney shall be signed by at least one attorney of record in the attorney's individual name, whose address shall be stated. An unrepresented party shall sign the request, response, or objection and state the party's address. The signature of the attorney or party constitutes a certification that to the best of the signer's knowledge, information, and belief, formed after a reasonable inquiry, the request, response, or objection is:

(A) consistent with these rules and warranted by existing law or a good faith argument for the extension, modification, or reversal of existing law;

(B) not interposed for any improper purpose, such as to harass or to cause unnecessary delay or needless increase in the cost of litigation; and

(C) not unreasonable or unduly burdensome or expensive, given the needs of the case, the discovery already had in the case, the amount in controversy, and the importance of the issues at stake in the litigation.

If a request, response, or objection is not signed, it shall be stricken unless it is signed promptly after the omission is called to the attention of the party making the request, response, or objection, and a party shall not be obligated to take any action with respect to it until it is signed.

(3) If without substantial justification a certification is made in violation of the rule, the court, upon motion or upon its own initiative, shall impose upon the person who made the certification, the party on whose behalf the disclosure, request, response, or objection is made, or both, an appropriate sanction, which may include an order to pay the amount of the reasonable expenses incurred because of the violation, including a reasonable attorney's fee.

Rule 29—Stipulations Regarding Discovery Procedure

Unless otherwise directed by the court, the parties may by written stipulation

(1) provide that depositions may be taken before any person, at any time or place, upon any notice, and in any manner and when so taken may be used like other depositions, and

(2) modify other procedures governing or limitations placed upon discovery, except that stipulations extending the time provided in Rules 33, 34, and 36 for responses to discovery may, if they would interfere with any time set for completion of discovery, for hearing of a motion, or for trial, be made only with the approval of the court.

Rule 32—Use of Depositions in Court Proceedings

(a) **Use of Depositions.**

At the trial or upon the hearing of a motion or an interlocutory proceeding, any part or all of a deposition, so far as admissible under the rules of evidence applied as though the witness were then present and testifying, may be used against any party who was present or represented at the taking of the deposition or who had reasonable notice thereof, in accordance with any of the following provisions:

(1) Any deposition may be used by any party for the purpose of contradicting or impeaching the testimony of deponent as a witness, or for any other purpose permitted by the Federal Rules of Evidence.

(2) The deposition of a party or of anyone who at the time of taking the deposition was an officer, director, or managing agent, or a person designated under Rule 30(b)(6) or 31(a) to testify on behalf of a public or private corporation, partnership or association or governmental agency which is a party may be used by an adverse party for any purpose.

(3) The deposition of a witness, whether or not a party, may be used by any party for any purpose if the court finds:

(A) that the witness is dead; or

(B) that the witness is at a greater distance than 100 miles from the place of trial or hearing, or is out of the United States, unless it appears that the absence of the witness was procured by the party offering the deposition; or

(C) that the witness is unable to attend or testify because of age, illness, infirmity, or imprisonment; or

(D) that the party offering the deposition has been unable to procure the attendance of the witness by subpoena; or

(E) upon application and notice, that such exceptional circumstances exist as to make it desirable, in the interest of justice and with due regard to the importance of presenting the testimony of witnesses orally in open court, to allow the deposition to be used.

A deposition taken without leave of court pursuant to a notice under Rule 30(a)(2)(C) shall not be used against a party who demonstrates that, when served with the notice, it was unable through the exercise of diligence to obtain counsel to represent it at the taking of the deposition; nor shall a deposition be used against a party who, having received less than 11 days notice of a deposition, has promptly upon receiving such notice filed a motion for a protective order under Rule 26(c)(2) requesting that the deposition not be held or be held at a different time or place and such motion is pending at the time the deposition is held.

(4) If only part of a deposition is offered in evidence by a party, an adverse party may require the offeror to introduce any other part which ought in fairness to be considered with the part introduced, and any party may introduce any other parts.

Substitution of parties pursuant to Rule 25 does not affect the right to use depositions previously taken; and, when an action has been brought in any court of the United States or of any State and another action involving the same subject matter is afterward brought between the same parties or their representatives or successors in interest, all depositions lawfully taken and duly filed in the former action may be used in the latter as if originally taken therefor. A deposition previously taken may also be used as permitted by the Federal Rules of Evidence.

(b) Objections to Admissibility.
Subject to the provisions of Rule 28(b) and subdivision (d)(3) of this rule, objection may be made at the trial or hearing to receiving in evidence any deposition or part thereof for any reason which would require the exclusion of the evidence if the witness were then present and testifying.

(c) Form of Presentation.
Except as otherwise directed by the court, a party offering deposition testimony pursuant to this rule may offer it in stenographic or nonstenographic form, but, if in nonstenographic form, the party shall also provide the court with a transcript of the portions so offered. On request of any party in a case tried before a jury, deposition testimony offered other than for impeachment purposes shall be presented in nonstenographic form, if available, unless the court for good cause orders otherwise.

(d) Effect of Errors and Irregularities in Depositions.

(1) **As to Notice.**

All errors and irregularities in the notice for taking a deposition are waived unless written objection is promptly served upon the party giving the notice.

(2) **As to Disqualification of Officer.**

Objection to taking a deposition because of disqualification of the officer before whom it is to be taken is waived unless made before the taking of the deposition begins or as soon thereafter as the disqualification becomes known or could be discovered with reasonable diligence.

(3) **As to Taking of Deposition.**

(A) Objections to the competency of a witness or to the competency, relevancy, or materiality of testimony are not waived by failure to make them before or during the taking of the deposition, unless the ground of the objection is one which might have been obviated or removed if presented at that time.

(B) Errors and irregularities occurring at the oral examination in the manner of taking the deposition, in the form of the questions or answers, in the oath or affirmation, or in the conduct of parties, and errors of any kind which might be obviated, removed, or cured if promptly presented, are waived unless seasonable objection thereto is made at the taking of the deposition.

(C) Objections to the form of written questions submitted under Rule 31 are waived unless served in writing upon the party propounding them within the time allowed for serving the succeeding cross or other questions and within 5 days after service of the last questions authorized.

(4) **As to Completion and Return of Deposition.**

Errors and irregularities in the manner in which the testimony is transcribed or the deposition is prepared, signed, certified, sealed, indorsed, transmitted, filed, or otherwise dealt with by the officer under Rules 30 and 31 are waived unless a motion to suppress the deposition or some part thereof is made with reasonable promptness after such defect is, or with due diligence might have been, ascertained.

Rule 34—Production of Documents and Things and Entry Upon Land for Inspection and Other Purposes

(a) Scope.

Any party may serve on any other party a request

(1) to produce and permit the party making the request, or someone acting on the requestor's behalf, to inspect and copy, any designated documents (including writings, drawings, graphs, charts, photographs, phono records, and other data

compilations from which information can be obtained, translated, if necessary, by the respondent through detection devices into reasonably usable form), or to inspect and copy, test, or sample any tangible things which constitute or contain matters within the scope of Rule 26(b) and which are in the possession, custody, or control of the party upon whom the request is served; or

(2) to permit entry upon designated land or other property in the possession or control of the party upon whom the request is served for the purpose of inspection and measuring, surveying, photographing, testing, or sampling the property or any designated object or operation thereon, within the scope of Rule 26(b).

(b) Procedure.

The request shall set forth, either by individual item or by category, the items to be inspected, and describe each with reasonable particularity. The request shall specify a reasonable time, place, and manner of making the inspection and performing the related acts. Without leave of court or written stipulation, a request may not be served before the time specified in Rule 26(d).

The party upon whom the request is served shall serve a written response within 30 days after the service of the request. A shorter or longer time may be directed by the court or, in the absence of such an order, agreed to in writing by the parties, subject to Rule 29. The response shall state, with respect to each item or category, that inspection and related activities will be permitted as requested, unless the request is objected to, in which event the reasons for the objection shall be stated. If objection is made to part of an item or category, the part shall be specified and inspection permitted of the remaining parts. The party submitting the request may move for an order under Rule 37(a) with respect to any objection to or other failure to respond to the request or any part thereof, or any failure to permit inspection as requested.

A party who produces documents for inspection shall produce them as they are kept in the usual course of business or shall organize and label them to correspond with the categories in the request.

(c) Persons Not Parties.

A person not a party to the action may be compelled to produce documents and things or to submit to an inspection as provided in Rule 45.

Rule 36—Requests for Admission

(a) Request for Admission.

A party may serve upon any other party a written request for the admission, for purposes of the pending action only, of the truth of any matters within the scope of Rule 26(b)(1) set forth in the request that relate to statements or opinions of fact or of the application of law to fact, including the genuineness of any documents described in the request. Copies of documents shall be served with the request unless they have been or are otherwise furnished or made available for inspection and copying. Without leave of court or written stipulation, requests for admission may not be served before the time specified in Rule 26(d).

Each matter of which an admission is requested shall be separately set forth. The matter is admitted unless, within 30 days after service of the request, or within such shorter or longer time as the court may allow or as the parties may agree to in writing, subject to Rule 29, the party to whom the request is directed serves upon the party requesting the admission a written answer or objection addressed to the matter, signed by the party or by the party's attorney. If objection is made, the reasons therefor shall be stated. The answer shall specifically deny the matter or set forth in detail the reasons why the answering party cannot truthfully admit or deny the matter. A denial shall fairly meet the substance of the requested admission, and when good faith requires that a party qualify an answer or deny only a part of the matter of which an admission is requested, the party shall specify so much of it as is true and qualify or deny the remainder. An answering party may not give lack of information or knowledge as a reason for failure to admit or deny unless the party states that the party has made reasonable inquiry and that the information known or readily obtainable by the party is insufficient to enable the party to admit or deny. A party who considers that a matter of which an admission has been requested presents a genuine issue for trial may not, on that ground alone, object to the request; the party may, subject to the provisions of Rule 37(c), deny the matter or set forth reasons why the party cannot admit or deny it.

The party who has requested the admissions may move to determine the sufficiency of the answers or objections. Unless the court determines that an objection is justified, it shall order that an answer be served. If the court determines that an answer does not comply with the requirements of this rule, it may order either that the matter is admitted or that an amended answer be served. The court may, in lieu of these orders, determine that final disposition of the request be made at a pre-trial conference or at a designated time prior to trial. The provisions of Rule 37(a)(4) apply to the award of expenses incurred in relation to the motion.

(b) Effect of Admission.

Any matter admitted under this rule is conclusively established unless the court on motion permits withdrawal or amendment of the admission. Subject to the provision of Rule 16 governing amendment of a pre-trial order, the court may permit withdrawal or amendment when the presentation of the merits of the action will be subserved thereby and the party who obtained the admission fails to satisfy the court that withdrawal or amendment will prejudice that party in maintaining the action or defense on the merits. Any admission made by a party under this rule is for the purpose of the pending action only and is not an admission for any other purpose nor may it be used against the party in any other proceeding.

Rule 37—Failure to Make Disclosure or Cooperate in Discovery: Sanctions

(a) Motion for Order Compelling Disclosure or Discovery.

A party, upon reasonable notice to other parties and all persons affected thereby, may apply for an order compelling disclosure or discovery as follows:

(1) **Appropriate Court.**

An application for an order to a party shall be made to the court in which the action is pending. An application for an order to a person who is not a party shall be made to the court in the district where the discovery is being, or is to be, taken.

(2) **Motion.**

(A) If a party fails to make a disclosure required by Rule 26(a), any other party may move to compel disclosure and for appropriate sanctions. The motion must include a certification that the movant has in good faith conferred or attempted to confer with the party not making the disclosure in an effort to secure the disclosure without court action.

(B) If a deponent fails to answer a question propounded or submitted under Rules 30 or 31, or a corporation or other entity fails to make a designation under Rule 30(b)(6) or 31(a), or a party fails to answer an interrogatory submitted under Rule 33, or if a party, in response to a request for inspection submitted under Rule 34, fails to respond that inspection will be permitted as requested or fails to permit inspection as requested, the discovering party may move for an order compelling an answer, or a designation, or an order compelling inspection in accordance with the request. The motion must include a certification that the movant has in good faith conferred or attempted to confer with the person or party failing to make the discovery in an effort to secure the information or material without court action. When taking a deposition on oral examination, the proponent of the question may complete or adjourn the examination before applying for an order.

(3) **Evasive or Incomplete Disclosure, Answer, or Response.**

For purposes of this subdivision, an evasive or incomplete disclosure, answer, or response is to be treated as a failure to disclose, answer, or respond.

(4) **Expenses and Sanctions.**

(A) If the motion is granted or if the disclosure or requested discovery is provided after the motion was filed, the court shall, after affording an opportunity to be heard, require the party or deponent whose conduct necessitated the motion or the party or attorney advising such conduct or both of them to pay to the moving party the reasonable expenses incurred in making the motion, including attorney's fees, unless the court finds that the motion was filed without the movant's first making a good faith effort to obtain the disclosure or discovery without court action, or that the opposing party's nondisclosure, response, or objection was substantially justified, or that other circumstances make an award of expenses unjust.

(B) If the motion is denied, the court may enter any protective order authorized under Rule 26(c) and shall, after affording an opportunity to be heard, require the moving party or the attorney filing the motion or both of them to pay to the party or deponent who opposed the motion the reasonable expenses incurred in opposing the motion, including attorney's fees, unless the court finds that the making of the motion was substantially justified or that other circumstances make an award of expenses unjust.

(C) If the motion is granted in part and denied in part, the court may enter any protective order authorized under Rule 26(c) and may, after affording an opportunity to be heard, apportion the reasonable expenses incurred in relation to the motion among the parties and persons in a just manner.

(b) Failure to Comply with Order.

(1) Sanctions by Court in District Where Deposition is Taken.

If a deponent fails to be sworn or to answer a question after being directed to do so by the court in the district in which the deposition is being taken, the failure may be considered a contempt of that court.

(2) Sanctions by Court in Which Action is Pending.

If a party or an officer, director, or managing agent of a party or a person designated under Rule 30(b)(6) or 31(a) to testify on behalf of a party fails to obey an order to provide or permit discovery, including an order made under subdivision (a) of this rule or rule 35, or if a party fails to obey an order entered under Rule 26(f), the court in which the action is pending may make such orders in regard to the failure as are just, and among others the following:

(A) An order that the matters regarding which the order was made or any other designated facts shall be taken to be established for the purposes of the action in accordance with the claim of the party obtaining the order;

(B) An order refusing to allow the disobedient party to support or oppose designated claims or defenses, or prohibiting that party from introducing designated matters in evidence;

(C) An order striking out pleadings or parts thereof, or staying further proceedings until the order is obeyed, or dismissing the action or proceeding or any part thereof, or rendering a judgment by default against the disobedient party;

(D) In lieu of any of the foregoing orders or in addition thereto, an order treating as a contempt of court the failure to obey any orders except an order to submit to a physical or mental examination;

(E) Where a party has failed to comply with an order under Rule 35(a) requiring that party to produce another for examination, such orders as are listed in paragraphs (A), (B), and (C) of this subdivision, unless the party failing to comply shows that that party is unable to produce such person for examination.

In lieu of any of the foregoing orders or in addition thereto, the court shall require the party failing to obey the order or the attorney advising that party or both to pay the reasonable expenses, including attorney's fees, caused by the failure, unless the court finds that the failure was substantially justified or that other circumstances make an award of expenses unjust.

(c) Failure to Disclose; False or Misleading Disclosure; Refusal to Admit.

(1) A party that without substantial justification fails to disclose information required by Rule 26(a) or 26(e)(1) shall not, unless such failure is harmless, be permitted to use as evidence at a trial, at a hearing, or on a motion any witness or information not so disclosed. In addition to or in lieu of this sanction, the court, on motion and after affording an opportunity to be heard, may impose other appropriate sanctions. In addition to requiring payment of reasonable expenses, including attorney's fees, caused by the failure, these sanctions may include any of the actions authorized under subparagraphs (A), (B), and (C) of subdivision (b)(2) of this rule and may include informing the jury of the failure to make the disclosure.

(2) If a party fails to admit the genuineness of any document or the truth of any matter as requested under Rule 36, and if the party requesting the admissions thereafter proves the genuineness of the document or the truth of the matter, the requesting party may apply to the court for an order requiring the other party to pay the reasonable expenses incurred in making that proof, including reasonable attorney's fees. The court shall make the order unless it finds that:

> (A) the request was held objectionable pursuant to Rule 36(a), or (B) the admission sought was of no substantial importance, or (C) the party failing to admit had reasonable ground to believe that the party might prevail on the matter, or (D) there was other good reason for the failure to admit.

(d) Failure of Party to Attend at Own Deposition or Serve Answers to Interrogatories or Respond to Request for Inspection.

If a party or an officer, director, or managing agent of a party or a person designated under Rule 30(b)(6) or 31(a) to testify on behalf of a party fails: (1) to appear before the officer who is to take the deposition, after being served with a proper notice, or (2) to serve answers or objections to interrogatories submitted under Rule 33, after proper service of the interrogatories, or (3) to serve a written response to a request for inspection submitted under Rule 34, after proper service of the request, the court in which the action is pending on motion may make such orders in regard to the failure as are just, and among others it may take any action authorized under paragraphs (A), (B), and (C) of subdivision (b)(2) of this rule. Any motion specifying a failure under clause (2) or (3) of this subdivision shall include a certification that the movant has in good faith conferred or attempted to confer with the party failing to answer or respond in an effort to obtain such answer or response without court action. In lieu of any order or in addition thereto, the court shall require the party failing to act or the attorney advising that party or both to pay the reasonable expenses, including attorney's fees, caused by the failure, unless the court finds that the failure was substantially justified or that other circumstances make an award of expenses unjust.

The failure to act described in this subdivision may not be excused on the ground that the discovery sought is objectionable unless the party failing to act has a pending motion for a protective order as provided by Rule 26(c).

(g) Failure to Participate in the Framing of a Discovery Plan.
If a party or a party's attorney fails to participate in good faith in the development and submission of a proposed discovery plan as required by Rule 26(f), the court may, after opportunity for hearing, require such party or attorney to pay to any other party the reasonable expenses, including attorney's fees, caused by the failure.

VI. Trials

Rule 43—Taking of Testimony

(a) Form.
In all trials, the testimony of witnesses shall be taken orally in open court, unless otherwise provided by an Act of Congress or by these rules, the Federal Rules of Evidence, or other rules adopted by the Supreme Court.

(d) Affirmation in Lieu of Oath.
Whenever under these rules an oath is required to be taken, a solemn affirmation may be accepted in lieu thereof.

(e) Evidence on Motions.
When a motion is based on facts not appearing of record, the court may hear the matter on affidavits presented by the respective parties, but the court may direct that the matter be heard wholly or partly on oral testimony or deposition.

(f) Interpreters.
The court may appoint an interpreter of its own selection and may fix the interpreter's reasonable compensation. The compensation shall be paid out of funds provided by law or by one or more of the parties as the court may direct, and may be taxed ultimately as costs, in the discretion of the court.

Rule 53—Masters

(a) Appointment

(1) Unless a statute provides otherwise, a court may appoint a master only to:

(A) perform duties consented to by the parties;

(B) hold trial proceedings and make or recommend findings of fact on issues to be decided by the court without a jury if appointment is warranted by

(i) some exceptional condition; or

(ii) the need to perform an accounting or resolve a difficult computation of damages; or

(C) address pretrial and post-trial matters that cannot be addressed effectively and timely by an available district judge or magistrate judge of the district.

(2) A master must not have a relationship to the parties, counsel, action, or court that would require disqualification of a judge under 28 U.S.C. § 455 unless the parties consent with the court's approval to appointment of a particular person after disclosure of any potential grounds for disqualification.

(3) In appointing a master, the court must consider the fairness of imposing the likely expenses on the parties and must protect against unreasonable expense or delay.

(b) Order Appointing a Master.

(1) **Notice.**

The court must give the parties notice and an opportunity to be heard before appointing a master. A party may suggest candidates for appointment.

(2) **Contents.**

The order appointing a master must direct the master to proceed with all reasonable diligence and must state:

(A) the master's duties, including any investigation or enforcement duties, and any limits on the master's authority under Rule 53(c);

(B) the circumstances–if any–in which the master may communicate ex parte with the court or a party;

(C) the nature of the materials to be preserved and filed as the record of the master's activities;

(D) the time limits, method of filing the record, other procedures, and standards for reviewing the master's orders, findings, and recommendations; and

(E) the basis, terms, and procedure for fixing the master's compensation under Rule 53(h).

(3) **Entry of Order.**

The court may enter the order appointing a master only after the master has filed an affidavit disclosing whether there is any ground for disqualification under 28

U.S.C. § 455 and, if a ground for disqualification is disclosed, after the parties have consented with the court's approval to waive the disqualification.

(4) Amendment.

The order appointing a master may be amended at any time after notice to the parties, and an opportunity to be heard.

(c) Master's Authority.

Unless the appointing order expressly directs otherwise, a master has authority to regulate all proceedings and take all appropriate measures to perform fairly and efficiently the assigned duties. The master may by order impose upon a party any noncontempt sanction provided by Rule 37 or 45, and may recommend a contempt sanction against a party and sanctions against a nonparty.

(d) Evidentiary Hearings.

Unless the appointing order expressly directs otherwise, a master conducting an evidentiary hearing may exercise the power of the appointing court to compel, take, and record evidence.

(e) Master's Orders.

A master who makes an order must file the order and promptly serve a copy on each party. The clerk must enter the order on the docket.

(f) Master's Reports.

A master must report to the court as required by the order of appointment. The master must file the report and promptly serve a copy of the report on each party unless the court directs otherwise.

(g) Action on Master's Order, Report, or Recommendations.

(1) **Action.**

In acting on a master's order, report, or recommendations, the court must afford an opportunity to be heard and may receive evidence, and may: adopt or affirm; modify; wholly or partly reject or reverse; or resubmit to the master with instructions.

(2) **Time To Object or Move.**

A party may file objections to–or a motion to adopt or modify–the master's order, report, or recommendations no later than 20 days from the time the master's order, report, or recommendations are served, unless the court sets a different time.

(3) **Fact Findings.**

The court must decide de novo all objections to findings of fact made or recommended by a master unless the parties stipulate with the court's consent that:

(A) the master's findings will be reviewed for clear error; or

(B) the findings of a master appointed under Rule 53(a)(1)(A) or (C) will be final.

(4) **Legal Conclusions.**

The court must decide de novo all objections to conclusions of law made or recommended by a master.

(5) **Procedural Matters.**

Unless the order of appointment establishes a different standard of review, the court may set aside a master's ruling on a procedural matter only for an abuse of discretion.

(h) Compensation.

(1) **Fixing Compensation.**

The court must fix the master's compensation before or after judgment on the basis and terms stated in the order of appointment, but the court may set a new basis and terms after notice and an opportunity to be heard.

(2) **Payment.**

The compensation fixed under Rule 53(h)(1) must be paid either:

(A) by a party or parties; or

(B) from a fund or subject matter of the action within the court's control.

(3) **Allocation.**

The court must allocate payment of the master's compensation among the parties after considering the nature and amount of the controversy, the means of the parties, and the extent to which any party is more responsible than other parties for the reference to a master. An interim allocation may be amended to reflect a decision on the merits.

(i) Appointment of Magistrate Judge.

A magistrate judge is subject to this rule only when the order referring a matter to the magistrate judge expressly provides that the reference is made under this rule.

VII. Judgment

Rule 54—Judgments; Costs

(a) Definition; Form.

"Judgment" as used in these rules includes a decree and any order from which an appeal lies. A judgment shall not contain a recital of pleadings, the report of a master, or the record of prior proceedings.

(b) Judgment Upon Multiple Claims or Involving Multiple Parties.

When more than one claim for relief is presented in an action, whether as a claim, counterclaim, cross-claim, or third-party claim, or when multiple parties are involved, the court may direct the entry of a final judgment as to one or more but fewer than all of the claims or parties only upon an express determination that there is no just reason for delay and upon an express direction for the entry of judgment. In the absence of such determination and direction, any order or other form of decision, however designated, which adjudicates fewer than all the claims or the rights and liabilities of fewer than all the parties shall not terminate the action as to any of the claims or parties, and the order or other form of decision is subject to revision at any time before the entry of judgment adjudicating all the claims and the rights and liabilities of all the parties.

(c) Demand for Judgment.

A judgment by default shall not be different in kind from or exceed in amount that prayed for in the demand for judgment. Except as to a party against whom a judgment is entered by default, every final judgment shall grant the relief to which the party in whose favor it is rendered is entitled, even if the party has not demanded such relief in the party's pleadings.

(d) Costs; Attorneys' Fees.

(1) **Costs Other than Attorneys' Fees.**

Except when express provision therefor is made either in a statute of the United States or in these rules, costs other than attorneys' fees shall be allowed as of course to the prevailing party unless the court otherwise directs; but costs against the United States, its officers, and agencies shall be imposed only to the extent permitted by law. Such costs may be taxed by the clerk on one day's notice. On motion served within 5 days thereafter, the action of the clerk may be reviewed by the court.

(2) **Attorneys' Fees.**

(A) Claims for attorneys' fees and related nontaxable expenses shall be made by motion unless the substantive law governing the action provides for the recovery of such fees as an element of damages to be proved at trial.

(B) Unless otherwise provided by statute or order of the court, the motion must be filed and served no later than 14 days after entry of judgment; must specify the judgment and the statute, rule, or other grounds entitling the moving party to the award; and must state the amount or provide a fair estimate of the amount sought. If directed by the court, the motion shall also disclose the terms of any agreement with respect to fees to be paid for the services for which claim is made.

(C) On request of a party or class member, the court shall afford an opportunity for adversary submissions with respect to the motion in accordance with Rule 43(e) or Rule 78. The court may determine issues of liability for fees before receiving submissions bearing on issues of evaluation of services for which liability is imposed by the court. The court shall find the facts and state its conclusions of law as provided in Rule 52(a).

(D) By local rule the court may establish special procedures by which issues relating to such fees may be resolved without extensive evidentiary hearings. In addition, the court may refer issues relating to the value of services to a special master under Rule 53 without regard to the provisions of Rule 53(a)(1) and may refer a motion for attorneys' fees to a magistrate judge under Rule 72(b) as if it were a dispositive pretrial matter.

(E) The provisions of subparagraphs (A) through (D) do not apply to claims for fees and expenses as sanctions for violations of these rules or under 28 U.S.C. § 1927.

Rule 55—Default

(a) Entry.

When a party against whom a judgment for affirmative relief is sought has failed to plead or otherwise defend as provided by these rules and that fact is made to appear by affidavit or otherwise, the clerk shall enter the party's default.

(b) Judgment.

Judgment by default may be entered as follows:

(1) By the Clerk.

When the plaintiff's claim against a defendant is for a sum certain or for a sum which can by computation be made certain, the clerk upon request of the plaintiff and upon affidavit of the amount due shall enter judgment for that amount and costs against the defendant, if the defendant has been defaulted for failure to appear and if he is not an infant or incompetent person.

(2) By the Court.

In all other cases, the party entitled to a judgment by default shall apply to the court therefor; but no judgment by default shall be entered against an infant or incompetent person unless represented in the action by a general guardian, committee, conservator, or other such representative who has appeared therein. If the party against whom judgment by default is sought has appeared in the action, the party (or, if appearing by representative, the party's representative) shall be served with written notice of the application for judgment at least 3 days prior to the hearing on such application. If, in order to enable the court to enter judgment or to carry it into effect, it is necessary to take an account or to determine the amount of damages or to establish the truth of any averment by evidence or to make an investigation of any other matter, the court may conduct such hearings or order such references as it deems necessary and proper and shall accord a right of trial by jury to the parties when and as required by any statute of the United States.

(c) Setting Aside Default.

For good cause shown the court may set aside an entry of default and, if a judgment by default has been entered, may likewise set it aside in accordance with Rule 60(b).

(d) Plaintiffs, Counterclaimants, Cross-Claimants.

The provisions of this rule apply whether the party entitled to the judgment by default is a plaintiff, a third-party plaintiff, or a party who has pleaded a cross-claim or counterclaim. In all cases, a judgment by default is subject to the limitations of Rule 54(c).

(e) Judgment Against the United States.

No judgment by default shall be entered against the United States or an officer or agency thereof unless the claimant establishes a claim or right to relief by evidence satisfactory to the court.

Rule 56—Summary Judgment

(a) For Claimant.

A party seeking to recover upon a claim, counterclaim, or cross-claim or to obtain a declaratory judgment may, at any time after the expiration of 20 days from the commencement of the action or after service of a motion for summary judgment by the adverse party, move with or without supporting affidavits for a summary judgment in the party's favor upon all or any part thereof.

(b) For Defending Party.

A party against whom a claim, counterclaim, or cross-claim is asserted or a declaratory judgment is sought may, at any time, move with or without supporting affidavits for a summary judgment in the party's favor as to all or any part thereof.

(c) Motion and Proceedings Thereon.

The motion shall be served at least 10 days before the time fixed for the hearing. The adverse party prior to the day of hearing may serve opposing affidavits. The judgment sought shall be rendered forthwith if the pleadings, depositions, answers to interrogatories, and admissions on file, together with the affidavits, if any, show that there is no genuine issue as to any material fact and that the moving party is entitled to a judgment as a matter of law. A summary judgment, interlocutory in character, may be rendered on the issue of liability alone although there is a genuine issue as to the amount of damages.

(d) Case Not Fully Adjudicated on Motion.

If on motion under this rule judgment is not rendered upon the whole case or for all the relief asked and a trial is necessary, the court at the hearing of the motion, by examining the pleadings and the evidence before it and by interrogating counsel, shall if practicable ascertain what material facts exist without substantial controversy and what material facts are actually and in good faith controverted. It shall thereupon make an order specifying the facts that appear without substantial controversy, including the extent to which the amount of damages or other relief is not in controversy, and directing such further proceedings in the action as are just. Upon the trial of the action the facts so specified shall be deemed established, and the trial shall be conducted accordingly.

(e) Form of Affidavits; Further Testimony; Defense Required.
Supporting and opposing affidavits shall be made on personal knowledge, shall set forth such facts as would be admissible in evidence, and shall show affirmatively that the affiant is competent to testify to the matters stated therein. Sworn or certified copies of all papers or parts thereof referred to in an affidavit shall be attached thereto or served therewith. The court may permit affidavits to be supplemented or opposed by depositions, answers to interrogatories, or further affidavits. When a motion for summary judgment is made and supported as provided in this rule, an adverse party may not rest upon the mere allegations or denials of the adverse party's pleading, but the adverse party's response, by affidavits or as otherwise provided in this rule, must set forth specific facts showing that there is a genuine issue for trial. If the adverse party does not so respond, summary judgment, if appropriate, shall be entered against the adverse party.

(f) When Affidavits are Unavailable.
Should it appear from the affidavits of a party opposing the motion that the party cannot for reasons stated present by affidavit facts essential to justify the party's opposition, the court may refuse the application for judgment or may order a continuance to permit affidavits to be obtained or depositions to be taken or discovery to be had or may make such other order as is just.

(g) Affidavits Made in Bad Faith.
Should it appear to the satisfaction of the court at any time that any of the affidavits presented pursuant to this rule are presented in bad faith or solely for the purpose of delay, the court shall forthwith order the party employing them to pay to the other party the amount of the reasonable expenses which the filing of the affidavits caused the other party to incur, including reasonable attorney's fees, and any offending party or attorney may be adjudged guilty of contempt.

Rule 57—Declaratory Judgments

The procedure for obtaining a declaratory judgment pursuant to Title 28 U.S.C. 2201 shall be in accordance with these rules, and the right to trial by jury may be demanded under the circumstances and in the manner provided in Rules 38 and 39. The existence of another adequate remedy does not preclude a judgment for declaratory relief in cases where it is appropriate. The court may order a speedy hearing of an action for a declaratory judgment and may advance it on the calendar.

Rule 58—Entry of Judgment

(a) Separate Document

(1)**Every judgment and amended judgment must be set forth on a separate document, but a separate document is not required for an order disposing of a motion:**

(A) for judgment under Rule 50(b);

(B) to amend or make additional findings of fact under Rule 52(b);

(C) for attorney fees under Rule 54;

(D) for a new trial, or to alter or amend the judgment, under Rule 59; or

(E) for relief under Rule 60.

(2) **Subject to Rule 54(b):**

(A) unless the court orders otherwise, the clerk must, without awaiting the court's direction, promptly prepare, sign, and enter the judgment when:

(i) the jury returns a general verdict,

(ii) the court awards only costs or a sum certain, or

(iii) the court denies all relief;

(B) the court must promptly approve the form of the judgment, which the clerk must promptly enter, when:

(i) the jury returns a special verdict or a general verdict accompanied by interrogatories, or

(ii) the court grants other relief now described in Rule 58(a)(2).

(b) Time of Entry.

Judgment is entered for purposes of these rules:

(1) if Rule 58(a)(1) does not require a separate document, when it is entered in the civil docket under Rule 79(a), and

(2) if Rule 58(a)(1) requires a separate document, when it is entered in the civil docket under Rule 79(a) and when the earlier of these events occurs:

(A) when it is set forth on a separate document, or

(B) when 150 days have run from entry in the civil docket under Rule 79(a).

(c) Cost of Fee Awards.

(1)Entry of judgment may not be delayed, nor the time for appeal extended, in order to tax costs or award fees, except as provided in Rule 58(c)(2).

(2) When a timely motion for attorney fees is made under Rule 54(d)(2), the court may act before a notice of appeal has been filed and has become effective to order that the motion have the same effect under Federal Rule of Appellate Procedure 4(a)(4) as a timely motion under Rule 59.

(d) Request for Entry.

A party may request that judgment be set forth on a separate document as required by Rule 58(a)(1).

VIII. Provisional and Final Remedies =

Rule 65—Injunctions

(a) Preliminary Injunction.

(1) **Notice.**

No preliminary injunction shall be issued without notice to the adverse party.

(2) **Consolidation of Hearing With Trial on Merits.**

Before or after the commencement of the hearing of an application for a preliminary injunction, the court may order the trial of the action on the merits to be advanced and consolidated with the hearing of the application. Even when this consolidation is not ordered, any evidence received upon an application for a preliminary injunction which would be admissible upon the trial on the merits becomes part of the record on the trial and need not be repeated upon the trial. This subdivision (a)(2) shall be so construed and applied as to save to the parties any rights they may have to trial by jury.

(b) Temporary Restraining Order; Notice; Hearing; Duration.

A temporary restraining order may be granted without written or oral notice to the adverse party or that party's attorney only if:

(1) it clearly appears from specific facts shown by affidavit or by the verified complaint that immediate and irreparable injury, loss, or damage will result to the applicant before the adverse party or that party's attorney can be heard in opposition, and

(2) the applicant's attorney certifies to the court in writing the efforts, if any, which have been made to give the notice and the reasons supporting the claim that notice should not be required. Every temporary restraining order granted without notice shall be indorsed with the date and hour of issuance; shall be filed forthwith in the clerk's office and entered of record; shall define the injury and state why it is irreparable and why the order was granted without notice; and shall expire by its terms within such time after entry, not to exceed 10 days, as the court fixes, unless within the time so fixed the order, for good cause shown, is extended for a like period or unless the party against whom the order is directed consents that it may be extended for a longer period. The reasons for the extension shall be entered of record. In case a temporary restraining order is granted without notice, the motion for a preliminary injunction shall be set down for hearing at the earliest possible time and takes precedence of all matters except older matters of the same character; and when the motion comes on for hearing the party who obtained the temporary restraining order shall proceed with the application for a preliminary injunction and, if the party does not do so, the court shall dissolve the temporary restraining order. On 2 days' notice to the party who obtained the temporary restraining order

without notice or on such shorter notice to that party as the court may prescribe, the adverse party may appear and move its dissolution or modification and in that event the court shall proceed to hear and determine such motion as expeditiously as the ends of justice require.

(c) Security.

No restraining order or preliminary injunction shall issue except upon the giving of security by the applicant, in such sum as the court deems proper, for the payment of such costs and damages as may be incurred or suffered by any party who is found to have been wrongfully enjoined or restrained. No such security shall be required of the United States or of an officer or agency thereof.

The provisions of Rule 65.1 apply to a surety upon a bond or undertaking under this rule.

(d) Form and Scope of Injunction or Restraining Order.

Every order granting an injunction and every restraining order shall set forth the reasons for its issuance; shall be specific in terms; shall describe in reasonable detail, and not by reference to the complaint or other document, the act or acts sought to be restrained; and is binding only upon the parties to the action, their officers, agents, servants, employees, and attorneys, and upon those persons in active concert or participation with them who receive actual notice of the order by personal service or otherwise.

(e) Employer and Employee; Interpleader; Constitutional Cases.

These rules do not modify any statute of the United States relating to temporary restraining orders and preliminary injunctions in actions affecting employer and employee; or the provisions of Title 28, U.S.C., 2361, relating to preliminary injunctions in actions of interpleader or in the nature of interpleader; or Title 28, U.S.C., 2284, relating to actions required by Act of Congress to be heard and determined by a district court of three judges.

X. District Courts and Clerks

Rule 77—District Courts and Clerks

(a) District Courts Always Open.

The district courts shall be deemed always open for the purpose of filing any pleading or other proper paper, of issuing and returning mesne and final process, and of making and directing all interlocutory motions, orders, and rules.

(b) Trials and Hearings; Orders in Chambers.

All trials upon the merits shall be conducted in open court and so far as convenient in a regular court room. All other acts or proceedings may be done or conducted by a judge in chambers, without the attendance of the clerk or other court officials and at any place either within or without the district; but no hearing, other than one ex parte, shall be conducted outside the district without the consent of all parties affected thereby.

(c) Clerk's Office and Orders by Clerk.

The clerk's office with the clerk or a deputy in attendance shall be open during business hours on all days except Saturdays, Sundays, and legal holidays, but a district court may provide by local rule or order that its clerk's office shall be open for specified hours on Saturdays or particular legal holidays other than New Year's Day, Birthday of Martin Luther King, Jr., Washington's Birthday, Memorial Day, Independence Day, Labor Day, Columbus Day, Veterans Day, Thanksgiving Day, and Christmas Day. All motions and applications in the clerk's office for issuing mesne process, for issuing final process to enforce and execute judgments, for entering defaults or judgments by default, and for other proceedings which do not require allowance or order of the court are grantable of course by the clerk; but the clerk's action may be suspended or altered or rescinded by the court upon cause shown.

(d) Notice of Orders or Judgments

Immediately upon the entry of an order or judgment the clerk shall serve a notice of the entry in the manner provided for in Rule 5(b) upon each party who is not in default for failure to appear, and shall make a note in the docket of the service. Any party may in addition serve a notice of such entry in the manner provided in Rule 5(b) for the service of papers. Lack of notice of the entry by the clerk does not affect the time to appeal or relieve or authorize the court to relieve a party for failure to appeal within the time allowed, except as permitted in Rule 4(a) of the Federal Rules of Appellate Procedure.

XI. General Provisions

Rule 81—Applicability in General

(a) To What Proceedings Applicable.

(1) These rules do not apply to prize proceedings in admiralty governed by Title 10, U.S.C. 7651-7681. They do not apply to proceedings in bankruptcy or proceedings in copyright under Title 17, U.S.C., except insofar as they may be made applicable thereto by rules promulgated by the Supreme Court of the United States. They do not apply to mental health proceedings in the United States District Court for the District of Columbia.

(2) These rules are applicable to proceedings for admission to citizenship, habeas corpus, and quo warranto, to the extent that the practice in such proceedings is not set forth in statutes of the United States and has heretofore conformed to the practice of civil actions. The writ of habeas corpus, or order to show cause, shall be directed to the person having custody of the person detained. It shall be returned within 3 days unless for good cause shown additional time is allowed which in cases brought under 28 U.S.C. 2254 shall not exceed 40 days, and in all other cases shall not exceed 20 days.

(3) In proceedings under Title 9, U.S.C., relating to arbitration, or under the Act of May 20, 1926, ch. 347, 9 (44 Stat. 585), U.S.C., Title 45, 159, relating to boards of arbitration of railway labor disputes, these rules apply only to the extent that matters of procedure are not provided for in those statutes. These rules apply to proceedings to compel the giving of testimony or production of documents in accordance with a subpoena issued by an officer or agency of the United States under any statute of the United States except as otherwise provided by statute or by rules of the district court or by order of the court in the proceedings.

(4) These rules do not alter the method prescribed by the Act of February 18, 1922, c. 57, 2 (42 Stat. 388), U.S.C., Title 7, 292; or by the Act of June 10, 1930, c. 436, 7 (46 Stat. 534), as amended, U.S.C., Title 7, 499g(c), for instituting proceedings in the United States district courts to review orders of the Secretary of Agriculture; or prescribed by the Act of June 25, 1934, c. 742, 2 (48 Stat. 1214), U.S.C., Title 15, 522, for instituting proceedings to review orders of the Secretary of the Interior; or prescribed by the Act of February 22, 1935, c. 18, 5 (49 Stat.31), U.S.C., Title 15, 715d(c), as extended, for instituting proceedings to review orders of petroleum control boards; but the conduct of such proceedings in the district courts shall be made to conform to these rules so far as applicable.

(5) These rules do not alter the practice in the United States district courts prescribed in the Act of July 5, 1935, c. 372, 9 and 10 (49 Stat. 453), as amended, U.S.C., Title 29, 159 and 160, for beginning and conducting proceedings to enforce orders of the National Labor Relations Board; and in respects not covered by those statutes, the practice in the district courts shall conform to these rules so far as applicable.

(6) These rules apply to proceedings for enforcement or review of compensation orders under the Longshoremen's and Harbor Workers' Compensation Act, Act of March 4, 1927, c. 509, 18, 21 (44 Stat. 1434, 1436), as amended, U.S.C., Title 33, 918, 921, except to the extent that matters of procedure are provided for in that Act. The provisions for service by publication and for answer in proceedings to cancel certificates of citizenship under the Act of June 27, 1952, c. 477, Title III, c. 2, 340 (66 Stat. 260), U.S.C., Title 8, 1451, remain in effect.

(b) Scire Facias and Mandamus.

The writs of scire facias and mandamus are abolished. Relief heretofore available by mandamus or scire facias may be obtained by appropriate action or by appropriate motion under the practice prescribed in these rules.

(c) Removed Actions.

These rules apply to civil actions removed to the United States district courts from the state courts and govern procedure after removal. Repleading is not necessary unless the court so orders. In a removed action in which the defendant has not answered, the defendant shall answer or present the other defenses or objections available under these rules within 20 days after the receipt through service or otherwise of a copy of the initial pleading setting forth the claim for relief upon which the action or proceeding is based, or within 20 days after the service of summons upon such initial pleading, then filed, or within 5 days after the filing of the petition for removal, whichever period is longest. If at the time of removal all necessary pleadings have been served, a party entitled to trial by jury under Rule 38 shall be accorded it, if the party's demand therefor is served within 10 days after the petition for removal is filed if the party is the petitioner, or if not the petitioner within 10 days after service on the party of the notice of filing the petition. A party who, prior to removal, has made an express demand for trial by jury in accordance with state law, need not make a demand after removal. If state law applicable in the court from which the case is removed does not require the parties to make express demands in order to claim trial by jury, they need not make demands after removal unless the court directs that they do so within a specified time if they desire to claim trial by jury. The court may make this direction on its own motion and shall do so as a matter of course at the request of any party. The failure of a party to make demand as directed constitutes a waiver by that party of trial by jury.

(e) Law Applicable.
Whenever in these rules the law of the state in which the district court is held is made applicable, the law applied in the District of Columbia governs proceedings in the United States District Court for the District of Columbia. When the word "state" is used, it includes, if appropriate, the District of Columbia. When the term "statute of the United States" is used, it includes, so far as concerns proceedings in the United States District Court for the District of Columbia, any Act of Congress locally applicable to and in force in the District of Columbia. When the law of a state is referred to, the word "law" includes the statutes of that state and the state judicial decisions construing them.

(f) References to Officer of the United States.
Under any rule in which reference is made to an officer or agency of the United States, the term "officer" includes a district director of internal revenue, a former district director or collector of internal revenue, or the personal representative of a deceased district director or collector of internal revenue.

Rule 83—Rules by District Courts; Judges Directives
(a) Local Rules.

(1) Each district court, acting by a majority of its district judges, may, after giving appropriate public notice and an opportunity for comment, make and amend rules governing its practice. A local rule must be consistent with—but not duplicative of—Acts of Congress and rules adopted under 28 U.S.C. 2072 and 2075, and must conform to any uniform numbering system prescribed by the Judicial Conference of the United States. A local rule takes effect on the date specified by the district court and remains in effect unless amended by the court or abrogated by the judicial council

of the circuit. Copies of rules and amendments must, upon their promulgation, be furnished to the judicial council and the Administrative Office of the United States Courts and be available to the public.

(2) A local rule imposing a requirement of form must not be enforced in a manner that causes a party to lose rights because of a nonwillful failure to comply with the requirement.

(b) Procedures When There Is No Controlling Law.

A judge may regulate practice in any manner consistent with federal law, rules adopted under 28 U.S.C. §§ 2072 and 2075, and local rules of the district. No sanction or other disadvantage may be imposed for noncompliance with any requirement not in federal law, federal rules, or the local district rules unless the alleged violator has been furnished in the particular case with actual notice of the requirement.

APPENDIX D

SEARCHING TECHNIQUES

L earning effective search techniques is one of the single most important things you can do as a forensic investigator. As anyone who has conducted an investigation on a large dataset can tell you, if you choose the wrong search criterion, you will either completely miss the data you are looking for or you will spend hours, if not days, searching through masses of false positives. To search effectively, you must consider not only the key phrases that you are looking for, but also the context in which they may be stored in the document. To search for the context as well as the keywords, you will have to understand something more than how to perform simple keyword searches.

REGULAR EXPRESSIONS

The easiest and quickest way to search effectively is by using regular expressions (regex). Most of the forensics tools available today support some subset of the regular expressions language. The most famous regex may be the old DOS holdover, `*.*`.. To translate loosely, this means any amount and kind of characters, a period, and then any amount and kind of characters after the period.

Theory and History

If theory isn't your thing, skip this section. Regular expressions were developed by an American mathematician named Stephen Kleene. They were created as a notation for an algebra that described what he called "the algebra of regular sets." This was later placed into what became known as the Chomsky Hierarchy of languages, which is a formal linguistics model that places every grammar from the regular expression language to the English language into a hierarchy. This hierarchy can then be used to tell how easy or how difficult it is to parse that grammar. Regular expressions are some of the easiest to parse, with the English language being one of the most difficult.

The Building Blocks

Before we start constructing regular expressions to see how powerful they are, let's look at some of the common operators that will be the fundamental building blocks.

Symbol	Meaning
?	Matches any character zero or one times.
*	Matches a preceding regular expression zero or more times; also known as the Kleene star.
+	Matches the preceding regular expression one or more times.
{number}	Matches the preceding regular expression *number* of times.
. (period)	Matches any character one time.

^	Matches the start of a string; also used in some languages for negation.
$	Matches the end of a string.
[]	Used to indicate a set; for instance, [0,1] matches all 0s or 1s.
[^]	Used to indicate an exclusive set; for instance, [^0-1] will match everything except for 0s or 1s.
" \ "	Used to escape special characters.
|	This is the regex equivalent of a logical or; A | B matches either A or B.
(...)	Matches whatever is inside the parentheses.

Constructing Regular Expressions

The following regex matches numbers in the format of currency ($2.50, for example). This shows that regular expressions can get messy and can become completely unreadable.

```
\\$[1-9][0-9]*(\\.[0-9]{2})?|\\$0?\\.[0-9][0-9]
```

Let's work with the symbols listed in the preceding table to see how to create effective searching tools. The utility that will be used throughout this appendix is called *grep*, the open source regex processor. It is extremely powerful and uses the same syntax that's used in Perl and other scripting languages.

Simple Text Matching

Let's start by doing a simple keyword search. If, for instance, we want to search for all HTML files, we would use the following:

```
\.html
```

Note the use of the \ operator to escape out the period (.), since the period itself is an operator. This works well enough for files ending in *.html*; however, some HTML files have the extension of .htm as well as .html, so we want to be able to search for both. In this case, we want to use the | operator, so this becomes

```
\.html | \.htm
```

This will give us all the files ending in either *.html* or *.htm*. Now, to extend this regex a bit, let's match only the files that are either index.htm or index.html. Two different regular expressions will match this:

```
index\.html | index\.htm
```

or

```
index\.(html|htm)
```

While the first example may be a bit easier to read, the second regex is less prone to error. We have also introduced the () operator. Think of this as the grouping operator. If we left it out, the regex would match either index.html or htm, but not index.htm:

```
Index\.html|htm
```

A lot of your problems when debugging these regular expressions will come because you are not grouping correctly. Practice makes perfect.

A More Complex Example

Let's construct an alternative regex to the one listed earlier that searched for financial numbers. First, we construct the regex to match $:

```
\$
```

Easy enough. Now to introduce the [] operator, which allows us to define a set of characters we want to match. To match a single digit, we use the regex

```
[0-9]
```

This will match and number 0 through 9. Let's combine the two regular expressions:

```
\$[0-9]
```

What we now have is a pattern that will match *$1* or any other number besides *1*. However, there is a "gotcha" here. This will check only for one digit, not multiple digits. If you want to do that, you must add either a + or a * to the end, as shown:

```
\$[0-9]*
```

Now we have something that will match an arbitrary number of digits, but will also match *$*, since the Kleene star allows for zero as a positive match. Be very careful when doing repetition operators like this. In this case, to reduce the number of false positives, we actually want to use the + operator, not the * operator, to force at least one number after the $.

```
\$[0-9]+
```

Say we want to enforce formatting where we know there is a decimal point and two trailing numbers ($250.00). To match this, we want to extend this regular expression a bit:

```
\$[0-9]+\.
```

This will match the *($250.)* part of the number. To add in the two places after the decimal, we can do it in one of two ways:

```
\$[0-9]+\.[0-9][0-9]
```

or

```
\$[0-9]+\.[0-9]{2}
```

The introduction of the { } operator shows another way the regex can be shortened and made even more unreadable. The number inside the brackets defines how many times the previous element can be repeated. In addition, if you want to do a range of repetitions, say two to four repetitions, you would write it like this:

```
\$[0-9]+\.[0-9]{2,4}
```

Here, the format is {x,y} with x being the minimum and y being the maximum number of occurrences.

APPENDIX E

THE INVESTIGATOR'S TOOLKIT

The entire forensic tool landscape is changing rapidly. As part of this book, you will find the latest information about each of these tools (and many more) on our web site, http://hackingexposedforensics.com.

Hackingexposedforensics.com follows the book's discussions of key concepts, tools, and methods to extend the reader's knowledge. The web site contains links to the latest information relevant to our field. We have chosen to pull together applicable experts, vendors, legal sources, and links to other sites focused on forensic science. You will find whitepapers, links to job aides, and information on how to contact the authors. Vendors have graciously worked with us to provide you with the latest working or demo version of each of the tools along with links to updated downloads.

FORENSIC TOOLKITS

There are a number of tools on the market either labeled as forensic tools or quite capable of performing as forensic tools. Keep in mind there are hundreds of software programs and hardware devices used by professionals for forensic purposes. A screwdriver becomes a forensic tool when you use it to open the case of a computer during an investigation. Again, keep in mind there are many more tools than those listed here. See the chapters and our web site for more information on other tools.

Guidance Software

http://www.guidancesoftware.com

EnCase Forensic Edition

EnCase Forensic Edition contains a large suite of tools based on the requirements of law enforcement, government, and corporations spanning the past seven years. Perhaps one of the strongest features of EnCase is the repeated industry and court validation and deep analysis capabilities. Guidance has provided ample materials to support the validity of the product. The tool's usage has been upheld in trial and appellate court decisions, and the company retains a reputable and accessible legal staff.

EnCase is capable of managing multiple cases simultaneously and has excellent searching, analyzing, and documenting abilities. EnCase supports a wide range of platforms, including Windows 95/98/NT/2000/XP/2003 Server, Linux, Unix, BSD, DOS, PALM OS, and Macintosh. The file systems supported at the time of this writing include NTFS, FAT 12/16/32, EXT 2/3, UFS, FFS, Reiser, CDFS, UDF, JOLIET, ISO9660, HFS, and HFST.

There are many special add-on modules for EnCase, some that are developed and marketed by EnCase and several that are not. Unfortunately, we don't have enough room here to discuss all the extras; however, one easy and inexpensive upgrade is to take advantage of the support for outside viewers such as QuickView.

EnCase Enterprise Edition

EnCase Enterprise Edition greatly extends the capabilities of EnCase Forensic Edition technology. Its secure network-enabled capability gives corporate and government investigators the ability to immediately—and centrally—respond to security breaches and conduct proactive and reactive investigations. One of the key features of EnCase Enterprise Edition is the ability to investigate a machine thoroughly without having to bring it offline, potentially disrupting business. EnCase Enterprise Edition also has a feature called Snapshot that captures quickly volatile data on Windows, Linux, and Solaris systems, including open ports, open files, active processes, live windows registry information, and network user information, allowing examiners to document the current state of a machine in a forensically sound manner.

Remote investigations technology brings you the flexibility to act immediately, which increases your effectiveness and bandwidth—always good in today's resource-strained market.

ASR Data

 http://asrdata.com/SMART

SMART

SMART is a computer forensics tool designed and optimized for the Linux platform. Integrating several advanced components into a lightweight package for Linux users, SMART offers advanced features such as the ability to mount forensic images as file systems at no extra cost. SMART also supports more than 40 file systems, including NTFS, FAT, HFS, UFS, E2FS, E3FS, and all other file systems, normally supported by Linux. SMART can multithread tasks and start, stop, and pause any process it launches. The tool allows you to use the inherent ability of Linux to mount media read only, and it supports networked imaging. SMART also comes on its own bootable Linux CD, giving you not only the full power of the Linux operating system, but also a fully functional SMART for acquisitions or preliminary analysis. Because of its excellent import and export features, SMART allows the examiner to take advantage of the large number of open source tools available.

Paraben

 http://www.paraben-forensics.com

E-mail Examiner

Paraben's E-mail Examiner is an all-inclusive e-mail examination tool with a wide variety of capabilities, including automatic reporting, task scripting, and much more. E-mail Examiner recovers active and deleted mail messages and has the ability to examine Groupwise, AOL 9.0, PST files, and over 14 other mail stores.

Network E-mail Examiner

Network E-mail Examiner allows you to inspect a large assortment of network e-mail archives. Network E-mail Examiner works hand-in-hand with E-mail Examiner. All output is compatible and can be loaded easily for more complex tasks.

Decryption Collection

Paraben's Decryption Collection is an advanced password recovery suite with extensive support for a wide variety of files.

PDA Seizure

Paraben's PDA Seizure is a comprehensive tool that allows Windows, Palm, and Blackberry PDA data to be acquired, viewed, and reported on, all within a Windows environment. The Blackberry capability is particularly interesting; definitely something to consider if you support Blackberry devices in your environment.

Cell Seizure

Paraben designed Cell Seizure to allow forensic acquisition of user data and portions of unallocated storage on mobile phones. Keep in mind that cell phone forensics is different from traditional forensics. Cell phones have unique issues because cell phone data storage is proprietary, based on the manufacturer, model, and system. Each device is different and should be dealt with cautiously. Paraben updates their list of supported models and devices constantly. As of the time of this writing, they offer the most complete package for examining mobile phones on the market.

NetAnalysis

NetAnalysis is an excellent tool for dealing with large amounts of Internet data. Developed by Craig Wilson, an outstanding investigator in the UK, this tool offers powerful searching, filtering, and evidence identification and supports a number of browsers. Currently, these include Internet Explorer 3, 4, 5, and 6, Netscape Communicator / Navigator up to 4.79 and Apple Mac Netscape Bookmark, Netscape up to 6.2 and the new Netscape 7, Mozilla Browser, and Opera.

Users like the extensive filtering, SQL integration, and keyword list support. Other useful features include bookmarks and comments for different entries, cache reconstruction, and the ability to recover deleted Internet history from unallocated space.

Access Data

http://accessdata.com

Forensic Toolkit

AccessData Forensic Toolkit is another multipurpose toolkit. FTK incorporates dtSearch on the backend to provide excellent correlation across artifacts after the evidence is indexed.

The downside is the time it takes to index the data, but the benefits can be enormous. After the evidence is indexed, FTK has excellent searching capabilities.

FTK also supports built-in viewing of more than 270 file types with Stellent's Outside In Viewer Technology. Other abilities include automatically generated logs and case reports. Another nice feature is the excellent integration with their Password Recovery Toolkit; after indexing a drive, you can add the strings from the drive to a password list for use in the toolkit. There are open source methods that will do this, but the integration is nice.

Supported file formats include NTFS, NTFS compressed, FAT 12/16/32, and Linux ext2 and ext3. Supported image formats include Encase, SMART, Snapback, Safeback, and Linux DD.

Password Recovery Toolkit

The Password Recovery Toolkit (PRTK) is an excellent corporate tool. If you or your users need access to encrypted files, then PRTK can likely help. Support is included for more than 50 file types.

The Sleuth Kit

http://www.sleuthkit.org

The Sleuth Kit

The Sleuth Kit runs on Linux, Mac OS X, Open & FreeBSD, Solaris, and CYGWIN. Its origin includes code from The Coroner's Toolkit (TCT). The Sleuth Kit contains command line tools for handling different types of media and performing forensic analysis of files. The media management tools identify the location of partitions and then extract them for analysis with file system tools. The powerful file analysis tools are able to recover deleted and hidden content across NTFS, FAT, FFS, EXT2FS, and EXT3FS file systems. The Sleuth Kit supports dd images. Additional features (there are many) include support for live incident response, deleted file recovery, organization by file type, file activity timelines, hash databases, thumbnail pages for images, and much more. For those who want an open source alternative to commercial toolkits, this is a powerful tool.

Autopsy Browser

The Autopsy Forensic Browser is an HTML-based graphical interface for the command-line digital forensic analysis tools in The Sleuth Kit. Together, The Sleuth Kit and Autopsy provide many of the same features as commercial digital forensics tools for the analysis of Windows and UNIX file systems. Autopsy allows for live analysis of media by running the tools from a CD. Features include an excellent graphical interface for viewing directory and file content, running hash database lookups, sorting files, creating activity timelines, performing searches, and much more. Autopsy also includes excellent case management and reporting features. Its client-server architecture lends itself naturally to several people working at the same time on data held on one large server. Autopsy is written in Perl and will run on many platforms.

GLOSSARY

The majority of the following definitions were extracted from the National Institute of Justice (NIJ) special report titled "Forensic Examination of Digital Evidence: A Guide for Law Enforcement," which was authored by more than 50 experts and was reviewed by more than 80 organizations. It can be found at http://www.ncjrs.org/ pdffiles1/nij/199408.pdf. In some cases, we developed the definitions from this document for clarity.

acquisition   The process by which digital evidence is duplicated, copied, or imaged.

analysis   The process of examining digital evidence for its significance and probative value to the case.

anticipation   For the purpose of this text, this is the examiner's homework and preparation for expected questions and issues encountered during the delivery of the findings.

archival   Method by which case materials and findings are recorded and held for future use.

articulation   The process by which your findings are documented and communicated in an accurate and understandable manner.

assessment   The process by which the investigator determines the scope of a case, identifies and preserves data, establishes custody, and in some cases previews data.

authentication   A process by which an acquired duplicate, copy, or image of digital evidence is verified against the original.

BIOS *Basic Input Output System*. The set of routines stored in read-only memory that enables a computer to start the operating system and communicate with the various devices in the system such as disk drives, keyboard, monitor, printer, and communication ports. The BIOS is stored in nonvolatile memory or as a permanent part of your computer. These routines are always available at a specific address in memory, so all programs can access them to perform their basic I/O functions. IBM computers contain copyrighted BIOS that only their computers can use; however, other companies such as Phoenix, Award, and American Megatrends have developed BIOSes for other manufacturer's computers that emulate or mimic the IBM instructions without using the same code. If you use a non-IBM computer, the BIOS company's copyright message and BIOS version number are displayed every time you turn on the computer.

CD-R *Compact Disc-Recordable*. This disc can be written to one time with a laser that irreversibly changes regions of the shiny silver polymer layer to a state that does not reflect light.

CD-RW *Compact Disc-Rewritable*. This disc can be written to and erased using a prestamped groove to guide a laser capable of changing the reflective nature of the writable alloy layer. A special drive is required to write to the disks, but they can be read by any CD player capable of detecting the low light levels resulting from the low reflectivity of the alloy. It is not as reflective as CD-R media.

CMOS *Complementary Metal Oxide Semiconductor*. Often used to describe the low-level hardware that contains a personal computer's BIOS setting and the computer's hardware clock.

compressed file A file that has been reduced in size through a compression algorithm to save disk space. The act of compressing a file will make it unreadable to most programs until the file is decompressed. Two common compression utilities are WinZip and PKZIP, with an extension of .zip. Other common compression extensions include .RAR, .BIN, .GZ, .TGZ, and .RPM.

copy An accurate reproduction of information contained on an original physical item, independent of the electronic storage device (for example, logical file copy). Maintains contents, but attributes may change during the reproduction.

deleted files If a subject knows incriminating files are on the computer, he or she may delete them in an effort to eliminate the evidence. Many computer users think that this actually eliminates the information. However, depending on how the files are deleted, in many instances a forensic examiner is able to recover all or part of the original data.

digital evidence Information stored or transmitted in binary form that may be used as reliable evidence in court.

duplicate An accurate digital reproduction of all data contained on a digital storage device (for example, hard drive, CD-ROM, flash memory, floppy disk, Zip, Jaz). Maintains contents and attributes (such as bit stream, bit copy, and sector dump).

electromagnetic interference   An electromagnetic disturbance that interrupts, obstructs, or otherwise degrades or limits the effective performance of electronics/electrical equipment.

encryption   Any procedure used in cryptography to convert plaintext into cipher text to prevent anyone but the intended recipient from reading that data.

examination   Technical review that makes the evidence visible and suitable for analysis; tests performed on the evidence to determine the presence or absence of specific data.

file slack   Space between the logical end of the file and the end of the last allocation unit for that file.

file structure   How an application program stores the contents of a file.

file system   The method used by the operating system to keep track of the files on the drive.

filename anomaly   Header/extension mismatch; filename inconsistent with the content of the file.

forensically clean   Digital media that are completely wiped of nonessential and residual data, scanned for viruses, and verified before use.

hashing   The process of using a mathematical algorithm against data to produce a numeric value that is representative of that data.

Host-protected area   An area that can be defined on IDE drives that meets the technical specifications as defined by ATA4 and later. If a Max address has been set that is less than a native Max address, then a host protected area is present. See also IDE.

IDE   *Integrated drive electronics.* A type of data communications interface generally associated with storage devices.

image   An accurate digital representation of all data contained on a digital storage device (for example, hard drive, CD-ROM, flash memory, floppy disk, Zip, Jaz). Maintains contents and attributes, but may include metadata such as cyclical redundancy checks (CRCs), hash values, and audit information.

ISP   *Internet service provider.* An organization that provides access to the Internet. Small ISPs provide service via modem and an integrated services digital network (ISDN), while the larger ISPs also offer private line hookups (such as T1 or fractional T1).

MAC address   *Media access control address.* A unique identifying number built (or burned) into a network interface card by the manufacturer.

MO   *Magneto-optical.* A drive used to back up files on a personal computer using magnetic and optical technologies.

network   A group of computers connected to one another to share information and resources.

original evidence   Physical items and the data objects that are associated with those items at the time of seizure.

password-protected   Many software programs include the ability to protect a file using a password. One type of password protection is sometimes called "access denial." If this feature is used, the data will be present on the disk in the normal manner, but the software program will not open or display the file without the user first entering the password. In many cases, forensic examiners are able to bypass this feature.

preservation order   A document ordering a person or company to preserve potential evidence. The authority for preservation letters to ISPs is in 18 USC 2703(f).

proprietary software   Software that is owned by an individual or company and that requires the purchase of a license before the software can be used.

remnant   A small part or portion of a file that remains after the main part of a file is deleted.

removable media   Items (such as floppy disks, CDs, DVDs, cartridges, tape) that store data and can be easily removed.

SCSI   *Small Computer System Interface*. A type of data communications interface.

steganography   The art and science of communicating in a way that hides the existence of the communication. It is used to hide a file inside another. For example, a child pornography image can be hidden inside another graphic image file, audio file, or other file format.

system administrator   The individual who has legitimate supervisory rights over a computer system. The administrator maintains the highest access to the system. Also can be known as sysop, sysadmin, and system operator.

unallocated space   Allocation units that are not assigned to active files within a file system.

write protection   Hardware or software methods of preventing data from being written to a disk or other medium.

Index

A

D

F

J

K

L

M

O

P

Q

S

▼ T

▼ U

X

 Y

 Z

INTERNATIONAL CONTACT INFORMATION

AUSTRALIA
McGraw-Hill Book Company
Australia Pty. Ltd.
TEL +61-2-9900-1800
FAX +61-2-9878-8881
http://www.mcgraw-hill.com.au
books-it_sydney@mcgraw-hill.com

CANADA
McGraw-Hill Ryerson Ltd.
TEL +905-430-5000
FAX +905-430-5020
http://www.mcgraw-hill.ca

GREECE, MIDDLE EAST, & AFRICA
(Excluding South Africa)
McGraw-Hill Hellas
TEL +30-210-6560-990
TEL +30-210-6560-993
TEL +30-210-6560-994
FAX +30-210-6545-525

MEXICO (Also serving Latin America)
McGraw-Hill Interamericana Editores
S.A. de C.V.
TEL +525-1500-5108
FAX +525-117-1589
http://www.mcgraw-hill.com.mx
carlos_ruiz@mcgraw-hill.com

SINGAPORE (Serving Asia)
McGraw-Hill Book Company
TEL +65-6863-1580
FAX +65-6862-3354
http://www.mcgraw-hill.com.sg
mghasia@mcgraw-hill.com

SOUTH AFRICA
McGraw-Hill South Africa
TEL +27-11-622-7512
FAX +27-11-622-9045
robyn_swanepoel@mcgraw-hill.com

SPAIN
McGraw-IIill/
Interamericana de España, S.A.U.
TEL +34-91-180-3000
FAX +34-91-372-8513
http://www.mcgraw-hill.es
professional@mcgraw-hill.es

UNITED KINGDOM, NORTHERN,
EASTERN, & CENTRAL EUROPE
McGraw-Hill Education Europe
TEL +44-1-628-502500
FAX +44-1-628-770224
http://www.mcgraw-hill.co.uk
emea_queries@mcgraw-hill.com

ALL OTHER INQUIRIES Contact:
McGraw-Hill/Osborne
TEL +1-510-420-7700
FAX +1-510-420-7703
http://www.osborne.com
omg_international@mcgraw-hill.com

Sound Off!

Visit us at **www.osborne.com/bookregistration** and let us know what you thought of this book. While you're online you'll have the opportunity to register for newsletters and special offers from McGraw-Hill/Osborne.

We want to hear from you!

Sneak Peek

Visit us today at **www.betabooks.com** and see what's coming from McGraw-Hill/Osborne tomorrow!

Based on the successful software paradigm, Bet@Books™ allows computing professionals to view partial and sometimes complete text versions of selected titles online. Bet@Books™ viewing is free, invites comments and feedback, and allows you to "test drive" books in progress on the subjects that interest you the most.

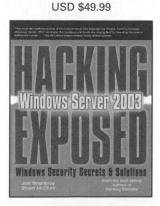